MW01097681

Vienna and Its Jews

The Tragedy of Success
1880s–1980s

George E. Berkley

Abt Books

Madison Books

Abt Books, Inc.
Cambridge, MA 02138

Madison Books
4720 Boston Way
Lanham, MD 20706

Printed in the United States of America

British Cataloging in Publication Information Available

Co-published by arrangement with Abt Books Inc.

Library of Congress Cataloging-in-Publication Data

Berkley, George E.
Vienna and Its Jews : the tragedy of success / George E. Berkley.
p. cm.
"Co-published by arrangement with Abt Books Inc."
1. Jews—Austria—Vienna—History. 2. Vienna (Austria)—Ethnic
relations. I. Title.
DS135.A92V5214   1987
943.6'13004924—dc 19   88–1521 CIP
ISBN 0–8191–6816–5 (alk. paper)

All Madison Books are produced on acid-free
paper which exceeds the minimum standards set by the National
Historical Publications and Records Commission.

Abt Books

Madison Books

To
the two most remarkable women
I have ever known.

My mother,
Anita Weinstein

My aunt,
Louise Nevelson

Contents

vi

Acknowledgments

So many people helped so generously with this book that I hardly know where to begin when it comes to acknowledging their aid. Most of them are listed in the back of the book under "Personal Communications," but some deserve special mention.

Hilde Wang Massler not only told me of her own experiences, but introduced me to Joseph Meisels and gave me introductions to other friends in Vienna and Israel. Among those friends in Vienna was Luise Papo who arranged for me to meet Sidoni Korelek and another lady who wishes to remain unnamed. All three were valuable sources of information.

My neighbor Benno Weiser Varon answered endless questions and gave me copies of his many articles on Vienna. Harry Zohn also patiently answered numerous questions, loaned me books from his well-stocked library, pointed out errors in the initial draft of the manuscript, and referred me to others including Ellen Taxer Sommer and Alfred Hoelzel. Meanwhile, his sister Fritzi, along with Max Alter, Rhoda Kalman and William Geisler, voluntarily called me when the *Jewish Advocate* kindly published my appeal for information from former Vienna Jews.

In Vienna, Jonny and Glen Moser proved most hospitable, inviting me to their home, answering my questions and providing, as well as pointing out, other sources of information. (Glen Moser subsequently helped me with my research but no errors in the book should be blamed on her or any others mentioned here.) Also in Vienna, Kurt Schubert twice interrupted his schedule to meet with me and gave me copies of materials published by his Institute for Jewish Studies; Fritz Hodek xeroxed copies of *Gemeinde* reports and supplied other information; and Marta Halpert and Lucian Meysels provided interesting and informative interviews.

My request for information in *The Jerusalem Post* produced many responses, not only from Israel but from around the world. Among the non-Israeli respondents I am especially grateful to the following: Charles Richter who subsequently sent me copies of his own article on Vienna's Orthodox Jews and on Hollensteiner's *Gutachten*; Harry Chameides who sent me copies of his parents' emigration documents and who later called me from New York; and Helly Frost Barzilay who sent me a copy of a group picture with Aron Menczer, together with information about him.

But most of the responses came from Israel, and I soon set off for Jerusalem. There Professor Jacob Metzer and his wife Etti brought me together with Ambassador and Mrs. Michel Elizur, and Professor and Mrs. Mahum Gross, gave me the names and phone numbers of Raphael Gat and Kurt Weigel, referred me to published sources of information, and were generally kind and helpful. Manachem Menczer, Jacob Metzer's uncle, invited me to his Kibbutz, Sde Nehemia, where I spent an exciting twenty-four hours going over his materials (copies of which he gave or loaned me), talking with him, his gracious wife Esther, and their fellow-Kibbutznik Lisa Gidron, and touring their most impressive Kibbutz. Also in Israel I became endebted to Herbert Rosenkranz, Max Diamant, Ben Shimron, Eliahu Fried, and Raphael Gat for interviews. Dr. Gat subsequently sent me a most helpful bibliography.

It was Lisa Gidron who told me of Louis and Ditta Lowy who actually live only a mile or so from my home. I promptly called them on my return. (Mrs. Lowy had not been deported from Vienna until the fall of 1942 and I had been searching desperately for someone who had remained in the city that long.) At about this time I also called Raul Hilberg who has written what many consider to be the most definitive work on the Jewish Holocaust, and he not only answered my questions but referred me to Leonard and Edith Ehrlich who willingly shared their information on Rabbi Murmelstein. (Professor Ehrlich teaches at my own university, but at a different branch, and I did not know of his research.) I also at this time read Edward Schechter's book, phoned him, and got from him among other things the phone number of William Stricker who not only freely answered my questions but, without ever having met me, voluntarily loaned me one of his two remaining copies of a privately printed book about his father.

Finally, I must mention some of the many who are not listed at the back of the book but who also assisted in its creation. They include Pat Berkley who not only encouraged me but allowed me to raid the family coffers to finance trips to Vienna and Israel; Diane Cleaver, my agent, who strongly supported the project; Victor Levine who first suggested it; Adelle Robinson who so proficiently typed the manuscript; Françoise Rosset who sent me helpful materials as she came across them in Geneva; Dr. Robert Rudy who xeroxed portions of his copy of Bilroth's book; Stanley Schwarz who referred me to Mrs. Massler; and David Shaw who sent me a list of libraries likely to have information.

I have sought to repay all the many who helped me so generously in the only way I know: by writing, within the limitations of my time and talents, the best book I could.

Foreword

When I learned that an American-born professor at the University of Massachusetts in Boston was working on a book about the Jews of Vienna, my first reaction was one of relief: "Good! Now *I* won't have to write it!" In the ensuing months and years, as I continued to write and lecture on various aspects of my native city, I was privileged to see Professor Berkley's manuscript in its various stages. While the emphasis of this book differs somewhat from my own more personal, less dispassionate approach, its many virtues effectively complement other writings on this important subject. Because George Berkley is a teacher of political science, his book properly gives pride of place to the historical, economic, political, and social situation of Viennese Jewry. It is thus a welcome addition to such scholarly studies as *The Austrian Mind* by William Johnston, *Fin de Siècle Vienna* by Carl Schorske, *Wittgenstein's Vienna* by Allan Janik and Stephen Toulmin, *A Nervous Splendor* by Frederic Morton, and *The Jews of Austria*, edited by Josef Fraenkel.

Professor Berkley's research was prompted by his recollection of a wartime encounter with a nostalgic Jewish lady from Vienna who averred that before 1938 she had lived in a virtual Paradise. Such a statement only demonstrates once again the endless human capacity for illusion and self-delusion. Berkley relentlessly piles up evidence that the Vienna so glowingly remembered by that lady was at best a Paradise of Fools. In fact, the author paints such an unrelievedly cheerless picture that the Paradiso is barely visible through the Inferno, and one almost wishes that his ex-Viennese informant (who was later joined by others) had a chance to state her case.

To briefly state my own view, I remember a Viennese childhood in an economically, politically, and socially parlous period that was reasonably happy. My father, who is mentioned in this book, was one of Vienna's best-known sign painters, but in the late 1920s and early 1930s many of his customers had the unfortunate habit of declaring bankruptcy before paying him for his work. Apart from the difficulty of making ends meet, anti-Semitic taunts and occasional brawls were a fact of life, a "given" for my generation. I remember attending games of the lower-division Jewish soccer team Hakoah, played in working-class districts, which touched off anti-Semitic incidents indicating that the self-bestowed "golden heart of the Viennese" was of baser stuff. However, none of this ever stirred thoughts of emigration. Even Sigmund Freud, that prime exemplar of a *Hassliebe* (love-hate relationship) for Vienna, could not imagine living elsewhere and became a very reluctant refugee in 1938. The Jews of my circle and time were good enough Austrians to exemplify the old local adage that the situation was desperate but not serious.

What is not fully brought out in Professor Berkley's book is the great fascination exerted upon Jews by the German language, especially its Viennese variant, and the intellectual, cultural, spiritual, ideological, and aesthetic values embodied in this language and this dialect. The author does mention the great contributions made by Jews to literature, music, commerce, sports, and indeed nearly every aspect of life in that exceptionally beautiful and livable city. These include the winegarden songs in which the Viennese tirelessly celebrate their city and their unique lifestyle.

Berkley cites this pertinent insight by Christopher Morley: "The writing on the wall grew so large that finally the wall fell down." Yes, the handwriting was clearly on the wall, but Vienna's Jews preferred to avert their eyes. In 1898 the Jewish writer Jakob Wassermann, a native of Franconia, came to Austria; he was to spend the rest of his life there. He found the banks, the press, the theater, the literature, and the social organizations of Vienna in Jewish hands. In his autobiography, *My Life as German and Jew*, first published in 1921, Wassermann severely criticized the Jews of Vienna for their servility, lack of dignity, and self-serving opportunism — qualities that Theodor Herzl had also identified as being part of a ghetto mentality. Wassermann's animadversions foreshadowed (or echoed) the alarm sounded in 1912 by Moritz Goldstein, a German-Jewish journalist, who warned (fruitlessly) that the Jews were acting as the self-appointed guardians of a cultural heritage to which their right was in doubt. Among the Jews of Vienna there was no Gershom Scholem to point out forcefully that the German-Jewish symbiosis there had no future. (And even if there had been such a prescient person, he would not have been heeded any more than Scholem was in World War I Germany.)

Both before and after the advent of political Zionism, Viennese Jewry sought salvation in ever greater acculturation and adaptation, often including conversion. These Jews' loyalty to the Empire and its capital city (and later to both the Social Democrats and the Fatherland Front) endured and survived crises, conflicts, and cataclysms. Professor Berkley mentions *3rd November 1918*, a play by F. T. Csokor, for which a good English title would be *The Army That Never Returned*. In it Colonel Radosin commits suicide when he realizes that multinational aspirations and cooperation will now be replaced by an atavistic, crude, know-nothing nationalism and particularism. Another such patriot (albeit a survivor) is Grün, the Jewish army doctor. After the dissolution of the Empire, many of the Gentile soldiers went to live in the successor states, but because of the unbearable anti-Semitism in the provinces of a truncated postwar Austria, the Jews were perforce limited to Vienna.

One *Ostjude* (Eastern Jew), the gifted novelist Joseph Roth, identified with Old Austria to such an extent that he intoned dirges for a bygone world, affected the stance of an Austrian army officer, called himself "a Catholic with a Jewish brain," and once signed a letter as "Moishe Christus." After 1918 he was torn by conflicting loyalties and sought spiritual refuge in monarchist ideology. But his Catholic leanings coincided with a fresh creative interest in his Jewish heritage, and he strove to create a special synthesis between *imperium* and *shtetl*. In his book *Juden auf Wanderschaft*, Roth viewed the Zionist movement as the direct result of internal conflicts within the Habsburg realm. Roth could not achieve a synthesis between his Jewish origins, his fixation on the lost empire, and his desire to embrace the predominant Catholic religion of Austria; he drank himself to death and died in Paris in 1939 at age forty-five.

The old story of progressive Jewish attenuation and disaffection is exemplified by the cloth and silk merchant Isak Löw Hofmann, born in 1759, who became Edler von Hofmannsthal in 1835, and thus ennobled co-founded the *Kultusgemeinde* (Jewish Community Council) of Vienna. His son was already baptized, and his great-grandson, Hugo von Hofmannsthal, one of the giants of modern Austrian literature, was a Catholic man of letters whose writings rarely contain any vestiges of a Jewish sensibility. Not only marginal Jews but also "professional Jews" were deeply attached to Austria and Vienna. The Yiddish writer Avraham Goldfaden spoke of *dos gebentshte Estreich* (blessed Austria); Hebrew writers including Smolensky, Broides, Brainin, and Bialik lived and flourished in Vienna, as did noted rabbis Jellinek, Güdemann, Chajes, Grünwald, and Taglicht.

Berkley details some of the great contributions made by Viennese Jews to literature, especially in the period of "Young Vienna." Fourteen of the eighteen writers I included in a collection of *fin-de-siècle* Austrian literature "happened" to be Jewish or of Jewish descent. More recently I compiled a list of Jewish authors associated with Vienna and found almost six hundred who published one or more books. Curiously enough, Jews made no great contribution to Viennese art and architecture; there was no Jewish Klimt, Schiele, Kokoschka, or Loos. Richard Gerstl, born in 1883, was a promising

xvi VIENNA AND ITS JEWS

artist of early expressionism whose savage, manic bitter paintings were in the mainstream, but he worked in isolation and took his own life at age twenty-five. Another painter of Jewish descent was Max Kurzweil, a suicide in 1917 who is remembered for his portrait of the young Herzl.

Berkley displays a fine eye for the internal and external confusions and contradictions of Jewish life in Vienna and writes with considerable empathy and imagination. If he neglects its amenities and more satisfying aspects, it is probably due to his concentration on the road to (and from) the *Anschluss* (annexation by Germany), which meant the *Ausschluss* (exclusion) of the nearly 200,000 Jews in the first Austrian republic and a tragic *Schluss* (conclusion) for tens of thousands of them. The author is quite hard on the Viennese and Austrian Gentiles, and not undeservedly so, for there were "*zu wenig Gerechte*" (too few righteous people) among them, and there is evidence that "the Holocaust from Hitler on down was more of an Austrian phenomenon than a German one." There is no faulting Berkley's conclusion that "the fierce attachment of so many Jews to a city that through the years demonstrated its deep-rooted hate for them remains the greatest grim irony of all." The story of the Jews of Vienna is the story of what may be the most tragically unrequited love in world history.

What about the Jews living in an Austria that not long ago elected Kurt Waldheim as its head of state? Today between six thousand and ten thousand Jews live in Vienna and a small number in provincial cities. Very few of the several hundred who survived the Holocaust in the city are still alive, so most of these Jews are survivors of the death camps (or their offspring), Hungarian Jews (who came in 1956), and a small number of remigrants from Israel, England, the United States, and other countries of exile. On my first visit to postwar Vienna in 1955 I gained the impression that this was a superannuated, moribund community, but in recent years its character seems to have changed. In the fall of 1984 I was able to observe, and even participate in, a series of events through which the Jewish community of Vienna attempted to put itself on the map of world Jewry again. The prime mover of the *Versunkene Welt* (Sunken World) programs was Leon Zelman, a survivor of the Mauthausen concentration camp who has for decades been an effective mediator and spokesman for Vienna's Jewry. A Jewish photographic exhibit, Jewish films, and an international symposium at the City Hall attracted large audiences, as did the monumental *Traum und Wirklichkeit* (Dream and Reality) exhibit (later seen in part at the Museum of Modern Art in New York), where viciously anti-Semitic posters and handbills antedating the Hitler period by many years provided a necessary context and motivation for Herzl's Zionist quest. In 1984 I attended the festive opening of the Chajes School in the refurbished building of the old Chajes Gymnasium, located a few steps from the Leopoldstadt house in which I was born. The Austrian government has generously supported these and other projects, and many accomplished Viennese Jews have been honored with titles and decorations. Symposia on Herzl, Beer-Hofmann, and Kraus in 1985 and 1986 seemed to lend credence to a wag's witticism that Vienna does not mind celebrating its Jews provided they are safely dead.

Though hardly any of today's Jews could have regarded Vienna as a Paradise, a new and hopeful spirit of ecumenism, tolerance, neighborliness, and cooperation seemed to have taken hold, until Kurt Waldheim's campaign for the presidency and his election poisoned the atmosphere and drew worldwide attention to the qualities and attitudes that seemed to make him a man right after Austrian hearts. Leon Zelman ruefully remarked that decades of work had apparently gone down the drain and that he had been "selling" an illusion. Many other Jews were aghast at the expression of latent anti-Semitic sentiments by so many of their fellow Austrians. The volume of hate mail received by Jewish officials and journalists exceeded the messages of sympathy and remorse. The future of Vienna's Jewish community must be regarded as uncertain, but one good result of Waldheim's opportunism and insensitivity may be the *cheshbon hanefesh* (soul-searching) that has at long last been initiated in a population that, from the Moscow Declaration of 1943 (which in effect exculpated the Austrians) to the Russian State Treaty of 1955 and beyond, has salved its conscience without coming to terms with a past that is so searingly set forth on the pages of this book.

That is why Professor Berkley's study has an important contribution to make. This long and copiously documented cautionary tale deserves to be widely read and pondered in the English-speaking world and even more in German-speaking countries.

Harry Zohn
Brandeis University
June 1987

Prologue

The Questions

While a student in New York City in the late 1940s, I happened to meet and talk with a middle-aged woman whose accent clearly bespoke a Central European background. I don't recall much of our conversation, but I do remember vividly one remark she made about her past. "Before the war," she said, "I lived in a virtual paradise." The statement was impressive not only because of what she said but the way she said it, for as she uttered those words her face lit up and her voice took on an almost ecstatic tone.

The lady was Viennese, and this glorification of her native city puzzled me. Here was a mature and educated woman who still treasured glowing memories of the city that had forced her and her fellow Jews to flee for their lives. I had never heard German Jewish refugees speak with such rapture about their native cities. Vienna, I therefore reasoned, must have been very different.

This impression was reinforced a few years later when I embarked on a Dutch freighter for a graduation trip to Europe. For those willing to put up with dormitory accommodations and a thirteen-day voyage, this vessel offered the cheapest passage across the Atlantic. Among my fellow passengers was a good-humored, sophisticated Jewish man in his sixties who had once been a business executive in Vienna and who was now going back there to spend his remaining days. Although his main reason for doing so was the city's lower cost of living — he had little more than his meager social security check to live on — one could see from the animated way he spoke that he still harbored fond feelings for Vienna. Even as an elderly semi-pauper, he was eagerly looking forward to returning to the city that had impoverished and expelled him.

This second encounter convinced me to put Vienna on my list of places to visit. In fact, I now became quite excited over the prospect of experiencing a German-speaking city that had so enchanted its Jews that their recollections of it had remained warm and positive despite all they had suffered there.

My initial reaction to Vienna paralleled those of the two refugees. Although still under four-power occupation and by no means recovered from the effects of the war, the Austrian capital seemed picturesque and socially pleasant. As a young American speaking a poor but generally intelligible German, I easily struck up acquaintanceships with its gregarious inhabitants. But whenever I mentioned that I was Jewish — it usually came when people asked me how I had learned German and I remarked that having been raised in a Yiddish-speaking family had helped — the atmosphere abruptly changed. Those to whom I was talking would suddenly become less animated, their eyes would shift away, and all warmth and spontaneity would drain out of our conversation. Indeed, the conversation itself would soon end.

I attributed this reaction to their feelings of awkwardness and guilt over what had transpired a few years before. I therefore began to avoid telling people I was Jewish and instead raised the subject in another way. For example, I remember having a lively conversation with a middle-aged couple on the train. We were laughing, joking, when I told them about the elderly Viennese Jew I had met who was so eagerly looking forward to returning to his, and their, native city. I thought they might be pleased to hear of such devotion to Vienna, but instead they replied, without any change in their good humor, "Oh, let him go to Israel. Yes, he should go to Israel." It was obvious that they did not consider my friend from the freighter Viennese and certainly did not want him back in their midst.

In later years I visited Germany several times and there I found a markedly different attitude. Although there was no shortage of anti-Semites in Germany, one did come across many Germans who immediately expressed genuine guilt and shame when the subject of the Jews came up. Yet to this day I have never heard an Austrian do the same.

Of course, one cannot draw any firm conclusions on the basis of subjective impressions from a few isolated incidents. Still, the subject continued over the years to intrigue me. A remark by a young German psychologist particularly piqued my curiosity. In the course of a conversation on an entirely different matter, he off-handedly noted how the Austrians "were ten times better Nazis than we were." He seemed amused by this observation, as if he thought the Austrians had in some clever fashion pulled the wool over the world's eyes.

Was this true? Were the Austrians "better" Nazis, or at least more ardent anti-Semites, than the Germans? On the other hand, did the Jews of Austria, ninety percent of whom lived in Vienna, believe they were living in a near Paradise before the war? If the answers to both these questions are yes, how does one explain the contradiction involved? How could the Jews of Vienna become so enchanted with the city that hated them so much?

In 1985 I finally set out to seek the answers to these questions. What follows is what I found.

Part I

Vienna, 1900: Dream and Reality

*Like you I have an uncontrollable
affection for Vienna, but unlike you
I know her deep abysses.*
— Sigmund Freud to a friend

Chapter 1

Vienna Gloriosa

Picture a city of stately buildings and spacious parks, elegant boulevards and elegant people, a city bounded on three sides by a wooded green belt and, on its fourth, by Europe's second largest river. Picture a city so brimming with culture, science, and scholarship that visitors come from all over the world to hear its concerts, consult its doctors, and study under its professors. Picture a gay, carefree city reveling in the colorful and yeasty diversity that befits the capital of a huge multinational empire that stretches from the Swiss to the Russian borders. Picture Vienna, the *Vienna Gloriosa*, of 1900.

This popular image of fin-de-siècle Vienna does not lack substance. The city in 1900 could claim to be all these things and even more.

To begin with, Vienna was universally acknowledged as the music capital of the world. During the century just ended it had given the world the operetta and the waltz. More importantly, it had provided Beethoven, Brahms, Schubert, and other musical giants with a place to live, work, and reap public acclaim. The dawn of the new century found Gustav Mahler, the leading conductor and composer of his time, directing the city's opera while such trailblazers of modern music as Arnold Schönberg and Alban Berg would soon add to the city's musical fame. At a more popular level stood a host of well-known and highly esteemed composers headed, until his death the past year, by Johann Strauss.

Certainly Vienna seemed to offer a most congenial setting for a composer or conductor to practice and develop his art, for the Viennese truly loved music. They thronged their opera house and their numerous concert halls, listening, often with close attention, to four hours or more of music at a time. The opera house even provided a special stall to accommodate on-duty army officers in their boots and swords. For the lower classes there were park concerts, dance halls, and other places where music could be enjoyed. Moreover, all the city's musicians, whether they played in dance halls or concert halls, knew they faced critical, discerning audiences who demanded the best.

Vienna in 1900 was also enjoying a rising reputation for art and architecture. Three years earlier a group of artists and aesthetes had launched a rebellion known as the Vienna Secession. Calling for a bold new art in step with a bold new age, they had staged a strikingly successful exhibition. Out of the ranks of the Secession would come such painters as Oskar Kokoschka and Gustav Klimt, and such architects as Otto Wagner, Josef Hoffman, and Adolf Loos. The latter two are today considered precursors of the famed *Bauhaus* school.

Literature was also flourishing. Writers such as playwright/novelist Arthur Schnitzler and lyric poet Hugo von Hofmannsthal had given Vienna a literary luster that equaled, if it did not exceed, that of any German-language city of its time. Nor did the Austrian capital take a back seat to Berlin when it came to theatre, for even Berlin critics considered Vienna's Adolf von Sonnenthal the best actor in the German-speaking world.

Stimulating and supporting all these artistic activities was a host of publications headed by the *Neue Freie Presse*. This influential daily newspaper stood without peer in its devotion to cultural matters. Its music critic, Eduard Hanslick, imposed — and so great was his influence that imposed is not too strong a term — rigorous standards on the city's musical community, while its cultural editor, Theodor Herzl, had become widely known for the elegance of his own literary sketches as well as for his talent in selecting those of others. (By 1900, Herzl had become much better known for his other activities, but these must await a later chapter.)

As might be expected, musicians, writers, and especially opera singers and actors enjoyed celebrity status far beyond that of noblemen, politicians, and business magnates. A playwright fortunate enough to have a play produced by the Imperial Theatre would find himself so showered with invitations to functions at the Royal Palace that he ended up becoming a virtual guest of the imperial household. "There is hardly a city in Europe," recalled Stefan Zweig in his later years, "where the drive toward cultural ideals was as passionate as it was in Vienna."

But Vienna's claim to eminence rested on more than its cultural refinements and artistic achievements. Its doctors and clinics had become celebrated for treating all manner of ailments, including the growing problems of "nervous" or "mental" disease. Among those breaking new ground in this area was the controversial Sigmund Freud, whose landmark work, *The Interpretation of Dreams*, was published just as the nineteenth century drew to a close.

The University of Vienna, where Freud held a teaching position, had become a hotbed of intellectual ferment. Its economists, especially Karl Menger, were ringing down the curtain on classical economics with the development of such new ideas as marginal utility theory. Its philosophers, including Felix Brentano and his pupil Edmund Husserl, and the development of phenomenology, would influence much twentieth-century thought. Two younger men then studying philosophy at the University, Martin Buber and Ludwig Wittgenstein, would also go on to achieve worldwide renown.

In scientific discovery and technological innovation Vienna had also played its part. In 1864 a Viennese engineer named Siegfried Marcus built an internal combustion engine, and by 1875 he was driving the world's first automobile through the city's streets. Other Austrian inventors had given the world its first typewriter, sewing machine, screw propeller, and in the work of a mild-mannered Augustinian monk named Gregor Mendel, the basic laws of biological inheritance. As the century ended, enterprising Viennese were making motion pictures, experimenting with power-driven airplanes, and conducting research that would later lead to supersonic flight.

Presiding over this remarkable outburst in science, scholarship, and the arts was the Empire's august sovereign, Franz Joseph. He would seem to be a most unlikely ruler for such an intellectual and cultural Camelot for since assuming the throne at the age of eighteen he had read no book save the army register. When someone called his attention to the publication of Krafft-Ebing's daring *Psychopathia Sexualis* in 1875, Franz Joseph merely muttered that it was about time someone had written a new Latin grammar. When he attended an opera or concert, Franz Joseph usually left at the first intermission, having slept through much of what had already been played. Franz Joseph, in fact, slept easily, retiring sometimes as early as nine and never later than eleven in order to rise at five the following morning to direct the affairs of his polyglot empire.

As a ruler, Franz Joseph had little vision of the future and lacked insight into much of what was going on in the present. Still he did not lack compassion and administrative competence. Despite his limitations, he governed both responsibly and responsively, and by 1900 had been governing longer than any monarch in Europe's history except for France's Louis XIV. (Franz Joseph eventually would break Louis' record.) He made an ideal father figure to his people. His tall, erect figure, bald head, and mutton-chop whiskers, along with his frugal habits (he slept on a narrow cot, bathed in a portable wooden tub, and smoked the cheap cheroots of the government's tobacco monopoly), plus his devotion to duty provided the people with a reassuring picture of stability and solidity. The good citizens of Vienna could sleep soundly at night knowing that in his palace on the Ringstrasse Franz Joseph was doing the same.

The Ringstrasse was perhaps Franz Joseph's most tangible and visible contribution to Vienna's aesthetics. It consisted of a series of linked boulevards that formed a two-mile-long horseshoe around the inner city. Along its two-hundred-foot-wide tree-lined route were government buildings, including the emperor's palace, various cultural edifices such as the opera, the Imperial Theatre, and the University of Vienna, together with well-groomed parks and expensive stores. Sigmund Freud lived only a few blocks away, and walking along the Ringstrasse provided a pleasant form of daily exercise. For young Adolf Hitler, visiting Vienna for the first time in 1905, the Ringstrasse seemed "like magic from the Arabian nights."

Vienna offered other scenic delights as well. There were its magnificent cathedrals, including towering St. Stephen's, the easily accessible Vienna Woods that girded the city, and of course, the Danube.

It would seem the Viennese certainly had much to sing about, for in addition to all the cultural achievements, they also enjoyed favorable economic, social, and political developments. The city's population had grown faster than that of any major city in Europe during the previous fifty years, and the Viennese label in clothes and craftsmanship was held in international esteem. Socially, the Viennese benefited from health and accident insurance laws which even Viktor Adler, the leader of the country's fledgling and fiercely oppositionist Social Democratic party, admitted were the world's best. Politically, they could cite their country's constitution that guaranteed all the Empire's citizens equality before the law.

There were the numerous festivals and rituals which contributed color, drama, and good feeling to everyday life in the city. These included the daily changing of the guard at the imperial palace, the Corpus Christi celebration, the May Day Festival at the Prater, the city's amusement park, and the pre-Lenten festivities known as Fasching when as many as fifty balls might be held in a single evening. In 1879 the city's residents dressed up in Italian Renaissance costumes to celebrate the silver wedding anniversary of their emperor and empress.

Rituals also embellished and enhanced the more ordinary routine of daily life. In meeting a friend or acquaintance, a Viennese would customarily say *servus*, the Latin word for "your servant." On the tramways a rider who could afford it gave a tip to the conductor, who in turn would treat the rider with effusive courtesy. Titles were highly valued and lavishly used. Every general automatically received a "von" in front of his name. So did every high-placed civil servant after ten years in rank. For that matter, so did virtually any banker who managed to reach retirement without going bankrupt more than once.

It was customary in addressing someone to give him the rank one degree higher than the rank he held. Thus a section chief would be addressed as a department head, a policeman would be called Herr Inspektor, and a waiter would be called Herr Ober, a shortened version of Mr. Headwaiter. The Herr Ober, in turn, would address his customer as Herr Baron, Herr Doktor, or simply Mein Herr, depending on the quality of the customer's clothes and the size of his tip.

Despite their deference to established and hierarchical values, the Viennese could still laugh at themselves. They could also manifest a certain charming quirkiness. Where else but in Vienna would a Doctor Schmecktgut (taste good) petition the court to change his name to Doctor Schmecktbesser (taste better)?

All in all, it would seem that the Vienna of 1900 had a right to its reputation for enjoyable, indeed joyful, living. To go to Vienna, wrote the Prague author Max Brod, was always a "Fest." Is it any wonder, then, that by 1900 Vienna had inspired more songs than all the world's other major cities combined? And is it any wonder that no one sang them more lustily than the Viennese? Young Thomas Mann went through a small inheritance in four days in fin-de-siècle Vienna and never regretted it. "After an evening at the theatre or May Day in the Prater," writes historian William Johnston, "a Viennese might with equanimity regard his city as the pivot of the universe. Where else did appearance so beguilingly sweeten reality?"

Chapter 2

Vienna Dolorosa

Just what was the reality that, in Johnston's words, appearance so beguilingly sweetened? How much substance actually underlay the near-idyllic image that existed at the time, and exists today, of fin-de-siècle Vienna?

To obtain a truer or at least more complete picture of the Vienna of 1900, we must turn back to the Vienna of 1800. At that critical juncture in its history, the city was the capital of the largest and in some respects the most powerful empire on the continent. This empire had been governed by one family, the Habsburgs, since the Middle Ages.

The Habsburgs' record of rule was not only long but proud. They had, admittedly with outside help, turned back the Turks at the gates of Vienna, thereby keeping those Asian intruders from overrunning Europe. They had also stopped the Protestant Reformation from spreading into southern Europe and had even converted the lower German states back to Catholicism. As a result, most of the few Protestants remaining in Austria lived only in small towns which the Counter-Reformation had bypassed. Finally, the Habsburgs had spread the blessings of Western civilization into the Balkan states.

For four hundred years a Habsburg had also headed that collection of mostly German states known as the Holy Roman Empire. This did not give him, or in one case her, much actual power since those states remained essentially sovereign, but the title did acknowledge the supremacy of Austria in central Europe.

But then came Napoleon who, after defeating the Austrian armies with comparative ease, did what the mighty Turkish armies had failed to do more than two centuries earlier: occupy Vienna. He also overran all the other German states and in the process dissolved the Holy Roman Empire. No longer would Austria's sovereign preside over this largely powerless but still prestigious confederation.

The wave of revolutions that swept through Europe in 1848 buffeted Austria and its capital once again. The Viennese rebelled, as did the residents of so many other European cities. Yet, with some exceptions, the Viennese did not actively seek to exercise power. Rather, they confined themselves largely to demanding concessions from their rulers. As Golo Mann would later point out, "They did not want a revolution in the French sense . . . the people wanted freedom to be granted by traditional authority."

Another incident that occurred during the revolt reveals another facet of Austrian or at least Viennese character. At one time a huge crowd gathered at the Ministry of War protesting the despatch of troops to put down an uprising elsewhere in the Empire. The crowd soon broke into the building, dragged out the Minister of War, and then hanged the sixty-eight-year-old man from a lamppost while freely stabbing and slashing him. The crowd ripped the clothes from his body, and as women dipped handkerchiefs in his blood, several men, to the crowd's delight, tore the genitalia from his dangling corpse.

These episodes from the tumult of 1848 indicate that the good-humored *gemütlich* Viennese *could be vicious as well as servile when the appropriate occasion arose.** Such occasions would come again, especially ninety years later, with tragic effects for both Vienna and its Jews.

Franz Joseph assumed the throne in 1848, and despite his youth he and his advisors succeeded in suppressing the revolt. But in 1859 new problems arose, and this time the young emperor did not fare so well. His empire then included most of northern Italy, and these provinces, inflamed with the spirit of nineteenth-century nationalism, now rebelled. With the help of the French, the Italians defeated the Austrians in two costly battles, thereby forcing the Empire to relinquish much of its Italian territory.

This setback in the south was followed seven years later in 1867 by an even greater one in the north when Prussia, having baited Austria into war, defeated her in seven weeks at Sadowa. It marked the quickest defeat of a major military power in world history. Although the German Chancellor Bismarck proved a fairly generous victor when it came to dictating the terms of peace, Austria — once preeminent among the German states — found itself permanently reduced to subordinate status.

---

*Schiller in one of his plays has a general remark that the Viennese would sooner forgive him for losing a battle than for depriving them of the joy of watching a traitor being hauled off to the gallows.

Following another seven-year interval, catastrophe once again struck Franz Joseph's empire. This time it took the form of a financial debacle. The year after its war with Germany, Austria enjoyed a bountiful harvest while the rest of Europe suffered a poor one. This greatly increased the country's exports, bringing a fresh supply of money and a fresh spirit into the Austrian economy. The country which had lagged behind Germany and other countries in industrial growth now began to catch up. Railroad construction rose sixfold in six years. Other activities also boomed and the Ringstrasse, started in 1859, rang with the sounds of new construction as foreign capital poured into the country.

But the upsurge spiraled out of control and turned into a speculation spree. Banks, most of them greatly undercapitalized, proliferated. Paper-thin corporations bloomed, some of them promising to pay their "investors" dividends of fifty percent. From the nobility to the more marginal members of the middle class, Austrians cashed in their savings to help fuel the speculative orgy.

In May 1873 the bubble burst. While the collapse helped trigger a worldwide depression, no country suffered as severely as the Habsburg Empire. Of the seventy-two banks operating in Vienna when it occurred, only fourteen remained in business five years later. Insurance companies, iron mills, and other businesses were also swept away.

The crash, compounded and magnified by a cholera epidemic, plus a series of poor harvests, brought Austria's economy to a state of semiparalysis. Moreover, laws hastily enacted after the crash curbed not only speculation but economic growth as well. The government began nationalizing railroads, clamping tariffs on imports, and curbing competition in various trades — measures which tended to thwart economic development. So many had been so badly burned that they henceforth shunned investments altogether.

Eventually Austria's economy began to struggle back to its feet. But the recovery came slowly and depended heavily on foreign capital. While other European nations, including Germany, were exporting capital in the late nineteenth century, the Austrian Empire was importing it. French investors financed two important railroads, the Germans developed the country's electricity, and British firms owned and operated Vienna's streetlighting system and its waterworks. Vienna became the only major city in Europe to have such basic municipal services in foreign hands.

Much of the city's phenomenal population growth came through annexation. The rural unemployed, their numbers mounting, drifted toward the city, settling on the outskirts where they made homes for themselves in hastily built huts and shanties or even abandoned railroad cars. Since they constituted a cheap and plentiful labor supply, factories and other businesses gradually began to appear. These factory communities eventually required city services to sustain themselves and so the city incorporated them.

Most of the factories that emerged during this time were small — only a few had one thousand or more workers — and many were oriented to producing luxury goods, or goods for the local economy. Even cottage industry was still common in late nineteenth-century Vienna, long after it had all but disappeared in other metropolitan areas.

Vienna's workers, many of them Czechs, may have benefited from some advanced social laws, but they labored long hours for low wages, for only on those terms could the city's industrialists meet foreign competition. Many put in eleven-hour days, sustaining themselves largely on bread and coffee and sharing bed space with others who worked different shifts. By 1900 Vienna had become almost as famous for its flophouses, some of which a few years later would shelter the would-be artist Adolf Hitler, as it had been for its concert halls and parks.

More than most cities, Vienna had been a city of small tradesmen and craftsmen. Despite growing proletarianization, it remained so. But most of its tradesmen and artisans fared only marginally better than its workers. According to a government study at the time, four out of five Viennese shoemakers in the early 1890s were earning less than the bare minimum deemed necessary to support a family.

To be sure, income taxes were light — small tips to the state was how one contemporary writer characterized them — while government bonds paid high interest. But such expedients were necessary to generate the funds that the government needed to sustain itself and the economy needed to grow. Despite these inducements to investment, the Empire's per capita income in 1900 was only forty percent of Germany's.

But if the Empire's economy was still struggling as the twentieth century dawned, its polity was actually foundering. To understand what was happening, we must first comprehend the demographics of Franz Joseph's crazy-quilt empire.

The Empire's fifty million inhabitants included eleven different nationalities plus numerous national subgroups. German-speaking Austrians made up the largest single group, yet they numbered less than one-quarter of the whole. Next in size were the Magyars (Hungarians), who constituted almost a fifth (ten million). Then came the eight million Czechs and Slovaks, the five million Serbo-Croatians, the five million Poles, and the two and one-half million Jews. Although the Jews were nearly five percent of the population, they were not considered to be, and did not for the most part consider themselves to be, a separate ethnic group.

Each member of Franz Joseph's cabinet owned twenty uniforms so that he could wear the appropriate one when visiting a particular ethnic region or when receiving its dignitaries in Vienna. Franz Joseph himself had over two hundred uniforms as befitted a sovereign who was emperor of Austria, King of Hungary, King of Bohemia, King of Dalmatia, King of Transylvania, King of Croatia and Slovenia, and Archduke of thirty other different places.

This diverse array of nationalities had brought the Empire diversity and vitality. But by 1900 it had brought it to the brink of political and economic collapse. The Empire's various ethnic groups, ignited by the nineteenth-century wave of nationalism, were increasingly demanding independence and in so doing they were fighting not only their emperor but also each other.

It all began with Italy. That country's successful bid for independence sparked the Hungarians who, taking advantage of the monarchy's weakened position following its defeat by Prussia, forced Franz Joseph to grant them a substantial degree of autonomy. The Hungarian Settlement of 1867 made Hungary a semi-independent country with its own prime minister and cabinet. The Empire's name was changed to Austria-Hungary and the Emperor himself now had to take a separate oath as King of Hungary.

As might be expected, Hungary's achievement of quasi-independence stirred many of the Empire's other nationalities to seek similar status. The crash of 1873, in creating widespread discontent, added impetus to this movement. The German liberals, who stood for a business-oriented economy, lost support, and their seats in Parliament increasingly fell to militant nationalists who spent much of their time and energy fighting each other.

Adding to all the dissension and disarray were the complaints of the more zealous clerics and laypeople of the Catholic Church. In 1855 Franz Joseph had signed a concordat with the Vatican, giving the Church widespread control over education, marriage, and other aspects of society. Gradually, under pressure from the liberals and others, he began whittling these powers away. Finally, when the Church proclaimed the doctrine of papal infallibility in 1870, Franz Joseph claimed the Church's new doctrine had changed the nature of the other party to the concordat and canceled it altogether.

This still left the Church with substantial powers and prerogatives. It continued to register births and deaths and to regulate marriage among Austria's predominantly Catholic majority. It could even count on the state to enforce certain Church laws. When philosopher Felix Brentano, an ex-priest, announced his intention to marry Ida Lieben, a baptized Jewess, the University of Vienna acted on Church laws forbidding former priests from marrying and ousted him from his chair. (The University later hired him back, but only as a lecturer.)

Priests were paid by the state to give religious instruction in the schools, but this was not enough to please the Church militants. Protestants and Jews now had equal rights, and therefore regulated their own affairs, while the state paid ministers and rabbis to teach religion to children of their faiths in the schools. What really rankled the clerical forces was the government's refusal to finance Catholic schools. This meant that Catholic schoolchildren were now exposed to occasional Protestant and, especially in Vienna, occasional Jewish teachers. Many Catholics regarded this situation as outright oppression. With twenty priests plus numerous staunch laymen in the lower House of Parliament, and with every bishop automatically a member of the non-elected upper House, militant Catholics became increasingly insistent that the situation be changed.

All of these tensions were coming to a head in the 1890s. A militant Catholic party made a bold bid for control of Vienna, a move that would eventually have serious and saddening consequences for the city's Jews. But at the national level, it was the fight between Austro-Germans and Slavs that created the most tension. An effort to make Czech a government language in the Czech province of Bohemia, or even an attempt by a Slovene minority living in an Austro-German province to have its own school, would set off riots in both German and Slavic communities throughout the Empire. As Viennese wits liked to quip, Austria was neither a democratic state nor an autocratic state, but a state of emergency.

As a result of all this ethnic squabbling, the Austrian Parliament degenerated into pandemonium, literally as well as figuratively. Its various factions began bringing drums, cymbals, horns, and other musical instruments to the sessions, playing them as loudly as possible whenever someone they opposed rose to speak. Since few could actually play their instruments and none was interested in making music, the result was a near constant din. One parliamentarian, during a filibuster, held the podium for twelve hours straight, but though his lips were moving, no one could actually tell whether he was speaking because of all the noise. Mark Twain, who attended a session or two of Parliament at about this time, did not need to embellish what he saw in order to write his humorous sketch entitled "Stirring Times in Austria."

Franz Joseph himself became so disgusted that he finally sent the members home in 1897 and governed without Parliament for ten years. In any case, Austria's Parliament had only modest powers and this, plus the fact that it was split not into coherent parties but into nationalist factions, made it a poor place to prepare its members and their constituents for the difficulties of democratic rule which lay ahead.

In his mounting struggle to hold his disintegrating empire together, Franz Joseph relied heavily on his army and his bureaucracy. He was particularly fond of the army, giving it generous sums from the Empire's none-too-plentiful resources. The army's uniforms had actually won prizes for their design and style. But, as George Marek notes, if Austria had the best-dressed military force in Europe, it may also have had the least effective one.

The army's shortcomings had become woefully apparent in 1859 when, despite having more troops and cannon than the combined French and Italian forces arrayed against it, it suffered stunning defeats at Maragenta and Solferino. It is not difficult to understand why. The general in command at Maragenta, for example, owed his position solely to the personal favor of Franz Joseph's mother. This commander's military prowess was demonstrated by his having previously ordered all his men to wear black mustaches, requiring those who were blonde to dye their mustaches black and those who were still beardless to paint their mustaches on. At Solferino, Franz Joseph himself insisted on taking command but could not find his staff officers, or they him, until the fighting was almost over.

At both battles, supplies arrived late and weapons frequently failed to function. The army's more disastrous loss to Prussia in 1866 stemmed partly from its refusal to buy the new breach-loading rifles which the Prussians had adopted but which the Austrian military had sneered at as unworkable. As Zweig once remarked, "The army had more great bandmasters than it had great generals."

The military was essentially controlled by the nobility, who disdained technology, loved the cavalry (the Austrian army had the highest proportion of cavalry of all European military forces), and pushed their favorites into high positions regardless of talent or merit. Its largely Austro-German officer corps led their mostly non-German, and non-German speaking, troops with a prescribed seventy-word list of German commands. Even Hungarian officers commanding Hungarian troops had to use the same all-German word list in giving orders to their men.

The military enjoyed great prestige, at least among the Austro-Germans. The army *is* Austria, Franz Grillparzer, the country's greatest pre-Hofmannsthal poet, had said. Consequently, it remained a powerful force in Austrian society. When a civilian met an officer on the street, the civilian had to give way if he did not want to fight a duel.

Thanks to the army, dueling had remained a vital element in the life of the better-off classes. Failing to fight a duel would lose an officer his commission, and most educated and socially elevated men held commissions in the reserve. For example, when a colleague of Sigmund Freud was called *Saujud* (dirty Jew) by a Gentile doctor in the course of a disagreement over a medical matter, the Jewish physician felt compelled to issue an immediate challenge to the Gentile since both held reserve commissions. Arthur Schnitzler, a physician as well as a writer, was courtmartialed and stripped of his reserve commission when he wrote *Lieutenant Guste*, a piece which discredited dueling.

Despite its shortcomings, the army could suppress riots and demonstrations, and by the turn of the century Franz Joseph increasingly called upon it to do so. As his crown prince had written a decade or so earlier, the army was "the single central thread which in this chaos still stands for the Empire." At the same time, the army both reflected and reinforced many of the Empire's great and growing problems.

If the army's impact on Austrian life was significant and largely deleterious, the impact of the country's bureaucracy was even more so. Built up since the eighteenth century to bind the Empire together, it had by 1900 become a major contributor to its disintegration.

The bureaucracy had become overly centralized. Its officials wore the same uniforms, followed the same procedures, and generally spoke the same language (German) from one end of the Empire to the other. At an earlier stage this may have made the bureaucracy a unifying force, but with time such centralization made it a disruptive one. The administration of such a geographically and ethnically variegated empire required flexibility in the field to accommodate disparate conditions and cultures. Yet field officers had little official discretion to adapt procedures and programs to the needs of the areas and groups they served.

While most bureaucracies tend to become stodgy and stultified, Austria had become virtually encrusted with outmoded ways of thinking and acting. In Vienna, a single ordinary tax payment was handled by twenty-seven separate officials. Most headquarters, to say nothing of field offices, still lacked typewriters and telephones in 1900 and even minuscule matters produced lengthy meetings and memoranda, with decisions continually put off until too late. As Viktor Adler put it, "The government of Austria is as incapable of performing acts of justice as it is incapable of performing acts of oppression. . . . We have government by indolence."

Two further and related characteristics of Austrian bureaucracy added to its aggravations: *Protektion* and *Schlamperei*.

Protektion can be translated as patronage or pull. While most of Western Europe's bureaucracies were evolving toward the democratic or at least quasi-democratic norm of impartiality, Austria's officials remained highly vulnerable to personal influence. While outright bribery was relatively rare, at least at the higher levels, favoritism of one kind or another was rife. The nobility that controlled the bureaucracy provided the model for such favoritism, and those beneath them faithfully followed their example. All too often, people were promoted, charges were launched or dismissed, and projects were either sanctioned or suppressed on the basis of who, not what, was involved.

Such favoritism even extended to the University of Vienna. A respected chemist waiting years for a professorship suddenly received one after marrying a professor's daughter. Freud obtained his long overdue promotion to full professor only after one of his patients, acting on his behalf, contributed a valuable picture to a new gallery that the Minister of Education was setting up.

Schlamperei, the other and still more pervasive trait of Austrian administration, is best translated as sloppiness. Files were lost, letters went unanswered, and petitions ended up in the wrong bureau. Here too the higher echelon set the example. Once, when a new minister of war was appointed, the cabinet order notifying the appointee was sent to one of his cousins who happened to have the same name. The cousin showed up at the ministry office, was sworn in, and served for some time as Austria's war minister before the mistake was discovered and corrected.

Given the dominant role that the bureaucracy played in Austrian life, and given its heavy-handed officiousness, its *Protektion* and its *Schlamperei*, the Empire's administrative apparatus was the despair of its citizens. Even the poet Grillparzer who made his living as a bureaucrat — he rose to the high position of *Hofrat* or Imperial Counselor — voiced concern over its workings, while the novelist Franz Kafka would later use the Austrian bureaucracy as a basis for his novel *The Trial*.

The bureaucracy's effect on the average citizen was profound. "Under bureaucratic rule," writes Johnston, "citizens of Austria continued their habit of carping (*Raunzerei*) at authority without resisting it, reinforcing a political flaccidity that survives to this day." Later, this attitude of lethargic disgruntlement would facilitate the death of Austrian democracy, and along with it, the destruction of the most brilliant Jewish community of modern times.

Like the army, the bureaucracy mirrored and magnified some of the basic aspects of Austrian society. One of these was its deep-rooted conservatism.

This may sound strange in view of all the artistic, scientific, and scholarly innovations noted earlier, but the Empire and its capital were actually highly resistant to innovation. Not only were telephones, typewriters, and elevators rare in Vienna in 1900, but the city's streetcars were still not electrified. Many homes, including Franz Joseph's own palace, lacked even gas lighting. In fact, until the 1890s, doctors at the Vienna General Hospital were still performing operations by candlelight. The typewriter, the screw propeller, the sewing machine, the automobile, and other inventions may have been made in Austria, but almost all of them were developed elsewhere. Consequently, Gregor Mendel may have been wise in hesitating to publish in Austria the findings that would make him the father of modern genetics.

The Viennese medical community, for all its esteemed brilliance, hounded Semmelweiss out of the city and eventually into a mental hospital when he dared tell physicians to wash their hands. Most of Vienna's doctors also refused to believe in male hysteria, decades after data compiled in France and even in Vienna had proven its existence. How could men become hysterical, they sneered, since every doctor knows that hysteria stems from a malfunction of the uterus?

As might be expected, Freud encountered a frosty reception when he sought not only to demonstrate and describe male hysteria but to go still further in exploring the human psyche. Most of the six hundred copies of his first book, *Studies in Hysteria*, were still unsold in 1900, six years after publication. Most of the eight hundred copies of his second book, *The Interpretation of Dreams*, would not be sold until eight years later. "In those days when one mentioned Freud's name in a Viennese gathering," one contemporary observer later reported, "everyone would begin to laugh as if someone had told a joke."*

But what about the Secession? Did this not represent a bold, exciting breakthrough in the world of art? Actually, the Secession drew much of its inspiration and support from abroad. Moreover, its better architects found few commissions in their native city. The majority of Otto Wagner's spectacular projects never got off the drawing board, while Josef Hoffman's masterpiece, the Palais Stocket, was put up in Brussels, not Vienna.

Even in music Vienna tended to resist anything smacking of originality. Although the waltz was created in Vienna, only after it became popular in Paris did the Viennese accept it. Mahler premiered all of his symphonies outside of Vienna, and when he later conducted them in the city itself, his numerous critics jeered at him. Schönberg's *Transfigured Night*, when finally performed in 1904, invoked a stormy reception and was not played again for many years thereafter. On New Year's Day, 1913, the Viennese Opera Orchestra refused to play Stravinsky's *Petrushka*, calling it *schmutzige Musik* (dirty music), although orchestras in London and Paris had already performed the composer's much more daring *The Rite of Spring*.

It should come as no surprise, then, that both Mahler and Schönberg left Vienna — Mahler went to New York and Schönberg to Berlin. Many of the prominent philosophers nurtured at the University of Vienna also emigrated: Husserl moved to Germany, Buber to Germany and then Israel, and Wittgenstein to England. Moreover, the Empire's only two writers of lasting international fame — Kafka and the poet Rainer Maria Rilke — were both born in Prague and neither ever spent much time or showed much interest in Vienna. Although a great bastion of culture, the city was not always respectful of or receptive to genuine genius.

This tendency to disavow the new also permeated many other sectors of Viennese life. The aristocracy clung zealously to their old ways, fiercely resisting

---

*The Viennese Medical Society at one of its gatherings in the early 1900s staged a parody of Molière's *The Imaginary Invalid*. In their version the quack doctor says, "If the patient loved his mother, it is the reason for his neurosis; and if he hated her, it is the reason for his neurosis. Whatever the disease, the cause is the same. And whatever the cause, the disease is the same. And so is the cure: twenty one-hour sessions at fifty kronen each."

the currents of change. Though an aristocrat would often turn up as a member of the board of directors of a new bank or business firm, rarely would he contribute much of anything to the enterprise beyond his name and occasional presence. No artist to speak of and only a few patrons of the arts came from aristocratic ranks; most of them were much more interested in developing fine horses than fine painters and musicians.

Even the more enterprising bourgeois were conservative in demeanor and deportment. Stefan Zweig recalls never having seen his father, a self-made industrialist, run up or down a set of stairs or do anything in a noticeably hasty fashion. "Speed was not only thought to be unrefined but indeed was considered unnecessary, for in that stabilized bourgeois world with its countless little certainties, well palisaded on all sides, nothing unexpected ever occurred." He further notes how his father would never have lunch at Sacher's, the city's leading hotel, for the elder Zweig did not think it proper for a man in his position to do so. Everything had its place, and the place of an upper middle-class Jewish businessman was not sitting next to aristocrats at Sacher's.

Lower middle-class males found their place in the numerous cafes where a man could read the daily papers and chat or play cards with friends. The workers, of course, were too busy trying to scrounge a living to worry about their lifestyles. Thus Austria, said Zweig, "was an old state, dominated by an aged emperor, ruled by old ministers, a state without ambition that hoped to preserve itself unharmed in the European domain solely by opposing all radical changes."

One effect of this near mania for stability was a glorification of age and a corresponding denigration of youth. A man of thirty was considered young, while even a man of forty was not considered truly ripe. When Mahler became director of the Imperial Opera at the age of thirty-eight, the Viennese expressed alarm over the city's foremost musical podium being entrusted to "so young a man." They had apparently forgotten that Mozart and Schubert did not even live to that age.

With youth a handicap to all careers, young men exerted every effort to look older. They affected long, black frock coats, beards, and gold eyeglasses whether or not they needed them. The desirability of a middle-aged appearance even made it fashionable to cultivate some portliness, a goal that the heavy, rich Viennese diet certainly facilitated.

The educational system did its part to repress youthful energies. Teachers, all of them male, sat on raised platforms, were addressed as professor even if they taught first grade, and rarely engaged a pupil in private conversation. The youngsters were drilled rather than taught, for rote learning was the chief method of instruction.

The atmosphere changed at the University, but only because academic work was now too easy. After eight semesters a student took an exam and handed in a dissertation. A bright student could fulfill this requirement in a year of solid effort, and even a not-so-bright student could do so if he studied law. This may have been one reason why nearly half of the University's students were law students.*

Virtually all the students were male. Although many universities in Europe had begun to accept female matriculants, the University of Vienna still discouraged them. No legal obstacle prevented women from enrolling, but many practical impediments effectively barred their path. They received no preparation for the entrance exams, and they had to overcome opposition from their families, as well as harassment from teachers and male students. (Peter Drucker relates that when his mother reached college age at about this time and expressed a desire to become a teacher, her guardian, "a certified, grade A liberal," tried desperately to talk her out of it, saying that a university education would scare off every eligible suitor in sight.)

In 1897 a young woman named Gabriele von Posner became Austria's first female doctor, but she had completed her studies in Switzerland. Since the University of Vienna couldn't believe that a woman could or should be a doctor, it made her take the exams all over again. Then, a few years later, a woman named Gertrude Bien passed the medical school entrance exam. Forced to admit her, the school told her to sit in the last row, ask no questions and make no comments, and in order to be less conspicuous, dress in men's clothing. She was always addressed as Herr Bien and her M.D. diploma was awarded to Herr Doktor Gertrude Bien. (She eventually became chief of staff and medical director of one of the city's better hospitals.)

Antifeminism in this sense permeated all sectors of the population from peasants who threw stones at women riding bicycles, to Catholic priests who occasionally refused to preach to women. Mahler and Freud both wanted their wives to be, as Freud put it to his fiancée, "an adored sweetheart in youth and a beloved wife in maturity." Mahler refused to allow his wife to compose music, telling her, "I want you for a wife, not a colleague."

The lot of middle-class women was not helped by what Janik and Toulmin call "the business character of bourgeois marriage." As they explain it, many marriages were arranged solely for financial reasons, with little or no regard for the desires of the partners. Such unions "guaranteed frustration, especially for women, in so straitlaced a society."

But was Viennese society so straitlaced? The answer is yes and no. For single women of the middle and upper classes, it is distinctly yes. They were continually watched and warned of the dangers of sex. This left them so fearful and naive that they frequently could not cope with married life. Zweig reports

*Drucker says it was not uncommon for a student to be asked, "Are you a real student or are you studying law?"

how one young woman came pounding on her parents' door at 1:00 a.m. on her wedding night, sobbing how her bridegroom had turned out to be a perverted beast. He had actually tried to undress her.

Once safely embedded in wedlock, a woman might discover pleasure in sex and go on to have extramarital affairs. But this often filled her with such feelings of guilt that it created more problems than it resolved. This was particularly true of Jewish women raised in families imbued with the traditional Jewish aversion to extramarital sex.

Far worse off, of course, were lower-class women, many of whom drifted into affairs with better-off men in the hope of improving their miserable existence. Quite a few fell into outright prostitution, and in the poorer working-class neighborhoods women could be picked up at any time of the day or night for hardly more than the price of a newspaper. Furthermore, although a prostitute could obtain a police license by undergoing a medical examination twice a week, she still lacked legal rights. For example, she could not sue a customer who had solicited her favors and then refused to pay for them.

Although men obviously enjoyed a much better existence, Vienna's moral ambiguities and exaggerated double standard created problems for them, too. They rarely could afford to marry before their late twenties or later, and indulging their libidos outside of marriage could prove difficult, if not dangerous. Zweig wrote, "I cannot recall a single comrade of my youth who did not come to me with pale and troubled mien, one because he was ill or feared illness, another because he was being blackmailed for arranging an abortion, a third because he lacked the money to be cured without the knowledge of his family, a fourth because he did not know how to pay hush money to a waitress who claimed to have borne his child, the fifth because his wallet had been stolen in a brothel and he did not dare to go to the police."

As one might expect, syphilis and gonorrhea had spread throughout the population, even touching, it is now believed, the royal family itself. One could hardly walk a block in the Austrian capital without seeing a shingle advertising a specialist who treated such maladies.

Vienna had other health problems as well. Tuberculosis had become so prevalent that it was sometimes referred to as Vienna's endemic illness. One study in the 1890s found nearly one out of every nine of the city's shoemakers and tailors suffering from it. Vienna's infant mortality must have been high since Austria as a whole had the highest rate of infant deaths in Western Europe. Finally, and for our purposes most importantly, Vienna suffered the distressing distinction of being the suicide capital of the Western world.

In *Die Fledermaus*, that most Viennese of all operas, there is the phrase, "Happy is the one who forgets about what cannot be changed." This expresses a fundamental problem of Viennese society. As historian Klemens von Klemperer puts it, "The Austrian capital in the last decades before the First World War had its way of coping, or rather not coping, with political and social realities. Life was pleasant and amusing, because the Viennese had a superb gift for looking away. There was a great deal of political wisdom but no one to apply it; there was much talent, but it was untapped and purposeless, with no will to act and no sense of power."

Lacking a sense of power and purpose, caused in part by historical, social, political, and economic factors examined earlier, large numbers of Viennese succumbed to a general malaise. Their high suicide rate was one symptom of this sickness. Their intense pursuit of pleasure was another. The city's balls and dance halls, the theaters and horse shows, and its citizens' delight in card playing, gossip, and sexual dalliance can all be seen not as an expression of life's joys but as an escape from its realities. Even when it came to loftier pursuits such as music, literature, and art, the Viennese generally preferred the role of carping critic to that of enthusiastic participant.

The exaggerated role that food played in daily Viennese life is also revealing. In his youth Franz Joseph was more admired for his large appetite than for anything else, and it was said that the only thing besides opera that started on time in Vienna was the midday meal. Heavily sugared foods were especially popular, and the city had become almost as celebrated for its pastries as for its music. Sweets can be a way of assuaging pains other than those of mere hunger.

So great was the Viennese drive for distraction that it could on occasion overcome the hostility to innovation. Thus in 1897, Vienna — a city with horse-drawn streetcars and gaslit offices — erected a giant Ferris wheel in its Prater. A decade or so later it inaugurated the largest roller coaster in Europe. Comments historian Johnston, "It was as though the Viennese wished to confine technological advance to an amusement park."

Another indication that all was not well with Viennese society can be seen in an anecdote reported by Zweig. One day when he was young, his family's cook burst into the living room, her eyes streaming with tears. She had just learned of the death of Charlotte Wolter, the city's most prominent actress. "The most grotesque thing about her wild mourning," Zweig said, "was obviously the fact this this elderly, semiliterate cook had never seen Wolter either on the stage or elsewhere."

To Zweig, her grief signified Vienna's unity and strength, showing that even those who had never seen the actress perform considered her part of the collective property of the community. But in light of what we know now about human behavior, another interpretation offers itself. The grief-stricken cook had, like so many other Viennese, fallen prey to simple celebrity worship, and was identifying with the illustrious as a way of compensating for the barrenness of her own life. It can scarcely be seen as a healthy social phenomenon.

There were also more direct manifestations of discontent and social decay in turn-of-the-century Vienna. Its residents spent inordinate amounts of time and energy grumbling, complaining, and bemoaning their fate. "Life is like a chicken-coop ladder," ran a saying of the time, "short and shitty." The Viennese expressed loud and frequent dissatisfaction with their government, their economy, and other ethnic and religious groups, as well as with their relatives, friends, and neighbors. They would even criticize themselves, although generally they would take the opposite tack if anyone openly agreed with them. George Marek quotes one contemporary writer as saying, "A Viennese is one who is dissatisfied with himself, who hates the other Viennese but who cannot live without them," and he quotes still another writer of the period as remarking how a Viennese "lives for his leisure occupation" for "Vienna is a city of people who have chosen the wrong profession."

Some commentators went still further, condemning their countrymen for a slew of delinquencies and deficiencies. "Laxity, multiplied by Slavic slovenliness, raised to the second power by spiritual and secular misgovernment, indolence, frivolity, moral degeneration, indescribable knavishness" were some of the terms used by the Viennese writer Ferdinand Kürnberger to describe his fellow countrymen, while another writer, Hermann Bahr, claimed that in Vienna "the man of character draws back; actual life is in the hands of the fraudulent for all is deceit and illusion." Such sentiments led many to agree with contemporary critic Karl Kraus that Vienna was "the proving ground for the world's destruction," and that its glory and splendor only signified what still another writer, Hermann Broch, called a "gay apocalypse."

Of course, intellectuals frequently find fault with their societies, but the feelings voiced by so many Viennese critics as the nineteenth century turned into the twentieth indicate that something deep-seated had gone amiss in the fabled city of dreams. Too few of its people were engaged in the kind of purposeful effort that leads to constructive achievement, and from there to feelings of healthy self-confidence and pride. Too many had succumbed to sluggishness and self-indulgence, practices which can lead to low self-esteem and eventually a need for scapegoats.

One particular defect of the Viennese character, a failing that many contemporary Viennese writers commented upon, warrants special attention. The Viennese at all levels of society had apparently become masters at dissimulation, saying one thing while thinking and doing another. "In this country," wrote Robert Musil, perhaps the greatest novelist the city has ever produced, "a man always acted differently from how he thought and thought differently from how he acted." Hermann Bahr, one of Musil's older contemporaries, had noted earlier "no one knows how a Viennese will ever act. . . . His conduct is incalculable."*

In his novel, *The Road to the Open*, Arthur Schnitzler describes an incident based on a real-life episode in which a member of Parliament calls out, "Yid, shut your mouth," to a Jewish member who is making a speech. But when the session ends, the two parliamentarians go out for a convivial drink together. This incident is then reported to a character in the novel who professes to find it unbelievable. "Unbelievable?" replies the one who related the episode. "No. Austrian. With us, indignation is as little genuine as enthusiasm. Only our delight at the misfortunes of others and our hatred of talent are honest."

This, then, was the Vienna of 1900, a city rich in fascination and glory, but one also rife with problems and perversities, and ripe for the horrors that lay ahead.

---

*As an example one can cite the poet Grillparzer who switched from being an ardent democrat to being an ardent supporter of the status quo when it became apparent that the democratic revolt of 1848 had been suppressed.

Part II

A Troubled Triumph

*. . . the Vienna Jews, you know, do not suffer from a persecution
complex but from a mania for security. A persecution complex,
by comparison, is harmless. You are aware of danger, real or
imagined, so your animal instincts rise to your defence.
A security complex lures you to destruction.*
— Arthur Schnitzler, *The Road to the Open*

Chapter 3

The Emergence of Jewish Vienna

Nestled alongside the Danube at a juncture where the Austrian Alps dissolve into a broad plain that sweeps into the Balkans, Vienna has long been a natural gateway between East and West. In medieval times the city's location made it a prime trading center, and this may help to explain why the Jews of medieval Europe, confined as they were to earning their living as traders and moneylenders, found the city so attractive. In 966, less than a century after the name Vienna first appears on historic documents, the phrase "Jews and other legitimate merchants" shows up on one of the city's commercial edicts.

Over the next four centuries, Vienna's Jewish community grew rapidly; by the 1300s a contemporary observer remarked, "There are more Jews in Vienna than in any other German city familiar to me." The Jewish community had grown in distinction as well, for Vienna had become known throughout the Jewish world as a center of learning with its rabbis and Hebraic scholars often referred to as the "sages of Vienna."

But the growth and prosperity of the Viennese Jews, along with their alien rituals and habits, had aroused the hostility and suspicion of their fellow townsmen. In 1421 the Viennese Gentiles launched a devastating, officially sanctioned pogrom. All Jews who refused to become Christians (the vast majority) were either executed or expelled. Their goods were expropriated and their children were forcibly baptized. For the first but not the last time in modern history Vienna destroyed its Jewish community.

A few Jews survived in hiding while many of those who were banished settled as close to the city as they could. During the next few centuries, many gradually drifted back to Vienna, for subsequent rulers of the city found increasing need for their financial and commercial services. By the mid-1600s a Jewish community of some five hundred families was living along the banks of the Danube in a small ghetto called Leopoldstadt, named after the reigning sovereign, Leopold I.

Although known as "court Jews" and given certain privileges, residents were also subject to numerous privations. They could circulate through the city only during business hours, they had to say their prayers softly lest they contaminate Christian ears, they could not host visiting Jews, and they were required to pay a high tax for residence permits, which in all cases were limited to five to ten years.

Despite these disabilities, this new Jewish community flourished like its predecessor. But like the earlier ghetto, it aroused the hostility of the other Viennese and in 1670 Leopold expelled the city's Jews. He converted their synagogue into a church and stamped out all other signs of their presence.

By 1693, the financial loss to Vienna from their absence had become so great that Leopold permitted a small number to return. Although they had to make heavy initial payments for settling in Vienna and then pay stiff annual taxes thereafter, and although they could now pray only in private houses, the Jews were again playing a critical role in Austrian life. Indeed, the death of their leading member, Samuel Oppenheimer, in 1703 plunged the Austrian empire into a grave financial crisis.

The 1700s brought increasing restrictions on these "tolerated" Jews. An ordinance issued in 1721 required them to wear a Jewish Star of David and a later edict forbade Jewish men to shave off their beards lest they look too much like Christians. Yet their importance to the Empire and its rulers did not diminish. Empress Maria Theresa, who ruled from 1740 to 1780, detested Jews. She once said, "I know of no greater plague on the state than this nation which, through deception, usury and cheating, brings people into beggary." She nevertheless appointed Adam Isaac Arnsteiner as her court purveyor.

Maria Theresa's death brought her son Joseph to the throne. A true child of the Enlightenment, Emperor Joseph issued a Tolerance Ordinance in 1781 that swept away many of the impositions on Vienna's Jews. They could now send their children to Christian primary and secondary schools, become apprentices and master craftsmen, carry on all kinds of trades providing they kept their records in German instead of Yiddish and Hebrew, and employ Christian servants. They could also leave their homes before noon on Sunday, visit places of amusement, and even wear swords if they held the rank of wholesale merchant or its equivalent. These were "privileges" that they had not hitherto enjoyed. Emperor Joseph claimed that his edict's goal was "to make the Jewish nation useful and serviceable to the state, mainly through education and enlightenment of the Jews as well as by directing them to the sciences, the arts, and the crafts."

Although Joseph maintained that "by these favors we place the Jewish nation on an almost equal level with adherents of other religions and associations in respect to trade and use of civil and domestic facilities," many restrictions remained. Jews still had to pay a special tax for being tolerated as well as a special levy when they married. They could not own homes or land, and they could not import books, including the Scriptures. Furthermore, their entry into the crafts was effectively nullified by the refusal of Christian master craftsmen to apprentice them.

Joseph hoped through his actions to bring about Jewish assimilation. This became evident in several subsequent, less benign decrees that abolished rabbinical judicial autonomy, required Jews to adopt German or German-sounding first and last names, and required them to perform military service. Although some better-off and better-educated Austrian Jews welcomed these new laws, the majority viewed them as an attempt to destroy their traditions, their religion, and their way of life. Thus was born a conflict that, in one form or another, would rend the Viennese Jewish community until its third destruction in 1938.

These efforts to encourage Jewish assimilation aroused much more anger and alarm among the Empire's other 400,000 Jews than it did among the more modernized Jews of Vienna, who still numbered only about 600. Especially upset were the 200,000 Jews who lived in Galicia, a Polish province that Austria had acquired in 1772. They were now supposed to set up their own schools, which they could not afford to do, or send their children to Christian schools, which they most decidedly did not want to do. Even provisions that allowed Jewish youths to keep their heads covered in class, to come after and leave before prayers, and to refrain from writing on Saturday failed to mollify the Galicians. They also objected to military service, which required their sons to eat non-kosher food and prevented them from observing the Sabbath and Jewish holidays. By 1800, a division between the traditional Jews of Galicia and the more integrated Jews of Vienna was already becoming apparent.

Helped by Emperor Joseph's tolerance decree, the Jewish presence and influence in Vienna's commercial life increased. The Jewish population rose to over 1,000 grouped into some 130 households. (The city's total population at the end of the eighteenth century was about 300,000.) More significantly, the number of Jewish visitors, most of them merchants coming to trade, swelled to over 10,000 a year.

Almost inevitably a reaction arose against this "Jewish invasion." In 1792 Joseph's successor established a *Judenamt* or Jewish bureau to restrict Jewish immigration. Toleration permits became more difficult to obtain and more expensive to retain. Special taxes were imposed on kosher meat, candles, and other items. Jewish visitors to the city could stay only a limited number of days. No Jewish scholar could tutor a Christian child, and no Jewish midwife could deliver a Christian baby except in emergencies, at the request of the woman in labor, and with a Christian woman present.*

Many Jews found ways of getting around these restrictions. Visiting merchants sometimes claimed illness or even got themselves arrested to prolong their stay in the city. From their sickbeds and jail cells they would continue to transact business. Many would get permits for three days, then continually leave and re-enter the city, paying a fixed bribe to the border guards each time.

Although they had to put up with far more impositions and restrictions than did their brethren in France, the Jews of Austria backed their country unreservedly during the Napoleonic Wars. In fact, they supported the Austrian side so fiercely that Napoleon, occupying Vienna, penalized them with special taxes. Two Jewish banking houses in Vienna, Arnstein-Eskeles and Hertz-Leidersdorf, had provided much of the army's munitions and provisions, while in Prague a Jewish wool merchant named Lamel was the only citizen of that city to respond to the bankrupt government's desperate plea for funds in 1807.

An estimated 35,000 Jews (including Lamel himself, who volunteered for military service at the age of forty-three) fought in the Austrian army during the Napoleonic Wars. Apparently they served with distinction, for one Austrian field marshal later said, "In all my years of service I have never seen an Israelite officer who did not ably fill his position. They combine a great deal of knowledge and much zeal with the highest sense of duty, and this leads them to self-sacrifice in facing the enemy."

But despite such contributions to their country's cause, the post-Napoleonic period brought the Jews of Austria little immediate relief from their disabilities. Although five Jews were ennobled and the wife of one of them, Fanny von Arnstein, developed one of the most highly regarded salons in Europe, restrictions on residence, land ownership, trade, and even on religious organizations remained in force. So did the special taxes they had to pay. Crippled or invalided Jewish veterans received no exemptions from these burdens while those who stayed in the army in peacetime encountered frequent discrimination. In the Eastern Army not one Jewish soldier was promoted from the end of the Napoleonic Wars to the Revolution of 1848, a period of over thirty years.

---

*In Bohemia, a province that included Prague, the Habsburgs in 1786 decreed that only the eldest son in Jewish families could marry. This restriction, designed to limit the growth of the Jewish population in Bohemia, was not abolished until 1848.

Such practices and policies contrast sharply with those pursued by Prussia during this time. As far back as 1787 the Prussians had abolished their head tax on Jews, and by the end of the century Berlin's Jewish community had its own newspapers and other institutions. Whenever Shakespeare's *Merchant of Venice* was performed in Berlin, a member of the cast would appear before the curtain to remind the audience that Shylock was not meant to be typical of his co-religionists.

In 1812 Prussia officially emancipated its Jews, and though the decree was only gradually put into effect, by 1847 Prussian Jews could pretty much live where they wished, marry when they wished, and pursue a wide variety of careers. Berlin had no *Judenamt*, for Berlin, unlike Vienna, had no need for one. In 1847 the Prussian king Frederick Wilhelm IV received a delegation from the Jewish community of Berlin and told them, "I count you among the best of my citizens."

The situation of the Jews in many other German states, as well as in most other West European countries, was roughly the same. By 1848 Austria had become the only major power in the Western world that was still imposing medieval restrictions on its Jews.

Austrian history books concerned with the modern era make frequent use of the term *Vormärz*. The word means "before March" and refers to the period before March 1848 when the revolutions erupted. The fact that Austrian historians have in effect created a new word to describe the time prior to the Revolution of 1848 indicates what a watershed it constituted in their country's development.

The Revolutions of 1848 also marked a major watershed in the development of Austria's, and especially Vienna's, Jewish community. To begin with, a Jewish physician named Adolf Fischhof played a major role in sparking the uprising by delivering an impassioned speech to a crowd in a Viennese street. But Fischhof, despite his oratorical skills, was no demagogue. Elected to Austria's first Parliament, he impressed his fellow members and even the government with his gift for reasonableness and persuasion. Although the revolutionary Parliament was soon dissolved, Fischhof's reputation survived. One of his Gentile contemporaries described him as "the only statesman of those days."

Other Jews also participated in the events of that year. Several were elected to Parliament along with Fischhof, and two of the fifteen Viennese killed during the first day of the revolt were Jews. At their funeral, Vienna's only rabbi said, "I pray for both our Christian and our Jewish brothers for they are all, one and another, dear to us." Thus the Revolution of 1848 enabled Vienna's Jews to participate directly in their nation's political life alongside their Christian countrymen. It even permitted them to provide a national hero whom both Christian and Jew could respect and admire.

But the Revolution of 1848 marked a turning point for Austria's Jewry in another and much more important way, for despite its speedy repression, many revolutionary ideals and principles subsequently became law. Among these was emancipation from the ghetto.

The grant of full rights to the Austrian Jews began in 1849 when Franz Joseph promulgated a new constitution which stipulated that "civil and political rights are not dependent on religion." The lifting of specific restrictions and taxes on the Jews soon followed. Heretofore, the only learned profession they could pursue had been medicine; now a wide variety of career options began to open up for them. Jews could also have Christian servants, own real estate, and live anywhere. Some Jews were even elected to the Vienna City Council. Finally, in 1867, a new constitution was adopted that, while still maintaining Austria- Hungary as a Christian country, proclaimed freedom of religion and civil rights for all the Empire's peoples.

The emancipation of the Jews took place gradually and did not occur without opposition. In particular, the Catholic Church and, in Vienna, the shoemakers' guild, opposed it. The Church went so far as to call emancipation a threat to the Catholic religion. Yet most Western nations had already taken such a step and Franz Joseph was determined to create a multinational empire on the basis of political and civic equality. Moreover, the Jews in Hungary, by then a semi-independent nation, had already achieved such status, thanks in large part to their numbers. (In Budapest they constituted nearly one-quarter of the population and almost one-half of the eligible voters.) The rest of the Empire thus felt the pressure to follow suit.

Another aspect of the emancipation is also worth noting. Many Austrians who had enjoyed, and who would continue to enjoy, close relationships with individual Jews firmly opposed Jewish emancipation. Among them were Dingelstedt, the director of the Burg Theater, and the poet Grillparzer. Grillparzer had once dedicated a poem to a prominent Jewish family, the Todescos, at whose house he was a frequent guest. Yet on the occasion of the emancipation, he wrote another poem which read:

> For a long time, your race will, with justice, be
> Burdened with hate, vengeance and shame;
> Now all rights of citizenship are yours,
> But you nevertheless forever Jews remain.

The contrast between Grillparzer's point of view, as expressed in these words, and his personal behavior points up once again the Austrian penchant, deplored by so many of the country's writers, for saying one thing and doing another, or, to put it more bluntly, for acting in a two-faced fashion. This particular trait would figure prominently in the ultimate fate of the Vienna Jews.

The lifting of restrictions on Jewish residents in Vienna produced a flood of Jewish immigrants into the city during the last half, and especially the last quarter, of the nineteenth century. The first wave consisted largely of Jews from Hungary. They were followed by an influx of Czechoslovakian Jews from Bohemia and Moravia. The final and largest wave consisted mostly of Jews from Galicia along with some other *Ostjuden* (eastern Jews) from territories held by Russia.

As a result of this immigration, Vienna's Jewish population shot up from around 6,000 in 1860 to 147,000 in 1900, or nearly nine percent of the city's total population. Both in absolute numbers and as a percentage of its total population, Vienna at the turn of the century had the largest Jewish community of any city in Western Europe. In all Europe, in fact, only Warsaw and Budapest had more Jewish residents.

We should note that throughout Europe during the nineteenth century the Jewish population increased at twice the rate of the non-Jewish population. This remarkable growth resulted not from a greater birth rate but from reduced infant mortality. Jewish communities had lower rates of illegitimacy, venereal disease, and alcoholism; these favorable factors, plus the greater status accorded to mothers and the greater care lavished on children, and the increased charitable or communal aid given to the needy, enabled a much higher proportion of Jewish children to survive. As a result, the Jewish population in other parts of the Austrian Empire increased rapidly, and this helped fuel immigration to the capital.

Many other forces also spurred the migration to Vienna. Jews found increased opportunities for economic, educational, and cultural activities in the city. Vienna's luster conferred a measure of status on those Jews who moved to or even visited the city. Joseph Wechsberg, a Moravian-born Jew who eventually became a writer for *The New Yorker*, mentions in his memoirs how some Moravian Jews "stayed up late at night trying to discover a relative in Vienna whom they might visit just as a start."

But as the century drew to a close, the biggest impetus behind this Jewish immigration was growing anti-Semitism elsewhere. In Russia the government had begun encouraging pogroms, prompting increasing numbers of Russian Jews to flee. While most of them went to the United States or to other European cities, some drifted into Vienna. Then the Empire's own *Ostjuden* began to feel intensified anti-Semitic pressure in their home areas. This was especially true in Galicia, which accounted for forty percent of the Empire's Jews. Galician Poles had begun excluding Jews from farmer co-operatives, and in 1893 a Catholic convention in Galicia proclaimed an economic boycott against Jewish merchants and tradesmen. Since over eighty percent of Galician Jews were desperately poor to begin with, increasing numbers of them now felt they had no recourse but to pack up their few belongings and seek what they hoped and thought would be a better life in their country's capital.

Population figures alone fail to tell the whole story of Vienna's emerging Jewish community. Indeed, they may be its least impressive and least important aspect. For it was not their numbers but their energy and abilities that enabled the Jews of Vienna to move to the forefront in so many areas of Austrian life.

Most noticeable, especially to their enemies, was the part they played in powering the Austrian economy. While Austria had lagged behind many other Western European nations in economic growth, its Jews could claim much of the credit for any gains, and they were certainly not negligible. It was largely the Jews who had built the country's steel mills and railroads, who had developed its textile, sugar-refining, meat-packing, and numerous other industries, and who were drilling the recently discovered oil deposits in Galicia. They had also established most of Vienna's leading banks — according to one source they owned all but one of the major banks in downtown Vienna — and erected most of the fashionable stores along the city's Ringstrasse. Even an anti-Semitic journalist of the time would later admit that it was the Jews who had given Viennese clothes and other consumer goods their international reputation.

At the center of many of these endeavors were the Rothschilds, who had founded the largest and soundest bank in Austria. But other Jewish businessmen also played important roles. One of them was Karl Wittgenstein, who graduated from the Technological Institute, gained some business experience in America, and then began the long-overdue rationalization of Austria's industries. Although he made his greatest contribution to the steel industry in which he became the most prominent figure, he helped transform numerous other failing industrial concerns into successful enterprises. While Wittgenstein is best known today as the father of some highly gifted children, including his philosopher son Ludwig, he probably did more than any other individual to modernize Austria's industrial base.

While many factors favored the emergence of the Jews as the dominating force in the Austrian economy, including their long history as financiers, one factor warrants special attention. This was the absence of entrepreneurial skills and drive among the Austro-Germans, a situation which left a vacuum that the Jews hastened to fill. This contrasts rather sharply with the situation in Germany where Gentiles had developed and still controlled most of the largest factories, as well as the strongest banks.

Religion undoubtedly was a factor in this situation; the successful firms in Germany were largely owned and controlled by Protestants, and several writers, including Max Weber, have pointed out how Protestantism fits far more compatibly with the capitalist ethos than does Catholicism. Austria's Protestants not only made up a mere three or four percent of the country's population, but lived largely in small, out-of-the-way villages. In Vienna, born and believing Protestants — the reason for making such a distinction will be seen later — were almost invisible.

From their earliest days, Vienna's Jewish business families showed a desire to contribute to their country's well-being. While establishing and maintaining many Jewish charitable institutions, they also sponsored and supported many non-Jewish organizations. Fanny von Arnstein raised money to found St. Mary's Hospital on the outskirts of Vienna, and in her will left funds for a host of Christian charities. The Rothschilds founded a hospital for contagious diseases. Jewish bankers, merchants, and other businessmen gave large sums to put a new roof on one of Vienna's most famous churches, to repair the steeple of another, and to establish such facilities as the Vienna Merchants' Hospital. In the Austro-Prussian War of 1866, the city's Jewish congregation established Austria's largest military hospital to care for the wounded.

Jews were also starting to enter the country's political life. In 1861 Franz Joseph appointed Anselm Rothschild to the *Herrenhaus*, a body roughly equivalent to Britain's House of Lords. The Constitution of 1867 brought Jews into the lower House of Parliament as well. In 1890 some fifteen elected Jews sat in the Reichstag, although by 1900 their number had diminished to eleven. Jews also appeared on the Vienna City Council and the legislature of Lower Austria, the province of which Vienna was a part. Moreover, during the late nineteenth century a speaker of the lower House of Parliament and a mayor of Vienna both had Jewish wives.

During the 1890s Jewish participation in Austrian politics increased with the formation of the country's Social Democratic party. Organized by the Jewish physician Viktor Adler, the party attracted many Jews, some of whom became Party functionaries. Although its mostly working-class membership could not yet vote — the franchise was still limited to those who paid a certain minimum tax — the party was already making itself felt in Vienna and elsewhere.

When it came to administering the country, the Jewish presence was far less conspicuous. But even here there were two notable exceptions. The first was in the administration of justice where Jewish, or at least Jewish-born, lawyers had given Austria its basic criminal and civil procedures, and a chief justice for the Austrian Supreme Court. The second area of Jewish participation in governmental administration was much more significant. Although Jews numbered only about four and one-half percent of the Empire's total population in 1900, they made up eight percent or nearly double their share of the Empire's military officers. These Jewish officers included a vice field marshal, five brigadier generals, and seventeen colonels. Austria's small navy had a Jewish admiral and three of its warships were commanded by Jewish captains. Austria-Hungary was the only country in the world where the proportion of Jewish military officers exceeded the proportion of Jews in the overall population.*

Emancipation also brought large numbers of Jews into the liberal professions. By 1881, at a time when Freud was starting his medical career, sixty percent of Vienna's physicians were Jews. By 1900 Jewish doctors held the majority of clinical chairs at the University's medical school, and the majority of medical directorships in the city's major hospitals. The Surgeon-General of the Army, the personal physician to the Emperor, and the obstetrician to the ladies of the imperial family, were all Jewish. Many of these Jewish doctors had helped to give Vienna its standing as the world's medical center. Among them were Bela Schick, whose diphtheria skin test paved the way for immunization against that fearful disease, and Josef Breuer, an internist whose "talking cure" influenced Freud and helped lay the basis for modern psychiatry. (Breuer treated a helplessly paralyzed girl known in psychiatric literature as "Anna O." by simply letting her talk to him over a period of one and a half years; at the end of that time she was cured.)

Jews had a later start in the legal profession, for unconverted Jews were barred from the law until the 1860s. But once the barriers fell, they soon made up for lost time. By 1888 a majority of Vienna's attorneys were Jewish.

But the profession that the Jews of Vienna had penetrated most heavily was journalism. They not only owned several leading newspapers, including the *Neue Freie Presse*, but made up an overwhelming majority of all editors and reporters. Furthermore, the government's own press department, according to Wolfdieter Bihl, a historian, "remained from its establishment in the 1860s to the First World War a province for German-Jewish journalism."

The Jewish influx into the liberal professions reflected, and resulted from, a determined drive for education. The majority of Vienna's young people did not go on to high school in 1900, but, despite Saturday classes and large crucifixes hanging on classroom walls, the majority of Vienna's Jewish youngsters did.

About thirty percent of the city's high school population was therefore Jewish and, since the Jews tended to live in certain districts and not others, some high schools actually had a Jewish majority. This was especially true in the schools for female students, for when it came to women the discrepancy in educational orientation between Jew and non-Jew widened considerably. Jewish girls constituted a full half of the city's female high school students in 1900.

*However, when the British sought to send a Jewish captain, Mathew Nathan, as their military attaché in Vienna in the early 1890s, the foreign office refused to accept him because he was a Jew. A few years earlier the foreign office had rejected an American ambassador who had a Jewish wife.

A somewhat similar situation existed in higher education. The University of Vienna and the Technological Institute drew students from all over the Empire where Jews on the whole were proportionately less numerous than they were in Vienna, but nevertheless Jewish youths made up over one-third of all students at the University and nearly one-quarter of all students at the Technological Institute. Only at the Agricultural Institute did Jewish representation fall to a mere three percent, a fact that anti-Semites were already exploiting to show that Jews did not want to dirty their hands with "real" work.

Their zeal for education propelled Jews into academic and cultural fields as well. The philosophers Husserl, Buber, and Wittgenstein all had Jewish backgrounds, as did a startling number of Vienna's writers, composers, musicians, actors, directors, and cultural critics.

This last group has given Vienna's Jewish community its greatest claim to international renown. And well it might. In music it includes Mahler, Goldmark, Schönberg, and many others. It also includes some of the more popular composers, including Johann Strauss, who historians now say was of partly Jewish ancestry. Indeed, many of the numerous songs celebrating Vienna were written by Jews, including the popular "*Fiakerlied*" or "Coachman's Song."

The list of Jewish actors was headed by von Sonnenthal, who was considered the best practitioner of his craft in the German tongue. As for writers, Schnitzler was Jewish and von Hofmannsthal was partly Jewish (Hofmannsthal's great-grandfather had been a founder of the city's first new temple). Most of the city's promising young writers, who called themselves "Young Vienna," were Jewish in whole or in part. They included Richard Beer-Hofmann, whose poem to his infant daughter Miriam had been set to music and had become one of the most popular lullabies in German Austria. They also included Felix Salten, whose *Bambi* would charm children and quite a few adults for generations to come.

The list of critics was also a long one, including not only Theodor Herzl and Eduard Hanslick of the *Presse*, but also the unique figure of Karl Kraus. Kraus had founded his own one-man publication *Die Fackel* (The Torch) in 1899 when he was twenty-five. This slender periodical seized the fancy of cultural Vienna so quickly that within two weeks 30,000 copies had been printed and sold. The beardless, bespectacled young man with a high-pitched voice almost instantly became "the intellectual conscience of Vienna."

Finally, we should note the part Jews played in sponsoring and supporting cultural Vienna. With Austria's nobility more interested in breeding horses or speculating in land, the Jews had become the foremost patrons of the arts. It was primarily they who showed up in such large numbers at concerts and plays, bought intellectual journals and books, and stalked the art galleries and formed the great art collections (many of which eventually ended up in the city's museums). At a later period when some anti-Semites attempted to form an "Aryan" theatre free of Jewish influence, the enterprise collapsed in a few years for lack of authors, actors, and audience. As Zweig would later recall, "Nine-tenths of what the world celebrated as Viennese culture in the nineteenth century was promoted, nourished, and even created by Viennese Jewry."

We must not lose sight, however, of the non-Jewish contributions. If most of Vienna's leading writers were wholly or partly Jewish, Robert Musil, whom some consider the city's greatest writer, was not. The first volume of his major work, an unfinished novel entitled *The Man without Qualities*, would not be published until 1911, but he had already begun to write and publish by the end of the nineteenth century. In the visual arts, most of the luminaries of the Secession were non-Jewish. A notable exception is Richard Gerstl, often considered Austria's first modern painter, who cut short his promising career by committing suicide at the age of twenty-five. There were several highly regarded non-Jewish philosophers, though none would quite acquire the international fame of Husserl, Buber, and Wittgenstein. Nearly all of the trailblazing economists of the so-called Vienna School were Gentiles, including the great Carl Menger.

In technology, while automotive pioneer Siegfried Marcus was Jewish, those Austrians who had invented the screw propeller, the typewriter, and the sewing machine were not. In medicine there were many brilliant non-Jewish physicians, including Theodor Billroth, who was considered the city's best. (Billroth's own personal physician, however, was the Jewish internist Josef Breuer.)

One acknowledges the substantial achievements of these and many other non-Jewish Austrians, but the amazing accomplishments of the Viennese Jews cannot be denied. They were not only disproportionately represented in most fields but dominant in many. "The history of Austrian Jewry in the modern age," writes the Gentile historian Karl Stadler, "is the history of Austrian scholarship and culture, and of the country's economic and social progress."

The Jews quite naturally came to feel an intense attachment to the city that had given such scope to their energies and talents. "Emigrate?" asked Martin Freud. "Who dreamed of leaving beautiful Vienna where they flourished under the protection of a benign and powerful emperor?" When the Viennese Jews vacationed, they usually stayed in or close to the city's outer suburbs. When they did go abroad they became homesick, it was said, as soon as they lost sight of St. Stephen's spire, and didn't really feel comfortable until they saw it looming once again on the horizon. One of the few who did leave the city was Gustav Mahler, but though he was not a native of Vienna and had had many problems during his tenure as conductor of its opera, nevertheless, when fatally stricken in New York, Mahler begged his wife to take him four thousand miles back to Vienna to die, a request she willingly granted.

With the possible exception of the Jews of fifteenth-century Spain, no Jewish community in history, Zweig says, ever achieved a more fruitful and harmonious attachment to their surroundings than did the Jews of Habsburg Vienna. The historian Hans Tietze, in writing of this period, said, "Without the Jews, Vienna would not be what it is, and the Jews without Vienna would lose the brightest era of their existence during recent centuries."

But if the Viennese Jews had contributed so much to Viennese life, what had they contributed to Jewish life? To what extent did their religious achievements match their worldly ones?

At the beginning of the nineteenth century little in the way of an organized Jewish community existed in Vienna, for the Habsburgs still prohibited the city's Jews from erecting a temple. The Jews had, however, established a burial society that performed some religious and secular functions. Furthermore, a Hebrew printing press had started up in 1793 and it soon attracted Hebrew writers and scholars to the city. Some earned their living as proofreaders while others worked as tutors in wealthy Jewish households. In their spare time they carried on their scholarly work. By 1810 or thereabouts, Vienna, a city still without synagogues or Hebrew schools, had nevertheless become a center for Hebrew scholarship and publishing.

The Jews repeatedly asked for the right to erect a house of worship and sometime in the mid-1820s Emperor Francis II finally consented. On April 9, 1826, Vienna's first Jewish temple was consecrated on the *Seitenstettengasse*, a narrow, curved street in a section where most of the city's Jews had their homes and businesses. (It is the only temple still functioning in Vienna today.)

For their first rabbi the Jews chose the Danish-born, German-educated Isaac Noah Mannheimer. Only thirty-three, Mannheimer had already earned a reputation in the Jewish world for his learning and, more controversially, his innovations. The Reform movement had already begun to sweep through the German-speaking world and Mannheimer had responded to its influence.

For his new congregation, however, Mannheimer settled on a middle course between Orthodoxy and Reform. He preached in, and translated prayer books into, impeccable German. But he made no changes in the content of these prayer books and he retained Hebrew as the main language of the religious service. Mannheimer emphasized music — though he ruled out the use of the organ — even going so far as to seek a cantata from Beethoven for the temple's dedication. Beethoven considered the proposal carefully before rejecting it. Mannheimer's innovations became known as the Vienna Ritual and were adopted by congregations in Holland, Denmark, and many other countries.

The choice of a cantor for the new temple was easily made, for an outstanding candidate was available. He was the twenty-six-year-old Solomon

Sulzer from the province of Vorarlberg on Austria's Swiss border. Despite his youth, Sulzer was already well-experienced; thanks to his extraordinary talent he had held a cantor's position since he was thirteen years old.

Mannheimer and Sulzer made an impressive duo. One who heard them later wrote, "The old Mannheimer — I still see his gaunt, intelligent head with the fluttering hair — preached as Sulzer sang. The same mastery of the material, the same strange and yet sweeping passion, the same inspired spark in their eyes and voices. They delivered the most glowing service I have ever experienced, both in words and tones."

Sulzer proved to be not just an extraordinary singer but also an exceptional composer, music director, and choirmaster. Under his direction the temple's choir, despite the lack of instrumental accompaniment, became famous throughout the musical world. Franz Liszt, after attending a service in the synagogue to hear it perform, wrote, "Their majestic, triumphant sounds proclaimed the power of the God of Abel and Noah, of Isaac and Jacob, and it was impossible not to join with all the sympathies of one's soul in the invocation of this fire which carried — as if on gigantic shoulders — the burden of so many thousands of years of tradition, of so many divine benefactions, of so many rebellions and chastisements and of such indestructible hope."

Many non-Jewish composers now gladly accepted the temple commissions, among them Franz Schubert, whose *Tov l'hodot*, Psalm 92, for unaccompanied choir, was written for Sulzer's ensemble. Sulzer himself, among other works, wrote *Shir Zion* which became the basic text on Jewish liturgical music.

The Revolution of 1848 brought an institutional strengthening to the Jewish community, for the government officially created the *Israelitische Kultusgemeinde*, or Jewish Community Council, and authorized it to handle Jewish affairs. The Council was to establish and maintain synagogues, supervise the production of kosher meat and matzoh, and oversee the operation of ritual baths, cemeteries, and other Jewish institutions. It would henceforth keep all records and vital statistics, including Jewish births, marriages, conversions, and deaths.

To discharge these responsibilities the Council would receive governmental subventions, as did Catholic and Protestant institutions that performed comparable functions for members of their faiths. The *Gemeinde* would also receive funds from a special tax levied on its members, but although all Jews were automatically members of the *Gemeinde*, only those who could afford it had to pay a tax. By 1900, only one-third of Vienna's Jews fell into this taxpayer category. The *Gemeinde* was governed by an elected board of twenty, which was later expanded to twenty-four.

When Mannheimer died in 1865, his thirty-five-year-old assistant, Adolf Jellinek, succeeded him. Jellinek soon acquired even more eminence than

Mannheimer, and was known throughout the Jewish world as a speaker, writer, and scholar. But he lacked both the talent and the desire to be the community's spokesman. As the historian Tietze was later to observe, "He handed over the rabbinical role of community leadership to the past and to the future."

Despite this lack of rabbinical leadership, Jewish institutions sprouted and thrived in Vienna, both during Jellinek's time and, after his death in 1890, under his successor, Moritz Güdemann. Numerous synagogues and prayer halls came into existence, often organized by immigrants from various parts of the Empire or in some cases by occupational groups. Jewish porters, for example, had their own place of worship. So did Vienna's Sephardic community, which had built an impressive temple with fifty-six-foot-high walls topped by a huge, meticulously planned and executed cupola. Although the Sephardic community itself was quite small, crowds of Jews turned out for its more picturesque observances, especially its lively observance of Simchat Torah, the festival that begins the yearly reading of the Torah.

Vienna's extensive network of Jewish institutions also included Jewish hospitals, homes for the aged, a school for the blind and deaf, a home for waifs and strays, and numerous special organizations, such as one to help poor Jewish artisans and another to assist "the poor suffering Jews of Galicia." Although all Jewish children received two hours of state-paid Jewish religious instruction a week in the public schools — Catholic and Protestant school children, of course, received similar instruction in their faiths — the Jewish community operated its own kindergartens and *cheders* for after-school religious teaching. A rabbinical seminary was established in 1893 and two years later a B'nai B'rith lodge was formed. The lodge counted Sigmund Freud among its charter members. Indeed, the already quite well-known and controversial physician attended its biweekly meetings faithfully and urged his friends to join as well.

This institutional growth was facilitated by the tendency of the Viennese Jews to cluster in certain neighborhoods. The most heavily Jewish district was Leopoldstadt, a section that had once been a Jewish ghetto and which by 1900 had, in a *de facto* sense, almost reverted to that status. It was the center of Jewish activity, although the offices of the *Israelitische Kultusgemeinde* were housed in the community's first synagogue on the Seitenstettengasse, in the inner city. The Viennese Jews not only tended to live together but to socialize and do business with each other. Says Martin Freud, "Rich and poor . . . we moved in Jewish circles. Our friends were Jews, our doctor was Jewish, our lawyer was Jewish. If one was in business, one's partner was Jewish. One read a newspaper that was written and directed by Jews and went for holidays to places where Jews were in the majority."

In surveying these formal institutions and informal living arrangements, one might easily conclude that the Jews of Vienna were vigorously affirming their religious and/or ethnic identity, that Judaism had remained a vital force within them. But such a conclusion would have been seriously, grievously wrong.

Chapter 4

Divisions, Dissensions, and Doubts

Early in the nineteenth century the Reform movement began to divide Jewish communities throughout Western Europe, as many of the more "enlightened" and active members responded to the liberalizing currents of the time. The Reform movement, or at least its spirit, quickly made its influence felt within Vienna's Jewish community. As early as 1810, a German-language text for religious instruction that appeared in the city omitted all mention of a Messiah to lead the Jews back to the Promised Land, although such a concept had been an integral part of Jewish belief since the *Diaspora* dispersion.

A year later some of Vienna's Jews apparently were having second thoughts about the need for a temple. Although the community asked for permission to build one that year, their spokesman felt obliged to note that "the liberal expresses his concern lest the establishment of such an organized community lead to a separation between Jew and Christian in the capital city of Vienna."

When the temple finally came into existence fifteen years later, it represented a compromise between Orthodox- and Reform-minded Jews. This is evident in Mannheimer's decision to exclude the organ and retain Hebrew prayers, while at the same time preaching sermons in German. But as the community developed, its Reformist or progressive elements became more assertive. Most of the community's leaders came from this group, for Reformism appealed to the wealthier, better-educated, and more integrated Jews who quite naturally comprised the community's leadership corps. From 1871 on, no Orthodox Jew was elected president of the *Kultusgemeinde* and few were elected to its governing board.

But the Orthodox Jews were not prepared to abandon the struggle, and for the rest of the century disputes between the two groups flared up continually, some of them culminating in court cases. One source of irritation was the desire of the Reformists to exclude from religious services all mention of the Messiah and a return to Palestine. Eventually, a compromise was reached whereby the *Gemeinde* would not subsidize any house of worship that used an organ, but would sanction the exclusion of all oral prayers for a return to the Holy Land. Individual worshippers could silently say such prayers if they wished, and mention of the Holy Land was left in the prayer books.

Such compromises failed to create peace, for the two factions represented very different perspectives on what it meant to be a Jew. To the Reform-minded, being a Jew meant adherence to a particular set of basic beliefs. For the Orthodox, it meant adherence to a way of life. The Reform Jew sought to identify with the greater community, while the Orthodox Jew sought to maintain a separate identity. Historian Marsha Rozenblit accurately divides the two groups into integrationists and nationalists. (With the advent of Zionism in the 1890s the term "nationalist" would take on a somewhat different coloration.)

The large-scale immigration into Vienna during the second part of the century obviously affected the balance of power between the two groups. Most of the Hungarian and Czechoslovakian Jews, i.e., those from Bohemia and Moravia, quickly joined the integrationists. Since they had come to the capital to take advantage of its many opportunities for entering the larger society, this was to be expected. But the Galicians and other *Ostjuden*, including those from Russia and Russian-occupied Poland, behaved quite differently. These Jews were by and large fleeing persecution and often acute deprivation. They were coming to Vienna not to shed or even modify their Jewish identity but to acquire the freedom and means to maintain it.

The *Ostjuden* were generally appalled at the Jewish life they found in Vienna. In 1864 Rabbi Solomon Spitzer resigned his paid position with the *Gemeinde* and together with a band of followers established a *schul* (synagogue) on the Schiffgasse dedicated to a "torah-true" *Yiddishkeit* ("Jewishness"). Many others worshipped at a Hungarian synagogue that still maintained some ties to Orthodoxy, but when the Hungarians in 1880 refused to admit a Galician to their governing board, the *Ostjuden*, whose numbers now began to swell, began setting up various synagogues and prayer rooms of their own. Soon they had built a substantial subculture in the Leopoldstadt. The *Schiffschul* even asked the government to establish a second *Kultusgemeinde* to administer and support their religious affairs, a request that the government, not wishing to be bothered with such internal disputes, firmly rejected.

If the Galicians and other East European Jews were dismayed by the integrationist Jews, the integrationists were likewise dismayed. These eastern Jews in black kaftans and beards seemed to lack all the refinement and urbanity that the integrationists had acquired. While the Hungarian and Czechoslovakian Jews could usually speak an acceptable German, the Galicians spoke Yiddish, a language that sounded to an integrationist like an abominable German. Even when the Galicians attempted to speak German, their speech was often so harsh, guttural, and ungrammatical that it still sounded like Yiddish.

In his memoir, *Last Waltz in Vienna*, the Viennese-born but now British journalist George Clare (born Klaar) mentions how once he unthinkingly addressed his father as *Tateh*, the Yiddish word for father. His usually mild-mannered father reacted by giving him a stinging slap across the cheek. "Don't you ever dare call me *Tateh*," his father hissed. "Never, you hear, never."

The incident happened in the late 1920s, and the elder Klaar had grown up in late nineteenth- and early twentieth-century Vienna — his reaction reflected the forces already in evidence at that time. As Clare puts it, "That brief and ugly scene, over in less than a minute, encapsulated the entire conflict dividing central European Jewry. . . . This bitter conflict, anchored deeply in the Jewish soul, affected every Jew in Austria."

Clare himself admits sharing this aversion to East European Judaism. "I was already a second-generation Viennese and Vienna-born Jews felt resentment toward the less assimilated Jews from the East." Clare not only felt disgust at his Galician grandmother's way of speaking but, he confesses, even resented his mother's having been born in Galicia.

By 1900 the Galicians and other *Ostjuden* made up about twenty-five percent of Vienna's Jews. While this was a formidable number, it still made them a minority within the Jewish community. Moreover, though most *Ostjuden* sought to keep their way of life, some — especially the younger ones and their offspring — had already strayed into the integrationist fold.

Their numerical weakness was aggravated by other disadvantages. Although some *Ostjuden* had become rich, most had remained poor. But perhaps their greatest handicap was their inferior social standing. Other Jews, and sometimes their own children, simply did not want to be associated with them. The relief efforts that the Viennese Jewish community mounted during this time to aid the Galicians, and the Jews fleeing the pogroms of Russia and Poland, were designed primarily to help these unfortunates remain where they were or emigrate to other countries, principally America, and thereby keep them from coming to or remaining in Vienna.

No one was more conscious of their social standing than the *Ostjuden* themselves. Most clung stubbornly and proudly to their way of life, while others became apologetic. In 1893 when a group of wealthy Galician Jews in Vienna decided to organize a synagogue, they felt compelled to assure the integrationists that it would be a "bright and clean" building that would not in any way stand as a "fortress of opposition to religious enlightenment."

The *Ostjuden*, and any nationalist allies they could find among other Viennese Jews, did manage to oust their greatest enemy from the board of the *Gemeinde* in 1889. The rise of anti-Semitism in the 1880s and the coming of Zionism in the late 1890s also tended to strengthen their position. Yet, by 1900 they still suffered from their inferior status both within and without the Jewish community. "Such a Jew has no power in the city of Vienna," commented the non-Jewish writer Hermann Bahr at about this time. And, added Bahr, "What a pity! Vienna could use his diligence, his industry, and his serious view of life."

If one tie bound the Jews of Vienna and indeed all the Jews of Austria together, it was their devotion to their emperor. No group in Austria loved Franz Joseph more than the country's Jews. Those members of the faith who attended services only three times a year to worship their God on the High Holy Days often went a fourth time to pay homage to the Emperor on his birthday.* Pictures of Franz Joseph hung in nearly every Jewish home, and many Jews named their first son after him (among them the Prague butcher Hermann Kafka). Martin Freud recalls how he and his brothers and sisters "were all stout royalists, delighting to hear and see all we could of the royal court." His grandmother, in transposing her birthday from the Jewish to the Christian calendar, made the date coincide with the birthday of Franz Joseph.

The love the Jews had for Franz Joseph was certainly well-founded, for almost from his first days on the throne he had acted as their protector. In 1849 he officially ended Austria's ghettos and, when several cities appealed his action saying that their Jewish ghettos were based on decrees issued by Maria Theresa, the nineteen-year-old monarch replied, "We are not living in the days of the Empress. All my subjects have equal obligations and therefore equal rights."

One often-repeated story tells how Franz Joseph, in reviewing his troops, noticed a heavily decorated soldier who held only a corporal's rank. "What is that soldier's name?" he asked the commander. "Abraham Schwartz, Your Highness," replied the latter. "Why is he only a corporal?" asked Franz Joseph.

---

*Nearly all synagogues held such services, one of the few exceptions being Vienna's Sephardic congregation who, having placed themselves under the protection of the Sultan of Turkey, held services on the Sultan's birthday instead. But they, too, on this occasion offered prayers for the Austrian monarch. Franz Joseph, who wished to maintain good relations with Turkey, did not object and sent a cabinet minister and a general to attend the observance.

"But he's a Jew," replied the surprised commander. The answer enraged the young emperor. "In the Austrian army there are no Jews, only soldiers. And a soldier who deserves it becomes an officer," said Franz Joseph. He then ordered Schwartz to come forward and in his hearing said to his commander, "This soldier should carry an officer's sword."*

Actions such as these had enabled the Vienna Jews to flourish and had endeared Franz Joseph to them. Yet despite their sincere professions of loyalty and love, many Viennese Jews were seriously compounding their sovereign's most aggravating and threatening problem.

As we saw earlier, Franz Joseph's greatest problem was the spirit of nationalism which had gripped most of the Empire's diverse and numerous ethnic groups. But the most troublesome national group was his own, the Austro-Germans. Comprising less than a quarter of the Empire's population, the Austro-Germans insisted on a supremacy over the others. Many of them had never fully accepted the Hungarian Settlement which had given the Hungarians their own government. As the century drew to a close, many more were fiercely resisting the granting of similar rights to other national groups.

Economic self-interest supplied some of the motives for their attitude, for greater deference to the other nationalities would curtail opportunities and even create hardships for Austro-Germans. If the government allowed Czech to be an official government language in Bohemia, German civil servants in that region would be placed at a disadvantage, for no matter where they lived in the Empire, few German bureaucrats had learned, or wished to learn, any other language than their own.

Another impetus to Austro-German intransigence was their own growing ardor for Germanism. Spurred on by the unification of Germany and its startling successes on the economic and military fronts, growing numbers of Austro-Germans were becoming more conscious and proud of their Germanic roots and ties. They wore Bismarck's emblem, the blue cornflower, in their buttonholes, sang "The Watch on the Rhine" in their taverns, and joined German national societies. That Bismarck was a Protestant who for a while waged a *Kulturkampf* or cultural war against German Catholicism did not seem to bother these nominally Catholic Austro-Germans. Nor did they seem to mind that Bismarck held a low opinion of them.

---

*In a communication to the author, Professor Richard Geehr cautions against exaggerating Franz Joseph's philo-Semitism. He points out that the Emperor did withhold some privileges from the Jews that he had granted to other groups, and once wrote the Empress that he saw merit in anti-Semitism but deplored its excesses. Still the Emperor did protect his Jewish subjects, especially when they had proven themselves on the field of battle. Franz Singer, himself a World War I veteran, says his great-uncle Alexander Eiss rose to brigadier general during the Italian campaigns, and when Eiss later retired, Franz Joseph offered him the war ministry if he would convert. His uncle replied, "I cannot sell my religion for my career," whereupon Franz Joseph stepped down from his throne and embraced him.

The move to forge closer ties with largely Protestant Germany was especially pronounced at the universities, where it even attracted some Catholic seminarians. Many adults were affected, or infected, as well, since the increasing tendency of the Empire's other national groups to assert their ethnic identity spurred on the Austro-Germans to do the same.

Among those who succumbed to the spirit of Germanism were the integrationist Jews. Fischhof, the hero of 1848 then living in retirement, counseled his co-religionists not to identify too closely with any national group, but his advice was largely ignored. Chief Rabbi Adolf Jellinek observed that Jews by background and education were inclined toward Germanism, and he voiced no displeasure at this fact. Indeed, he seemed to approve of it.

The integrationist Jews loved the German language and the literature it had created. They worshipped Lessing, who had written a pro-Jewish play, *Nathan the Wise* (*Nathan der Weise*), and Goethe, who for them stood as a symbol of humanistic enlightenment (although Goethe had opposed Jewish emancipation). But beyond that, the Jews wanted to identify with Western civilization, and Western civilization in the Austrian Empire seemed to have reached its zenith among the Austro-Germans. "The Jews loved German," a later Zionist writer would observe, "because to them the German people in Austria were the symbols of freedom and progress."

Thus, Jews joined the German National Union in droves before it became racially anti-Semitic. There, for as long as they were permitted to be members, they would raise their voices loud and clear in singing *"Deutschland, Deutschland über Alles,"* while one of the union's younger members, the then music student Gustav Mahler, played the piano accompaniment. They also flocked to the German Liberal party. Heinrich Friedjung, a brilliant Jewish historian who had become a professor at the age of twenty-three, founded and edited *The German Weekly* and later became editor-in-chief of the official organ of the German Caucus in the Austrian Parliament. A Jewish lawyer named Ignaz Kuranda headed the German Liberal party for a time, and on his seventieth birthday in 1882 he spoke proudly of having spent forty years fighting for Germanism in Austria. As a Galician rabbi would later put it, "The Jews of Austria absolutely sided with the so-called liberal (German) constitutionalists and were attracted to them for better or for worse, so much so that any divergence was looked upon not only as heresy but as treason against the Jews."

Their devotion to the German Liberal party and their admiration for Bismarckian Germanism put the Jews on a collision course with the Catholic Church, which was fighting to maintain and extend its privileges and powers within the Empire. In 1864 Pope Pius VII had said, "The Church could not and should not be reconciled to progress, liberalism, and modern civilization." In fighting so prominently alongside the Austro-German bourgeois, professionals, and intellectuals to extend these features and to curtail the rights of the Church, the Jews were only adding to the Vatican's already plentiful store of anti-Jewish sentiment.

Their ardent, almost reverent pro-Germanism had also put the Jews on a collision course with their own beloved emperor. In his struggle to give the various Slavic groups a stronger voice in the Empire, Franz Joseph frequently found the integrationist Jews joined with the German Austrians in opposing him. Count Taafe, who served as Franz Joseph's prime minister for nearly two decades, tried to get the Jews to go along with the Emperor's efforts to reduce the dominance of the Austro-Germans and to give the Slavic groups more rights and privileges. Personally not anti-Semitic, Taafe had smuggled a subsidy for the rabbinical school into the government budget — he actually inserted it somewhere in the naval account — and repeatedly offered to help squash the rising anti-Semitic movement if the Jews would side with the government on the nationalities question. But the integrationist Jews, who formed a majority of the Jews in Parliament, spurned such offers. As one of them said, "I refuse to let my German heart be torn out of my bosom."

This pro-Germanism was not confined to Viennese Jews but extended to those parts of the Empire from which most of the integrationists had come. In Bohemia, a majority of the Jews gave German as their first language in the 1890 census, and even many of those who spoke Czech at home, such as Franz Kafka's father, sent their sons to German schools. Some of Prague's German schools were in fact almost exclusively Jewish. Much the same situation was true in Budapest also. In the Moravian provincial legislature, Jews consistently sided with the German representatives to give the Germans a majority. But in Galicia and other easterly parts of the Empire, Jewish Germanism diminished considerably. As Kurt Grünwald notes, "Only the Galician Jews regarded themselves as Austrians. The Jews of western Austria considered themselves Germans."

The affinity and affection that the Czech and Hungarian Jews showed for Germanism cost them dearly, since it made them doubly despised. They were frequently persecuted, not just for being Jews but also for being Germans. In December 1897, a group of Czech students at the University of Prague went on an anti-German rampage, smashing and sacking the city's more prominent German businesses and cultural establishments. This done, they turned on the Jews, smashing and looting synagogues and Jewish-owned stores and beating everyone who looked remotely Jewish. Franz Joseph had to declare martial law and send in the army to restore order.

Faced with such reactions, many Jews in Hungary and Czechoslovakia began abandoning or at least downplaying their pro-Germanism. In the 1900 census a majority (though only a bare majority) of Prague's Jews declared

Czech their national language. In Vienna of course there were no anti-German riots and the Jews continued, though with increasing desperation in the face of rising hostility from the Austro-Germans, to affirm their German identity.

We have seen how the Viennese Jews disdained and sought to distance themselves from their more religious and more ethnically oriented Jewish brethren from the East. We have also seen how they identified with, and immersed themselves in, German culture. It should therefore come as no surprise to find that large numbers of Viennese Jews were becoming less and less interested in being Jews. They were still, to a limited degree, establishing Jewish institutions, but behind such efforts lay an increasing lack of interest in Judaism itself.

After-school Hebrew instruction for Jewish boys began to disappear after 1880, and synagogue attendance also declined. The rabbinical seminary, which had been established by a Galician scholar, drew most of its students, especially the better ones, from the eastern areas of the Empire, and most of these students left the city once they had finished their studies. N.H. Tur-Sinai, one of the school's teachers, would later report, "Studies at the college had no connection with the city or with the Viennese Jewish community. The Jews of Vienna were not concerned with Jewish studies and showed no interest in the college, which existed in a kind of ghetto of its own. No public lectures were given there, and no one asked for them." Those who wished to present a paper or give a lecture on a Jewish subject normally had to go to Prague to find an audience.

The two hours of weekly Jewish instruction in the public schools continued but became, in the words of Tur-Sinai, "hollow, a mere matter of appearances. . . . There was nothing in it to attract the pupils' sympathies nor yet the teachers'." Students whispered among themselves or read and studied other materials, while their state-paid religious instructors droned on. This may help explain why as late as 1900 Vienna still did not have a single rabbi who had been born in the city.

To be a rabbi in Vienna was, in any case, a mixed blessing, for the Jewish community did not even allow its rabbis to vote in *Gemeinde* elections. When the government introduced a proposal to correct this, a Jewish baron in the upper House opposed it, saying that the Jewish community did not want its rabbis to exercise the same authority as rabbis did in Galicia. The *Gemeinde*, it is recalled, was state-supported and therefore a quasi-governmental body. No other Jewish member spoke for the measure and so it promptly died.

In the 1890s the problem of prayers for Palestine surfaced once again. Although the compromise worked out earlier with the nationalists had eliminated all prayers for return to the Holy Land, the *Gemeinde* board now wanted to go further and remove all mention of Palestine from the prayer-books. Chief Rabbi Moritz Güdemann desperately opposed this step, but only when he threatened to resign did the board finally back down.

There were now Jewish newspapers in Vienna, but in contrast to those in London and Paris, none was written in Yiddish. Moreover, none of Vienna's Jewish newspapers made any reference to Jews or Judaism in their titles. Nor, in contrast again to what was happening in London, Paris, and other cities, was any significant Yiddish literature being published in Vienna, although two Yiddish theaters were operating in the Leopoldstadt.*

When Herzl started the Zionist movement in the late 1890s, he had to shift the site of one of his early conferences from Vienna to Munich, in part because Munich had kosher restaurants while Vienna, with a much larger Jewish community, had none. "These fin-de-siècle Jews," writes Grünwald, "took absolutely no interest in Judaism. As long as their environment did not remind them of their Jewish heritage, it caused them no inner discomfort."

In some respects, Grünwald's finding may be too sweeping, for Jewish nationalists and Jewish nationalism were certainly in evidence in Vienna at that time. Yet Grünwald grew up in the Jewish Vienna of this period and his conclusion seems essentially correct. He points out that whenever a subject concerning Jews came up in Parliament, and such subjects were being raised with increasing frequency during the century's last twenty years, the Jewish members either managed to be absent, or, if present, buried their heads in the papers before them and pretended not to know what was going on. When the Speaker of the House once graciously suggested postponing a session that fell on Yom Kippur, the holiest day in the Jewish calendar, Jewish members of Parliament vigorously opposed the move.

This drawing back — one could even call it a retreat — from Judaism could be seen in the frequency with which Jewish homes displayed Christmas trees in December and dispensed Easter eggs in April. It could also be seen in the frequency with which Jewish children sang in church choirs and joined in the Corpus Christi procession.**

The parliamentarians who fled from Jewish issues and wanted sessions held on Yom Kippur, the families that decorated Christmas trees, and the children who sang Christian hymns remained, for the most part, officially

---

*Interestingly enough, many Yiddish words, such as *mishpoche* (family, clan), *meshuggah* (crazy), *tzores* (sorrows), *nebbish* (pitiful person), and *ganif* (thief), had entered the Viennese dialect, where most of them remain to this day.

**In his memoirs Martin Freud reports how "our festivals were Christmas, with presents under a candlelit tree, and Easter, with gaily painted Easter eggs." When he married in the 1920s, Martin Freud caused a great deal of consternation by repeatedly taking off his hat during the synagogue service. He had never been in a synagogue before. To be sure, his father had no love for any religion and had raised the children in a secular home. Still, Sigmund Freud did assert his Jewish identity — he was, it is recalled, a founding member of Vienna's B'nai B'rith lodge — and nearly all of the family's friends were Jewish. Martin Freud's experience cannot be considered unusual or even atypical.

Jewish. That is, they remained on the *Gemeinde*'s records as members of the community. But increasing numbers of their fellow Jews were going a step further and severing their ties to Judaism completely. Some of them had officially declared themselves *konfessionslos*, or without religion. Others, a greater number, had converted to Christianity.

Conversion had long provided Jews with what seemed to be an entree into mainstream society, and over the centuries a fair number had taken advantage of it. During the nineteenth century as Jews became more immersed in and influenced by the larger Christian society around them, conversion rates rose. In Germany, thousands of Jews became Christians. But although Berlin's conversion rate was high, Vienna's rate was higher still. By 1900, in fact, the Viennese Jews had the highest conversion rate of any Jewish community in the world.

The trend had actually begun before the Revolution of 1848 when both the Arnsteins and the Eskeles, the two most prominent Jewish families in the city, had their children (though not themselves) baptized. (The Arnsteins were also the first Jews of Vienna to have a Christmas tree, a step that shocked their fellow Jews at the time.) The conversion pace picked up in Vienna as it did elsewhere during the second half of the century. From 1868 to 1903, according to Professor Rozenblit, over nine thousand Vienna Jews renounced Judaism. During roughly the same period, she says, less than three thousand Berlin Jews took such a step.*

One half of all Viennese Jews who left Judaism became Catholics, one-quarter turned to Protestantism, while the remaining quarter simply declared themselves without religion. The relatively high number who became Protestants, given Vienna's minuscule number of those born into that faith, meant that in some circles most of the Protestants one encountered were actually baptized Jews.

These apostates included some of the leading luminaries of the Jewish community. Among them were Mahler and Schönberg; Karl Wittgenstein and his gifted children; Husserl; the critic Karl Kraus who converted first to Catholicism, then Protestantism, and finally became *konfessionslos*; and two unrelated Adlers — Alfred, the psychologist, and Viktor, the organizer and head of the Social Democratic party. Also included were Viktor's wealthy parents, who had been personally received into the Catholic Church by the Pope. (Viktor himself, however, had opted for Protestantism.)

---

*Rozenblit does say that the Jewish intermarriage rate in Vienna was less than ten percent, substantially below that of Berlin's. Professor Wolfdieter Bihl of the University of Vienna, however, reports the intermarriage rate of Viennese Jews in 1901 as 14.9 percent, which would put it on a par with the Jewish intermarriage rate of Berlin. Many complications surround the use of the data available from this period, so it is possible for serious and astute scholars, such as Rozenblit and Bihl, to come up with somewhat different figures. In any event, the intermarriage rate for Viennese Jews had certainly reached significant proportions by 1900.

Few of these assimilated Jews found happiness in their new status, for Jews who converted rarely succeeded in shedding their stigma. As Mahler once bemoaned (to his wife), "I am three times homeless, as a native of Bohemia in Austria, as an Austrian among the Germans, and as a Jew throughout the world. Everywhere I am an intruder, never welcome." Schönberg, in fact, would return to Judaism in 1933 following his racially motivated dismissal from the Prussian Academy of Arts in Berlin.

Was conversion really necessary for a Jew who wanted to get ahead? Mahler certainly believed so, for he wanted the post of conductor at the Viennese opera and believed that his Jewishness would block his way. When it became known that the opera house was considering him for the position, and Richard Wagner's widow publicly expressed outrage over the idea of a Jew conducting her husband's music from such a prestigious podium, Mahler responded by having himself baptized.

But in most instances adherence to the Jewish religion, while a hindrance, could hardly be called a barrier to success. Most Jewish doctors, lawyers, and businessmen had many Christian clients. Only certain high posts in the government and the judiciary actually required a baptismal certificate. Anti-Semitism was growing, and it was becoming more racially or ethnically focused. Changing one's religion was becoming a less effective way of avoiding it, although many Jews had yet to realize this fact.

No, the appeal of assimilationism resulted less from a need to overcome anti-Semitism's economic and professional effects than from a desire to counter its social and psychological impact. Most of Vienna's Jews wanted to integrate as much as possible into the city they so passionately loved. That they could not do so remained a continuous source of frustration and chagrin.

In his memoirs Felix Braun, a Jewish writer who became a devout Catholic, tells of his shock when his parents, in discussing an anti-Semitic incident, told him he was a Jew. Until then, he had believed he was no different from anyone else. Later, in school, when the Jewish boys left the room for their twice weekly religious instruction — the Catholic boys, being the majority, would receive their religious instruction in the classroom — he remained rooted at his desk. When his teacher, smiling at his naiveté, told him he would have to join his co-religionists, it marked a turning point in his young life. As Braun put it, "I wanted to be where I had no right to be, and I had to go where I did not want to go."

Despite the record high conversion rate, most Vienna Jews remained officially and ostensibly Jewish. The comparatively large number of baptisms does not signify a wholesale exodus into Christianity. Rather, it reveals something much more widespread and damaging: the growth of *Jewish* anti-Semitism.

Self-hatred is Jewish patriotism, the Hungarian Jewish writer Arthur Koestler once sardonically observed, and, if so, then such perverted patriotism had begun to seep through Jewish Vienna, affecting convert and nonconvert alike.

Arthur Schnitzler points out that by the late 1860s his own parents, uncles, and aunts had not only abandoned any real belief in Judaism, but that some of them openly mocked their ancestral religion. Schnitzler tells us he had a friend named Louis Friedman, whose virulent anti-Semitism made him vow never to beget children lest he perpetuate the hated Jewish blood that flowed through his veins. In his novel, *The Road to the Open*, Schnitzler has a Jewish intellectual remark, "It doesn't take much to arouse the self-contempt that is always lying dormant within us, and when that happens we readily, and quite sincerely, join forces with any rascal or rogue in attacking our very selves."

Such Jewish anti-Semitism had begun to affect all strata of Jewish society. The Rothschilds employed few Jews in their banking firm, and Nathaniel Rothschild, when he retired, kept no Jews on his personal staff. His private secretary reportedly voted for an anti-Semitic party. Moreover, Rothschild invited no Jews to his lavish receptions. When a distinguished Austrian nobleman, Prince Schwarzenberg, was urged by a fellow peer to attend one of these receptions with the assurance that he would meet no Jews there, the Prince declined, saying, "Nathaniel Rothschild does not associate with Jews; no more do I."

Next to Rothschild, Vienna's richest Jew was probably Baron Maurice de Hirsch, a railroad builder and banker. "All our misery comes from Jews who want to climb too high," said the Jewish Baron. "We have too many intellectuals. I want to prevent Jews from pushing ahead too much. They should not make such great strides." Hirsch gave over $100 million to Jewish philanthropy before his death in 1896, but most of it was directed to resettling Jews outside of Europe, principally in Argentina. One cannot help wondering whether his primary purpose was to help his countrymen or to remove them to a place where their presence would no longer bother him.

If Rothschild and Hirsch were displaying anti-Semitic tendencies, so were some of their sworn enemies, the Social Democrats. The Party's newspaper, edited and largely written by Jews, spoke with hostility about "Jewish interests" and directed its sharpest editorials at Jewish capitalists. It referred to the bourgeois press as "a conspiracy in favor of the Jews" and called the battle cry of a rising anti-Semitic party, "Down with the domination by the Jews," sympathetic and very understandable.

In the intellectual and cultural world, few Jews wished to be associated with anything openly or obviously Semitic. Mahler asked his Gentile wife not to wear her hair up, for it made her look too Jewish, and he asked her to tell him when he gesticulated too much lest he look too Jewish. Jewish comedians in the city's numerous cabarets made fun of Jews, and self-deprecating Jewish jokes achieved wide circulation:

Two strangers, one Jewish, one Gentile, introduce themselves on the train. The conversation goes as follows: "Von Bradow: lieutenant in the reserve." "Lillenthal: permanently unfit."*

In several instances, such Jewish self-hatred reached grotesque proportions. One such case was the friend of Arthur Schnitzler, noted earlier. Another was that of Hermann Schwarzwald, a young civil servant whose remarkable brilliance and ability had enabled him to triumph over an unprepossessing manner and appearance, and become one of the rising stars of the Austrian bureaucracy. He had a bony build, a high-pitched voice, and a badly deformed left leg that forced him to "slither" about on a cane. Although a Galician, Schwarzwald despised Judaism so much that every year he made a pilgrimage to Germany to lay a wreath on the grave of the viciously anti-Semitic German writer Eugen Duhring.**

Then there was the critic Karl Kraus, whom one historian has described as "an exquisitely Jewish anti-Semite." Claiming the Jews constituted an oriental enclave in Western civilization, Kraus called on them to jettison all their beliefs, rituals, mannerisms, and other evidence of their Jewishness. In his periodical *Die Fackel*, Kraus not only wrote anti-Semitic articles of his own, but published articles by Gentile anti-Semites as well. These included pieces from France that derided the claim of Captain Alfred Dreyfuss that he was innocent of the espionage of which he was accused.

Perhaps the most outspoken and bizarre Jewish anti-Semite in turn-of-the-century Vienna was Otto Weininger, whom Sigmund Freud would later describe as a "highly gifted and sexually disturbed young philosopher." At the age of twenty-three, Weininger published *Sex and Character* (*Geschlecht und Charakter*), a book that consisted of a lengthy diatribe against both women and Jews. Weininger maintained that both groups stood in opposition to the "masculine principle" which in his view represented all that was good and noble in human history. He blamed Judaism for the decadent materialism of the

*Another joke tells of a boy coming home from school who tells his father that the teacher had said that the Jews killed Jesus. "Yes," replies the father, "but those were the Jews of Mattersdorf, not from our Korbersdorf."

**Schwarzwald did, however, refuse to undergo "the formality of baptism" when he came up for promotion to Imperial Counselor. Franz Joseph himself became interested in the case and wrote Schwarzwald a personal letter saying that while he "never dictated the choice of religion to any of my subjects," he had taken an oath to maintain a Christian country, and therefore felt he had to require all government officials who had access to him to be Christians. Franz Joseph then asked Schwarzwald to reconsider his refusal. "I am a much older man than you and you might yield if only to old age," the Emperor said. Schwarzwald stood firm and eventually won his promotion anyway, becoming not only the first non-Christian but, at the age of thirty-five, the youngest non-nobleman ever appointed to such a position.

times, and he viewed the struggle between Aryan Christianity and Judaism as a battle between the masculine and the feminine or, more straightforwardly, as a battle between good and evil.

Weininger committed suicide less than a year after his book appeared, but he could hardly have done so in despair over its reception, for *Sex and Character* became an almost instant best seller. The book eventually went through twenty-eight editions and was still being seriously discussed in the 1930s.

One may be tempted to believe that characters such as Kraus and Weininger represent quirky oddballs whose anti-Semitic writings made them outcasts from Jewish society. However, such was far from the case. Jews were the principal subscribers to Kraus' periodical, and they found Weininger's book a source of continuing interest. And lest one conclude that such extreme self-hatred was limited only to the Jewish intelligentsia, there are numerous indications that it was not. In the 1896 municipal elections in Vienna, for example, an avowed anti-Semite carried a heavily Jewish district in the Leopoldstadt.

Arthur Schnitzler mentions a joke that circulated in the city in the early 1880s. Anti-Semitism became popular in Vienna, so it went, only when the Jews themselves took it up. In this chapter we have seen how the Jews had taken it up. In the chapters that follow we will see how popular it had become.

Part III

The Attack Begins

. . . *in Vienna, before Berlin or Frankfurt, hatred of the Jews
was to become a political force; Austria would prove the
nursery for those who saw history in racial terms.*
— Desmond Stewart

*If any city in the world may claim to be the cradle of modern
political anti-Semitism, it is Vienna.*   — Peter G.J. Pulzer

*Anti-Semitism [as an ideological force] reached its most
articulate form in Austria.*   — Hannah Arendt

Prelude

A New Kind of Anti-Judaism

Anti-Judaism has existed ever since there have been Jews, and especially since there have been Christians. But through the centuries such anti-Judaism focused almost completely on Jews as a religious group. Those Jews who cast off their ancestral religion and converted to Christianity usually shed their stigma as well.

Anti-Semitism or hostility to Jews based on ethnicity or "race" is for the most part a creation of the nineteenth century, specifically the late nineteenth century. Its emergence confronted the Jews with an insidious and perplexing problem, one that could not always even be detected, let alone combatted. Ironically, development of the problem followed closely in the wake of what had become the greatest boon bestowed on the Jews since the Diaspora: emancipation from the ghetto and the acquisition of equal, or near equal, rights. The day so long in coming and so desperately desired had dawned only to bring with it new problems and anxieties.

The causes of this new form of Jew-hatred were many. One source lay in the new biology pioneered by Darwin but perverted by some who came after him. Darwin had spoken of superior species. This encouraged others to speak of superior "races," and races often became synonymous with sub-races or ethnic groups. More importantly, such "races" also became synonymous with the races to which the spokesmen for this new biology belonged. A forerunner of this new thinking was a French count named de Gobineau who claimed that racial composition determines the fate of nations and, indeed, whole civilizations. Aryan societies must remain racially pure, he said, for mixed breeding robs the nation of its vitality and propels it toward debasement and corruption.

De Gobineau's theories found many champions, especially in Germany. One was the composer Richard Wagner. Another, far less known today but greatly influential in his time, was the lawyer-turned-economist, Karl Eugen Dühring. In *The Jewish Question as a Racial, Moral and Cultural Question*, Dühring attacked the Jews as a despicable racial, cultural, and economic group that was threatening Western civilization with disaster.

Another factor fostered this new form of Jew-baiting. Capitalism itself was coming increasingly under attack in the late nineteenth century despite its apparent success in raising overall living standards and extending human freedom. The long deflation beginning in 1873, the failure of living standards to rise as rapidly as expectations, the inevitable failure of the majority to rise to the top, the plight of European peasants who saw their markets being eroded by exports from the United States — all these and countless other problems generated increasing skepticism toward industrial capitalism and what seemed to be its largely illusionary promises. The prominent part that Jews were playing in advancing and profiting from capitalist enterprise helped make them the most frequent targets of this new and rising anti-capitalist sentiment.

But capitalism had done more than simply create economic dislocation. Perhaps more significantly, it had broken up existing social and cultural arrangements, creating in the process the uprooted, urban individual who, while substantially better fed than his forebears, seemed at the same time more forlorn as well. Having lost many of his traditional ties to family, community, and church, nineteenth-century man began reaching out for anything that would overcome his sense of what sociologists had begun calling "anomie." Nationalism provided one readily available remedy, and the late nineteenth century saw an outburst of national sentiment. Such sentiment quite naturally fed in turn the theories of racism that had emerged earlier. Since the Jews, even the more emancipated ones, were still viewed as a group apart, anti-Semitism became an integral part of most ultra-nationalist movements.

Socialism, linked to the trade union movement, also offered an antidote to anomie. The socialists preached internationalism and urged their followers not to think in terms of national concerns but of the class struggle. But this message, while it helped in some instances to stem the rise of anti-Semitism, fell far short of erasing its influence even among the socialists themselves. For one thing, class solidarity failed to exert the same emotional pull as national pride. Industrial workers were ready to follow their leaders in demanding better pay, shorter hours, and other benefits, but they proved far less eager to abandon their national flag, their national traditions, and their overall sense of national identity.

To make matters worse, the identification of Jews with capitalism tended to blur the distinction between anti-Semitism and anti-capitalism among the socialists. Even Karl Marx, though he was the son of converted Jews and a neighbor of the Chief Rabbi of his native city, referred to his long-time ally, Ferdinand Lassalle, as a "Jewish nigger," and in one of his articles for the *New York Daily Tribune*, he railed against "loan-mongering Jews." Marx's most trenchant attack on Jews came in his essay, *The Jewish Question*, which bristles with such passages as:

What is the world religion of the Jew? Huckstering!
What is his worldly God? Money!

Socialism never fully succeeded in casting off its ambiguous attitude toward the Jews. In the Dreyfus case, for example, the German socialist press sided against the Jewish captain since he came from a wealthy family, while the French socialist leader, Juarez, initially complained that Dreyfus had received a "light" sentence — life imprisonment on Devil's Island! — because of the influence of the Jewish bourgeoisie.

Yet the fact that Marx and many of his followers were Jews also increased the anti-Semitism of anti-Marxists, especially of the Christians, and most especially of the Catholic Church. The Church, of course, had long held the Jews responsible for the death of Christ, and more recently had also held them partly responsible for the French Revolution, which had dealt such a blow to French Catholicism while emancipating French Jews. Now the Jews seemed to be threatening the Church still more by advocating a materialistic and atheistic doctrine, Marxist socialism.

But the Catholic Church linked the Jews not only to socialism but also to capitalism, and this association only added to its rancor. The Church had customarily held most of its assets in, and derived most of its income from, land. But as agricultural surpluses made land ownership less lucrative, and industrialization made other investments more promising, the Church, according to historian Gaetano Salvemini, began to change its investment policy.

Unfortunately, the Catholic businessmen to whom Church authorities entrusted their funds frequently proved no match for their Jewish rivals. An especially notable event was the collapse in 1882 of the *Catholic Union Generale*, a Parisian bank backed by the Church. It had been organized to put the Rothschilds out of business, but had obviously failed to do so. Such economic setbacks understandably angered and alarmed many Church leaders. The fact that many enterprising Jewish business and professional men supported parties and policies aimed at curtailing Church influence over, and subsidies from, the state only added to their concern.

But the Catholic Church remained committed only to anti-Judaism, not anti-Semitism. Opposition to the Jews on racial grounds conflicted with basic

Catholic doctrine that preached the conversion of all peoples to the one true faith. Furthermore, Jesus and his early disciples were ethnically Hebrew. A racially based anti-Semitism would require the Church to repudiate its own founders. Finally, quite a few Jews, including some wealthy ones, had converted to Catholicism, and the Church did not want to deter others from following them.

Despite these considerations, the Church's problems with Jewish capitalists and Jewish socialists often made many of its adherents, including the lower clergy, lose sight of the distinction between anti-Judaism and anti-Semitism. The dividing line between the two forms of hatred was not always clear and, in most cases, not very wide.

There were additional and more specific, but not necessarily less serious, spurs to Western European anti-Semitism in the late nineteenth century. Many Jews in Russia and Russian-occupied Poland began fleeing westward in the 1880s, attempting to escape the persecutions of their Slavic rulers and to enjoy the blessings of emancipation. Many continued on to America, but others settled on the Continent. Their distinctive dress, lifestyle, and mannerisms not only alienated West Europeans, but reinforced the notion that Jews were not just a separate religion but a separate nation. Also, the entry of Jews into business and the liberal professions antagonized some of their earlier supporters. The many lawyers, doctors, journalists, and professors who — caught up in the wave of early nineteenth-century liberalism — had backed the emancipation of the Jews began having second thoughts, as the beneficiaries of their efforts began competing with them for customers, clients, and public positions, including university professorships.

Finally, there is the more subtle question regarding the twofold nature of assimilation. In the rush to become integrated members of their societies, many Jews tried to discard everything, or nearly everything, that had made them Jews. Some went the full distance, changing their names, their habits, and even their religion. Others retained the rudiments of religion but sought in other ways to appear and act like their Gentile neighbors and confreres. But psychology teaches us that the person who fails to respect himself will almost never gain the respect of others. Jews who were trying to cast aside their Jewish identity as if it were a badge of shame were only encouraging others to treat them as if they were indeed shameful. As William A. Jenks has observed, "There is considerable reason to suppose that the emancipated Jew who tremulously reached out his hand for the trappings of Gentile culture was more hated than the Jew who kept to his ghetto and his orthodoxy." Regrettably, the Jews of Europe, and especially those of Austria, would not realize this until too late.

With such negative factors and forces at work, it is perhaps surprising that anti-Semitism did not gain more ground than it did. Although it did create a great deal of unrest (the Dreyfus case in France was perhaps the most sensational single example), it was, as a political force, largely contained. By the end of the century, Germany's small anti-Semitic party was consistently losing votes and seats in Parliament. In France, Dreyfus' innocence, although still not officially recognized, was now fairly established and a substantial portion of the non-Jewish population supported him. In Great Britain no political party had shown any inclination to include an anti-Semitic plank in its platform. In Scandinavia and the Lowland countries anti-Semitism had acquired almost no political thrust. As Hannah Arendt points out, "Whereas anti-Jewish sentiments were widespread among the educated classes of Europe throughout the nineteenth century, anti-Semitism as an ideology remained, with very few exceptions, the prerogative of crackpots."

Unfortunately for the Vienna Jews, one of these "very few exceptions" would be Austria.

Chapter 5

Seeds of Storm

If the Catholic Church throughout Europe had reasons for fearing and hating the Jews, the Austrian Catholic Church would seem to have had cause for feeling especially imperiled by their presence and activities. To begin with, many Jews, as we saw earlier, had played a leading role in Austria's aborted Revolution of 1848, an uprising that the Church correctly regarded as a threat to its position. Many of the newspapers that sprang up to back the insurgents were edited by Jewish journalists who did not hesitate to attack the Church directly. The Catholic press responded by denouncing "arrogant, insolent Jews" and the "perfidy of Jewish writers."

Although Franz Joseph suppressed the revolution and thereafter signed a concordat with the Vatican, such moves brought no lasting abatement in the Church's animosity, for a Liberal party soon emerged and most of Vienna's Jews flocked to its banner. The Liberals waged unremitting warfare against the concordat, claiming that it delivered Austria into the hands of the Pope. The Party's Jewish members fully joined in this fight; several Jewish journalists and writers became particularly outspoken in voicing opposition to the pact. Understandably, the clergy's rancor continued to rise, and when Franz Joseph finally abolished the concordat, clerical hostility grew still more.

Developments in the economic sphere were also adding another, more dangerous dimension to the country's attitude toward the Jews. Austria was at long last entering the Industrial Revolution, and in Austria, much more than in other countries, the Jews were emerging as its leaders. "The coming of the

Industrial Revolution [in Austria] was to a large extent a Jewish enterprise," writes Peter Pulzer. "Most of the country's bankers and many of its industrialists were . . . Jews."

There were many reasons for this. First, the Austro-Hungarian Empire had a larger percentage of Jews than any other Western European nation. Jews made up over four and one-half percent of the Empire's population while they constituted less than one percent of the populations of Germany, France, and Great Britain. Moreover, while ninety percent of the Empire's Jews lived in Hungary, Galicia, and the Czechoslovakian provinces, more and more of their enterprising members were moving to Vienna. In the imperial capital they found outlets for their entrepreneurial energies, and they became a more conspicuous presence for the eyes of the Empire were naturally fixed on its capital city.

The fact that Austria was primarily a Catholic country also fostered Jewish enterprise. Catholicism, in comparison to Protestantism, was far less conducive to capitalist activities and attitudes. Historian Robert Wistrich points to the "absence of a dynamic, indigenous middle class animated by the Protestant ethic of capitalism" as having facilitated Jewish entrepreneurship in the Habsburg Empire.

Finally, Austria's own particular ethos encouraged Jewish economic leadership, for the country's aristocrats were more interested in breeding and racing horses than in building factories, while its tradesmen were more devoted to playing cards than scrounging for business. Such habits left a vacuum that the newly emancipated Jews hastened to fill. To their later discomfort and dismay, they filled it all too well.

As a result of all these circumstances, capitalism became more closely identified with the Jews in Austria than in most other countries, and the association did little to encourage friendly feelings. In creating a new economy, the primarily Jewish capitalists were causing all kinds of stress and strain. The aristocrats saw Jews buying ancestral estates, and many aristocrats who did not sell their estates heavily mortgaged them to Jewish bankers. Farmers had also borrowed heavily from Jewish banks. But shopkeepers and artisans suffered the most, for they were threatened by Jews from both above and below.

The threat from above came from Jewish-owned factories that were turning out clothes and other consumer goods at a cheaper cost than the tradesmen could produce them. Also threatening were the new, large stores that Jewish merchants were erecting throughout Vienna and in many other Austrian cities. The threat from below came from Jewish peddlers and artisans who were aggressively hawking their wares and services from door to door. When these peddlers and artisans opened permanent places of business, they continued to underbid their non-Jewish competitors, making up the difference by working harder and longer. From 1865 to 1890, some thirty-five thousand independent Viennese tradesmen were driven out of business, while many others were reduced to eking out a bare livelihood.*

The expansion of Jewish economic influence was aided by new laws that not only gave the Jews near equal rights but weakened the power of the trade guilds to restrict competition. An additional irritant was the desire on the part of some Jews to encourage more of their co-religionists to enter manual trades. The Society for the Promotion of Handicrafts Among Native Israelites had been formed as early as 1840 and, subsidized heavily by Baron Hirsch, it was sponsoring fifteen hundred Jewish apprentices by 1890. It is one of the many ironies of Jewish Vienna that a movement designed to discourage anti-Semitism by showing that Jews could and would work with their hands only increased anti-Semitism.

The stock market crash of 1873 and the devastating depression that followed gave a further boost to anti-Semitism. The speculation spree that preceded the debacle involved nearly all sectors of Austrian society, from the aristocracy to the lower middle class. Many members of Parliament as well as the upper bureaucracy were also involved. Unwilling to accept any responsibility for the disaster, they found a scapegoat in the Jews.

To be sure, many Jews had played a part, but what really aroused the ire of the non-Jews was that many had not. The Rothschilds, for example, had publicly warned against the speculative mania and had wisely refrained from joining it. As a result, their bank remained standing after most others had disappeared. As a further result, they, and by extension all Jews, were thought to be profiteering from the crash. The Viennese press in publishing cartoon caricatures of speculators almost invariably gave them Jewish features. Many of these cartoons showed Jews gloating over the catastrophe; one depicts a Jewish speculator leading a group of his countrymen who, in turn, are carrying a banner emblazoned with the Star of David and the message, "Masters over the World."

Another development during the 1870s also helped set the stage for the coming outburst of anti-Semitism. As noted earlier, the new interest in biology and anthropology had awakened the concept of the Jews as a "race" rather than as a religion. This idea gained intellectual respectability in 1876 when Theodor Billroth, the city's most esteemed physician, published his book, *The Teaching and Learning of Medical Science.*

Billroth had become disturbed by the number of Jews who were entering the University's medical school. He was especially upset because many of

---

*A further irritant was the presence of Jewish moneylenders operating in the working-class districts of Vienna. They charged ten or eleven percent interest, while the downtown banks charged only four or five percent. The fact that such charges reflected the greater risks, collection costs, and other expenses — most of their own capital was borrowed — or the fact that Christian moneylenders charged the same, did little to soften the hostility these Jewish moneylenders provoked.

these students were Galician Jews who pursued their studies while selling firewood on the streets of Vienna. He did not understand that these students were forced into this sideline by extreme poverty, for impoverished Gentile youths rarely enrolled in medical school. Consequently, he concluded that Jews were racially addicted to making money. Jews were a "sharply distinctive nation" who could never be Germans, Billroth said, for the "gulf between purely German and purely Jewish blood" was simply too great to be bridged.

Billroth later repudiated his racial ideas and even became something of a philo-Semite. But this renunciation came too late; his ideas had found a fertile field in which to take root and grow, and grow they certainly did.

The first organized expression of *racial* Jewish hatred in Austria erupted at the University of Vienna. Certainly Billroth's book helped prepare the way, but other forces also contributed.

By the 1870s, the Empire's loss of the Italian provinces, its settlement with the Hungarians, and its stunning and sudden defeat by the Prussians, plus the lagging pace of economic growth, had stripped it of any real claim to greatness as a political power. This in turn weakened the national ability to arouse patriotic idealism among its youth. Consequently, many young Austro-Germans began to identify with Germany and to assert their Germanism. Other national groups within the Empire had also begun to assert *their* own nationalities, and this encouraged the Austro-Germans to do the same.

In embarking on this course, the students and some of their professors as well became anti-Habsburg, anti-liberal, and also anti-capitalist, for they regarded capitalism as an internationalist institution whose practitioners eagerly trampled over national boundaries and repudiated national identity in a ruthless quest for profits. Given the identification of Jews with capitalism, this provided more fodder for anti-Jewish sentiments.

Opportunistic considerations also stimulated the anti-Semitism of the Austro-German students. Many were relatively uninterested in learning. They had only enrolled in the University to acquire an entree into the bureaucracy or the professions, and spent far more time fencing and drinking than studying. The Jews generally disdained such activities, preferring instead to work hard in preparing themselves for the careers now becoming available. They thus posed an increasing threat to the future career prospects of the Austro-Germans.

Jewish baptism, far from allaying this threat, only increased it, for a baptized Jew could compete even more successfully than could a nonbaptized one. Many Austro-German students planned careers in the bureaucracy and the judiciary, and higher positions in these branches of government remained closed to professed Jews but open to baptized ones.

All these circumstances converged to make students ripe for the new anti-Semitism and, with the writings of Billroth, Dühring, Wagner, and others as intellectual justification, they launched their attack.

Most Austro-German students belonged to one of a group of fraternal societies called *Burschenschaften*, student clubs that sponsored various activities ranging from lectures and libraries to duels and drinking bouts. (The latter two activities were by far the most popular.) In 1878 one of these *Burschenschaften*, ironically called *Libertas*, decided henceforth to exclude Jews whether they were baptized or not. By 1890 all the other *Burschenschaften* had done the same.

The case of *Albia*, one of these groups, is of special interest. *Albia* had only three Jewish members when it began deliberating its position on the question. One of the three, Theodor Herzl, became so disgusted at what he was hearing and experiencing that he resigned. One of the other two suggested that the association allow him and the other Jewish member to remain, and simply not accept any more Jews. For a while, *Albia* did so but finally decided to rid itself of its existing Jewish membership. By this time, however, only one Jew remained, for the student who had suggested the exclusionary compromise had committed suicide.

In the spring of 1883 the Union of German Students held a memorial meeting to honor Richard Wagner who had died recently. A gifted twenty-year-old student named Hermann Bahr was selected to give the eulogy. Bahr chose to eulogize not Wagner the composer but Wagner the anti-Semite, and his eloquence caused the whole assembly to turn into an anti-Semitic riot. Fortunately, the gathering took place in a concert hall outside the University so the police could intervene and rescue the Jewish students caught up in it.*

Another incident around this time further illustrates the ugly mood enveloping the country's prized citadel of learning. The University's medical school had a society for financially assisting poor and deserving students. Most of those helped were impoverished Jewish students from Hungary, Galicia, and other outlying parts of the Empire, since they were almost the only ones who qualified. In addition, most of the money for such aid came from the contributions of Jewish doctors.

There had been little problem with this system until the early 1880s when, at the association's annual meeting, some Austro-German students began demanding that henceforth only Germans receive assistance. Nothing was said initially about excluding Jews per se, but the proposal, if enacted, would have effectively done so. The proposal was approved with some of its more

---

*Bahr would later become one of Vienna's foremost writers and, like Billroth, would abandon his anti-Semitism.

enthusiastic endorsements coming from baptized or assimilated Jews. Liberally-oriented student members of the executive committee, among them the later physician and writer Arthur Schnitzler, were voted out of office and an anti-Semitic committee elected in their place. The issue apparently flared up again, for at a later meeting anti-Semitic students began beating Jewish students with clubs and canes as they left the chamber, forcing the University to disband the association altogether.

Violence against Jewish students was not restricted to meetings or special occasions. As the 1880s progressed, it became almost routine. The *Burschenschaften* would spend Saturday afternoon marching up and down the University courtyard singing German national songs; groups would then frequently break up to attack Slavs, Italians, Hungarians, and especially Jews.

The German national students also came up with a couplet to express their opinion that Jews remain Jews regardless of whatever religion they might profess. The couplet in English went as follows:

> What religion the Jew professes is of no account. Swinishness lies in the race itself.
> (*Was der Jude glaubt ist einerlei. In der Rasse liegt die Schweinerei.*)*

This little rhyme soon swept Vienna, signaling as well as supporting the new attitude toward the Jews. As historian Karl Stadler has observed, "It was the University that made anti-Semitism intellectually 'respectable,' and the 'intelligentsia' which fed it to a troubled populace."

While economic factors played only a limited though significant role in the growing anti-Semitism at the University, such factors dominated the concerns of the small tradesmen. Jewish competition in fact had become a troubling phenomenon as early as the late 1860s when it prompted eight thousand Vienna shoemakers to petition against the emancipation of the Jews. Claiming that Jewish competition threatened their existence, they asked for the reinstitution of the pre-1848 restrictions, a step which would effectively place the Jews back in the ghetto.

The tradesmen's cry for help found a ready response in the Catholic Church, which, as we have seen, had many reasons of its own for becoming alarmed over Jewish economic success. So the Church joined forces with the tradesmen in an all-out attack on the growing economic and what, to them, seemed to be the growing political might of the Jews.

This attack gained greater force as well as respectability in 1875 when the *Vaterland*, a paper of the Catholic hierarchy, acquired a new editor. He was

---

*Harry Zohn contributes a rhymed translation of this couplet: "What the Jew believes is all the same/It is his race that is a dirty shame."

Baron Karl von Vogelsang, a Protestant-born nobleman from Germany who had moved to Austria and converted to Catholicism. Like so many converts, he was prepared to defend his new faith with unmatched zeal.

Vogelsang hated capitalism as much as Karl Marx did. Moreover, his reasons, to some degree, paralleled those of Marx. Vogelsang claimed that under capitalism economic activity became an end in itself and not merely a means to other, more noble, ends. He also shared Marx's view that Jews were unwholesomely wound up with capitalism. Indeed, he even on occasion quoted from Marx's essay on the Jewish question to prove his point. "Never will we revile the religion of the Jews," said Vogelsang in one of his editorials, but "we must demand that the Jews cease their evil business practices. Through such practices they so poison trade and commerce that an honorable Christian can hardly create a place for himself." Vogelsang's writings also represented the thinking of Austria's aristocracy, which felt itself challenged economically, socially, and culturally by a rampaging free enterprise led by the Jews. Consequently, the aristocrats became natural allies with the small tradesmen, the clergy, and others who had suddenly found their way of life, if not their very existence, imperiled by the country's delayed entry into the Industrial Revolution.

In the fall of 1880 the artisans and small tradesmen of Vienna held a giant rally to protest Jewish competition. Two years later they formed the Austrian Reform Union to protect their interests. Increasingly they viewed such protection largely in terms of curbing the Jews. The Union quickly set up its own newspaper whose official slogan, carried under its masthead, read, "Buy from Christians."

The new organization grew rapidly in numbers and strength. Its mounting influence, along with the growth of anti-Semitism in general, was greatly helped by a new election law that came into effect the same year. The new law lowered the amount of tax an Austrian male had to pay in order to vote. The new minimum figure, while still high enough to exclude most industrial workers, was low enough to permit tens of thousands of small tradesmen to join the electorate. So Vienna's newly organized and enfranchised lower middle class now possessed the weapons and allies it needed to curtail if not crush the Jewish threat.

One of the leaders in this attack was Ernst Schneider, a skilled mechanic who had taught himself several languages and had written articles for Vogelsang's publication. Undeniably gifted, he was also undeniably unscrupulous. During the course of his career, he was accused of forgery, ballot tampering, and eliciting false testimony. He was also a heavy drinker. Yet his abilities as an organizer and orator enabled him to move to the forefront in the fight against the Jews.

With the help of the new election laws and with the financial assistance of a leading aristocrat, Schneider was elected to Parliament, where he soon became a member of that body's executive committee. His wife became office manager of the Catholic Women's League. (To his chagrin, his daughter married a Jew, and his son became a wastrel, forcing his parents to take out ads disclaiming responsibility for his debts.)

Schneider not only proposed various laws to curb the influence and restrict the rights of Jews, but encouraged and urged people to embrace outlandish methods of Jew-baiting. For example, with his blessing and probably at his behest, the Reform Union began selling silver effigies of a Jew being hanged. These were to be worn on watch chains, and Schneider and his still small band of extreme anti-Semitic parliamentarians immediately began flaunting them on their vests in the lower House of Parliament. The Austrian historian Hawlik, commenting on the wave of anti-Semitism sweeping Austria in the mid-1880s, writes: "One could not yet foresee the direction in which it would develop and whether the dam of reason would prove strong enough to contain it."

Chapter 6

A Cause and a Champion

Although Vogelsang had pledged never to "revile the religion of the Jews," attacks on the Jewish religion also began to increase, for racial and religious anti-Semitism naturally nourished each other. In 1871 a priest who was also a professor of theology at the German University of Prague published a short book, called *Der Talmudjude* or *The Talmud Jew*. In it the author — Father August Rohling — claimed (among other things) that the Talmud describes Christians as animals.

Given the mood of the times, Father Rohling's book became immensely popular, going through six editions in six years. One Catholic organization distributed 38,000 copies free of charge.

The Jewish community sought at first to ignore the book, but in the spring of 1882 an event occurred that made this impossible. It began when an agitator named Holubek addressed a group of Christian tradesmen and claimed that the Jews "are no longer our fellow citizens but have become our masters, oppressors, and tormenters." He then went on to say that the Talmud describes Christians as a "herd of pigs, dogs, and asses."

Some months later the public prosecutor of Vienna, acting probably at the behest of Franz Joseph's government, brought Holubek to trial on charges of disturbing the peace. The defendant's attorney quoted from Rohling's book to show that his client was only speaking the truth, and the jury quickly, and unanimously, acquitted the accused man.

The case made front page headlines in Vienna, and the city's Jews, most of whom had no idea of what was in the Talmud, turned to their rabbis for help. Chief Rabbi Jellinek and his assistant Moritz Güdemann issued a three-sentence statement saying that "the Talmud contains nothing hostile to Christianity" and that any claim to the contrary was an "absolute untruth." But the sigh of relief that swept the Jewish community on the issuing of this statement proved short-lived. Six weeks later Rohling published a series of articles in a Vienna newspaper citing what he claimed were passages from the Talmud that proved his point. He accused the two rabbis of "cunning knavery" for having dared to say otherwise.

The newspaper covered the city with red posters advertising the articles, and each edition that carried them sold out. Subsequently, the articles were reprinted as a book which sold an extraordinary 200,000 copies. The Vienna Jews were mortified; many believed that the passages Rohling cited did appear in the Talmud after all. This fear grew when no further reply came from Jellinek and Güdemann to repudiate them.

At this point, a mini-Messiah of sorts appeared in the form of a feisty, brilliant, Galician-born rabbi named Samuel Bloch. Largely self-educated, for he'd been forced to shift for himself at an early age, Bloch had not only earned a rabbinical certificate but had also picked up a bona fide doctorate degree. He was, at the time, serving a congregation in Floridadorf, a poor working-class suburb located on Vienna's southern edge. (The city would incorporate it in the early 1890s.)

When Bloch saw that Jellinek and Güdemann had no stomach for continuing the fight — such squabbles were simply not something they enjoyed — he wrote a massive rejoinder to Rohling in twenty-four hours, and three days before Christmas found a paper to publish it in a separate edition.

Bloch's reply scored an immediate success. It even sold 100,000 copies in Germany and eventually was translated into all of the Empire's major languages. As Bloch would later say in his memoirs, "I awoke one morning to find myself famous." When Rohling sought to counterattack with a further article, Bloch challenged him, saying he would deposit 3,000 Gulden in a bank for him "should you be able to read and translate correctly one single page of the Talmud." He then added, "My dear sir, you cannot do it." (It was his assurance on this point that enabled him to issue such a challenge; at the time Bloch possessed nothing close to 3,000 Gulden.)

As Bloch predicted, Rohling declined to accept his challenge and, for a time, the theologian kept silent. But only for a time, for another, more ancient and even more inflammatory issue would soon re-emerge and place the Jews once again at bay.

The Church had never abandoned its belief that Jews engaged in ritual murder. As its hostility to Jews increased in the late nineteenth century, some

Church officials began to show increased interest in this subject. From early 1881 to late 1882 the Jesuit magazine *La Civita Cattolica* published a series of articles on this allegedly Jewish practice. In one article, which appeared in its March 4, 1881 issue, it said that "every practicing Hebrew is required even now, in conscience, to use in food, drink, circumcision and in other rituals of his religious and civil life the fresh or dried blood of a Christian child." An incident a little over a year later would put this belief to the test.

The incident was the Tisza Eszla case, which has become something of a landmark in modern Jewish history. A teenage girl had disappeared from a Hungarian village and the local authorities charged a group of Jews with having murdered her for ritualistic purposes. The evidence came largely from the testimony of the fourteen-year-old son of the synagogue sexton, who had been coerced into saying that he had seen the local kosher butcher slaughter the girl. The trial lasted for six weeks, an unusually long time for even a murder trial in the Austria of those days, but the case against the Jews was so flimsy — no body was ever discovered and some witnesses reported having seen the girl alive in Vienna — that all four judges, including one who was an outspoken anti-Semite, voted for acquittal.

During the course of the trial, however, Rohling testified for the prosecution, saying under oath that "the religion of the Jews requires them to despoil and destroy Christianity in every way possible," and that "the shedding of a Christian virgin's blood is for the Jews an extraordinarily holy event." Bloch immediately and publicly denounced Rohling as a liar and a perjurer.

The rabbi's new attack on the priest could not go unanswered; silence in the face of such a charge would constitute an admission of guilt. Court actions for slander were quite common in those days — they are by no means rare today — and Bloch had purposely framed his charges to compel Rohling to file a suit against him. Bloch was by now a member of Parliament, elected to a vacant seat from a Jewish district in Galicia after his first reply to Rohling had made him famous. As such he was immune from libel actions. But the new champion of Austrian Judaism waived his immunity thereby removing any excuse Rohling might have for failing to take legal action.

Rohling finally did file the complaint and Bloch, with the financial help of a Jewish coal magnate, immediately set about finding a highly respected Christian attorney to defend him and some respected non-Jewish Hebraic scholars from Germany to testify in his behalf. His action scared off Rohling who, shortly before the case was scheduled to come to trial, suddenly withdrew his suit. Since this action was considered an admission of guilt, he was dismissed from his professorship. Bloch, and with him the Jews of Austria, had won.

But the triumph proved to be something of a pyrrhic victory. Rohling's book continued to sell well, as many Gentiles held fast to the ideas it espoused.

Not one Christian had publicly repudiated Rohling, although a few had privately written sympathetic letters to Bloch. The belief in the blood libel, along with so many other negative notions about the Jews, had simply become too ingrained and, perhaps, too comfortable and convenient for many Christians to give up.

How did the Vienna Jews respond to this upsurge in hostility coming so soon and so unexpectedly after their long-awaited emancipation? At the University a small group of mostly Galician and other Eastern European students banded together to form the first Jewish student organization in the history of the Diaspora. They called their organization Kadimah, a word which in Hebrew literally means eastward, but which figuratively also means forward.

On March 21, 1883 Kadimah posted a statement in all of Vienna's institutes of higher education. Addressed to "Ethnic Comrades" (*Stammesgenossen*), the first part of the message read as follows:

> Since the eighteenth century the Jewish people has lost its independent existence and has become subject to increasing persecution whose goal is the destruction of Jewry. In this endeavor our enemies are unfortunately supported by our fellow Jews. The indifference from inside the Jewish community competes with animosity from outside it in the effort to achieve this goal.

The statement then ended with an appeal to fellow Jewish students to join in working for "the regeneration of the Jewish people."

Unfortunately for Kadimah, and for the future of Vienna Jewry in general, few non-Galician students responded to the appeal. The sons of well-to-do Vienna Jews had begun instead to join the German Liberal Students Association, which was rapidly becoming the only organization at the University that would accept them. To their horror they soon found themselves making up a majority of the Association which, with the gradual departure of the Gentile members, became virtually a Jewish organization and therefore less than useless as a means of achieving integration. Nevertheless, most Jewish students continued to cling to a German identity regardless of the fact that virtually all German national groups would no longer accept them, baptized or not.

As one step to counter anti-Semitism, both the integrationist and the nationalist students began to study fencing. The *Burschenschaften* placed a great deal of emphasis on saber duels where heavily padded contestants tried to inflict saber wounds on each other's faces. The nationalists took up fencing for self-protection, while the integrationists did so with the hope that it would make them more acceptable to their Gentile fellow students. Gradually, more and more Jews began fighting duels, and, as they became increasingly proficient, more began winning them as well.* Their new powers with the saber failed to achieve what the integrationists had hoped. Indeed it angered the German nationalists still more by depriving them of the one activity in which they had heretofore demonstrated an absolute superiority to the Jews. The fact that members were even on occasion losing duels to Jews prompted the *Burschenschaften* to adopt the following resolution in 1896:

> Every son of a Jewish mother, in whose veins circulates Jewish blood, is by dint of birth without honor. . . . He cannot distinguish between dirtiness and cleanliness. . . . Since any Jew cannot be insulted, he can therefore not ask for satisfaction.

The *Waidhofer Resolution*, named for the town in which it was drawn up, allowed Gentile students to avoid the danger of fighting and thereby possibly losing a duel with a Jew. It also allowed the Jews to see that their efforts to prove themselves in any area would not create greater regard and rapport with the German students, but would only encourage greater animosity. This lesson, unfortunately, would remain unlearned.

The flareup of anti-Semitism in the 1880s jolted adult Jews even more than it did the students. Passionately pro-German, they were caught off balance by the sudden surge of hostility from those they had regarded as their fellow Germans within the Empire. "I had in truth already forgotten that I was a Jew," Sigmund Meyer Kaufmann would later say. "Now anti-Semitism brought me to this unpleasant discovery."

Nevertheless most stubbornly refused to abandon their German identity. They continued to support the Austro-Germans in their all-too-successful efforts to squelch government attempts to make concessions to the Empire's Slavs and other minorities. That the Austro-Germans were not only disavowing the Jews but seeking to repress them as well did not discourage large numbers of Jews from continuing to assert their Germanism.

In the summer of 1882 some progressive, mostly Jewish, Austrians sought to form a genuinely multinational party that would include and represent liberal elements from all the ethnic groups in the Empire. But a band of Jewish students led by the passionately pro-German Jewish historian, Heinrich Friedjung, showed up at the meeting called to consider formation of the party.

---

*A few years later, when a brilliant young anatomist with the rather comical Jewish name of Zuckerkandl gave his first lecture at the University of Graz, the German nationalist students organized a noisy demonstration against him. But Zuckerkandl had been an earnest fencer while a medical student in Vienna, and he promptly reached into his coat pocket, took out a bunch of his calling cards, and flung them at the demonstrators saying, "I challenge you all to a duel." None accepted, and henceforth he was allowed to lecture in peace.

Together with some German nationalist Jews present, Friedjung's group squashed the whole effort by voicing vigorous opposition to any step that would endanger the privileged position that the Germans held in the Empire. Adolf Fischhof, the Jewish hero of 1848 now living in retirement outside Vienna, had supported the mutinational endeavor, seeing in it a way to head off the coming calamity. Its collapse caused him to comment, "The Vienna Jews do not realize what an awful reaction will break out, and that it will certainly engender violent anti-Semitism. . . . The Jews themselves have prevented this attempt to save them."

The election of Schneider and twelve other extreme anti-Semites in 1884 did force some Jews to rethink their position and to recognize the danger that confronted them. Earlier Bloch had called for an organization to combat anti-Semitism. Now a group of younger Jewish business and professional men decided to listen to him.

In the spring of 1884 several of them met to form the Union of Austrian Israelites. They expressed particular concern over the youth of the Jewish community, who "are more ashamed of being Jewish than of anything else." The organization's first president, a lawyer named Sigmund Zins, defined his primary task succinctly and, it would seem, accurately. "If anti-Semitism is to be fought, we must begin with Jewish anti-Semitism. Our first mission is to raise Judaism in our own eyes as well as in the eyes of others, to battle against humiliation and abasement."

But Zins, in what had become an all-too-typical twist in Jewish thinking, refused to sever the links that he saw as existing between the Jews and the Austro-Germans, for while he emphasized "the duties of Austrian Jews to a straightforward Austrian patriotism," he also stressed their "political brotherhood with the people and nation among whom they are born and raised, in whose literature they prefer to be educated and in whose cultural and economic life they participate."

Despite such concessions to Germanism and its integrationist stance generally, the Union evoked opposition from some of the more ardent Germanists, such as Friedjung, who called it a political ghetto. But in 1886 it came officially into existence and gradually became a major force within the Jewish community.

If many Jews had qualms about the Union, many more had qualms about its primary instigator, Dr. Bloch. While they recognized his valiant and certainly valuable efforts in fighting the anti-Semites, they also felt uneasy over having such an outspoken and orthodox Galician serving as their spokesman. When Prime Minister Taafe, who had developed an admiration for Bloch, wanted to appoint the rabbi as Professor of Hebrew Antiquities at the University of Vienna, some Jewish leaders told him they would consider Bloch's appointment a provocative act against the Viennese Jews. Bloch himself later recalled how the president of one Jewish organization, the Israelite Alliance, told him, "You defend the Talmud too much. We don't know it and don't want to have it anymore."

In the political arena the Vienna Jews continued to support the German Liberal party, which, like most liberal parties in nineteenth-century Europe, believed in civil liberties and equal rights but also in untrammeled free enterprise. Their support would prove disadvantageous on two counts. First, the Liberal party had become less and less interested in protecting Jewish interests. Second, the Party was now on its last legs. The broadening of the franchise in 1882 had sounded its death knell, for the lower middle class, who could now vote, had no intention of voting for free enterprise. Instead, this new electorate wanted to curtail the power of big business and restrict competition even within its own ranks. The Jews' continued allegiance to the liberals gained them few friends, while it heightened their identification in the popular mind with a ruthless, rampaging capitalism.

Faced with the fading of the Liberal party and its unwillingness in any case to further champion their cause, and faced also with the developing anti-Semitism of the other parties, many Jews began avoiding politics altogether. This was especially true of the wealthier ones, who feared that any moves they might make would only whip up a new storm of controversy and hate.

Most of those who remained in the political arena adopted an ostrich policy as far as anti-Semitism was concerned. Jewish members of the Vienna City Council, for instance, took a joint pledge to ignore the worst ravings of the anti-Semites. "The Jew was to appear before the public as a man, not as a Jew," writes Max Grunwald. Whenever a Jewish issue arose in Parliament, most Jewish members tried to be absent or, if that were not possible, would bury their heads in the papers on their desks and feign disinterest in what was going on. When the president of Parliament once suggested rescheduling a session which fell on Yom Kippur, it was the Jewish members who objected to the idea.

Such behavior was further encouraged by the largely Jewish-owned popular press, which sought to downplay to the point of ignoring the rising clamor of Jew-hatred. The *Neue Freie Presse*, for example, continued to concern itself with cultural or weighty state affairs. A foreigner reading the *Presse* would never have known that anti-Semitism even existed in the Habsburg Empire. "Despite the growing electoral strength of the anti-Semites in the 1880s and 1890s," writes Rozenblit, "the Jewish establishment refused to acknowledge the need for Jewish politics or a Jewish vote. While they hoped for a spirited defense of Jewish rights against the anti-Semites, they were unwilling to admit that there were Jewish issues in politics."

Chapter 7

Cresting Wave

The anti-Semitic tide gathered force as the decade progressed, faced with only limited efforts by the Jews, and almost no efforts by the non-Jews, to contain it. Groups of all kinds became involved in the issue. In 1888 the Austrian Society for the Protection of Animals called for an end to kosher slaughtering, claiming it was inhumane. Prime Minister Taafe set up a commission to study the subject and, when the commission found no cruelty in the process, the government rejected the society's proposal.

In Parliament anti-Jewish bills, some frivolous, some not, bobbed up in profusion. Among the former was a proposal by Schneider to put all the country's Jews on a big ship, send it to the middle of the ocean, and sink it. This, he said, would end the Jewish problem for good.

More serious measures sought to abridge Jewish rights, especially in the economic sphere. Bills restricting the immigration of Jews fleeing Czarist pogroms in Russia also received keen attention. The German Nationalists even proposed a complicated measure designed to make it much harder for Jews to change their names. Since all these proposals contradicted the country's constitution, as well as the wishes of its emperor and his prime minister, they made no headway. Yet they indicate the atmosphere that had engulfed Austria's Lower Chamber, supposedly its most democratic institution.

Anti-Semitic motions and measures had not only become commonplace but had also become a source of fun. On one occasion when a member moved to take up a Jewish measure before some of the more general measures on the agenda, the Speaker of the House ruled out the request, saying, "No, my good sir, business before pleasure."

The atmosphere within Parliament accurately reflected the atmosphere without. The Pan-Germans had formed a political party pledged to fight the Habsburgs, the Catholic Church, and the Jews. Shortly thereafter, in 1887, a group of Catholics formed a party of their own. Called the Christian Social Union, it centered its fire on capitalism and Judaism, two isms regarded as more or less interchangeable by the aristocrats, tradesmen, and lower clergy, who constituted the new party's main support. One Christian Social newspaper, the *Illustrierte Wiener Volkszeitung*, proudly bore under its masthead the subtitle, *Das Organ des Anti-Semitismus*.

The Christian Socials and the Pan-Germans formed an alliance called Christians United to sponsor joint candidates in the Vienna City Council elections in 1889. The alliance platform called for the exclusion of Jews from the civil service, the judiciary, the teaching of non-Jewish pupils, medicine, the law, pawnbrokering, grocery store ownership, and the sale of alcohol. It also demanded severe restrictions on Jewish immigration.

The year 1889 would prove a fateful year for the Vienna Jews in two other ways as well. In January, Crown Prince Rudolf and his lover Mary Vetsera committed suicide at the Prince's estate at Mayerling. This has become the most celebrated double suicide in history, and has generated countless books and several movies. But largely left out of all that has been written and spoken of the event is its effect on the situation of the Vienna Jews.

The Crown Prince was liberally-oriented and a foe of anti-Semitism. His best friend was the Jewish newspaper publisher Moritz Szeps, and Rudolf wrote anonymous articles for Szeps' newspaper in which he occasionally denounced anti-Semitic agitation within the Empire. While virtually no one knew of the prince's writing activity, his cordial attitude toward Jews had become public knowledge. Only a few months prior to his death he had taken the visiting Prince of Wales, the future Edward VII, to a luncheon at Sacher's with Baron Hirsch. The news of the two Crown Princes lunching with a Jewish baron became the talk of Vienna.

From all we know, the Prince was quite popular with the Viennese. He was also, of course, only a heartbeat away from the throne. These factors had probably helped restrain the growing power of the anti-Semites. Now this restraint was gone. Franz Joseph still held an umbrella over his Jewish subjects, but he was in his sixtieth year. Moreover, the man he eventually chose as his new heir apparent, his nephew the Archduke Franz Ferdinand, was a determined anti-Semite. Though most of Vienna's Jews seemed oblivious to it, the chain of events had weakened their position and made them more vulnerable to their enemies.

The other event of special significance to the Vienna Jews which occurred in 1889 passed unremarked by almost everyone, Jew and Gentile alike. Three months after Rudolf's death, in the border village of Braunau, a son was born to Alois and Klara Hitler.

In March 1891, a few days before Passover, a Jewish horse dealer in one of Vienna's suburbs was preparing to drive out to work when he heard a noise under his wagon seat. He lifted the seat lid and found a boy of six or seven crouching under it. When the youngster would not say why he was there, the horse dealer quickly guessed the reason. Anti-Semites had planted the lad in the wagon with instructions to cry out, "The Jews are kidnapping me," once the wagon had started down the street. The incident had been scheduled for a few days before Passover to help substantiate a subsequent charge that the horse dealer was taking the boy away for a ritual murder.

The horse dealer had no trouble surmising what was afoot for such incidents were becoming increasingly common in Vienna and elsewhere in the Empire. In another example, a thirty-year-old woman offered her infant daughter to a childless Jewish couple. The couple, their suspicions instantly aroused, reported the offer to the police. Under questioning, the woman confessed she was planning to charge the pair later with kidnapping the child. In Bohemia two maids claimed their Jewish employer entered their bedroom at night and drained blood from their wrists while they slept. They later recanted, saying the idea for making the charge had been suggested to them by others.

In Galicia kidnapping cases involving Jews often took a different twist. Here it was becoming fairly common for anti-Jewish zealots to abduct Jewish children and hand them over to convents to be raised as Catholics. The convent would give the child a new name, making it difficult for the parents to trace the youngster's whereabouts. If the parents succeeded in locating their children, they usually found the convent unwilling to release the child and the provincial authorities reluctant to intervene. In one case involving a twelve-year-old girl named Rachel Steiglitz, the Church did agree to return the girl to her parents, but only if the mother converted to Catholicism and the father renounced paternal rights.

Such incidents did not occur in western, i.e., German Austria, for here the flow of hate against the Jews rested increasingly on racial grounds. But since the Church was still encouraging Jewish conversions, this sometimes produced awkward and even ludicrous situations. A group of Church authorities inspecting a Catholic school were shocked to see a boy with a prominent, Semitic nose sitting in the front row of the classroom. "What is that Jewish child doing here?" they asked the teacher. They were even more shocked when the teacher replied, "But that is Dr. Schwarz's child." They had forgotten that

Dr. Kaspar Schwarz, the president of the local Catholic School Association, was a converted Jew.

One incident illustrates the new racial anti-Semitism, and its greater effect on German Austria than on other parts of the Empire. This event involved the choice of an archbishop in one of the Czech provinces, a particular See that had the right to elect its own archbishop. The position fell vacant in 1892, and when the factions supporting the two contending candidates became stalemated, they compromised by selecting a respected Catholic scholar, Monsignor Theodor Kohn, for the post.

Kohn is a German form of Cohen, and the new prelate was indeed a converted Jew. But while his election may have unsettled many Czech Catholics, it outraged most German ones. When the new archbishop sought to address a Catholic Congress in Salzburg in 1896, he was greeted with catcalls and jeers. Eventually the Vatican asked him to resign, saying his name had caused too much controversy.

In keeping with this new approach, the Christian Social party was making less and less distinction between religion and race in its ongoing crusade against the Jews. The Party focused most of its fury on what it regarded as Jewish economic crimes, and its strictures strongly implied that such supposedly criminal behavior was more racial than religious in origin. Ernst Schneider had become one of the Christian Social party's leading orators and, with the Party paying his expenses, he traveled throughout the Empire, whipping up what seemed more and more to be racial hate.

Buoyed by the reception he was receiving, Schneider became increasingly outspoken and outrageous. At a party meeting in Kremes, he called on the government to pay a bounty to anyone who killed a Jew. Since the government pays a bounty for killing predatory animals, reasoned Schneider, it should do the same for those who killed predatory people. The audience roared its approval.

On at least one occasion, however, Schneider failed in his mission. When he arrived at a trade fair at Lemberg in Galicia, a huge man with a beard and caftan stepped up to him and asked, "Are you the Schneider from Vienna?" When Schneider, looking up at his questioner, who towered over him, answered with a weak "Yes," the man, whose name was Rosenstein, replied, "Well, I am the *Schneider* (tailor) of Lemberg. I hope you will have a quiet time during your stay here." The Lemberg tailor then gave the visitor from Vienna a meaningful look and stepped away. Schneider, who like most bullies was a natural coward, complied completely. Indeed, in true Viennese fashion, he sought to ingratiate himself with the Jewish tradesmen who were attending the fair.

But the poison Schneider and his allies were spreading was rapidly permeating all sectors of Austrian society. Even puppet shows were not immune. One of the plays at the Prater's puppet theater featured Wuerstel the

Clown and a figure identified only as *Jude*. During the skit Wuerstel hits Jude repeatedly over the head with a hammer, and at the play's end strikes him dead. It had become one of the puppet theater's most popular plays.

Not all Austro-Germans were willing to abet or even accept the swelling stream of vituperation against their Jewish countrymen, and in 1891 some of them formed the Society to Combat Anti-Semitism.

The organizers of the Society were a husband-and-wife team, Gundacar and Berta von Suttner, both members of the nobility. A count and two barons were among the Society's founding members, along with several Viennese luminaries, including Johann Strauss and Theodor Billroth, who had completely changed his earlier point of view. Another charter member was Hermann Nothnagel, an internist famous for, among other things, his statement that "only a good human being can become a great doctor."

Nothnagel, in addressing the Society's first general meeting, called anti-Semitism a disgrace. "Its origins are rooted in the murky and hateful qualities of human nature. Its existence is the annulment of humanity and righteousness. Its affirmation is the caricature of the noble and the good. Its consequences are moral barbarism. Our fellow Jewish citizens are exposed to the most outrageous insults and even violence. Daily we see and experience this with anger and shame."

Despite such strong and sincerely meant words, the Society did little to achieve its purpose. The von Suttners were pacifists who were becoming too involved in the emerging world peace movement to provide the Society with the leadership it needed. Lacking such leadership, it languished. Today one finds little mention of it in history books beyond reports of its founding.

Another organization that came into existence at the beginning of the 1890s might have been expected to provide a more effective barrier to anti-Semitism. This was the Austrian Socialist party, organized by the Jewish physician, Viktor Adler. (More properly, he might be called the ex-Jewish physician since he no longer practiced either his profession or his religion.)

Socialism disavowed anti-Semitism as simply another manifestation of the nationalism that the reactionaries were using to deflect the workers from the class struggle. One socialist, Bebel, even called anti-Semitism "the socialism of fools."

But socialism and socialists throughout Europe were shying away from fighting anti-Semitism and indeed were even showing signs of sympathizing with it. This had proven to be doubly true in Austria, for although many Jewish intellectuals as well as the Jewish poor (and there were far more of the latter than the anti-Semites realized) enrolled in its ranks, Austria's new Socialist party displayed little desire to confront the issue. On the contrary, the socialist newspaper, *Gleichheit* (Equality), preferred to attack the country's rich Jewish capitalists, often expressly designating them as Jewish. It showed still greater zeal in attacking the Jewish-owned liberal newspapers which it collectively and contemptuously referred to as the *Judenpresse*.

In mounting such attacks, the Socialists did seek to distinguish between rich Jews and poor ones, and to stress that only the former warranted the people's animosity. They also taunted the Christian Socials with being only against Jewish capitalists while leaving the Christian capitalists alone. Yet, on balance, the greatest Socialist fire was leveled at Jewish bankers, industrialists, and journalists, rather than at the anti-Semites.

The reasons for their doing so were numerous. For one thing, they had to compete, and compete vigorously, with the anti-Semitic parties, especially the Christian Socials, for mass support. As the socialist theoretician Karl Kautsky put in in a letter to Engels, "We have problems keeping our own people from establishing brotherly ties with the anti-Semites. . . . The anti-Semites are now our most dangerous enemies, more dangerous here than they are in Germany, because here they oppose the rich and hence seem democratic." Adler himself acknowledged the popularity of Jew-baiting in noting that "whoever participates in Austrian politics is hard put not to turn anti-Semitic."

The fact that so many Socialists were Jews provided a further basis for the Party's behavior. Socialist leaders, and especially their party's mostly Jewish writers and editors, felt compelled to exert every effort to disassociate their party from Judaism and to show that they could be as harsh on the Jews as anyone else. They were terrified at the prospect of seeing their party mocked by its enemies, especially the Christian Socials, as a Jewish organization. When some East European comrades attending the Second Socialist International at Brussels in 1891 proposed holding a sympathy demonstration for the Jewish workers of Russia, Adler, who headed up the Austrian delegation at the conference, vehemently opposed the idea.

The Socialist Jews found it easy to encourage the Party's at best ambivalent, and at worst accepting, attitude toward anti-Semitism, for many of them were apostate and even self-hating Jews. They failed to realize, however, that their own disavowal of Judaism actually weakened their position. Adler won election to the provincial legislature of lower Austria in the early 1890s, but when he first arose to address that body, he was repeatedly heckled with calls of "Jew, Jew, Jew." After trying in vain to ignore the cries, he said, "Now tell me frankly: aren't you getting bored with this Jew, Jew, Jew business? I most certainly am." But his obvious discomfort only encouraged his hecklers, including a Catholic priest, to jeer him all the more.

Adler had made himself vulnerable to such attacks by renouncing his religion in favor of Protestantism. Although he only did so, as he on another occasion said, to protect his children from the disadvantages of being Jewish, still such a step had made him more susceptible to anti-Semitic scorn. If, for example, he had chosen to become an openly devout Jew, probably no one would have dreamed of shouting "Jew, Jew, Jew" at him since he would have made no move to hide such a fact. Their flight from Jewishness had made Adler and his fellow Jewish Socialists more vulnerable to anti-Semitic attack.

While the Union of Austrian Israelites was slow in getting started, its organizer, Rabbi/Doctor Bloch (the anti-Semites referred to him by the first title, the Jews by the second) continued to fight on. The doughty Galician had virtually become a one-man Jewish Defense League.

Thanks to his good relations with Taafe, who even sent him cheeses from his estate, Bloch was able to remedy many of the injustices being committed against Jews in the provinces. Among his accomplishments was the return of Rachel Steignitz to her parents. Many times he came knocking on the Prime Minister's door with a list of grievances, and seldom did he leave empty-handed.

On the floor of Parliament he battled continuously against the outpouring of anti-Semitic proposals and petitions. When some parliamentarians still wanted to outlaw kosher slaughtering as cruelty to animals — the City Council of Graz had already passed a resolution to this effect — Bloch claimed the practice was humane and that the Jews had enacted the first regulations in history to safeguard animals from cruel treatment. He challenged the anti-Semites to clamp down on hunting if they really wanted to protect wildlife. (Hunting was, and still is, Austria's favorite outdoor pastime.)

When some Christian Socials protested that almost no Jewish corpses appeared among the bodies of paupers turned over to the medical school for dissection, Bloch reminded them that the Jewish community sees to it that every Jew, no matter how poor, receives a decent burial. "Why don't you Christians set up burial societies of your own?" he retorted. When the anti-Semites expressed outrage over the arrest of a few Galician Jews for procuring prostitutes, Bloch quickly silenced them by running down a long list of Austro-Germans who had been found guilty of the same offense. "You Germans just don't want any competition," he scoffed.

His most spectacular victory, however, came outside Parliament. In 1893 an apostate Jew with a criminal past told a prominent Viennese priest, Father Joseph Deckert, that he had witnessed a ritual murder committed in Russia. The priest had already published a book of his own on this subject, and was overjoyed to have eyewitness confirmation that the practice still existed. He paid the renegade Jew to write up his story, complete with gruesome details, and then published the account in a Catholic newspaper. Given the atmosphere prevailing in Vienna, the "eyewitness acount" created an immediate sensation.

At first there seemed little that Bloch or any other Jew could do to counter the story. Since the alleged event took place in Russia, no Viennese Jew could claim injury from the story's publication, and therefore had no grounds to bring a suit. But Bloch was undeterred. With some difficulty, he located the town where the ritual murder was supposed to have taken place, and found that while the alleged perpetrator was now dead, some of his relatives were still alive. He persuaded these relatives to bring suit in a Viennese court for slander.

The ensuing trial exposed the whole episode as a hoax, and its perpetrator, the "eyewitness," ended up in prison. But, as in the fight with Rohling, Bloch's victory produced at best mixed results. Though the Viennese Jews were pleased to see this new attempt to perpetuate the ritual murder myth crushed, most of them still shied away at identifying too closely with a man who identified himself so openly and outspokenly as a Jew. (Though Bloch wrote and spoke perfect German, he, like most Galician Jews, refused to identify with German culture. Instead he called himself an Austrian. It was sometimes said that the Galicians and other East European Jews were the only real Austrians in the Empire, for all other citizens identified with their own particular nationality.)

As for the anti-Semites, the embarrassing setback in no way diminished their fervor for their cause. In a subsequent parliamentary session some of them claimed that the Kol Nidre prayer that Jews offer on Yom Kippur absolves Jews from observing oaths of any kind. When Bloch denounced this distortion of the observance, he found himself surrounded by anti-Semites shouting at him and even threatening him personally.

His foes soon succeeded in making good their threats, at least as far as Bloch's parliamentary career was concerned. They persuaded the chairman of Parliament's Polish caucus — Bloch as a representative from Galicia was a member — to ask the Jewish firebrand to resign. When Bloch refused, they found a corrupt Jewish mayor in his district to run against him and, thanks to a variety of intimidating and manipulative tactics, succeeded in engineering his defeat at the next election. Only one newspaper expressed regret at Bloch's loss of office. It was a Jewish newspaper published in Berlin.

Chapter 8

The Mayor and the Knight

Both the Pan-German and Christian Social movements brought forth a leader. Each was a dominating figure who would have a determining impact on Austria's character and destiny. Each would also have a determining impact on that Austrian who would bring about the final destruction of the Vienna Jews.

The Pan-German leader was Georg Ritter von Schönerer, a name that even today can stir strong emotions in Austrians, Jew and non-Jew, who have a sense of their country's history. As his name indicates, he was a nobleman — Ritter in German means knight. But his title was a relatively new one, having been acquired, along with considerable wealth, by his father who had served as chief engineer to the Rothschilds in construction of the North Railway.

The younger von Schönerer was thirty-one when he entered the lower House of Parliament in 1873. He was a liberal and a rather left-wing liberal at that. Soon he was sponsoring progressive legislation of all kinds, including workmen's compensation and minimum wage laws. But von Schönerer's hostility to capitalism, his sensitivity to the mood of the times, and possibly some psychological problems involving his father (who, as we have seen, owed his wealth and title to the Rothschilds) induced him to turn against the Jews. In his 1879 re-election campaign, von Schönerer called for an end to "Semitic control over money and word" ("word" referred to the heavily Jewish presence in the Viennese press). He also began expressing concern over the influx of Jewish refugees from the East.

The year following his re-election von Schönerer invited some like-minded allies and supporters to a meeting in Linz. There they drew up an eleven-point program calling for various left-wing measures such as a progressive income tax, the nationalization of the railroads, and social laws to protect workers and, on the other hand, for various pro-German measures, such as the recognition of German as the Empire's only official language and the establishment of a customs union with Germany.

The Linz Program, as it was called, contained no anti-Jewish clauses. Indeed, despite von Schönerer's previous anti-Jewish pronouncements, Heinrich Friedjung and Viktor Adler helped him draw it up. But the next year, von Schönerer added a twelfth point, stating that "the removal of all Jewish influence from every section of public life is indispensable for carrying out the intended reforms." Von Schönerer had now become, and for the rest of his life would remain, a rabid anti-Semite.

His contacts with both the students and the Viennese tradesmen had helped fuel his fight against the Jews. He attended the students' stormy mourning service for Wagner, and when the police arrived to break up the ensuing brawl they found him standing on a chair brandishing a sword and calling on the students to resist. He had also spoken at a meeting held by the Viennese tradesmen to protest the Jewish peddlers, and had eagerly championed their call for putting the Jews back in the ghetto.

Von Schönerer seldom let any opportunity go by to attack what had become his favorite foe. When the United States enacted its Chinese Exclusion Act, von Schönerer had it translated into German with the word "Jew" substituted for the word "Chinese." He then offered it to Parliament as a piece of model legislation. He also sponsored a bill to segregate Jewish schoolchildren, while requiring that their education be overseen by Christians. The German National Union supported such proposals, for in 1882 it had adopted an Aryan clause, thereby forcing the departure of Friedjung, Adler, Mahler, and other Jews from its ranks.

Von Schönerer made it clear at all times that his hatred of Jews was racial, not religious. As he remarked on one occasion, "Our anti-Semitism is not directed against the religion of the Jews, but against their racial peculiarities which have not changed under past oppression or present freedom."

His hostility to the Jews, so he felt, went hand-in-hand with his adoration of Germany and its Chancellor Bismarck. He and his followers wore Bismarck's blue cornflower in their lapels. Yet Bismarck had a Jewish doctor and a Jewish banker who looked after his health and wealth splendidly. The German Chancellor had once even spoken half-seriously of pairing off "German stallions with Jewish mares," i.e., encouraging impecunious Junker army officers to marry rich Jewesses. At the Congress of Berlin Bismarck had sharply reproved the Russian representative for the latter's denigrating remarks about the Jews.

Not only did Bismarck not share von Schönerer's anti-Semitism, he disagreed with the Pan-German desire to join Austria to the German Reich. Bismarck wanted to preserve the Habsburg Empire as a device for preventing the Russian Czar from uniting all the Slavs under Russian hegemony. Furthermore, he apparently had little regard for the Austro-Germans themselves — he once characterized a Bavarian as a cross between a man and an Austrian.

The fact that his idol disdained his ideas and his movement did not deter von Schönerer, but rational behavior was never his strong point. Once, with all seriousness, he proposed a new calendar whose year would begin not on January first but on the date of a battle in which the German tribes had defeated the Roman legions. More significantly, in terms of his political future, he also urged his followers to renounce Catholicism for Protestantism as a way of showing their support for, and strengthening their ties to, Bismarckian Germany.

Von Schönerer's weakness for alcohol precipitated the pivotal event that marked his political decline. He and a group of cronies were sitting in a tavern in the spring of 1888 one night when a Jewish-owned newspaper came out with an extra edition announcing the death of the German Kaiser. The Kaiser had lingered near death for some time, so the news came as no surprise. But at midnight, two hours later, the paper came out with still another extra edition, saying that the previous announcement had been premature and that the German Emperor still lived. Von Schönerer and his companions, now well along in their cups, became enraged at what they thought was a cheap stunt to sell extra papers. They stormed the newspaper's offices, beating up the "Jewish pig scribblers," breaking up the furniture and type fonts, and wrecking the fixtures.

The publisher filed charges against von Schönerer, and although four thousand enthusiastic supporters chanting "Death to the Jews!" accompanied him to his trial, the charges stuck and the government packed him off to prison for four months. More importantly, he was stripped of his title and deprived of all right to hold political office for five years.

At this point, von Schönerer disappears from our story. But he will reappear, and though he would never again personally acquire the political clout and visibility he once possessed, his basic ideas and attitudes would endure and eventually prevail.

The Christian Social Union grew out of a series of evening meetings that Catholic editor Karl Vogelsang began holding at his home in the mid-1880s. Priests and noblemen, along with professionals and politicians, made up most of the attendees. Their underlying, unifying purpose was to mount a Catholic response to the challenge of the capitalist-industrialist revolution, a phenomenon that they blamed largely on the Jews.

One evening a member showed up with a Viennese city councilor who had recently won election to Parliament. The name of the new guest was Karl Lueger.

Of humble origins (his father had been a building custodian), Lueger could not speak until he was four years old. But once in school he showed remarkable brilliance, moving quickly to the head of his class and staying there. His academic achievements helped secure him a scholarship to the city's most prestigious *gymnasium* or high school, the Theresianum, and from there he easily moved on to the University to study law. Despite his early muteness, he became an adroit speaker and was soon carving out a successful career in politics.

At first glance, Lueger would seem an unlikely candidate for Vogelsang's group, for his mentor for many years had been a radical Jewish physician and city councilor named Ignaz Mandl. With Mandl, Lueger had denounced corruption and championed democratic reform in Vienna's city government. In addition to being Mandl's protégé and ally, he was also his friend, and a friend to the physician's brother and father as well. He frequently played cards with the family and sometimes stayed overnight in their house. Lueger had also offered his services to Rabbi Bloch in the Rohling libel suit and had urged the Vienna City Council to send a special greeting to Adolf Fischhof, the Jewish hero of 1848, on the latter's seventieth birthday. Said Lueger at the time, "None of the gentlemen in this hall can hold a candle to Fischhof in terms of integrity and service to the city of Vienna."

Fischhof did not seem ready to return Lueger's admiration. The elderly revolutionary had advised Bloch not to let Lueger defend him, saying, "I warn you to beware of Dr. Karl Lueger. He now goes with you but may abandon you in the end and even put you in danger before the jury."

Fischhof had evidently sized up the politician correctly for Lueger's attitude toward the Jews had started to change. He had become aware of and, one may assume, become genuinely sympathetic to the plight of Vienna's large lower middle class. He had also become aware of the political power this group had acquired thanks to the voting-law changes of 1881. Lueger spoke at an early meeting of the Austrian Reform Union in 1882 and two years later shared a platform with von Schönerer at a giant rally called to demand the nationalization of the Rothschild-owned North Railway. Elected to Parliament in 1885, he began showing increasing sympathy and support for the more serious proposals of the anti-Semites.

Lueger had many political gifts. His ability as a speaker was matched by his adroitness at one-on-one encounters. He was the first Austrian politician who knew how to "press the flesh." That he could easily and naturally express himself in Viennese dialect obviously didn't hurt; nor did his striking good looks, which had earned him the sobriquet of "Handsome Karl."

These qualities, in addition to his clever, quick mind, soon catapulted him to the forefront of Vogelsang's group. With Vogelsang's death in 1890, Lueger became the leader of the still small but rapidly growing Christian Social Union.

The Union, to those who think of the political spectrum in modern terms, seems a curious affair, consisting as it did of noblemen, priests, professionals, small tradesmen and artisans, and even some fledgling Christian labor leaders. What held it together, besides a common religious base, was its hostility to capitalism in general and to the Jews in particular. As we have seen, in 1889 the Union formed an electoral alliance with the Pan-Germanists and other groups to elect candidates to Vienna's city council. As one of the Union's young enthusiasts later recalled, "The foundation stone of the United Christian Alliance was anti-Semitism, the recognition that our people must be rescued from their cultural and financial bondage to the Jews."

But after 1889, the Christian Socials went their own separate way, for they did not share the Pan-Germanists' desire to unite with Protestant Germany. They also went much further in favoring numerous welfare measures to rescue the working class from destitution. The Party was in many ways a party of Christian socialism.

Lueger's life as its leader became a continuous campaign. Elected to the provincial legislature in 1890, he now used his three legislative offices to wage an all-encompassing battle in behalf of "the little man" against the Jewish capitalists. "Only fat Jews can survive the murderous competition of economic freedom," he said on one occasion, "Christian people must be protected from insatiable capitalism." On another occasion he said, "I stand by what the Bible says: Give to Caesar that which is Caesar's. But where in the Bible does it say, 'Give to Rothschild that which is Rothschild's.'" He willingly helped sponsor Schneider's still more virulent form of anti-Semitism, sharing the speaker's platform with him on numerous occasions. While Lueger usually refrained from expressly endorsing his colleague's more outlandish proposals, he once in a parliamentary speech repeated without a hint of disapproval Schneider's suggestion of sending all the country's Jews out on a ship to drown. Lueger was also among the deputies who surrounded Bloch in a menacing manner after the latter's speech on the Kol Nidre oath.

By the early 1890s Lueger and his Christian Socials had acquired adherents at the city, provincial (state), and national legislative levels. The Christian Social Union was now a well-organized political party with a most promising future. But though warmly embraced by most of Vienna's parish priests, it was arousing anxiety within the Church hierarchy. The upper clergy felt that Union policies smacked of materialism. Furthermore, they could not go along with Lueger's racial anti-Semitism which, as noted earlier, ran counter to the Church's ideas and interests. Lueger also despised Hungarians and made no bones about saying so. This too disturbed the Church fathers, for it endangered the Church's position in Hungary. Indeed, the whole Christian Social movement seemed under Lueger to have become a rebellious, destructive force that was unsettling the lower clergy along with their parishioners.

Alarmed at the growing support for the Christian Social Union, those elements in the Church hostile to Lueger sent a letter to Pope Leo XIII asking him to disavow the Party. As grounds, they mentioned its racial anti-Semitism.

The Pope was in no mood to heed such a request. He had recently issued an encyclical calling on the Church to involve itself more fully in the economic and social problems besetting its communicants. He was also aware that the Christian Social Union had reversed the trend toward declining Church attendance. Parish priests affiliated with or supporting the Party were now using the pulpit to denounce the Jewish capitalist oppressors and, as a result, their services were drawing throngs of enthusiastic worshippers. As Albert Fuchs later put it, "Thanks to the Christian Social Union, the Catholic Church in 1890 began exercising its full weight and authority in public life."

When the Christian Social Union leaders heard about the letter from the hierarchy to the Pope, they sent a letter of their own, answering the hierarchy's charges against the Party. With respect to the Jews, the Union letter said, "We do not countenance a certain racial anti-Semitism directed against the Jewish race." This was enough to reassure Pope Leo, who wrote back to Lueger, saying, "The leader of the Christian Social Union may know that he has in his Pope a true friend who blesses him and treasures the Christian Social effort."

This reply removed virtually all opposition within the Church to the Christian Social Union and thereby eliminated its greatest obstacle to power. Meanwhile, a scandal in the Liberal party created a propitious occasion for the Union to make its bid for power in Vienna.

The city's Liberal party mayor had died suddenly in the fall of 1894. The first vice mayor was ready to take over when a scandal concerning him came to light. He had renounced Catholicism to marry a Jewess, but sometime afterward, while testifying in a court case, he had declared himself a Catholic. Only his immediate reconversion to Catholicism enabled him to escape a charge of perjury. The second vice mayor was elected instead but, although he was not involved in any scandal, he too had a Jewish wife and in addition was a Mason.

In the spring of 1895, shortly after the Christian Social Union had received the Pope's blessing and the Liberals had suffered a discrediting blow over the mayoralty succession, the city held a new election. Since the newly created Social Democrats disdained municipal politics, and could not have effectively participated in any case since the minimum tax requirements still prevented most workers from voting, the fight was essentially between the declining Liberal party and the rising Christian Social Union. The number of council seats won by the Christian Social Union shot up from forty-three to sixty-six. This still left the Party two seats short of the sixty-eight won by the Liberals, but the latter now lacked a majority since independents had won the remaining eight seats.

With no party able to govern effectively, a new election was scheduled for the following September. The Christian Socials, sensing potential victory, threw their whole effort into the campaign. The Party staged rallies, parades, and demonstrations throughout the city, with bands playing their new campaign song, "The Lueger March." (The words of the song had both an official and unofficial version. In the unofficial and most popular version, there was a line that went, "Lueger will live and the Jews will croak.") Mobs sometimes assaulted Liberal councilors on the streets in their frenzy to elect *their* party.

On election day, which happened to fall on Rosh Hashonah eve, Party enthusiasts gathered at various polling places to shout "Jew" and "Jew lackey" at voters known to cast Liberal party ballots. "The mood among the Jews is one of despair," reported Theodor Herzl in his diary. "One sees looks of hatred everywhere."

Herzl toured some of the polling places that day, and while he was at one of them, Lueger himself showed up. Immediately the crowd broke into wild cheers, while housewives waved kerchiefs from their upstairs windows. As one ecstatic member of the throng exclaimed to Herzl, "That is our *Führer*" (leader). Wrote Herzl afterwards, "More than all the oratory and abuse, these words showed me how deeply anti-Semitism is rooted in the heart of these people."

The tabulation of the votes startled even the Christian Socials. Lueger and his party had won 92 of the 138 council seats at stake. Vienna had become the first major city in the Western world to fall under control of a political party openly and officially committed to hating the Jews.

Part IV

The Vienna of Herzl and Hitler

*Vienna gave me the harshest but also the most thorough
education of my life. In that city I acquired a point of view,
and a political approach which . . . has never left me.*
— Adolf Hitler

*In this city of Vienna one day I tore myself loose from the
whole circle in which I lived, from all my friends and
acquaintances, and, as a lonely man, devoted myself
to that which I considered right.*
— Theodor Herzl

Chapter 9

The Reign of Karl Lueger, Hitler's Mentor

When news of the Christian Socials' smashing victory became known, a wave of jubilation swept Vienna. Strangers embraced on the street, some of them literally weeping with joy. Friedrich Funder, a young, Catholic, and passionately pro-Lueger journalist at the time describes the mood:

> What just a few years ago seemed unimaginable had happened. The power of a ruling group, alienated from and injurious to the people, had been shattered. It had been beaten in its very center, the imperial capital, by an opposition which had had to fight against high finance and the stock exchange, all the big newspapers, the liberally-oriented bureaucracy and influential court circles.

As Funder's words indicate, the typical Lueger supporter considered himself a victim of the Jews and those allied with them, and looked to Lueger and his anti-Semitic party to release him from bondage. This feeling of victimization, so characteristic of anti-Semites generally, would characterize the Austro-Germans for the next half century.

But while most Viennese were reveling in what they regarded as their liberation, a few were packing their bags. For Lueger and his party were not just anti-Semitic but anti-capitalist, and those who fell into both categories were especially alarmed. The Jewish wheat dealers started transferring their operations to Budapest, while the Rothschilds and other businessmen began muttering threats to do the same. Writes Pulzer, "Only a guarantee from the Emperor that he would protect them prevented a mass exodus of wealthy Jews."

The new city council at its first meeting promptly elected Lueger as mayor. But no one could govern the Emperor's city without the Emperor's approval. What would the Emperor do?

Franz Joseph may have appreciated the way Lueger had deflected, and to some extent defused, the Pan-Germanist drive to join Austria with Germany, but he could hardly appreciate Lueger's potential ability to stir up racial hatred, throttle the city's economy, and disrupt western Austria's relations with Hungary. The Hungarian government in fact lost no time in sending Franz Joseph a telegram saying it would regard Lueger's confirmation as an unfriendly act. Furthermore, the Emperor, so it seems, despised Lueger personally, regarding him as a hate-mongering demagogue whose personal popularity threatened his own. So when the papers bearing Lueger's designation as mayor arrived at the imperial palace, he sent them back without the imperial signature and seal. "You may count on it," said Franz Joseph to one of his aides, "as long as I reign, I will never confirm Lueger as mayor of my imperial and residential city."

The Emperor's veto produced a sigh of relief in Jewish and business circles. Shares on the stock exchange that had been plummeting immediately shot up. Sigmund Freud, though he had not bothered to vote in the election, wrote to his friend and fellow physician Wilhelm Fliess, "I am keeping to my resolution [to give up cigars] but on the day of the Emperor's veto I lit one up out of sheer joy." (It was Freud's concern over rising anti-Semitism that had induced him to help found Vienna's first B'nai B'rith Lodge during the same year.)

The Emperor's veto outraged Lueger's supporters. A stony silence now greeted Franz Joseph when his carriage rode through the city, and some of the more zealous Luegerites threatened to march on the imperial palace. Within the palace itself, a battle raged over the Lueger issue. The Emperor's new prime minister, Count Badeni, along with most of his cabinet, urged him to stand fast. They feared Lueger's destructive effect on the Empire, and sensed in him a challenge to their own authority. But the Archduke and heir apparent Franz Ferdinand, the Papal Nuncio, and the widow of Crown Prince Rudolf all pleaded Lueger's case. So, for that matter, did Theodor Herzl who, in a call on Badeni, urged Lueger's confirmation. Sensing the mood of the city, Herzl told Badeni, "If you fail to confirm him, you will have to call out the army to keep the peace."

The Emperor stood firm while the city council elected Lueger a second time, then a third, then a fourth. Finally, when the council in the spring of 1897 chose Lueger for a fifth time, the Emperor called in the Christian Social leader for an interview. The sixty-five-year-old monarch and the upstart politician conferred in private for an hour, an unusually long time for an imperial audience. Nothing is or probably ever will be known about what transpired between the two men, but afterwards Franz Joseph cleared the way for Dr. Karl Lueger, champion of Vienna's anti-Semitic masses, to become the city's mayor.

If the sweep of Lueger's election victory had surprised his fellow citizens, then the thrust of his administration surprised them even more. In his inaugural speech he ignored the "Jew question" completely. Instead, after paying glowing homage to his emperor, Lueger went on to stress the urgent necessity for improving the city's services. Once in office, he lost no time in doing so.

For the next thirteen years, until his death in 1910, Lueger busied himself in building roads, bridges, parks, a second aqueduct, some one hundred schools, an orphanage, a tuberculosis sanatorium, an insane asylum, a beach along the Danube, and other needed or desirable facilities. His administration also took over the city's privately-owned utilities and extended and improved their services. The city even bought up and operated two undertaking establishments, and established city-operated agencies for housing, employment, and life insurance along with a savings bank which eventually attracted 100,000 depositors. Lueger also thought of constructing an underground subway as Budapest was doing, but Franz Joseph vetoed the idea, saying the area under the ground belonged to the dead and the living had no business there.

In carrying out his sweeping programs, Lueger did not neglect the simple human touches. Thus, his schools were light and airy, and in the poorer areas served free lunches. He equipped his parks with playgrounds and even had a tub of flowers placed around each lamppost.

While engaged in this seemingly endless array of municipal improvements, Lueger maintained close contact with the people. A bachelor who lived with his two maiden sisters, he spent his evenings, weekends, and even some of his workdays going to christenings, funerals, anniversaries, banquets, and meetings of all kinds. One tabulation shows that in his first seven years in office he attended 1,372 golden wedding anniversaries, an average of four a week. As a personable and poised "Herr Doktor" who spoke Viennese dialect as fluently as a street sweep, and who could down a stein of beer with the gusto of an Austrian "little man," he received a warm welcome everywhere.

As might be expected, Lueger became enormously popular. Soon replicas of his handsome head adorned paperweights, salt shakers, and walking stick handles. His Christian Social party continued to gain popularity not only in the city council but in Parliament as it began attracting votes from the countryside. The early 1900s must be considered the Lueger era in politics.*

*In carrying out his projects the mayor could count on several fortuitous factors. These included an excellent chief engineer with some well-drawn plans ready for implementation. Lueger also benefited at the outset from three of the mildest winters in Vienna's history. This facilitated

But he was also a man of contradictions. Authoritative at City Hall, at home he was ordered around by his sisters and even by his servants. Capable of spending millions of the city's funds without blinking an eye, he would complain frequently of being overcharged on small personal bills and became enraged when he lost a few cents playing cards. (Like most Viennese, including Freud, card playing was his favorite distraction.) While demonstrating a clear commitment to helping the "little man" he wooed him with demagoguery and deception. There was in his speeches, says Boyer, "a clear difference between what he said and what he meant."

This contradiction also characterized his Jewish policies. Once in office he made no overt attempt to oppress or suppress the Jews. Instead he did business and even socialized with Jewish businessmen. When asked how he could be so friendly with members of this accursed race, he answered, "Just who is and who is not a Jew is something I determine for myself." Privately, he admitted that "The Viennese Jews aren't so bad and we cannot get by without them. My Viennese always want to take it easy; it's the Jews who keep things going." As for anti-Semitism, he described it as "a very good means of creating a stir in order to make headway in politics; but when one is at the top one no longer has use for it. This is a sport for the lower breeds."

Other factors also restrained him. He was still operating under the Emperor's shadow, and Franz Joseph would not have tolerated any outright oppression or incendiary talk from the mayor of his capital. The Vatican may also have cautioned him on this issue. Furthermore, as Lueger himself admitted, he needed the Jews for they not only maintained the city's economy but many of its social services as well. It was largely Jewish contributions that kept Vienna's vitally needed shelters for the poor in operation.

As a result, the Jews continued to flourish under the Lueger administration. In some respects they fared better than under the Liberal party administration it replaced. A generation later Stefan Zweig would look back on Lueger as an able leader whose "official anti-Semitism" never prevented him from being helpful and friendly to his former Jewish friends. Hannah Arendt goes further and describes the Lueger era as "actually a kind of Golden Age for the Jews." The only Viennese Jew of any prominence who took Lueger's anti-Semitism seriously, says Arendt, was "the 'crazy' feuilleton editor of the *Neue Freie Presse*, Theodor Herzl."

construction while holding down other municipal costs. We should also remember that public utilities, including public transportation, made money in those days, and by taking them over and extending their services, he enriched the city treasury. Finally, and most important from the standpoint of what would later occur, Lueger did little to improve the city's housing supply. In fact the severe property taxes he imposed, coupled with continued immigration, especially from Czechoslovakia, made the situation worse, not better. Young women would sometimes sell themselves just to get a place to sleep, and the sleeping place where they had to compensate their "benefactors" would usually be a crowded, communal room.

Was Herzl so crazy? We should note that Lueger never disavowed anti-Semitism in any way. On the contrary, his cynical statement "Just who and who is not a Jew is something I determine for myself" clearly implies that Jewishness is discreditable if not condemnable, but that it may be overlooked in individual cases when it is personally convenient to do so. (The Viennese have always loved this remark and it has become the best-known political one-liner in Austria's history.)

Although as mayor Lueger toned down his anti-Semitism, he by no means abandoned it. He made frequent rather sneering references to Jews, especially Hungarian Jews, and decried "Jewish cliques" at the University. He gave subsidies to the "Aryan" theater but when once asked to approve a grant for scientific research, he rejected it saying that "Science is something one Jew cribs from another." On one occasion he even espoused the ritual murder myth.

Such behavior hardly helped to reduce the anti-Semitic sentiments of his vast legion of admirers. Says Hawlik, his most recent, and, for the most part, adulatory biographer, "In considering his position on anti-Semitism, one cannot absolve Lueger of the charge of helping prepare the climate which permitted the terrible germination of the National Socialist Jewish Program."*

If Vienna under Karl Lueger proved less of a fount for anti-Semitism than many had feared, other sources in the city kept the stream of racial hate flowing. The University in particular remained a bastion of *Judenhetze*, for the Austro-German students, though they would on occasion attack students of other nationalities, still made the Jews their favorite and most frequent target. They would enter a lecture hall shouting "*Juden heraus*," keeping up the refrain until the Jewish students gathered up their books and trooped out of the room. Since the Austro-Germans would resort to violence on the least provocation, and sometimes without provocation, Jewish students learned how and when to use side doors and back entrances. They did not always succeed, however, in avoiding physical harm.

Although most of the press was still Jewish-owned, two fairly popular newspapers feverishly backed the anti-Semitic cause. There were also a bevy of lesser periodicals devoted to Jew-baiting. One of them was the *Ostara Hefte*, a monthly that viewed the castration knife as the only real solution to the Jewish problem.

The lower clergy, despite occasional admonitions from Rome against racial hate, remained convinced that "The Jew was guilty." A particularly

---

*Hawlik points out that Lueger's library, examined after his death, was found to be full of anti-Semitic hate literature. One item was a caricature depicting a group of Polish Jews at a railroad station leaving for Herzl's Jewish state. The name on the railroad station happened to be Oswiecim. Oswiecim is the Polish name for Auschwitz.

forceful expounder of this view was Father Josef Scheicher, a former professor of theology, a prodigious writer, and the editor of a Catholic review on social and economic matters. All during the Lueger era Father Scheicher kept up a stream of vitriolic attacks against the Jews. His most famous work was a "Utopian" novel published in 1900. Entitled *In the Year 1920*, it depicted a paradisiacal Austria in which a facist-style government, through the hanging of hundreds of Jews every day, eventually drives all the remaining Jews from Vienna. As one later critic said of this man of God, "He would sooner have renounced the divine blessing on his soul than suppress an anti-Semitic remark."

Another and much more influential book than Scheicher's novel was also published in 1900. It was written by Houston Stewart Chamberlain, an Englishman. A zealous Germanophile, Chamberlain had married Wagner's daughter and settled in Vienna. In his book *Foundations of the 20th Century*, he said the Germans would soon lose their greatness if they did not protect themselves against the Jews, for the Jews were utilizing their unique racial qualities to destroy and conquer the Aryan world. Chamberlain's work helped confer intellectual respectability on the anti-Semitic cause, and affected the course of Jewish history not only in Austria but in Germany. Kaiser Wilhelm II was so impressed by Chamberlain's work that he read parts of it to his children and thought about using it as a text in the nation's military academy. Vienna was now nourishing anti-Semitism in Berlin.

An underlying hostility to Jews permeated Vienna's lively cultural scene. In 1898 the German National Theatre started up with the avowed aim of presenting plays written, directed, and performed by non-Jews. Despite subsidies from the Lueger administration, the theater lasted only five years. When Hamburg in 1909 made plans to put up a monument to the Jewish poet Heinrich Heine, Viennese anti-Semites published a leaflet depicting their own proposed design for such a monument. It showed Heine riding a pig. Some garbled lines from Heine were added to show how his poetry had polluted the German language.

Anti-Semitism also played a role in the constant criticism being leveled at Gustav Mahler, and was a factor leading to his unprecedented step of resigning from the podium of the Viennese Opera. It will be recalled that Mahler said on one occasion, "I am three times homeless — as a Czech in Vienna, as an Austrian among the Germans, and as a Jew throughout the world. Everywhere an intruder, nowhere welcome."

Anti-Semitism elsewhere in the Austrian Empire helped nourish, and in turn was nourished by, the Jew-hatred of Vienna. The three or four Jewish members of Parliament from Galicia and Bukovina had long belonged to Parliament's Polish caucus, but during the late 1890s, they, like Rabbi Bloch, found themselves excluded from its ranks.

In the spring of 1899 a ritual murder case arose in Czechoslovakia when the body of a nineteen-year-old girl was found in the Jewish quarter of her native village. A young shoemaker's assistant named Leopold Hilsner was charged with the crime and on the thinnest of evidence was convicted and sentenced to death. Fortunately, a philosophy professor from Prague, Thomas Masaryk, became outraged over the proceedings and intervened in Hilsner's behalf. While he failed to reverse the verdict, he got Hilsner's death penalty commuted to life in prison. Masaryk, who later became Czechoslovakia's first president, described the case as an example of "Viennese anti-Semitism and its Prague twin."

When art student Adolf Hitler arrived in Vienna in 1906, the Jewish question was, from all we know, the last thing on his mind. His earlier contacts with Jews had been limited but remarkably positive. As he would later say in *Mein Kampf*, "There were very few Jews in Linz and over the centuries they had taken on a European and human [sic] look. Yes, I even looked upon them as Germans." The only thing that seemed to make them different in Hitler's eyes was their religion and "the fact that they had been persecuted on that account (as I believed) turned my aversion against slurring remarks made against them into abhorrence." He could even recall coming to the defense of a Jewish boy in his school who was being abused by others because of his religion.

Hitler does not mention, but his biographers point out, how Jews had been among his benefactors. A Jewish doctor had treated his mother's breast cancer without payment. Jewish art dealers had encouraged his efforts to paint and bought some of his works.

In Vienna Hitler also had several personally positive experiences with Jews. He had not only received help from Jewish-financed charities, but had made some Jewish friends in the flophouses where he so frequently stayed. One such friend gave the threadbare young artist a long cummerfrock coat and Hitler later referred to him as "a very decent man." Most of his paintings sold in Vienna went to three Jewish art dealers, prompting Hitler to say on one occasion that he preferred doing business with Jews "because they were willing to take chances."

Yet when the twenty-four-year-old Hitler left Vienna for Munich five years later, he was a committed anti-Semite. Why?

We may never know all or possibly even the most important reasons for his conversion. Various psychological factors undoubtedly entered in, including the very real possibility that he himself was one-quarter Jewish. (His father was the illegitimate son of a servant girl who was employed in a Jewish household with two young sons when she became pregnant.) But the reasons he gives us in *Mein Kampf* are still of interest.

Hitler's conversion started, so he says, when he encountered on the street in Vienna an Orthodox Jew complete with caftan and black curls. With his experiences with the Linz Jews in mind, he asked himself, "Is this also a Jew?" This question led eventually to another. "Is this man also a German?"

After pondering these questions he concluded that "The Jews were not Germans with a special religion but an entirely different race." He then began to view Jews in a different light. For one thing, he said, they were so unclean that you could detect the presence of a Jew with your eyes closed. Hitler also held Jews responsible for all the trashy billboards, the trashy literature, and even for Vienna's prostitution and vice. (Many prostitutes did operate out of the Leopoldstadt which, despite its large Jewish population, was still sixty percent non-Jewish.)

Two things in particular incensed the young Hitler. First that the Jews seemed to control the theater, the fledgling movie industry, advertising, and the media in general. He then began to see the press as a giant conspiracy that criticized German authors and artists while favoring their Jewish counterparts. A second major trouble was more factual. Much of Vienna's Social Democratic party was under Jewish leadership. Hitler despised socialists not because they advocated socialism but because they espoused internationalism.

Hitler from youth had been an ardent German nationalist. The internationalist orientation of Austria's Socialist party, and of the world's Socialist movement in general, disgusted and alarmed him. The fact that Jews had become so deeply involved with this movement offered further proof to Hitler of their non-nationalist, and therefore non-German, character.

As might be expected, Hitler had been an early admirer of von Schönerer. In school he wore the Pan German blue cornflower in his buttonhole and longed for the unification of the two countries. In Vienna he lived for a while on the street where von Schönerer's newspaper was published, and the frequency with which some of the newspaper's pet terms for Vienna – such as "ethnic conglomerate" or "ethnic Babylon" – pop up later in *Mein Kampf* has led historians to conclude that he read the paper regularly, perhaps every day. (Hitler also probably read the *Ostara Hefte* whose proposed answer to the Jewish problem, it will be recalled, was the castration knife.)

In *Mein Kampf* Hitler praises von Schönerer for having seen the "inevitable end of the Austrian state." But he also faults him for failing to understand the need for mass support. "A point of view may in general only hope to achieve victory if the broad masses take it up and fight for it." Von Schönerer did not know, and did not seem to want to know, how to reach and manipulate the masses. Indeed, he showed little awareness of political considerations at all, and in Hitler's eyes this seals his political doom.

Hitler might not have so fully discerned von Schönerer's weaknesses had not another politician been present to point them out. This was Lueger, who ruled Vienna during four of the five years Hitler spent in the city.

Lueger knew how to move the masses by appealing to "those strata whose struggle for existence was most seriously threatened." He did so by undertaking extensive public works, by joining socialism with anti-Semitism, and by political demagoguery and opportunism. Consequently, despite the fact that Hitler considered Lueger totally wrong in supporting an independent Austria, and that he considered the mayor's hatred of the Jews to be somewhat half-hearted, he joined most other Viennese in mourning the mayor's death in 1910.

Lueger, said Hitler in *Mein Kampf*, was "The last great German" to be produced by the Austrian Empire, and "what he achieved as mayor of Vienna was immortal in the best sense of the word." Hitler's own extensive use of Lueger's strategies and tactics – his demagoguery and opportunism, his impressive public works, his shrewd blend of socialism and anti-Semitism – show that the mayor whose reign provided a "Golden Age" for the Vienna Jews also provided a model for the man who would later destroy them.

Chapter 10

Herzl: The Unwelcome Messiah

The upsurge in nationalism that swept through Europe during the late nineteenth century could hardly help but cause some Jews to think about Jewish nationalism as well. The increasing realization that the tearing down of the Ghetto had not ended the Jewish problem but had only given it a new and, in some respects, more troublesome dimension also encouraged this trend. But the greatest specific stimulus to Jewish nationalism lay in the pogroms that began breaking out in Russia in the late 1870s and early 1880s. In 1882 a Russian-Jewish physician, Leon Pinsker, published a book, *Self-Emancipation*, which called for the colonization of Palestine. Two years later forty representatives, most of them from Eastern Europe but a few from Germany and England, met in Kattowitz to draw up a program designed to achieve such an aim.

No Viennese Jews attended the Kattowitz Congress of 1884 but the sentiments that produced it had not left the Austrian capital completely untouched. As we have seen, a group of students at the University formed Kadimah in 1882 and called on their "ethnic comrades" to join them.

Although most of Kadimah's membership consisted of Galician and other East European Jews, one of its leaders was the Viennese-born Nathan Birnbaum. He soon became the moving spirit not only behind Kadimah but of Viennese Jewish nationalism in general. In 1885 he established a journal called *Selbst-Emancipazion* in which he introduced for the first time the word *Zionism*.

Meanwhile, as the pogroms in Russia and Russian-occupied Poland continued, the move to return to Palestine also gained momentum. The Bilu movement arose to encourage immigration to the Holy Land, and thousands of Jews responded to its call.

Few Viennese Jews joined these early immigrants, but Birnbaum and his small group lost none of their enthusiasm. In fact they grew bolder and began dreaming not just of colonizing Palestine, then part of the Turkish Empire, but of making it into a Jewish state. In 1893 these Kadimah alumni, along with a few other sympathetic Jews, formed an organization in Vienna called Zion: Union of Austrian Societies for the Colonization of Palestine and Syria. Birnbaum also published a pamphlet entitled *The National Rebirth of the Jewish People in Their Own Country as a Solution to the Jewish Question.*

The Birnbaum group issued a call for an international congress to achieve this new goal of Jewish statehood, and the following year such a congress convened in Paris. But attendance was weak and the ideas of those who did attend were too varied and vague to produce any meaningful results. The new champions of Jewish statehood were floundering for want of a leader. But eighteen months later they had one.

If in 1895 one set about looking for someone to head a Jewish nationalist movement, the last person one would have picked would have been Theodor Herzl. For the former attorney turned minor playwright and successful journalist seemed the very epitome of the totally Europeanized Jew.

Born in Budapest, where he attended German schools, Herzl earned excellent grades in German literature and strikingly poor ones in religion. His parents belonged to the city's most liberal temple, and though they gave their only son a bar mitzvah, they did not use this term on the invitations they sent out. Guests were invited to Theodor's *Konfirmation* instead.

At the University Herzl joined a Burschenschaft and fought the obligatory saber duel (which he won). He twice volunteered for army service only to be rejected as unfit. He was something of a dandy and a playboy both before and after his less than satisfactory marriage. He did not bother to have his son circumcised and at Christmas the Herzls would gather around a large Christmas tree to sing carols. In July of 1895, just weeks before he would plunge into the work that would make him the most outstanding Jewish political leader of the Diaspora, Theodor Herzl wrote in his diary, "If there is one thing I should like to be, it is a member of the Prussian nobility."

Herzl was not even free of the taint of anti-Semitism. He expressed distaste and disdain for "the wrong kind of Jew" and once spoke of attending a soiree in Berlin where he found "thirty or forty hideous little Jews and Jewesses. No comforting sight." He preferred Nordic-looking women and chose one for his wife. Says Schorske, "He generated his highly creative approach to the Jewish question not out of immersion in the Jewish tradition but out of his vain efforts to leave it behind."

But there was another side to Theodor Herzl. At the University he had offered his resignation to his *Burschenschaft* after the Wagner memorial meeting had stirred up anti-Semitism. (He was, however, surprised and hurt when his fellow members accepted it.) He gave up the practice of law, which he enjoyed and was good at, when he saw he could not become a judge without converting to Christianity. If he rarely attended religious services, and knew almost no Hebrew, he still remained a registered, tax-paying member of the Jewish *Gemeinde*.

In 1882 Herzl, then twenty-two, read Dühring's book on the Jewish question and realized that, as he put it, "It has now become a matter of race." He saw racial anti-Semitism as "the modern petrol" which would once again put Jews to the stake. The anti-Semitic tide swirling around him reinforced these impressions. On two occasions, once in a German music hall, another time while riding in a carriage in Vienna, he was jeered at for being Jewish by people he did not know. These incidents showed Herzl that it was his physical appearance, not his religion, that mattered.

Finally there was the Dreyfus trial whose proceedings and culmination he covered for the *Neue Freie Presse*. He would never forget the sight of the Jewish army captain vigorously but vainly protesting his innocence while being publicly stripped of his rank, sword, and epaulets, and while being vilified by shouts of "death to the Jews" from the crowded stands. In his Paris hotel room, Theodor Herzl, "integrated" Viennese Jew par excellence, began writing what would become the most important political document in the two-thousand-year history of the Jewish Diaspora.*

The Jewish State appeared in February 1896, surprising and shocking Jewish Vienna. Herzl had paid for the printing. It was one thing for a small band of Galician students to call for a Jewish state; it was another thing for the literary editor of the *Neue Freie Presse* to do so. As Harry Zohn notes, Herzl was "the great amateur of Zionism," but, Zohn adds, "in this perhaps lay his strength."

As might be expected, the most positive response came from the members of Kadimah. One of the group's activists, Isador Schalit, later recalled running to Herzl's home and exclaiming "Herr Doktor, what you have written is our dream, a dream of many young people. . . . Come with us and lead us." Two days later Herzl met with the group and gratefully received its support.

But support from other Jewish groups in Vienna did not come so easily. The city's small number of deeply religious Jews believed they must wait for the Messiah to lead them back to the Promised Land. What Herzl was

*At the time he plunged into the Jewish question, Herzl was dissatisfied with his career as a playwright as well as with his marriage. Desmond Stewart believes these two factors played a significant role in his decision to take on a wholly new line of activity.

preaching seemed tantamount to sacrilege. The much larger number of integrationists reacted at first with disbelief. Herzl, as if anticipating the animosity with which Jewish Vienna would greet his ideas, had published an abridged version of his manuscript ahead of time in the *Jewish Chronicle* of London. When the *Chronicle* asked the executive secretary of the *Gemeinde* whether Herzl was truly the author of this work, the secretary expressed disbelief saying he had always known Herzl to be a reasonable person. (When Herzl later told the official that he had become a Jewish nationalist, the official replied, "You're fooling yourself.")

As it became apparent that Herzl meant what he said, reaction turned into ridicule mixed with rancor. The editor-in-chief of one of the city's leading newspapers called his ideas "totally confused nonsense," while one of Herzl's own colleagues at the *Presse* wondered if he was not indulging in fantasy, and called him a Jewish Jules Verne. Another colleague wrote a short poem, the second stanza of which ran somewhat as follows:

> He sees a goal, a faraway goal
> in dreams and while awake.
> He thinks he can, in times like these,
> out of Jews a state to make.*

Many Jews regarded Herzl's *mashugana* (crazy) ideas as not only foolish but dangerous, for in espousing Jewish nationalism he was only furthering the claim of the racial anti-Semites that the Jews were a people apart.

As the Jews were desperately insisting that they were simply Austrians of a different religion, along came one of their own to dispute them. "Herzl had damaged the basis of Jewish existence for he had opened up the Jewish question and thereby committed a deadly sin," one later Zionist would say. "There was only one policy for the Jews, the ostrich policy."

By August 1896, the first anti-Zionist pamphlet appeared. It was followed by other writings designed to discredit the movement and its originator. Especially vitriolic, indeed vicious, was Karl Kraus who weighed in with a pamphlet entitled *A Crown for Zion*. In it he scoffed at Herzl's attempt to remake "hooked noses into badges of merit." While Zionism might suit certain "victims from the mud puddle of Galician culture," it offered central European Jews "the unpleasant spectacle of clumsy hands scratching at the two-thousand-year-old grave of an extinct people."**

---

*The German original contains a double entendre, for "to make a state" means also in German "to make a big impression."

**Harry Zohn has pointed out, however, that Kraus later modified his position when Herzl's posthumously published diaries convinced him of Herzl's sincerity.

Kraus called Zionism's founder "King Herzl I" and the label became popular throughout Jewish Vienna. When Herzl walked down a theater aisle, Jews would nudge each other and hiss "the King has arrived." They also hissed Herzl's comedy *I Love You* when it premiered in 1900, and the author's Zionism may have been more responsible for their disapproval than the weakness of the play itself.

Of particular distress to Herzl were the reactions of Vienna's chief rabbi and of his employers at the *Presse*. He had consulted with Rabbi Güdemann before publishing *The Jewish State*, and thought he had elicited the Rabbi's warm support. But once the short book appeared, and the storm over its message broke, the Rabbi backtracked. Motivated in large part by a desire not to disrupt the Jewish community at such a perilous time, Güdemann joined the opposition. While supporting continued colonization of Palestine for those *Ostjuden* (eastern Jews) who wanted or needed such a sanctuary, he labeled Herzl's call for a Jewish state a *Kuckucksei* or cuckoo's egg that would only isolate the Jews and lead them back to the ghetto. It would also defeat what he saw as the civilizing mission of Judaism. Said Güdemann, "A Jewry equipped with cannons and bayonets would exchange the role of David with Goliath and be in itself a travesty."

The *Neue Freie Presse* took another approach. It simply ignored the whole issue. Despite Herzl's pleadings, its two Jewish editor-publishers refused to allot any space to the movement. When Herzl died prematurely in 1904, the *Presse* printed a lengthy, glowing obituary extolling his achievements as writer, journalist, and editor. Only at the end of the eulogy, buried deep in the middle of the paper, appeared the single sentence, "The deceased devoted much time and energy to the Zionist cause."

Not all Viennese Jews turned their backs on Herzl. Besides the students of Kadimah a few others joined his cause. Meetings were held, headquarters were established, and a Zionist weekly *Die Welt* (The World) was launched. It should also be noted that the reception that Herzl and his ideas received from Jews in other countries was far from uniformly benign. Throughout Europe, rabbis, community leaders, and others denounced the new movement.

Still, Vienna's reaction differed markedly from that of London, Paris, or even Berlin. In these other cities Herzl and his cause won *some* influential supporters or at least well-wishers. They included Lord Rothschild in England and the Chief Rabbi of Paris. In accounts of the initial Zionist congresses we also see numerous German Jews playing active roles, but except for Herzl himself we almost never see any Viennese delegates doing so. Despite the fact that under Herzl Vienna served as Zionism's headquarters, the movement had attracted only 862 dues-paying members there by 1902. This poor response prompted Lord Rothschild to accuse the Vienna Jews of indolence because, he said, "They don't listen to Dr. Herzl who may be an enthusiast but who is also a great man."

But perhaps the greatest evidence of the predominantly hostile attitude of the Viennese Jews to Zionism is what happened to Zionist headquarters after Herzl's death. The practical step would have been to keep the headquarters in Vienna, for Austria had the largest Jewish population of any country in Europe with press freedom. Furthermore, it was not only geographically close to the large masses of Eastern European Jews but, in its provinces of Galicia and Bukovina, included over a million of them within its own borders. Yet soon after Herzl's death, the Zionist headquarters were shifted to Berlin while the offices of *Die Welt* were transferred at first to Cologne and then subsequently to Berlin. Vienna had not produced a single Zionist of sufficient stature to lead either the movement or its newspaper. One can understand why Chaim Weizmann, Herzl's eventual successor, says in his memoirs that he never fully appreciated Theodor Herzl until he saw Zionism's first leader in his Viennese milieu.

Chapter 11

The Prewar Years

Two years before Herzl issued his call to arms, the Jewish students at the University of Vienna had organized the *Jüdische Akademische Lesehalle* (Jewish academic reading/study hall). They did so more out of desperation than desire, for they were now barred from virtually all other student associations. The new *Lesehalle* functioned as a meeting place and lecture hall. In 1896 Sigmund Freud chose this forum to outline for the first time in public his interpretation of dreams.

The *Lesehalle* was followed by the establishment of a Jewish dormitory, a Jewish cafeteria, and eventually a Jewish employment service. All these activities received financial support from the Jewish *Gemeinde*.

This new Jewish consciousness, developed in reaction to and sometimes regenerating the new anti-Semitism, spread among Jewish youth outside the University as well. High school student associations sprang up, each of them affiliated with a Jewish club in the University. Outside of the University other Jewish national clubs arose. They included two for young women: One to aid the colonization of Palestine and the other to study Jewish history, literature, and the role of women in the Jewish past. The latter, a non-political group, was the most popular. By 1896 its forty members were holding bi-weekly meetings.

It is not surprising then to find young people making up the majority of the city's first Zionists. Moreover, they were, as the research of Professor Marsha Rozenblit has disclosed, mostly middle-class young people from integrationist families. Soon these young Zionists, along with the handful of Vienna's older Zionists, had set up chapters in half of the city's twenty-two districts. Some of these chapters were, and for a long time remained, paper entities, while others had over one hundred members. Gradually, more specialized Zionist groups emerged to supplement them, including a society for young women, Hadassah.

The movement's membership among the poorer, less integrated Jews, however, continued to lag. Although the Leopoldstadt housed thirty-six percent of the city's Jews, only twenty-seven percent of Vienna's Zionists lived there. To remedy this situation, and to improve the lot of their less fortunate fellow Jews, Vienna's Zionists decided to set up a settlement house. Called Toynbee Hall after the settlement houses established in memory of Arnold Toynbee in London, it opened its doors in December 1900.

At the opening ceremonies the chairman of the organizing committee declared that its purpose was to provide a place where "the prosperous and intelligent devote a few hours a day to the poor and less educated in order to strengthen them morally and spiritually for the battle in the coming days." Just two months later the new facility was offering within a single week lectures on the Bible, the economic condition of the Jews, the situation of the Jews in pre-Christian Italy, school hygiene, Jews and usury, Lessing's play *Nathan der Weise* (*Nathan the Wise*), and astronomy. By 1903 the list of offerings included such diverse subjects as dueling and the works of Charles Dickens.

The numerically and financially weak Zionist movement in Vienna, however, could not support such an ambitious program and Toynbee Hall fell into financial difficulties. But the city's B'nai B'rith Lodge, impressed by what the settlement house had achieved, took it over. In 1905 the Lodge opened a second such facility in another district. By 1910 these Jewish settlement houses were sponsoring courses, concerts, lectures, Sunday outings, special programs for children, and clothing and medical care for the needy.

While the settlement houses did not propagandize for Zionism, they could not help but encourage Jewish national consciousness, and the Zionist movement began gaining ground among the city's poorer Jews. By 1910 Zionist meetings in the Leopoldstadt were attracting hundreds of people, most of them young but some of them older Jewish workmen.

The Zionist presence at the University became more pronounced, although it continued to depend on the East European students for its basic support. In 1911 the University's rector noted how Zionist students on enrolling were refusing to give any language but Yiddish as their mother tongue. Their "fantastic fanaticism," he said, had even caused some of them to write threatening letters to those Jewish professors who had mocked the Zionist movement.

But for most Jewish students it was not the anti-Zionist professors but the Austro-German *Burschenschaften* who remained the real enemy. As we saw earlier, Jewish students by the mid-1890s had learned how to fight saber duels and by the early 1900s, according to the then Viennese correspondent of the London *Times*, Wilfred Steed, "The Jews were in a fair way to becoming the best swordsmen of the University." But the *Burschenschaften* had changed their tactics. Taking advantage of their better organization, their numerical superiority, and the fact that the police could not enter University property, they relied more and more on outright assault. The Jewish students, less violent by nature or upbringing and in any case always outnumbered, found themselves harassed and sometimes seriously harmed. In 1913 Martin Freud was knifed so badly in a brawl that he might have died if a University official who was also a physician had not appeared on the scene and treated his wounds.

On a later occasion the younger Freud came to the University to find another Austro-German-Jewish battle raging on the campus' ramps and steps while the police stood on the sidewalk patiently waiting for the first Jews to be tossed into their hands. But this was a genuine battle, for the Jewish students were fiercely fighting back. With heavy padding under their hats to protect their heads, the heavily outnumbered Jewish students were swinging clubs like the Austro-Germans and giving as good as they got. This time many an Austro-German fell into the arms of the police, who would arrest anyone who landed outside the University's precincts.

Delighted at this display of Jewish courage and combat prowess, young Freud made inquiries and found out that the fighting Jewish students were the mostly *Ostjuden* members of Kadimah. Martin Freud promptly joined the group. When he told his father about his decision, the elder Freud immediately approved. This in turn greatly pleased the son for even by 1913, so he later wrote, "Jewish citizens in distinguished positions had a strong prejudice against Zionism."

With the Zionists going their own way, the Austrian-Israelite Union remained the main fighting arm of the community's integrationist majority. In 1897 the Union set up a civil rights office to take legal action in defense of Jewish equal rights and to gather and disseminate evidence on individuals, newspapers, and groups attacking Jews. Many Jews felt uneasy in seeing the Union act so aggressively, for they believed the growing anti-Semitism that had swept Vienna for the past fifteen years represented a somewhat superficial and, hopefully, passing phenomenon. Reacting too aggressively to it, in their view, might only make it worse. But the Union's leaders ruled out such an ostrich policy, saying the time had come to speak up and make use of all legal means to defend Jewish rights.

The Union made some efforts to counteract the boycotts of Jewish stores. Such boycotts would be continuously, though not always effectively, launched by various anti-Semitic groups until 1938. It also helped the Jews in Galicia and Bukovina, and came to the aid of Leopold Hilsner, the youth accused of murdering a nineteen-year-old girl in Czechoslovakia. Unfortunately, the attorney the Union engaged to defend Hilsner felt he would be disloyal to the German Liberal party if he took a Czech attorney as co-counsel. So Hilsner was defended solely by German-speaking lawyers, which effectively insured his doom.

The Union never abandoned the young man and from time to time published reports on the case. It was never able to come up with the real murderer, however, and the hapless Hilsner remained in prison. The Union also intervened in other incidents involving anti-Semitism and often with greater success. Celebrating its twenty-fifth anniversary in 1910, it proudly claimed to have defended the rights of Jews in five thousand cases, and to have spoken out time after time against anti-Semitism. Neverthless many of its seven thousand members still seemed ambivalent over the desirability and need for asserting Jewish equal rights. Moreover, Union membership, though almost five times greater than that of the Zionists at this time, still represented less than ten percent of Vienna's eligible Jews.

All during this time the Union, and the integrationist Jews generally, had to contend not just with anti-Semitism but with the Zionist nationalists within the Jewish community. In 1896 Kadimah, emboldened by Herzl's manifesto, tried to transform the newly-established *Lesehalle* into a forum for Jewish nationalism. Integrationists beat back this attempt and the *Lesehalle* remained neutral on the subject. In 1900 Vienna Zionists began preparing a slate of candidates for election to the twenty-four-member board of the *Gemeinde*. The integrationists spoiled their efforts by adding twelve more seats to the board and stipulating that only the biggest tax payers, those who paid ten times the minimum tax of twenty kronen, could vote for the additional members. This helped keep the Zionists from winning a single seat, although at the end of the year the president of the movement's Leopoldstadt chapter was appointed to fill a vacancy.

In 1902 the Zionists tried again and won twenty-seven percent of the vote. Four years later they gained a startling thirty-two percent of the vote, and although this dropped to twenty-two percent in 1908 it rose to thirty-four percent in 1912. The percentages substantially overstate actual Zionist support within the community, because two-thirds of the *Gemeinde*'s tax paying members never bothered to vote, and probably most of these stay-at-homes would never have voted for the Zionists. Furthermore, since voting was largely for slates rather than for individuals, the Zionists during this time never elected a single board member. Nevertheless they had made themselves into a force to be reckoned with.

As might be expected, the Zionists accompanied their bid for power within the Jewish community with attacks on their integrationist foes. They accused the integrationists of refusing to confront the real issue, i.e., *racial* anti-Semitism. This was anathema to most integrationists, whose ideal self-image was that of a religious and cultural minority of ethnic, nationalist Germans. Even the Union, which represented only the more aggressive Jewish integrationists, balked at accepting the concept of a Jewish nationality, while the *Gemeinde* board itself was, in the words of one Zionist writer, "A sad caricature of a Jewish council" and "wanted to have nothing to do with Judaism." The Zionists also frequently accused the *Gemeinde* administration of corruption.

The integrationist leaders of the *Gemeinde* counter-attacked by accusing the Zionists of aping the anti-Semites in resorting to vituperation and demagoguery. The Zionists, they said, made more promises to the "little man" than did Lueger. As the decade advanced, the integrationists even began taunting the Zionists with being themselves insufficiently Jewish. When, for example, the Zionists derided a *Gemeinde* leader whose son had converted to Christianity, presumably to advance his career, the integrationists pointed out how the leader himself had said Kaddish (the prayer for the dead) for his mother faithfully three times a day. Most of the Zionists, sneered the integrationists, could not even intone a simple Hebrew prayer.

At times and on some issues the two groups could at least informally coalesce. One such issue was the colonization of Palestine, which the integrationists supported as a haven for the increasingly oppressed Jews living under Russian rule. (This solution would also, of course, prevent these Jews from coming to and settling in Vienna.) But in general the two sides remained divided, often bitterly so. The Zionists, despite their gains among the poorer Jews, remained both numerically and financially too weak to oust the integrationists from power. Still, they did influence the community's thinking and tactics. As Rozenblit puts it, "Their polemics precipitated a rethinking of the meaning of Jewishness and forced the Jewish establishment to a stronger assertion of Jewish identity."

It would be a dangerous oversimplification to divide the Vienna Jews of the early 1900s into merely two groups: integrationists and nationalists. A host of factions and organizations existed, some that overlapped the two main groupings, and others that did not.

The one group that most clearly demarcated itself from both the integrationists and the Zionists was the band of highly Orthodox Jews gathered around the *Schiffschul*. Although few in number and meager in resources, they managed to maintain a lively religious and communal existence. They had always repudiated the integrationists, and they now rejected the Zionists as well. In fact they found the Zionists even more distasteful, viewing them as Godless Jews who were turning their ancestral religion into a political movement.

Another group that warrants separate and special consideration is the socialists. In a technical sense they did not constitute a separate group for all of them could be classified as either integrationists, Zionists, or *konfessionslos* (without religion). The latter, who probably included the largest proportion of the truly committed Jewish socialists, were not, of course, part of the Jewish community at all. Still socialism was creating its own various divisions within and among the Vienna Jews.

For many reasons the socialist movement exerted an enormous appeal on the Jews of Vienna. It offered them a humanistic doctrine to replace the humanistic religion so many of them were abandoning or at least finding less and less attractive. It also offered a solution, at least on paper, to the problems of anti-Semitism since, according to its doctrine, anti-Semitism would vanish once socialism had replaced nationalism with a classless, internationalist society. Finally, and most importantly, it offered an opportunity to achieve a measure of immediate integration into Austrian society, for in the socialist party Jews could join with non-Jewish "comrades" in political and even in social and leisure activities. This became especially important for younger Jews as more and more Austrian youth organizations adopted "Aryan" clauses.

Socialist Jews early perceived the Zionist movement, with its emphasis on nationalism and its de-emphasis of class consciousness, as a threat, and in some places they moved aggressively to squash it. When Jewish Zionists held their first open meeting in Prague, Jewish Socialists broke it up. In the Galician city of Krakow, the police had to intervene when Jewish Socialists turned up at a Zionist meeting and fistfighting broke out.

In Vienna the Zionist movement was initially at least too small, too young, and too middle-class to pose much of a peril to the socialists, and the latter made no organized effort to crush it. Yet competition between the two movements soon became evident. A group of socialist students left Kadimah to found a socialist club called *Gemara* and sought to build ties to the proletarian *Ostjuden* in the Leopoldstadt. So, despite the frequently anti-Semitic tone of the Party's press, and despite the efforts of Viktor Adler (who felt his own Jewish origins were a hindrance to the Party) to discourage non-proletarian Jews from joining the Party, many of them did so and, given the Party's dearth of educated Gentiles, many became party functionaries and officials.

In 1907, in response to increasing socialist agitation that included demonstrations in downtown Vienna, Franz Joseph abolished the last tax paying requirement for the franchise. All males twenty-three and older could now vote. As a result, the Social Democrats garnered a large number of seats in the parliamentary elections that year, becoming one of the country's two major parties. (The Christian Socials were the other.) This of course only increased the Party's attraction to Jews attempting to shed their status as outsiders and enter the mainstream of Austrian life. The illusion of integration which adherence to the socialist Social Democrat party conferred would figure strongly in the ultimate tragedy of the Vienna Jews.

The Social Democrats had long recognized the need to accommodate the Empire's restless nationalities, and in 1899 had proposed transforming the Empire into a federation of member states. The proposed federation made no mention of the Jews, for it was assumed that they would remain citizens of the states in which they lived. In 1907 one of the Party's rising stars, a twenty-six-year-old Czech Jew named Otto Bauer, wrote a book on the nationalities problem that essentially restated the Party position. But in a brief appendix at the end of the book Bauer did take up the Jewish problem. He noted that historically the Jews were indeed a nationality and not just a religion. But, he maintained, as a result of capitalism and assimilation, this had ceased to be true. The Jews were no longer a separate nation and could not therefore be given separate nation status in the proposed socialist federation.*

The problems that the growing Social Democratic party created for the Zionists did not seem insuperable. Many Jews supported both movements, in the quixotic way in which socialists everywhere were continuing to respond to nationalist sentiments. The emergence of a socialist Zionist organization, *Poale Zion*, in Russia, and its establishment of a chapter in Vienna in 1907 helped keep some socialist-minded Jews within the Zionist fold.

The Social Democrats themselves indirectly and unintentionally often helped Zionist movements. Their party press, as noted earlier, competed with the Christian Socials in condemning Jewish capitalism, and this hardly helped attract more nationalistically-oriented Jews to their cause. Adler, who felt his own middle-class Jewishness was a burden to the party, sought to discourage other middle-class Jews from joining it. He also wanted nothing to do with Zionism. When *Poale Zion* applied for membership at the Second Socialist International, Adler led the fight in getting the application rejected, even though the Zionist Labor Group had endorsed a socialist, and anti-Zionist, candidate in the previous parliamentary elections in the Leopoldstadt. Jewish Socialists generally, but Viennese Jewish socialists particularly, tried to avoid the slightest gesture that would associate their party with anything Jewish.

---

*Bauer himself, however, despite his personal rejection of the Jewish religion and his disavowal of Jewish nationality, remained officially a Jew. That is, he did not remove his name from the *Gemeinde*'s registration rolls. When a Gentile colleague once asked him why, he replied, "How could you understand? You have never heard someone muttering 'dirty Yid' behind your back."

In the 1890s as Jews became excluded from the various national caucuses in Parliament, some began dreaming of creating a Jewish state within the Empire itself. A few called for recognition of Hebrew as the national language of the Jews and demanded that it be given equality with other languages in governmental affairs. In effect they were saying that, "If all the other nationalities are treating us as a separate nationality, then let us demand the rights and privileges which such a status confers." By the beginning of the 1900s a *domestic* Jewish nationalist movement was underway.

Domestic nationalism was not only rejected by the Social Democrats but initially by the Zionists as well. When Herzl had told his followers to "conquer the communities," he meant only that they should win their communities' support for a Jewish state in Palestine, not for a state within the Empire or any place in Europe. Indeed, he opposed all involvement in domestic politics, believing it would divert valuable energies from the true goal. Nevertheless, even before but especially after his death, many Zionists began to feel differently. A Jewish state in Palestine lay far in the future, and Herzl himself, with all his pleas to the Sultan of Turkey and various world leaders, had not made it seem much closer. But the need to protect Jewish interests and identity in the Empire was immediate.

A development in the Czech province of Moravia in 1905 gave a sudden impetus to the domestic Jewish nationalist movement. The province decided to allocate seats between the Germans and Moravians within its borders in proportion to their respective share of the population. A similar apportionment of positions was to be carried out in the provincial bureaucracy. This step spurred some Jewish nationalists to demand a similar arrangement for Jews. Like the other two groups, the Jews would have their own *Curia* or quota of seats, and would elect representatives to them from their own voting list.

The demand alarmed the integrationist Jews, especially those in Vienna, and the Union published two articles in its monthly journal attacking the idea. "The separate position assigned to the Jews through special *Curia* would only play into the hands of the anti-Semites," said the Union, for Jews could no longer claim to be members of the national groups among whom they lived. Germans, Czechs, Poles, and others would use the Jews' new official status to bar them from the free professions and various areas of commerce. A separate Jewish *Curia*, in short, would mean political and economic suicide.

While the demands for a Jewish official government representation died down in Moravia, the concept of Jewish national autonomy gained in other parts of the Empire. It also attracted the attention and support of Isador Schalit who had become head of the Austrian Zionist movement following Herzl's death. In 1906 Schalit and other Zionists concluded a formal alliance with Jewish nationalists in Galicia calling for a separate *Curia* for the Jews who made up over one-tenth of the provinces' population. Although the

Karl Lueger, Mayor of Vienna, 1897–1910. *Austrian National Library.*

Right, Karl Kraus, Austrian satirist, critic, and poet. *Lidor Press, Tel Aviv, Israel.* *From* Wiener Juden in der Deutschen Literatur, *by Harry Zohn, 1969.* Below, cartoon depicts an anti-Semitic brawl at the University of Vienna, 1897. *Austrian National Library.*

Hugo Bettauer, author of *The City Without Jews. Austrian National Library.*

Sigmund Freud, 1922. *Freud Collection, Library of Congress.*

Arthur Schnitzler, physician, playwright, and novelist. *Austrian National Library (photo by D'Ora, Vienna, 1931).*

Ostjuden on the Mathildenplatz (today, Gaussplatz), Vienna, around 1915.

A group of Jews in front of a clothing store in the Jewish quarter, Vienna 1915. *Austrian National Library.*

OSTJUDEN HINAUS!

Kulturlosigkeit – Barbarei – Reaktion – Pogrom!

So wird, wenn dieser Ruf erschallt, die gesamte Judenpresse und Judenmeute aufheulen. Nur gemach! Wie es mit dieser örtlichen Bettelei in Wahrheit steht, wollen **nicht wir** vorbringen. Es möge einfach **das** öffentlich wiederholt werden, was am 1. Jänner d. J. in einem der unverschämtesten Judenblätter, der "Wiener Sonn- und Montagszeitung", ein jüdischer Schmierfink zu schreiben wagte. Dort heißt es nämlich:

> Kaum hatten die Ghettobewohner Galiziens über Wiener Flüchtlingsquartiere bezogen, gingen die Männer schon auf die Straße, fremdartige Gestalten mit dem Ruf des Gebetes, (arme Haideln) mit tieferen Falten der Stirn und der Wangen, als wir bei bisher darin gesehen hatten, mit mieren orientalischen Sitten, mißtrauisch, ängstlich, jüdisch sprechend, entmurgelte Menschen, ruhig Gekreuzigte (von neu?), ruhig Bonberube [...]

Vermögen wuchsen in unheimlicher Progression

(sicher "ehrlich" erarbeitet), besonders als der fließende Geldwert die

Spekulation an der Börse

[...] aus schmierigen Massenquartieren in stattliche Wohnungen und Villen."

"Die Ostjuden ..."

Bankenbeherrscher, Industrielle, Geldkönige

[...] Also offene Aufforderung zur Korruption und Spekulation, Schieberei, Schwindel und Betrug! Wo bleibt da der Staatsanwalt, wo bleiben da die Volksvertreter, wo bleibt da die Volkssicherung in diesem "Freistaat"? [...] sich dort. Wir aber rufen das deutsche Wien auf zu den

3 MASSEN-VERSAMMLUNGEN

am Mittwoch, den 14. Februar 1923, um 7 Uhr abends,

in Weigls Dreherpark	in der	und im
Katharinenhalle	**Volkshalle**	**Drehersaal**
12. Bez., Schönbrunnerstraße	des Neuen Wiener Rathauses	3. Bez., Landstraße-Hauptstraße 91

in denen die endliche Durchführung strenger Maßnahmen gegen das Ostjudentum zum legitimed verlangt wird, ehe das betrogene und begaunerte Volk zur Selbsthilfe schreitet!

Der völkisch-antisemitische Kampfausschuß.

"Ostjuden Hinaus!" ("Eastern Jews, Get Out!") This February 1923 poster announces "three gigantic rallies against the Ostjuden," who are described as having no culture, committing unspeakably barbaric acts, and as reactionaries—unable to fit into Viennese and Austrian life. *Documentation Center of the Austrian Resistance, Vienna.*

Right, Theodor Herzl. *Lidor Press, Tel Aviv, Israel. Date of picture unknown.* From: Wiener Juden in der Deutschen Literatur, *by Harry Zohn, 1961.*

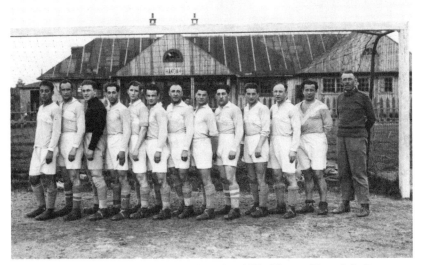

Above, Hakoah soccer team (thought to be 1927), Vienna. From left: Stross, Polak, Oppenheim, Hess, Stern, Posamer, Nemes-Henfeld, Mausner, Feldmann, Katz, Scheuer, Fried, Huber. *Austrian Institute for Contemporary History.*

Jewish front soldiers at a Rosh Hashana celebration, 1916. *From the catalogue,
"Judah in Ungarn Beth Hatefutsoth," The Nahum Goldmann Museum of
the Jewish Diaspora.*

Jewish soldiers at a religious service during World War I, Trient (now Tren-
tino, Southern Tyrol). *Austrian National Library.*

Ministry of Interior in Vienna rejected the idea, a Jewish Nationalist party emerged to contest seats not only in Galicia, but in those sections of Bukovina and Vienna where the Jews had a majority.

The Jewish Nationalist party elected four members of Parliament in the two eastern provinces, but its two candidates in the Leopoldstadt, one of them Schalit himself, received scarcely more than five percent of the vote. Of course, even these sections of Vienna had substantial numbers of non-Jews who probably voted for the more integrationist candidates. Nevertheless, it seems probable that the Nationalist/Zionist candidates received no more than one out of ten Jewish ballots.

The Zionists were neither crushed nor crestfallen at the results. They knew they suffered from lack of funds and experience, and that many of their supporters were under twenty-three and therefore could not vote. They felt they had at least pricked the conscience of the "assimilationists" and established themselves as a political force of some consequence. They were also pleased over the election of their four candidates from the East who promptly constituted themselves into Parliament's first Jewish caucus. (It would also be Parliament's last Jewish caucus.)

The success of the Jewish nationalists in the East spurred on other nationalist developments in that part of the Empire. In 1908, fifty Jewish writers held the world's first Yiddish language conference in Czernowitz. One of the attendees was Sholem Asch, who would become the leading Yiddish writer of the 1920s and 1930s.

The following year a Jewish theater society was formed in the same city and applied for official recognition, and therefore a state subsidy, as a national theater. When the Ministry of Interior rejected the request, the theater group took its case to the imperial court. The court, whose chief justice was a seventy-nine-year-old baptized Jew, decided after hearing lengthy arguments that the Jews were not a nationality and that Yiddish was not a national language. The justice pointed out that most Jews did not speak Yiddish and did not wish to declare themselves as a national group.

The issue came before the court again the following year when Galician Jews complained that their efforts to identify themselves as Jews by giving Yiddish as their mother tongue — national identity was ascribed according to language in the Austrian census — was frustrated by Polish officials who put them down as speaking Polish and therefore Poles. (The more Poles that could be counted in the census, the more benefit the Poles could receive from the government.) This time, with the chief justice absent, many of the other justices showed sympathy for the complainants. As the acting chief justice remarked, the Jews believe their position as a chosen people stems from the purity of their descent, and that "by baptism a Jew does not cease to be a Jew." Still the court decided that since Yiddish is not recognized by most Jews as their common language, it cannot be regarded as such by the government.

A much more inflammatory issue arose from what was called the Bukovina Settlement. For the 1910 provincial elections the Bukovina provincial legislature decided to follow the example of Moravia and set up a separate *Curia* or voting lists along national lines. The province consisted of a mix of nationalities with more than one out of eight of its residents being Jewish. Consequently the legislature assigned one of the five proposed election positions to the Jews.

The integrationist Jews of western Austria promptly spoke out in opposition. Theodor Gomperz, an internationally famous sociologist at the University of Graz, published an article saying the move would create an "election ghetto" and stir up chauvinistic sentiments. In Vienna the Union protested vigorously to the Minister of Interior who responded by vetoing the whole idea.

The following year brought new parliamentary elections and this time three of the four Jewish Nationalist members of Parliament lost their seats. The Nationalist and Zionist candidate for the Leopoldstadt, engineer Robert Stricker, doubled the vote received by Schalit at the previous election, but failed to oust the integrationist incumbent. Jewish nationalism had been dealt a serious but not, as we shall see, a fatal blow.

If the 1911 parliamentary elections were a severe setback to the Jewish nationalists, the results pleased many other Jews, for the Social Democrats had scored a major victory, becoming the largest single party in Austria. In Vienna where the Christian Socials (*Christlichsozialen Partei*) had not recovered from the death of Lueger the previous year, the Social Democrats emerged with an absolute majority. Although the Social Democrats had shown little zeal for defending Jewish interests, still the Party had many Jewish leaders — eight of its new parliamentary members were Jewish — and at least did not espouse an avowed anti-Semitic point of view.

The Jews could also take comfort from what seemed to be a gradual moderation of the Christian Social party's anti-Semitism. The Christian Socials had not only controlled the city government for nearly fifteen years but had also been represented in the Cabinet. Acquisition and exercise of power had made them more resonsible. The shrill cries of racial hate, once so characteristic of the party, had diminished though they had certainly not disappeared. Some improvement in the Austrian economy, plus a slight *relative* reduction in the city's Jewish population — the Jewish community was still growing but now the Gentile community was growing faster — may also have helped ease Jewish-Gentile tensions.

Emperor Franz Joseph for his part continued to protect and advance Jewish interests. During this time he apparently abandoned his policy of requiring Jewish army officers to convert if they wished to advance beyond the rank of brigadier general. In 1908 he appointed Edmund Schweitzer as Field Marshal. Schweitzer, whom Franz Joseph called "one of my best commanders," was a professed Jew who had been active at one time in the Jewish community of his native city of Budapest.

In the spring of 1910 the highly esteemed anatomist Emil Zuckerkandl died and even the *Reichspost*, the Christian Social official newspaper, joined the city's other major journals in mourning his passing. The following year Gustav Mahler returned from New York to die, and the papers who once attacked and mocked him reported his daily condition as though he belonged to the royal family. His numerous former enemies in the city's music world now spoke rapturously and longingly of the "Mahler era" at the Vienna Opera.

The slight easing of pressures from outside the Jewish community in these prewar years was accompanied by a similar easing of pressures from within. In 1912 the World Zionist Organization selected Vienna for its bi-annual congress the following year. It would be the first time the organization would hold such an event in the city of its founder.

In recognition of this decision, and in recognition of the position that the Zionists had established for themselves within the Jewish community, the integrationists made a conciliatory gesture; they offered to put two Zionists, Robert Stricker and Attorney Jakob Ehrlich, on their own candidates' list for the *Gemeinde* board elections. The Zionists accepted and thereby gained their first official voice on the *Gemeinde*'s ruling council. In 1913 virtually all Jewish groups joined forces to protest a new blood libel case in Russia known as the *Beilis* affair.

Several new Jewish organizations arose during these few relatively quiet years before World War I. Among them was *Agudas Israel*, an organization of Orthodox Jews which was founded in Kattowitz in 1912. Another was *Blau-Weiss*, a German Zionist youth organization. Although Vienna had relatively few Orthodox Jews and still did not have many Zionists, both organizations established active chapters in the city. In fact highly assimilationist Vienna became something of a center for the *Agudas Israel* movement. But the organization born during these years that came to mean the most to the Vienna Jews was a sports club, Hakoah.

From the 1890s on, Vienna's Jewish youth had displayed a great interest in sports. At the first Olympic Games in 1896 they had brought home to Austria gold and bronze medals in swimming. Four years later they earned bronze medals in both swimming and fencing and, in the following Olympiad, a gold and a bronze in swimming plus a silver medal in fencing. A Sephardic Jew, N.D. Alvalo, had reigned as the world's best distance runner during the early 1900s and some consider him the father of Austrian track.

Jews had also become active organizers and leaders of sporting clubs. Before the turn of the century a baptized Jewish general named von Joelson became president of the Austrian Steeplechase Society. Under his leadership Austria gained international recognition in this sport.

The exclusion of Jews from the Austrian branches of the German Gymnastic Association led to the formation in 1897 of the country's first Jewish sports organization, later known as Maccabi. Some ten years later, when the Austrian (though not the German) branches of the *Wandervogel*, a popular outdoor youth group, adopted an Aryan clause, the Jews set up a similar organization of their own. Then in 1909 a group of Zionist Jews formed a Jewish soccer team with the name Hakoah.

The leading organizer was an unusual attorney named Fritz Löhner. What made Löhner unusual was his double life, for under the pen name of Beda he had become a renowned operetta librettist and songwriter. A fierce Jewish nationalist, Beda had also written a booklet entitled *Israelites and Other Anti-Semites*, and every week he contributed a poem to the Zionist weekly, *Jüdische Zeitung*, taunting the *Assimilanten* (assimilationists). This lawyer turned librettist became Hakoah's first president.

Outfitted with blue and white uniforms bearing the Star of David, Hakoah's players (the word Hakoah in Hebrew means strength or power or force) started out as a fourth or bottom division team. As such they could use only the less desirable playing fields of the city's poor suburbs. They also had to play against teams whose members and fans were animated by more than just the usual desire to win, for Hakoah was not just an ordinary opponent. To lose to a team of Jews meant double disgrace; emotions ran high, and anti-Semitic abuse, both verbal and physical, and on the playing fields and in the stands, was frequent. Moreover, many Jews opposed the team's creation, believing that it only played into the hands of the racial anti-Semites. Furthermore, some existing Viennese soccer clubs had admitted Jews who were exceptionally qualified, and two-thirds of these Jewish players, at least initially, refused to leave their present clubs to join Hakoah.

Despite such difficult conditions, Hakoah began an upward march that would eventually make it one of Austria's, and indeed one of Europe's, top soccer teams, as well as the most outstanding Jewish sports team in the history of the Diaspora.

Contrary to the fears of integrationists, Hakoah did not slam the door shut on Jewish involvement in non-Jewish sports organizations. On the contrary, the easing of anti-Semitism during these years opened such doors a bit wider. In 1910 Hugo Meisl became the captain of the first Vienna Football Club while a Jewish attorney became the president of the Austrian Football League. During the next three years young Jewish athletes won the European championship in wrestling, the world championship in bicycling, such local events as *Quer durch Wien*, the city's most popular swimming competition, and such national events as Austria's heavily contested 100-meter dash.

But athletic awards were not the only things the Viennese Jewish community was winning in these comparatively calm days. For some years the work of Dr. Robert Barany on the inner ear had been attracting increasing acclaim, and in 1914 the thirty-eight-year-old physician brought home to Austria its first Nobel Prize. Unfortunately Austria and, as it would turn out, its Jewish population especially, had now much more worrisome things on its mind.

Part V

War Within, War Without

*One must remind the people that the situation is no longer
as harmless as in the days of Lueger, for we all confront
important decisions which could change the countenance
of the world fundamentally. One must remind the people
that . . . the comedy of the Lueger era was child's play
compared to the powerful upheaval that has just begun.*
— Felix Salten in 1927

*We are certain to suffer greatly in the struggle between the
classes because we stand in the most exposed position in
both the capitalist and socialist camps.*
— Theodor Herzl in 1902

Chapter 12

The Two-Front War

When news of Archduke Franz Ferdinand's assassination at Sarajevo on June 28, 1914 reached Vienna, it produced little grief or emotion of any kind among the Viennese public. When the band at one dance hall stopped playing to announce the news, the crowd listened and then went on dancing with no loss in its festive mood.

The heavy-jowled, heavy-handed heir-apparent had never been especially popular. Even his uncle the Emperor had seen as little as possible of him in recent years. When Franz Joseph first named Franz Ferdinand to be his successor, Viennese wits had wisecracked, "When he gets to be Emperor, we'll have nothing to laugh about." Now, they wisecracked, "He didn't get to be Emperor and we still have nothing to laugh about." It is one of history's many ironies that the killing of a man not particularly well-liked or even well-known in his own country could plunge Europe into devastating war.

When the war which Franz Ferdinand's death triggered arrived six weeks later, it set off large-scale demonstrations of public support throughout Europe's major cities. Vienna was no exception. When the Viennese learned that their government had broken off relations with Serbia, they "burst into a frenzy of joy, and huge crowds roamed the streets all night singing patriotic songs."

Most of the city's Jews apparently shared this mood of elation. Pleased to be joining with other Austrians in fighting for their country, they marched off willingly, indeed often eagerly, to battle. Jewish intellectuals justified their sudden martial ardor by such phrases as "He who cannot hate cannot really love." Jewish Social Democrats and Zionists justified theirs by noting that they were fighting against Russia, an anti-trade-unionist and anti-Semitic country.

Just how many Jews served and died for the Austro-Hungarian Empire in World War I remains unknown, for no systematic study of their participation has ever been done. But according to Professor Erica Weinzierl of the University of Vienna, "Their share of fighting troops was in part disproportionately high." Professor Weinzierl notes that a memorial tablet in the Leopoldstadt bears over four hundred names. In the small city of Klagenfurt, twenty-five Jewish men went off to war and five did not return. Though not too much can be read into one small sample of this kind, still it represents a casualty rate double that of the Austrian army as a whole.

One notable Jewish casualty of the war was the writer Hugo Zuckerman. He wrote "The Song of the Austrian Cavalryman" which became the favorite song of the Austrian troops. Zuckerman himself joined the army at the outbreak of war and died in battle shortly thereafter.

Many Jews received medals and/or promotions during the conflict. Among them was Martin Freud, who rose from private to lieutenant while winning the Military Cross. For professional Jewish soldiers, advancement to the army's upper echelons became much easier. Alfred Kornhaber, a Galician, became a field marshal while many others advanced to general officer rank.

One Jewish officer warrants special mention since he plays a role in the later history of the Jewish community. He is Emil Sommer, the son of a prominent Bukovina banker who had chosen not to follow in his father's footsteps but to become a professional soldier instead. The forty-year-old Sommer was serving as a captain when the war broke out. He was wounded twice during the early months of the war and taken prisoner by the Russians. But in 1917 he was released in a prisoner-of-war exchange. He promptly volunteered for further service at the front, and by war's end had won two decorations and the rank of colonel.

Austrian Jews were also active on the home front. Hermann Schwarzwald, the rather quixotic Galician who had become the first unbaptized Jewish imperial counselor, now became the highest ranking civil servant in the Ministry of Finance. As such he virtually ran the country's economy. Schwarzwald managed to keep Austria solvent without raising taxes through issuing voluntary bonds. "That Austria with its backward economy, small reserves, totally incompetent military and political leadership, and discordant nationalities fought four years is largely due to Schwarzwald's policies," says Peter Drucker.

Schwarzwald's wife Eugenie, already known for opening Austria's first school to prepare women for the University, and known as well for operating the country's foremost intellectual salon, also helped the war effort. She set up soup kitchens and cheap restaurants to feed hungry adults and established an office for sending Vienna's undernourished children to the country. Better-off Jews contributed generously to various war relief charities.

But despite their patriotism the war did not decrease the sentiment against Jews. On the contrary it whipped up such feelings to a level not seen since the 1890s.

To begin with, although most Jews fervently backed the war, a small but highly visible number did not. They included left-wing socialists such as the labor Zionist group *Poale Zion*. When some 200,000 hungry and weary Viennese workers went out on strike at the beginning of 1918, *Poale Zion* actively supported them. A large number of its members were arrested as agitators, and their Jewish names appearing in the newspapers lent substance to the anti-Semites' often-repeated charge that the Jews were betraying Austria.

Among the notable Jewish individuals who opposed the war was Karl Kraus, who gave pacifist talks and readings throughout the conflict, donating the proceeds to aid the war wounded. Another was Friedrich Adler, the pacifist son of Viktor Adler, who in October 1916 assassinated the country's prime minister Karl Stürgkh as Stürgkh was lunching at a popular restaurant. The Jewish writer Mannes Sperber later recalled standing near a crowd of adults on a street corner in the Leopoldstadt on the evening of that day. The adults were heatedly discussing the incident when young Sperber suddenly felt a sharp, searing sensation on his neck. Someone had pressed a burning cigarette against his flesh. He turned to see "a large man looking at me in a mocking manner" who quickly disappeared through the doors of a nearby Catholic hospital.

Another and more serious spur to anti-Semitism was the war-caused shortages, especially of food. As a group, the biggest beneficiaries of this situation were the farmers who profited considerably by selling foodstuffs on the black market. But many of the middlemen they sold to were Jews and, since the latter dealt directly with the consumer, they were the ones who reaped the public's wrath. In addition, the feeling grew that big business was somehow benefiting from the war; this belief, given the close identification of the Jews with big business in Austria, further inflamed public sentiment. Starting in 1916 and almost every week thereafter, leaflets appeared urging boycotts of Jewish merchants, doctors, attorneys, and others.

As to the charge of Jews becoming rich from the war, it is interesting to note that a full half of all Jewish burials in Vienna during the war years were at the Jewish community's expense. In other words they involved the deaths of Jews whose families were simply too impoverished to pay for their interment. Another thirty-three percent of all Jewish burials were of the fourth class, which was the least expensive category. That leaves only seventeen percent of all burials for the three remaining classes. Furthermore, a government survey during this time found eighty-two percent of all the city's Jews living in the lowest dwelling classification. Of course, most Viennese Gentiles were not aware of these figures, and probably would not have believed them in any case.

But the biggest cause for the heightened hostility was the refugee problem. Galicia quickly became the major battleground between Austria-Hungary and Russia, and much of it soon became a virtual no-man's land. Fighting raged in Bukovina as well. As a result, refugees from these areas began streaming into western Austria, particularly Vienna.

Jews made up a disproportionate share of these refugees for they were the most endangered. The Russians suspected the Jews on the eastern front of supplying information and otherwise helping the German and Austrian authorities, and either expelled them or made their lives so miserable that they left on their own accord. Native Poles, freed from the restraints of Austrian officialdom, gave vent to their deep-seated hatred of the Jews as well. By the end of 1915, 77,000 Jewish refugees were living in the city. Among them were some Chassidic rabbis who had come to Vienna bringing their flocks of supporters with them.

The refugees created immense problems for Vienna. As noted earlier, the city had long suffered from an acute housing shortage, and Lueger, despite his ambitious public works, had done little to alleviate it. The new arrivals aggravated the situation considerably. Although most of the refugees squeezed in with relatives — average densities in the Leopoldstadt reached six per room — or occupied space not otherwise being used, such as empty stores, the Viennese promptly blamed them for the constantly worsening housing shortage.

The new arrivals were also blamed for compounding the food shortage. They were, after all, being fed and their continued existence in the city meant less food for others.

In one illustrative incident, a Jewish woman with her suitcases had climbed aboard a wagon that was to take her to the railroad station where she was planning to take a train back to recently reoccupied Galicia. The wagon also contained numerous rice baskets which the wagon owner had used the previous day for transporting a consignment of food. A Viennese woman seeing her sitting there among the rice baskets shouted out, "See how our food is being carted off to Poland." An angry crowd quickly gathered and broke up only when a policeman investigated and found the rice baskets empty.

Jewish charities maintained the refugees, but sitting in cafes or standing on street corners in their enforced idleness, often clothed in black caftans, they annoyed the Viennese who accused them not just of causing food and housing shortages but of black marketeering and of avoiding military service. Most of Vienna's Jewish community also kept them at arm's length. "No one is interested in the *Ostjuden*," wrote the Jewish writer Joseph Roth. "Their cousins and fellow believers who sit in editorial rooms downtown are already Viennese and want no relationship with them. The Christian Socials and German Nationalists have made anti-Semitism a keypoint in their programs. The Social Democrats fear to acquire a reputation of being the 'Jewish party.'"

Many of the refugees returned to the East as the war ground to an end. By Armistice Day less than forty thousand remained. In a city of two million this would not seem to be an unmanageable number. Yet they formed a visible and vulnerable target for anti-Semitic agitators who for some years to come would take advantage of their presence to stir up racial hate.

One of the few Viennese Jews who *was* interested in the *Ostjuden* was Robert Stricker, the Zionist candidate in the last pre-war elections for Parliament. But then Stricker was interested in everything Jewish and in very little else. This unique man, who was already emerging as the leader of Viennese Zionism, and who would become the only notable political leader Viennese Zionism would produce after Herzl, was born in Czechoslovakia in 1879. Enrolling as an engineer student in Prague's German-speaking university, he had helped form and become the first president of Czechoslovakia's first Zionist student organization, and had co-authored at the age of nineteen the first Zionist pamphlet to appear in the Czech language.

Following graduation, Stricker went to work for the national railroad system. After a few years on the job, he wrote a series of anonymous articles for Prague's leading German newspaper criticizing the railroad's inefficient procedures and often scandalous practices in Czechoslovakia. The government's railroad minister investigated and, finding that Stricker was the author, gave the young engineer a position of authority at the ministry's Vienna headquarters.

In Vienna Stricker eventually met and married a widow with an infant son whom he quickly adopted. (The couple would also have a daughter of their own.) He continued his Zionist activities which included, besides running for election, writing a regular column for the Zionist weekly *Judische Zeitung*.

Jewishness, not Judaism, was Stricker's real religion. It was his political creed as well. He rejected right-wing politics for he believed that "an honest Jew cannot make peace with a reactionary government. He must stand where there is justice." But Stricker scorned the left as well since in calling for a class struggle it was, in his view, pitting Jew against Jew and thereby destroying the Jewish community. He was especially scornful of Jewish Social Democrats, contempuously referring to them as the "Red Assimilationists."

Unusual for an engineer, and an engineer of proven professional capability at that, Stricker was also a spellbinding speaker and a brilliant journalist. Next to Beda's poems satirizing the integrationists, Stricker's column was the *Judische Zeitung*'s most widely-read feature.

Stricker's fierce devotion to Jewish nationalism in Austria, and Jewish statehood in Palestine, at times drove him to take positions that, at least in hindsight, seem quite unrealistic. Some might view him as a modern Don Quixote, and with his tall figure and bushy goatee, he even resembled that earnest but naive champion of good causes. But Stricker's brilliance, devotion, and warm affection for all those who shared his dreams would earn him not just the respect but also the love of many of World Zionism's foremost leaders.

In 1915 Stricker and an associate set up the Jewish War Archives to document what was happening to the *Ostjuden* in their home areas. In reporting atrocity after atrocity he hoped to secure a better understanding and some sympathy for their plight.

The archival project continued for the next two years. But in 1917, with its work largely completed but its mission of promoting greater sympathy for the *Ostjuden* largely unrealized, a new development captured Stricker's attention. It also captured the attention of Jews throughout the world. Britain's foreign minister Lord Balfour issued his famous declaration pledging the British government to the establishment of a Jewish homeland in Palestine.

Palestine was then part of the Turkish Empire, which was allied with Germany and Austria as one of the Central Powers. Stricker quickly sent a memorandum to Austria's foreign minister urging the government to counter the British initiative by pressuring Turkey to issue a similar statement. Austria at that time was probably in no position to put pressure on any country to do anything, but the foreign minister did express sympathy for the idea of making Palestine into a Jewish state when he later met with a leader of the World Zionist movement.

For Stricker and the other Viennese Zionists, the Balfour Declaration marked a major advance. They would seek to capitalize on it in the difficult years that lay ahead.

Chapter 13

From Empire to Republic

Austria's greatest casualty of the war was Franz Joseph, who died in November 1916 at the age of eighty-six. Although his death deprived the Jews of their most powerful protector, they had, or felt they had, no immediate grounds for concern. In place of his murdered nephew, Franz Joseph had designated his grand nephew Karl as his successor, and this idealistic, twenty-nine-year-old Habsburg seemed well-disposed towards his Jewish subjects. One of the new Emperor's early moves was to free Leopold Hilsner, the Jewish youth convicted of a ritual murder in Czechoslovakia, from prison.

But while Karl I was well-intentioned, he was also politically naive. His uncle had liked him but had never included him in the actual administration of the nation. Distressed over what the war was doing to his country, Karl made an effort to negotiate a separate peace with the Allies in 1917, but he failed to follow through properly and the move misfired.

With the war drawing to a close in the fall of 1918, Karl sought to retain the framework of the Empire by transforming it into a federation of separate national states. But the move came too late, for the Czechs, Hungarians, Poles, and others were already asserting their absolute independence. The German-Austrians, meanwhile, were dreaming once again of uniting with Germany. So Karl appointed a provisional government and on Armistice Day, November 11, 1918, he renounced all personal participation in state affairs. Thus did six hundred years of Habsburg rule come to an end.

The next day the country's new provisional national assembly, consisting solely of German-Austrians (including socialist Jews who believed themselves to be such) unanimously declared Austria to be a "constituent part of the German Republic." The Social Democrats were the most vigorous champions of this idea, with one of their new leaders, Karl Renner, proclaiming, "We are a single race: one country in the face of destiny." The stenographic record reports his remarks being followed by a "standing ovation. Loud and prolonged applause and clapping from the floor and galleries."

In the following February, with the war now over but with the peace treaty still to be negotiated, the new Republic held its first elections. The Social Democrats emerged as the biggest winners with over forty percent of the vote, but they failed to gain an absolute majority, and were forced to organize a Grand Coalition with the Christian Socials and the German Nationalists. The forty-nine-year-old Renner, a former librarian and a Gentile, became prime minister, while two of the Party's Jewish leaders, Otto Bauer and Julius Deutsch, took over the posts of foreign minister and minister of defense, respectively.

Both Bauer and Deutsch had served in the army during the war with Deutsch rising to the rank of colonel by its end. (Viktor Adler had died just as the war ended.) Among the cabinet portfolios awarded the Christian Socials was the Ministry of Social Welfare, which went to Monsignor Ignaz Seipel, a brilliant professor of moral theology who had occupied the same ministerial position in Emperor Karl's provisional government, and who figures heavily in Austria's subsequent history. Municipal elections held three months later gave the Social Democrats an absolute majority and near absolute control in Vienna.

One of the first acts of the new parliament was to reaffirm the call for Austria's unification with Germany. A proposal to this effect swept through the 165-member body with only one "nay." Interestingly enough the vote on the measure occurred on March 12, the date when, nineteen years later and under quite different circumstances, Austro-German unification would finally take place.

The Allies, however, had other ideas. After dealing with Germany at Versailles, they turned their attention to Austria. A delegation headed by Renner went to Paris, where after a few weeks of negotiations they reluctantly signed a harsh peace treaty. As one Austrian negotiator put it, "We are forced to sign our own death warrant."

The Austrians knew they had already lost their non-German-speaking regions but they did expect to hold on to the German-speaking areas, for national self-determination had been a key point in Woodrow Wilson's peace plans. But the Allied negotiators, disregarding Wilson's principles and Austria's protest, stripped the country of over a third of its German-speaking inhabitants. Certain areas in the east, where Germans sometimes outnumbered Slavs by almost twenty to one, were given to Czechoslovakia and Yugoslavia. The South Tyrol, containing nearly a quarter of a million Austro-Germans and almost no Italians, was ceded to Italy on the grounds that thirty-eight million Italians needed a buffer zone to protect themselves from six and one-half million Austrians.

The Austria that remained after this dismemberment has been likened to a "mutilated trunk bleeding from every pore" and a "rump state." Even one of the British negotiators referred to the country he had helped create as a "pathetic relic," while Professor Pauley has called it "an impossible creation consisting of a huge world city and a few Alpine valleys."

Pauley's statement points up another peculiar and ultimately perilous feature of the new Austria. Its capital now comprised nearly one-third of the country's population. Some began to refer to Vienna as a hydrocephalic head perched precariously on the body of a dwarf.

Vienna had owed its size and status to its position as an imperial capital, but the loss of the Empire meant the loss of much of the city's economic underpinnings. It housed a vast army of bureaucrats, most of whom no longer had anything to administer. It also housed banks, insurance companies, and other concerns, many of whose branches and much of whose business had disappeared along with the Empire. Gone also were most of the factories and mines from the East that formerly nourished the country's western half.

Many wondered whether the new Austria was *lebensfähig* or viable. Such a situation naturally increased Austria's interest in uniting with Germany, but the Allies, fearful of seeing a new and greater Germany arise, required Austria to maintain her independence. Said Zweig, "It was the first instance in history, as far as I know, in which a country was saddled with an independence which it exasperatedly resisted."

Other restrictions imposed by the victors on Austria required payment of war reparations and limited the Austrian army to thirty thousand, about the size of the present day New York City police force. One clause that would be important for Jewish Austria required the country to grant equal rights to any national group within its now shrunken borders.

Austria did get some concessions from the Allies: they granted her the German sections of western Hungary and promised long-term and short-term credits. The clause forbidding unification with Germany left a little leeway for later modification. Furthermore, no one took the requirements for reparations seriously. The victors realized that if Austria was to remain independent, some assistance had to be given. Still the new state was born in a state of shock. The Austro-Germans found themselves no longer the dominant group of a vast empire but the rank-and-file population of a small and shaky republic. It was a bitter pill that many of them would never manage to swallow.

A year after the peace treaty the new Austrian Republic adopted a constitution. Drafted by Hans Kelsen, a Jewish professor of law at the University of Vienna, it created a federal state similar to that of Germany and the United States. Under its provisions each of the country's nine provinces would enjoy a great deal of autonomy.

Kelsen's constitution also set up a powerful national legislature elected by proportional representation. Such an electoral system allocated legislative seats according to the percentage of votes a party received. Since no party need secure an absolute majority or even a plurality in any district to acquire representation, proportional representation discourages compromise and hardens party lines. It can work reasonably well in countries where a basic consensus exists, such as Switzerland or Sweden, but in a fragmented society such as postwar Austria or present-day Israel, it encourages and indeed exacerbates fragmentation. Proportional representation plus federalism, plus a strong legislature versus a relatively weak executive, provided a fragile foundation for the already weak Republic.

A more formidable factor threatening the new nation was the emergence of extra-legal armies. The Social Democrats may have initiated this development when, during the last months of the war, Deutsch began preparing a secret organization called the *Volkswehr* or People's Defense Force among troops stationed in Vienna. His objective was to create a force that could crush any attempt by either communist or rightist elements to take over the government. Not without reason he feared efforts by both groups to destroy Austria's new democracy.

Deutsch later disbanded the *Volkswehr*, but in the meantime a new para military movement had sprung up in the countryside. Groups of ex-soldiers had banded together to defend farm property from hungry marauders from the city and to safeguard the country's borders from unwanted intruders from other countries, especially Yugoslavia. These groups gradually coalesced into a single, though loosely knit, organization which called itself the *Heimwehr* or Home Defense Force.

The *Heimwehr* started out with no particular political ties and even some Social Democrats initially belonged to it. But Deutsch, sensing its inherent right-wing orientation, set up a Social Democratic force called the *Schutzbund* or Protective League. As the *Schutzbund* took form and spread to Social Democratic centers outside Vienna, the *Heimwehr* became more or less allied with the Christian Socials, although unlike the *Schutzbund* it retained a separate status. It is a well-known fact of political life that no government can carry out its functions unless it retains an essential monopoly on the use of force. The presence of two virtual armies outside the control of government ensured a troublesome time for Austria's fledgling Republic.

With so many centrifugal forces at work, the Grand Coalition came to an end in the summer of 1921. The Social Democrats precipitated the split as they seized on a relatively minor issue to leave the government. Their decision to depart may seem strange since they held the dominant positions. But Austria was undergoing difficult days that required unpopular measures, measures that any party would be loath to take. Furthermore the Social Democrats now held Vienna, which gave them substantial power as well as opportunities for patronage. So they abandoned to the Christian Socials the task of governing "the state that no one wanted."

Although the Christian Socials had started out in Vienna, their center of gravity had by now shifted to the countryside. In the February 1919 elections the Party had won sixty-three seats, compared to sixty-nine for the Social Democrats. But in a new election, held a few months after they took over the government in 1921, they won eighty-two seats compared to sixty-six for the Social Democrats and a mere twenty for the German Nationalists.

The Party eventually chose Monsignor Seipel as chancellor, a position the Catholic prelate would hold through most of the 1920s. Though an admirer of Lueger whom he once called a "true leader," Seipel differed from Lueger in several respects. Bald and bespectacled in appearance, and aloof and ascetic in manner, he owed his rise to political heights to his great intellectual abilities and interpersonal skills. He disdained rabble-rousing in any form. As such he disdained demagogic and opportunistic anti-Semitism, describing it as something *für die Gasse* (literally, for the street or, more idiomatically, street-corner stuff).

Seipel had previously indicated that he would help safeguard equal Jewish rights in the new Republic. In 1917 he had said, "We welcome with genuine pleasure every step which promises to lead to closer connections and undisturbed cooperation with our fellow citizens of other persuasions, and we will gladly contribute, even at the price of sacrifice, toward cementing such connections." Three years later as the Christian Socials took over the government, Seipel said, "The time of religious wars is over."

Even before becoming chancellor, Seipel had leaned heavily on a Jewish bank executive named Gottfried Kunwalt for advice on economic and financial matters. The two men would meet frequently, often at Kunwalt's three-room apartment, for the banker suffered from polio and could get around only with difficulty. Once in office Seipel continued to consult with Kunwalt, and one occasionally saw the red-bearded banker being pushed in his wheelchair through the corridors of Parliament on his way to the Chancellor's office. To the extent that the new Christian Social government had an *eminence gris* for economic affairs, it was Kunwalt.

Yet despite his conciliatory pronouncements and his connections with Kunwalt, Seipel was a committed anti-Semite. To be sure, his anti-Semitism was more complex and finely nuanced than that of most members of his party. But despite its sophisticated trappings, it was anti-Semitism nonetheless.

Seipel saw the Jews as a nation without a fixed territory and therefore disposed to intrude into and adapt themselves to the environments of others. They had also, in his view, developed into a "commercial society of a certain kind" for they tended to make money without doing any "productive" work of their own. Moreover they tended to spread this commercial spirit through all areas of life. Austria, lying more to the east than other Western European countries, was more exposed to their influence and therefore, he felt, must take special steps against becoming "culturally, economically, and politically dominated by Jewry."

The fact that the Jews were playing a dominant role in Austria's Social Democratic party, and were leading the country's small communist movement as well, gave added urgency to the problem. Seipel viewed the Jews as "inclined to revolution," and regarded "the Bolshevik danger as a Jewish danger." Therefore, although Jews had produced some outstanding individuals, one must keep them separate, he felt, for they constituted a "decomposing element" in Austrian society.

Such were the views of the man who, more than any other, would guide the Austrian Republic during the first decade of its existence.

The political problems confronting postwar Austria were vastly overshadowed, and indeed almost completely dominated, by the country's near catastrophic economic situation. Austria had ended the war in a state of semi-starvation, and the Armistice, at least initially, brought little relief.

Stefan Zweig, who spent the last years of the war in Switzerland but who decided to return once hostilities ceased, has described the shock of changing at the border from a Swiss train to an Austrian one. It meant changing from a clean, shiny passenger car with all its accouterments intact, to a shabby, soot-filled wagon where almost nothing was whole. Window straps and whole sections of seat coverings had been stripped away to provide material for clothes, and all ashtrays had been stolen for the mite of nickel and copper they contained. Nightfall brought utter darkness for the light bulbs had been either stolen or smashed. Broken windows allowed cinders from the inferior soft coal fueling the locomotive to blow in. Since few trains were even running, every bit of space was occupied, with each passenger frantically holding on to his or her baggage and provisions lest they be stolen. After setting up residence in Salzburg, Zweig, though now a fairly wealthy man thanks to the royalties his books were earning abroad, had to write in bed in order to keep warm.

Such was the condition of an Austria deprived of Silesia's coal, Bohemia's textiles, Hungary's wheat, and other sources of economic nourishment, and saddled with a vast army of civil servants, pensioners, and other underemployed white collar people to support. Still, the new nation did have some resources to draw on. It contained much arable land, iron ore, and cheap hydro-electrical power potential. It could also count on tourist business as well as on relief assistance from the British and Americans, especially the latter.

Unfortunately the Social Democratic-dominated government of the immediate postwar years pursued policies that discouraged economic development. True to its principles, it raised wages, distributed relatively high unemployment benefits, decreed an eight-hour day, and imposed numerous regulations, as well as high taxes on business. Bread was subsidized while many other foods were rationed.

These policies produced budget deficits which in 1920 reached *150 percent* of the nation's gross national product. (By comparison, many Americans expressed alarm when their country's budget deficit in the early 1980s reached five percent of GNP.) More specifically, these policies triggered an inflation which, by the time it ended in 1922, had devalued Austria's currency by 12,000 percent. Money set aside in the morning to buy a suit would by afternoon cover only the cost of a waistcoat. People spoke of streetcar rides that were more expensive at the end of the ride than at the beginning. Money eventually became so cheap that paper currency was only printed on one side, and school children sometimes used the blank side as writing paper. In Salzburg a new type of "tourist" appeared — unemployed workers from Britain who found that their weekly dole, a mere pittance when reckoned in pounds sterling, enabled them to take up residence in the city's most luxurious hotels.

The roaring inflation brought widespread misery. Some of Vienna's more cherished treasures were not spared as the shivering Viennese began cutting down their famous Vienna Woods for fuel, and the government seriously considered selling the famed Gobelin tapestries in the imperial palace to feed its hungry populace. Top Viennese performing stars who before the war had disdained playing in the provinces now eagerly sought such engagements, hoping to find a decent meal and a heated room in the better nourished rural areas. A student would do another's homework for a slice of salami. The tuberculosis rate rose fifty percent above its prewar level, while the birth rate dropped fifty percent from the same level.

Roaring inflation, combined with regulated markets, produced wide-scale black marketeering. Farmers refused to sell their products at government-set prices and instead sold or, more frequently, traded them to hungry city dwellers who had begun scouring the countryside for food. Many a once poor peasant ended up owning valuable jewelry and antiques. But those who had little to trade had to contend with frozen potatoes and bread that often tasted like pitch. (In an effort to stop the bartering the government quarantined certain key areas with police and troops. This led to nightly pickups by truck which on more than one occasion produced battles involving revolvers and knives between the black marketeers and the forces of order.)

On becoming chancellor, Seipel moved as expeditiously as possible to change things. He stopped the treasury's printing presses, abruptly ending the inflation. He also negotiated a loan through the League of Nations. The terms of the loan, however, required the government to undertake two highly unpopular measures: discharge tens of thousands of civil servants, and agree unequivocally to maintain Austria's independence for at least twenty years. The loan, together with Seipel's other moves, brought a measure of economic stability and growth. But, in political and social terms, the new Republic paid a high price, one that would eventually help undermine its existence.

Chapter 14

The Solitary Scapegoat

The political instability and economic impoverishment that accompanied the birth pangs of the new Republic furnished, in themselves, ideal conditions for an upsurge of anti-Semitism. But more specific elements also helped unleash a new outburst of hate.

When the Austro-Germans ruled and largely ran a vast empire, they could look down upon a host of other nationalities. They could also blame them for many of their own grievances. Now they had no one to feel superior to, and no one to attribute their misfortunes to, except the Jews. The Jews had always been the primary internal target for Austro-German wrath; now they became the only target.

As might be expected, the country's economic problems ranked foremost in the Austro-Germans' long list of accusations against their Jewish countrymen. Postwar inflation wiped out the savings of the middle class while it enriched, at least temporarily, many speculators. The two most spectacular speculators were Camillo Castiglioni and Sigmund Bosel. Both men were Jews. Castiglioni, in fact, was the wayward son of the chief rabbi of Trieste.

Both speculators eventually went bankrupt, and their bankruptcies showed that numerous highly-placed and highly-respected Gentiles had actively assisted, and hoped to profit from, their wild schemes. Bosel's financial manipulations had even involved two prominent members of Seipel's cabinet, while Castiglioni had had dealings with a host of Christian Social leaders including a provincial governor. Jewish Social Democrats in Parliament had led the fight in exposing and excoriating their machinations, yet the finger of accusation remained pointed at the Jews and the oft-heard slogan of the 1890s, "The Jew is guilty," took on new life.

Many blamed the inflation itself on the Jews, whom they considered its biggest beneficiaries. Such a belief ignored several basic economic facts. Inflation hurts savers, and Austria's largely middle-class Jews were, if anything, greater savers than Austria's Gentiles. Inflation also hurts lenders who see their loans repaid in money that has lost much of its value. The inflation was one reason why ten of Vienna's twelve major banks went bankrupt during the early 1920s, and these banks were largely Jewish-owned.

The biggest beneficiaries of inflation are borrowers who can pay back their loans in less valuable money. In Austria such borrowers did include some Jewish speculators but many more were non-Jewish, among them the country's farmers whose mortgages and other debts were, in real terms, largely wiped out by the erosion of money values. Yet many Gentiles, including many farmers, claimed the Jews had produced and were profiting from the collapse in the country's currency.

Then there were the *Ostjuden* refugees who constituted both an economic and a social problem. As noted earlier, many of them sought to return to their homes with the winding down of the war. But many of those who did so ended up returning to Vienna, because after the Armistice Galicia once again became a no-man's land as war raged first between the Poles and the Ukranians, and then between the Poles and the Russians. Furthermore, the Poles did not allow embroilments with their neighbors to keep them from indulging in savage pogroms that during the first few months of "peace" killed over five hundred Jews. As a result, unemployed and unsettled Jewish refugees continued to congregate in the cafes and on the streets of the Leopoldstadt, provoking angry reactions from Austro-Germans, and from more than a few Viennese Jews as well.

In August 1920 the peace treaty signed in Paris a year earlier came into effect. Its terms gave all Jews and other nationals of the former empire now residing in the Republic the option of choosing Austrian citizenship. Most of the *Ostjuden* did so. Consequently, Vienna's Jewish population reached a high point of over 200,000 in the 1923 census (about ten percent of the population). Although this figure was only 25,000 more than the prewar figure, it did make Vienna more Jewish than it had been. Another 20,000 Jews lived in the rest of the country, giving Austria an overall Jewish population of about three percent. This was slightly larger than the prewar figure for the same area. Many of the new Jews in the countryside lived in the Burgenland, a section of prewar western Hungary which had been given to Austria in the peace treaty.

That over ninety percent of the country's Jews now lived in Vienna created additional problems, and these problems were compounded by the fact that the Social Democrats now ran the city.

Even before the war many rural Austro-Germans had viewed Vienna with a measure of distaste. The city's decadent sophistication, combined with its polyglot population, made it seem alien and even suspicious. In the new, postwar Austria, these feelings took on added dimensions. Vienna was now the bloated *Wasserkopf* (water head) that the rest of the country had to support. Even its geographical position argued against it, for in the new Austria it was no longer centrally located but situated at the far eastern end of the country. Austrians living along the western border were as close to Paris as they were to their own capital city.

In taking over Vienna the Social Democrats launched a series of public projects that would attract worldwide attention and admiration. They built well-designed housing complexes, kindergartens, funeral societies, sports centers, and other facilities. They even gave a *Waschpaket*, or laundry package of diapers and other infant necessities, to the parents of every new baby born in the city. Helped by the new federal constitution, whose decentralizing features they had originally opposed, the Social Democrats virtually transformed Vienna into a state within a state.

But all these expensive undertakings bore a price tag. To pay it, the Social Democrats imposed heavy taxes which fell largely though not exclusively on business and the more affluent. They taxed telegrams and telephone services, opera tickets and restaurant meals, and even windows and staircases. Twenty-five years earlier, when the city's capitalists felt threatened by Lueger's election, they threatened to shift their activities to Budapest. But Hungary was now an independent country and that option no longer existed. Most large businesses and most of the city's middle and upper classes were in effect now trapped in the capital and could do nothing but pay the levies.

The city's real estate owners were particularly hard hit, for the Social Democrats increased the already high property taxes of the prewar era, and at the same time imposed strict rent controls on residential property. One result was that during the inflation the price of a single dinner in a decent restaurant would cover the rent of a luxury apartment for a year. Another result was a swift decline in real estate values which allowed the city administration to buy up property for its own numerous projects at bottom prices. Since most property owners owned only a single building, the policies of the Social Democrats created a large group of deeply disgruntled people.

But better-off Viennese were not the only ones who had to pay for the Social Democrats' ambitious programs. The rest of the country also had to bear, at least indirectly, some of the burden, for the costs these programs imposed on business were to some degree reflected in the costs of goods and services, including government services, which only Vienna could supply. Most provincial Austrians felt that in some way they were being forced to shoulder the costs of Vienna's social experiments, and to some degree they were right.

The Social Democrats installed a Gentile, Karl Seitz, as mayor, but some key administrative posts were occupied by Jews. Chief among them was Hugo Breitner, a former bank executive who now became the city's finance director. Since it was Breitner who levied the onerous taxes necessary to carry out the Party's expensive programs, he soon became the focal point of middle- and upper-class rage. Even many of the middle- and upper-class Jews who increasingly voted for the Social Democrats — what other party could they vote for? — railed against Breitner and his financial policies. Christian Social election posters branded him as a "tax sadist." Thus it was Breitner the Jew, not Seitz the Gentile, who became the chief target of widespread wrath.

Aside from their financing, the programs and projects themselves generated controversy and complaints. A fortunate family allowed to rent a sparkling new apartment for ten dollars a month, and to send their children to nursery school for thirty cents a week, was expected to be loyal to the Social Democrats. If they knew or were related to a member of the admissions committee for the housing project involved, so much the better. Similar informal patronage guidelines governed the dispensing of the much-sought-after jobs in municipal agencies and enterprises. The use of public funds to reward the party faithful, and sometimes personal favorites among them, tarnished the luster of the Social Democrats' ambitious social welfare programs.

More importantly many of the city's projects offended the Catholic clergy. In building a municipal crematorium and in naming their biggest housing project (three-quarters of a mile long, it was the world's largest) after Karl Marx, the Social Democrats seemed to be going out of their way to confront and affront the Church. This at least was the Church's view, which increasingly regarded the Social Democrats as, basically, Bolsheviks intent on undermining organized religion and its values.

The Austrian Social Democrats were not Bolsheviks but their Jewish leaders especially did display an affinity for doctrinaire Marxism. This tendency was reinforced by their desire to squelch the country's budding communist movement by undercutting its position. In this they succeeded, for their left-wing orientation did prevent the communists from gaining the position in Austria that they acquired in Germany. But the Social Democrats paid a price in distancing themselves too far and too rigidly from the center and, since the Jews had become increasingly identified with the Party, they paid the price as well.

Thus, while municipal officials from all over Europe trooped to Vienna to marvel at the city's remarkable achievements, a large majority of Austrians, including a substantial number of Viennese, seethed with resentment and rage. Already too large for, and too isolated from, the rest of the country, Vienna had now become identified with the Jews and with all their alleged materialistic, parasitical, unethical, in short "decomposing" qualities. Even Social Democrats in the provinces spoke sarcastically of "the Jews in the Vienna headquarters," while many other Austrians looked on "Red Vienna" as an infected scab that needed to be lanced.

Shortly before the first postwar municipal elections of 1919, a then-famous anthropologist named P. Wilhelm Schmied warned his fellow Austrians that had the Turks captured Vienna in 1683, it would not have been so destructive and painful as the loss of Vienna today to "these Jewish hostile forces." Shortly after the elections that gave the Social Democrats control of the city, the Tyrol Farmers League held a rally in Innsbruck to urge "Freedom from Vienna." The chief speaker, a prominent Christian Social attorney, summoned them to fight against "the Asiatic overlords of Vienna" for "only a fundamental break with the spirit of Jewry and its disciples can save the German Alpinelands." His remarks were greeted with thunderous applause.

Not only domestic developments were undermining the position of the Jews in postwar Austria. International concerns were also playing a role.

The end of the war brought communist governments to Hungary and the state of Bavaria. Both governments were soon overthrown but the fact that Jews figured so prominently in their makeup, plus the fact that both states bordered Austria, drove home to many Austrians the Bolshevik peril which the Jews seemed to present. That so many Jews also seemed to be playing so great a role in the Bolshevik government of Russia further strengthened this fear.

But it was not just the notion of Jews as communists that acquired increased pervasiveness during these turbulent times. In 1920 a German edition of *The Protocols of the Elders of Zion* appeared. This trumped-up document, which supposedly proved a Jewish conspiracy to take over the world, did not arouse as much attention in Austria as in Germany, for many Austrians had long already believed in the existence of such a plot. But its remarkable acceptance elsewhere — the *Times* of London wondered if it was not true — certainly did nothing to diminish its appeal to Austrians.

The *Protocols* had made a deep impression on Henry Ford, who wrote and signed a series of editorials warning of the Jewish menace in his newspaper, the *Dearborn Independent*. Ford in some respects enjoyed a greater reputation in Europe than in America, and when his editorials appeared in book form, a German publishing house put out a German translation which went through several editions. Ford's opinions provided further confirmation that the Jews, whether capitalists or communists, represented a dangerous pestilence that the new nation must, at the peril of its own survival, crush or at least strictly control. So developments abroad joined with developments at home in setting the stage for a fresh storm of *Judenhetze* (Jew hate).

In June 1918, with Austria's war effort already starting to disintegrate, the Pan-Germans and Christian Socials joined to stage a German Peoples Day. Speakers included such Christian Social leaders as Richard Weiskirschner, Lueger's successor as mayor of Vienna; Leopold Kunschak who headed the Christian Workers League; and Heinrich Mataja who would become foreign minister in Seipel's cabinet. The event turned into a virtual competition in anti-Semitism as the speakers vied with each other in accusing Jewish Austrians of disloyalty to the Emperor, of profiteering from the war, and of causing virtually all of Austria's many and troublesome problems.

A week later the board of the *Gemeinde* replied by branding such charges misleading and false, and accusing the anti-Semites of trying to make loyalty to the Emperor synonymous with hate of the Jews. But in rather contradictory fashion, the integrationist-dominated board said, "The Jewish community considers it beneath its dignity to mount a defense against such deliberately false accusations."

In August the rector of the University of Vienna announced a quota system on medical students from Galicia and Bukovina, though both regions were still part of Austria. Since virtually all medical students from the two areas were Jewish, the intended effect was obvious. In the meantime, the Christian Social and Pan-German press kept up their drumfire against the Jews, publicizing, for example, the names of all Jewish businessmen arrested for illegal activity, while downplaying and even omitting the names of Christians apprehended for similar misdeeds. At the war's end the influential *Reichspost*, the official organ of the Christian Socials, began telling the peasants that the government was seizing grain and livestock to feed hundreds of thousands of idle Jews in Vienna, and that Jewish profiteers and Jewish Socialists bore responsibility for retaining war regulations regarding food.

In its first postwar election manifesto, issued on Christmas Eve in 1918, the Christian Social party stated that, "The corruption and lust for power which Jewish circles are manifesting in the new state compels the Christian Social party to call on the Austrian people to defend themselves as strenuously as possible against the Jewish peril. Recognized as a separate nation, the Jews shall be granted self-determination. But they shall never be masters of the German people."

Harsh as such a statement may seem, it appears almost mild alongside some of the individual pronouncements by the Party's leading dignitaries. A week earlier Kunschak had told a party conference that when it came to the Jews "nothing is being talked about more in recent years than the decisive hour in which the reckoning will begin. The Jews know that when the people are ready for this reckoning, it will be a judgment that will make them shudder." Richard Kralik, one of the Party's foremost writers, submitted a proposed text for the new Republic's national anthem. For the old anthem's words, "God protect and God preserve our emperor from harm," Kralik substituted the following: "God protect, God preserve our land from the Jews."

Violent words from on high were being matched by actual violence below. Groups of anti-Semites began staging sporadic riots on the streets of Vienna, giving the city's Jewish residents a taste of Russian- and Polish-style pogroms. The rioters seized and beat everyone who looked Jewish, sometimes stopping and searching trolleys in their hunt for suitable victims. Inevitably, mistakes occurred. In one instance they grabbed and beat an elderly Catholic priest whose long white beard not only gave him a rabbinical look but concealed his clerical collar. But on the same trolley a Jewish couple who did not look particularly Jewish escaped unscathed.

The riots usually erupted on the Franz Joseph Kai which lies in the inner city just across the Danube Canal from the Leopoldstadt. A group of some 150 Leopoldstadt war veterans hastily organized themselves into a Jewish defense force and were sworn in as auxiliary policemen. With the help of the regular police they succeeded first in containing and then in snuffing out the attacks.

But the calls for violence continued. As the February 1919 elections approached, anti-Semitic brochures were distributed before churches and coffee houses. The leaflets labeled the Jews the "refuse of humanity," and claimed that where Jews were concerned, God had canceled his fifth commandment, "Thou shalt not kill." Pogroms against them could and should be carried out with the "Joy of God." The Christian Social party did not, at least officially, sign or sanction such inflammatory material, confining its election campaign position largely to a call for a quota system within a generalized framework of political and economic segregation.

The Austrian-Israelite Union, the fighting arm of the integrationists, blamed the Christian Socials for whipping up such hate and called on their co-religionists to give their answer "with a ballot in the hand." The Jews responded by voting heavily for the Social Democrats, thereby giving the Party its narrow edge over the Christian Socials in the national elections.

While the semi-victory of the Social Democrats and the installation of a coalition government that they dominated checked some of the more outrageous anti-Semitic agitation, the wave of hostility continued. During 1919 it centered largely on the *Ostjuden* refugees, and on this issue the Social Democrats offered little help. When at the beginning of the year a Christian Social deputy submitted a resolution designed to crack down on the refugees, a Social Democratic deputy submitted an amendment to make his proposal more severe. Two months later, when a Pan-German demanded that all war refugees be stripped of their ration cards and prevented from doing business, the Social Democrats combined with the Christian Socials to draw up a somewhat less drastic series of measures to restrict the rights of the refugees. The Social Democratic newspaper *Arbeiter Zeitung*, in reporting this development, added rather sheepishly, "It would be nicer to be hospitable but naked self-preservation compels us to be otherwise."

Two days later a deputation from the newly organized Union of Eastern Jews called on Prime Minister Renner to protest. Renner glibly assured them that such measures were directed only against the Bolsheviks.

The Social Democratic press frequently launched its own attacks on the *Ostjuden*, demanding on several occasions expulsion for those engaged in illegal or unethical activities. (Some refugees, to be sure, were involved in such activities, but given their widespread poverty, their lack of German, and their lack of contacts in or even knowledge of the city, it is impossible to imagine that their numbers could have been very substantial, although highly visible. Many *Ostjuden*, however, conducted illegal business amongst themselves and many others tried to eke out a living by peddling without proper licenses. In May, the Social Democratic militia, the *Volkswehr*, joined with the city's police in raiding coffee houses frequented by *Ostjuden* and, to the delight of passersby, dragging them off to headquarters for interrogation. Most, however, were subsequently released.

On September 10, the Social Democratic governor of Lower Austria which included Vienna called for the removal of "all those not native to German Austria." He set September 20 as the deadline. When the day came, the police rounded up some of the refugees and hustled them off to the railroad station. But no trains were there to transport them, and, even if trains had been available, no coal was there for fuel. Three days later the provincial government admitted that it could not implement its order.

The failure to carry out the expulsion incensed the Pan-Germans especially, and on September 25 they held a mass rally in front of city hall. Fired-up speakers exhorted the crowd to equip themselves with sticks and staffs to drive the Jews out of the city. They set October 5 as the date for the next meeting, calling it the "day of reckoning."

But now for the first, and what would be the last, time, the Social Democrats came to the support of the Jews. Embarrassed over their provincial governor's fiasco and aware that the planned outrages could cut off American assistance currently being received by Austria, the Social Democrats called a rally of their own two days later. Using the quite spurious but reasonably effective excuse that the Pan-Germans were monarchists who were stirring up *Judenhetze* in order to restore the Habsburgs (actually the Jews with their memories of Franz Joseph were much more pro-monarchist than the Pan-Germans), the Social Democrats threatened counter-demonstrations. To their credit, they also deplored the call for Russian-style pogroms, calling such efforts a "cultural scandal" for German Austria.

The move emboldened two influential, Jewish-owned newspapers, the *Neue Freie Presse* and the *Abend*, to take a stand as well. The following day both papers pointed out that while some *Ostjuden* were black marketeers, most of them were desperately poor, while Austria itself was too poor to deport them. The *Presse* also warned that an outbreak of violence against them could jeopardize the American aid that the country would need to survive the coming winter.

Confronted with such resistance from the country's governing party and Vienna's major newspapers, the Pan-Germans backed down. They held their rally as scheduled but did not call for physical violence against the Jews. The Social Democrats then refrained from organizing counter-demonstrations of their own.

The Christian Socials had not officially participated in the Pan-German rallies but their spokesmen equaled and at times exceeded the Pan-Germans in anti-Semitic zeal. Chief among them was the Party labor leader Kunschak who called for the internment and deportation of all *Ostjuden* to the East. Some months later when anti-Semitic students at the University of Vienna raided the Jewish cafeteria and beat up the students, Kunschak called the incident "an outburst from the soul of an oppressed people," and he added, "we can now give the Jews a choice: either leave voluntarily or be put into concentration camps."

Conditions at the University were so serious that two years earlier Albert Einstein had initially rejected an invitation to lecture in Vienna. Professor Felix Ehrenhaft, a friend and admirer of Einstein, had urged him to come but Einstein declined, saying, "In view of the special situation in the Viennese academic world which has so spectacularly come to light in recent days, I do not think it advisable to give a lecture in Vienna in the foreseeable future." Ehrenhaft had persisted, saying that all the agitation was coming from the Germans attending the University, not the Austrian students. Although this argument would seem dubious indeed since Einstein was then experiencing no trouble lecturing regularly to the German students in Berlin, still the scientist finally agreed to give a talk at the *Konzerthaus* in October. Fortunately the hall lay outside the University and the police could act. They stationed a double cordon of uniformed policemen around the building several hours before the lecture, and allowed no one without a special invitation to enter.

The lecture itself went off smoothly and successfully. As one local professor said afterwards, "The Viennese like Einstein for they love a relative point of view." But the German ambassador sent back a report saying, "The official Austrian position towards Einstein is very reserved, since he is a Jew and is oriented towards the left. Neither the educational minister nor the rector of the University attended the lecture."

Outside Vienna anti-Semitic sentiment also raged. In September 1919 the provincial legislature of Upper Austria banned stays of "outsiders" for more than three days. (The legislators acted on a petition from a group of Salzburg housewives who claimed that such outsiders were aggravating the food shortage.) Two months later the Tyrolean legislature took similar action. It also banned kosher slaughtering, thereby forcing the province's few hundred Jews, most of whom lived in Innsbruck, to import their meat from Linz. In southern Austria, Jewish soldiers returning from Italian prisoner of war camps were occasionally roughed up as they tramped through rural villages on their way home.

Many Austrian resort communities began barring Jewish vacationers. The mayor of Maria Tafel issued the following proclamation on July 27, 1920:

> It has been repeatedly observed that Jews are finding lodgings and meals in Maria Tafel. Owners of hotels, coffee houses, and inns are requested not to cater to Jews. . . . Maria Tafel is the most famous health resort in Lower Austria and not a Jewish temple.

Another resort community, Erfinding, decreed that no Jew could stay in the town for more than twenty-four hours. In 1921 the German-Austrian Mountain Club, acting at the repeated urging of its Austrian branches, adopted the Aryan paragraph.

As these developments indicate, the agitation against the *Ostjuden* did not spell any diminution in the drive against all Jews. As national elections loomed again in the fall of 1920, the Christian Socials (to say nothing of the Pan-Germans) sought to lump the *Ostjuden* with Jews and Social Democrats into one perilous package. On September 22, a few weeks before the balloting, the *Reichspost* blazoned forth with a headline saying "Out with the Ostjuden — No Votes for the Jewish-Led Social Democrats — No Votes for a Party List Which Has a Jewish Candidate — German People Awake and Fulfill Your Holy Duty." In the supporting story the paper gave grossly falsified statistics on the number of Jews in Vienna both before and after the war, putting the prewar figure at 300,000 and saying that it "has assuredly more than doubled" with the influx of refugees. It then went on to blame the Jews for all the problems, both material and moral, besetting the country, and charged the allegedly Jewish-dominated Social Democrats with wanting "to create out of German-Austria a new Palestine, a land where their people, the Jewish people, rule and govern."

Christian Social party election posters adopted a similar tone. One showed a snake strangling the Austrian eagle. The serpent had a grotesquely humanized head which featured a long, hooked nose and was covered by a yarmulke.

The Christian Social/Pan-German government which the election produced took office two months after the peace treaty went into effect. One of its first moves was an all-out attempt to prevent the *Ostjuden* from obtaining Austrian citizenship. To do so the government decided to link nationality with language. Since most *Ostjuden* spoke Yiddish as their mother tongue, they could then be denied Austrian citizenship. The country's administrative court upheld this ruling, but the constitutional court struck it down.

Many young *Ostjuden* had begun to attend the University of Vienna and their presence prompted the University's rector in 1922 to express fears that the University was becoming "levantized." He publicly called for a quota system to halt this dangerous trend. The Vienna Technical Institute went still further, saying that henceforth it would admit Jews only in proportion to their numbers in the population.

On December 22 a delegation from the *Gemeinde* called on Seipel to protest these measures and the mounting violence against Jewish students generally. Seipel quickly assured them that no political party wanted to destroy "our country's reputation as a state of tranquility and order." The quotas never took effect – they probably would have been unconstitutional in any case – but the violence continued. After a series of student riots at the Vienna Institute of Commerce and World Trade (*Hochschule für Welthandel*) in 1923, the police confiscated some highly inflammatory anti-Semitic posters and other materials. (The Institute did not enjoy the University's immunity from police intervention.)

Preparations for the first postwar census brought a new government effort to isolate the Jews. The Interior Minister decided to include the question of race on the census form with the intent of designating Jews as a race separate from German Austrians. The Jews, however, took the issue to court to demand a clear definition of race. Basing a decision on precedents, the judges more or less said that a person belonged to the race that he believed himself to belong to. Liberal newspapers added to the Minister's frustrations by telling their readers to write simply "White" in the prescribed place on the census form. Anti-Semites, especially German nationals, grumbled that the incident proved how "Judaized" the press had become, and how cowardly the Jews themselves had become since they feared to admit their racial origins.

But such setbacks at the official level failed to curb anti-Semitism at lower levels. The beginning of 1923 brought a series of rallies and demonstrations. At one, a speaker claimed that Jews owned seventy-five percent of all apartment houses in Vienna and that every Viennese surrendered three-quarters of his earnings to Jewish bankers. At another, a speaker from Germany told his women listeners that whenever they see a German maiden with a Jew they should give the girl a hard box on the ears. The speaker was a schoolteacher named Julius Streicher who, in his own city of Nuremberg, was already actively supporting the activities of another Austrian anti-Semite, Adolf Hitler.

As the anti-Semitic fervor of the immediate postwar period continued into the 1920s, it became increasingly apparent that the Social Democrats would not, and indeed could not, mount an effective defense against it. The Party was plagued not only by the number of Jews in its own upper echelons, but also by the abundance of anti-Semites within its rank and file. After their election losses in the fall of 1920, the Social Democrats began resorting to a tactic they had previously used and never fully abandoned. Instead of trying to counter anti-Semitism, they sought to capitalize on it.

To begin with, they derided the Christian Socials for the number of converted Jews — many of them actually half Jews — within that party's own ranks. In March 31, 1921 the *Arbeiter Zeitung* spoke sneeringly of a Frau Dr. Maresch who worked in the Department of Education and who was born in Galicia. "A few drops of holy water and out of the Polish Jewess emerges a Christian Social leader," scoffed the paper. Seven months later the newspaper taunted the Party's Finance Minister Viktor Kienböck for having earlier, as a private attorney, defended a wealthy Galician Jew in a civil case. Said the paper, "Isn't it a fact, Herr Kienböck, that the money of the *Ostjuden* doesn't stink; only the *Ostjuden* stink?"

When Seipel the following year announced his new pro-business policy aimed at encouraging economic growth, the Social Democrats responded by trying to link the Christian Socials with Jewish capitalism. In the parliamentary debate on the new policy, Karl Seitz, who held a parliamentary seat in addition to being mayor of Vienna, claimed that Seipel had undergone his "conversion" to laissez-faire liberalism "with the help of the Jew press." In making this observation, Seitz adopted a pronounced Jewish accent modeled after the one Austrians used in telling anti-Semitic jokes.

On September 17, in a story headlined "The Zionists for Seipel," the *Arbeiter Zeitung* claimed that the Christian Social/Greater German Government had become "the executive organ of the bank Jews." In a subsequent edition the paper referred to the "Jewish plutocracy" as "protecting and directing" Seipel. Caricatures of capitalists in the Social Democratic press invariably sported long, hooked noses.

As new parliamentary elections approached in the fall of 1923, the Social Democrats stepped up this line of attack. Their publishing house issued a small book entitled *The Jewish Swindle* which trotted out nearly every anti-Semitic cliche available in railing against the Jewish capitalists, especially bankers, who were allegedly benefiting from Seipel's currency reforms. (Seipel was by now moving vigorously against the hyper-inflation.) The book labeled the Christian Social and German Nationalist parties as "the bodyguards of Jewish capitalism."

The Social Democratic press also took to mocking religious Jews, caricaturing not just their beliefs but also their appearance and dress. On at least one occasion it tried to link them with Jewish capitalism. This occurred during the summer of 1923 when *Agudas Israel* held its International Congress in Vienna and Seipel sent the delegates a perfunctory message of welcome.

Arbeiter-Zeitung published a cartoon showing a group of bearded, black-clothed Jews in Seipel's outer office. In the caption, the delegation leader says to an official, "We want to thank the Federal Chancellor for his friendly greetings to our *Ostjuden* organization *Agudas Israel* which was not even greeted by the West European Jews." The official then replies, "Don't mention it. The Chancellor has instructed me to thank you for supporting so generously our Christian election fund."

The cartoon's message was, of course, a travesty. Although many Jewish industrialists were contributing to the Christian Social party, largely through paying dues to various business organizations which themselves contributed to the Party, hardly any of these Jewish businessmen were members of *Agudas Israel.*

As the election day drew closer, the Social Democrats sought to make increasing use of Jew-baiting to further their electoral fortunes. Though their election posters were ostensibly directed only against Jewish capitalist and/or religious Jews, they rivaled those of the other parties in viciousness. Nevertheless the election saw the Party lose further ground to the Christian Socials, who won a near majority of the seats. One can argue that the anti-Semitism of the Social Democrats backfired and cost them votes. Unfortunately one can also argue, and perhaps with more plausibility, that had they not adopted such an approach, then, given the tenor of the times, they would have suffered even greater losses than they did.

Chapter 15

New Developments, Old Divisions

As in fin-de-siécle Vienna, so in postwar Vienna rampant Jew-baiting erected no unbreachable barriers to Jewish achievement. Ludwig von Mises founded an internationally known economics institute while Paul Lazarsfeld created the world's first market research organization. Arthur Schnitzler continued to write plays and stories, including his best-known play, *Reigen*; Stefan Zweig became Austria's most popular and most widely translated author. In the music world, although Fritz Kreisler had left Vienna for New York, where he was becoming the most acclaimed violinist of his time, other Jewish musicians and composers such as Oscar Strauss and George Fuld continued to pursue successful careers in Vienna. The same was true of Jewish theater producers, directors, and actors. Moreover all the editors of Vienna's leading daily newspapers, with the exception of the *Reichspost*, were Jewish, although most of them had long ceased to consider themselves as such.

In sports Fred Oberländer won the Austrian heavyweight wrestling championship while Willi Kurtz was showing the promise that would make him Austria's heavyweight boxing champion. Hakoah's soccer team was doing well while its field hockey team had won the championship of greater Vienna. Even the Republic's ragtag army provided a Jewish success story. When Austria encountered some opposition from Hungary in occupying sections of the Burgenland, Colonel Emil Sommer, who had remained in the army and who was stationed in Burgenland at the time, led his troops in a well-planned, well-executed maneuver which quickly drove the larger Hungarian forces out. Overnight, he became Austria's first postwar military hero.

The Jewish community itself was also flourishing as the influx of *Ostjuden* infused a new vitality into Jewish life. A private Jewish junior high and high school came into existence as did a Jewish daily newspaper. The works of Sholem Aleichem were translated into German; the Jewish museum had many visitors; and the Yiddish theater often played to packed houses. In 1919 Vienna boasted 120 Jewish organizations, about half of them devoted to charitable purposes. Among them was an association to provide clothes and other assistance to older men of the Jewish faith, another for assisting poor Talmud students, and another to help Jews left behind in Galicia.

As might be expected, Vienna's Orthodox community benefited especially from the presence of the *Ostjuden*. Soon the *Schiffschul* was operating a variety of institutions, including an orphanage and a weekly newspaper, *Judische Presse*. Money for such activities came largely from the *Schiffschul*'s thriving kosher food service since it still received no financial support from the *Gemeinde*. The local chapter of *Agudas Israel* was also flourishing, and in 1919 founded a youth association. Highly integrationist Vienna was becoming something of a center for Jewish Orthodoxy.

The immigration from the East also proved a boom for the city's Zionists since many of the less stringently Orthodox among the new arrivals strongly sympathized with the Zionist movement. But two other factors had also favored the Zionist cause: the Balfour Declaration in Britain and the appointment of Zvi Peretz ben Solomon Chajes as Vienna's chief rabbi.

Chajes' appointment surprised many since he was a Zionist, a Galician, and also a bachelor. (Unmarried rabbis, except when they are very young or very old, are almost unknown.) What, then, prompted the integrationist-dominated *Gemeinde* Board to choose him?

As to his bachelorhood, Chajes suffered from a congenital heart condition and had refrained from marrying for fear of passing it along to his children. Although he was born in Galicia he had been highly educated and spoke perfect German plus several other languages as well. He also acquired renown as a rabbinical scholar. While Chajes was still a student one of his teachers had said, "If, God forbid, the Talmud should be lost and Chajes' memory remained, everything could be reconstructed from that." He had gone on to become a professor at the University of Florence, and from there to become chief rabbi of Trieste. Such a record apparently sufficed to overcome his *ostjüdische* origins.

The biggest objection to Chajes would seem to have been his Zionism but here more than one factor may have been at work in causing the Board to overlook it. Many non-Orthodox rabbis had now become Zionists: finding a non-Zionist rabbi of any stature willing and able to come to war-torn Vienna in 1918 could not have been easy. Probably the main reason for Chajes' selection was the recommendation of his predecessor, Rabbi Güdemann, before his death. Professor Ben Shimron speculates that Güdemann may have felt remorse for having first encouraged and then turned his back on Herzl, and sought on his deathbed to make amends.

The new strength of both the Orthodox community and the Zionists was revealed in the *Gemeinde*'s first postwar election in 1920. The Orthodox, entering the election for the first time, won three seats on the thirty-six-member board of directors. The Zionists won thirteen seats, and one of their leaders, Attorney Desider Friedmann, became the *Gemeinde*'s vice president. But the increased support which both groups had demonstrated only exacerbated the rifts within the Jewish community. This was especially true of the surging Zionists who were becoming increasingly committed not just to fostering Jewish nationalism abroad but in Austria as well.

The leader and gadfly of this postwar nationalist movement was, predictably, Robert Stricker. In September 1918, with the war still raging, Stricker twice called on the country's prime minister to seek recognition of the Jews as a separate nation within the Empire. He asked for a state secretary for Jewish affairs, a separate Jewish school system, a separate Jewish *Curia* or voting list for Parliament, and for provincial legislatures and municipal councils. His requests were rejected. Stricker had no mandate to speak for the Jewish community, and in any case the whole issue was too difficult to deal with, especially at a time when the Empire was fighting for its very survival.

On October 1, 1918, with peace in the offing, Emperor Karl granted an audience to Rabbi Chajes. The rabbi did not go so far as Stricker, but he did ask the young monarch to regard the Jews as constituting a nation as well as a religion. He further urged his sovereign's support for Zionism, saying that on the international level the Zionists could prove helpful to Austria. The *Gemeinde*'s board of directors, still dominated by the integrationists, was greatly upset with Chajes for this intitiative and censured him for undertaking it. The Board's action, in turn, enraged the Zionists, especially the younger ones, who staged a noisy demonstration on the rabbi's behalf before the *Gemeinde*'s administration building.

On November 4, with the war virtually over, Stricker and forty-nine of his followers announced the creation of the Jewish National Council, and in what seems like a rather startling exhibition of Jewish *chutzpa*, they proclaimed the Council (which consisted solely of themselves) as the representative body for the Jews of German Austria. Within three months they had founded Vienna's first Jewish daily in the German language, *Wiener Morgenzeitung*, and put up three candidates for the upcoming parliamentary elections.

The integrationists sought to counter the nationalists by asserting their own identification with and loyalty to Austria. The nationalists, in forming their council, had made a similar pledge, but this action by the integrationists put them on the defensive. As the election approached, the integrationists confidently predicted that "the representatives of the Jewish National Council will be rejected by the overwhelming majority of the Jews."

The prediction proved essentially correct. In the February elections the nationalists won 7,760 votes out of well over 100,000 Jewish ballots cast. Only one of their candidates, Stricker himself, won a parliamentary seat. In the Vienna municipal elections the following May, they won three of 160 council seats, indicating that only one out of five Jews had voted for their slate.

Stricker took his place in Parliament as the only Jew in that body to expressly designate himself as such. In fact he began his first parliamentary speech by saying "I am a Jew." The occasion was the vote on whether to join Austria with Germany. In delivering the sole speech, and casting the sole vote, against this popular proposal, he warned of the dangers of German militarism which, he maintained, still constituted a power in Germany and a threat to Austria. The Jewish Social Democrats present in the chamber would live to rue their refusal to heed his words.

Stricker delivered his second speech when a bill came up that would give unused agricultural property to "capable" German Austrians. Commented Stricker, "You have always cast slurs upon the Jews for living by trade and usury, but now you want to enact a law that would prevent them from farming." Pointing out that six hundred Jewish war veterans were working on rural estates in lower Austria, he castigated the members for their two-faced attitude that would prevent these veterans from applying for the property that the bill would make available.

Stricker's persistent and strident championship of Jewish interests, and his bold defiance of the anti-Semitic majority, frequently made the Jewish Social Democrats present squirm in discomfort. Once he began a speech with, "*Meine Herren-Antisemiten* (Gentlemen Anti-Semites)." He also annoyed the integrationists outside Parliament, especially when he voted for the Christian Social motion to list the Jews as a nationality on the census form. Such a move, said the union, "would provide the basis for depriving the Jews of equal rights, and for creating special laws against them." It called Stricker's approach "anti-Semitism turned inside out."

Though a lonely, and somewhat quixotic figure in the Republic's first legislative body, Stricker was not totally ineffective. He challenged both the anti-Semites and the assimilationists by showing them that here was one Jew who was not ashamed to admit and even to assert his Jewishness. On one occasion Stricker actually defeated the coalition government. It had proposed a tax on horse racing which Stricker opposed, saying that no government should derive income from immoral sources. He proposed instead a motion banning all betting on racing and his motion carried by eight votes.

But Stricker's parliamentary career did not last long. Vienna's Social Democratic administration found a way to remove a heavily Jewish district from his constituency, while the national government enacted a new bill designed to make it more difficult for splinter groups to win parliamentary seats. (This municipal gerrymandering was almost certainly designed to get rid of Stricker.) Although he and his fellow nationalists almost doubled their vote in the 1921 election, obtaining 13,358 ballots, all of them were defeated. On election night Stricker cheered up his glum-faced supporters, most of them young, by telling them that they had upheld Jewish honor. "The day will not be far off," he added, "when the Jews will have to pay the bill in Austria in spite of their servitude to the national parties."

In 1923 the nationalists again entered the election list. This time they formed a "Jewish Election Association" which, among other things, distributed throughout the Jewish community a brochure showing four Social Democratic election posters with anti-Semitic connotations. The Association called on all Jews not to support the party that had printed them.

This move helped lower the Social Democratic vote while once again nearly doubling the nationalist vote, this time to over 25,000. But this was still not enough to elect a candidate under the new election law. Henceforth the Party declined, gaining only 10,717 votes in 1927 and dipping to 2,135 in 1930. After that it disappeared. Nevertheless the 25,000 votes the Party received in 1923 helped deprive the Social Democrats of their plurality. As a result, the Social Democrats would never again publish or publicize anti-Semitic campaign materials, although the Party's basic strategy of attacking Jewish capitalists and trying to link them with the two other parties would remain unchanged.

According to historian Jonny Moser, the Jewish National Council and the party it created failed to see that "German Austria was no longer one national entity among others, but was itself now a national state." As such there could be no real place for Jews unless they could identify themselves, and be identified, as German Austrians. The Strickerites were also not clear, says Moser, as to just how much recognition they wanted the Jews to have. Sometimes they requested merely simple recognition as a nation and at other times demanded full-scale autonomy. The dilemma that the Jews had confronted in the old Empire, that of being perceived by many as a separate nationality but one without a fixed territory, continued and indeed became magnified in the new Austro-German Republic.

This dilemma would be poignantly dramatized in a play written by Franz Theodor Csokor at the end of the 1920s. Entitled *3rd November 1918*, it depicts a colonel in the old imperial army who dies heartbroken at the end of the war as he watches the breakup of his multinational regiment. At his funeral a representative of each nationality in the regiment in turn throws a shovel of earth over his coffin, saying "Earth from Hungary," "Earth from Poland," "Earth from Slovenia," etc. When the turn of the regiment's Jewish doctor comes, he balks but finally accepts a shovel of earth. Then with great uneasiness and hesitation he says, "Earth from — earth from — earth from Austria."

The postwar wave of anti-Semitism reached its height during the winter of 1923. By early March rallies and demonstrations against the Jews were becoming an almost daily occurrence. The persistent agitation finally forced the fragmented Jewish community to unite. On March 3, Jews of all orientations turned out for a mass rally in front of city hall to protest the campaign of hate against them. Twelve days later leaders of various Jewish organizations held a press conference where, speaking with one voice for the first time, they vowed to take action against any further outbreaks. "These strong words seem to have made an impression on the anti-Semites," says Moser, "for anti-Semitic activity immediately began to subside."

The unity displayed on this occasion did not last. The feuds, especially the basic one between nationalists and integrationists, would soon reassert themselves. Nor did anti-Semitism in any way die out. As we have seen, all major parties, including the Social Democrats, made use of anti-Semitic materials in the fall election campaign. But the rallies and demonstrations which at times threatened to turn into mass pogroms became far less frequent.

A key factor in the gradually improving atmosphere was the change in the Christian Social party. Under Seipel it had become an essentially pro-business party dependent on campaign contributions from business groups, especially the Austrian Industrialists' Association. But the Jewish members of the Association had begun expressing annoyance over the vicious attacks and threatened to stop paying their dues. This, in itself, helped induce the Party to moderate its more extreme expressions of hate.

The responsibilities of governance had also tempered the Christian Socials' attitude. This was especially true regarding the international situation, for Austria depended heavily on foreign favor, and no other western nation, including Germany, was prepared to sanction and support policies that could lead to physical violence against Jews.

Another favorable factor was the fading away of the *Ostjuden* problem. Many of them had by now returned home; others had immigrated abroad. Those who remained in Vienna had, for the most part, established themselves in a legitimate line of work. The census of 1923 put Vienna's Jewish population at 201,500, less than 30,000 above its prewar figure. This put a damper on claims that the city was flooded with *Ostjuden*.

The Austrian economy was also starting to revive. Although unemployment was still high, and would remain high all through the inter-war period, it had gone down, while the hyper-inflation of the immediate postwar years had ended. Seipel's policies, a loan from the League of Nations, and the improved world economic situation generally were having a beneficial effect.

Life in Vienna was also recapturing some of its prewar gaiety. Dancing classes filled up as the Viennese abandoned the waltz for the Charleston. Bridge had also become the rage, at least among the middle class. Not only did the theater flourish but the city now became a center for motion picture production. By 1930 its studios would be grinding out over one hundred feature films a year, some of them large-scale spectaculars.

If 1924 was Vienna's best postwar year, then this was especially true for the Jews. With the city's economy partially revived and anti-Semitism apparently in abeyance, Max Reinhardt, considered the most exciting stage director of his time, returned from Germany to assume direction of one of Vienna's foremost theaters. In the new movie industry such promising directors as Eric von Stroheim, Josef von Sternberg, Fred Zimmerman, and Billy Wilder were launching their careers. Most would eventually go on to Germany, and from there to America, but not before they had helped Vienna establish a name and position for itself within their rapidly growing industry.

Karl Kraus, whose one-man journal *The Torch* had been stimulating intellectual Vienna since the turn of the century, now became something of a theatrical personality as well. His frequent readings at various halls drew packed houses. Kraus often read from his unproduced, and unproducible, 1800-page play, *The Last Days of Mankind*. As he railed against the corruption and mediocrity of the times, his largely Jewish audience responded with frequent, and feverish, applause. Even Elias Canetti, later a Nobel Laureate in literature but then a skeptical chemistry student, became one of his fans and attended over one hundred of Kraus' performances.

In sports, Hakoah's soccer team had gradually played and won its way to the top division. It had not been an easy ascent, for to move up a team had to finish first or second in its own division. (The bottom two teams of each division dropped to the next lowest division.) But by the early twenties the ascent had been completed.

The team had become vitally important to the Vienna Jews for, probably more than any of the community's other 120 organizations, Hakoah provided a unifying force. Both integrationists and Zionists turned out in droves to cheer the team on. Writes Edmund Schechter, "The idea that Jews could produce not only people with brain power but also strong and agile sports skills — and particularly in the most popular sport — was terribly exciting. Each Hakoah victory became another proof that the period of Jewish inferiority in physical activities had finally come to an end."

Although Jew-baiting had become a common side sport at Hakoah matches, the team occasionally created friendly feelings within the Gentile community. When Hakoah managed to defeat Prague's foremost team in a 6-to-5 game, all Vienna felt a measure of pride that a local team had beaten the Czechs.

On another occasion when Hakoah was playing a local team called Brigittenauer AC, the members of a third team, Vorwaerts 06, showed up to root for Hakoah. For if Hakoah won, Vorwaerts would retain its place in the first division and Brigittenauer would have to move down. When, in the final minutes of a 0-to-0 game, Hakoah forward Norbert Katz kicked in the winning goal, the Vorwaerts' spectators burst into frantic cheers, and, not knowing Katz's name, shouted lustily, "Hurray for Mr. Jew."

In the 1924-1925 season Hakoah culminated its fifteen-year march to the heights by winning the Austrian national championship. The sweetness of the victory was enhanced by its drama, for it came in the last minutes of the final game when a Hakoah forward playing with his arm in a sling — he had injured it earlier in the game and under the rules could not be replaced — kicked in the winning goal. The triumph brought all-night celebrations in Vienna's Jewish districts.

Yes, 1924 was a very good year for the Vienna Jews. They would never have such a good one again.*

---

*Hakoah toured the U.S. the following year and many of its best players decided to stay there. As a result Hakoah never won another national championship, although it remained a first division team.

Chapter 16

Summer Storms

Shortly after 1900, a group of German workers living in the Sudetenland, a section of northern Czechoslovakia bordering Germany, formed the German Workers party. Many were skilled craftsmen or railroad employees who hoped to ward off competition from Czechs who would work for lower wages. But despite the many Germans living in the area, the Party fared poorly at the outset. Then in 1908, a smooth-talking, politically astute lawyer named Walter Riehl joined the party ranks, and under his guidance the three deputies were elected to Parliament in 1911.

With the breakup of the Empire after World War I, many of these Sudeten Germans emigrated to Austria with 22,000 coming to Linz alone. Riehl moved to Vienna where he sought to keep the Party alive. Re-christened as the German National Socialist Workers party, it espoused socialism, unification with Germany and, above all, anti-Semitism. Its newspaper cited *Judenherrschaft* (Jewish domination) as Austria's number one evil.

The jovial, convivial Riehl became its leader, and in rather typical Viennese fashion did not allow the Party's, and his own, anti-Semitism to prevent him from freely mixing with Jews on a social basis. Meanwhile, the Party's chief theoretician, a young railroad engineer named Richard Jung, moved to Munich to set up the Party's counterpart in Germany. Board member number seven of the National Socialist Workers party of Germany was Adolf Hitler.

The Austrian National Socialists got off to a slow start. In the country's first elections in February 1919, they received only 28,000 votes, less than one percent of the total. Still, the Austrian party initially grew faster than its German offshoot. It won 34,000 votes in October 1920, and in the following three years its membership tripled. In March 1923, it won four seats on the Linz city council and in the following year it obtained sixty district council seats in the province of Styria in southern Austria.

At the outset, relations between the Austrian and German Nazis were quite cordial. Both parties adopted the hooked cross or swastika as their symbol and exchanged speakers. Hitler addressed the Austrian party conference in Salzburg in 1920 and returned the following year to speak to the party faithful in several cities. In 1922 he was the main speaker at the Party's first major public rally in Vienna. Riehl and Hitler wrote articles for each other's newspapers, exchanged letters, and addressed each other with the informal, friendly *du*.

By 1923, however, the Germans had begun to look upon their Austrian colleagues as poor relations, for the German party had now outstripped the Austrian one in local stature as well as size. Hitler had stopped answering many of Riehl's letters, and the German party contributed nothing to the interstate bureau that Riehl had established in Vienna.

The deteriorating relationship reached a critical point at the Austrian party's annual conference in Salzburg in August 1924. Four years earlier Austria's Pan-Germans, formerly split into several groups, had come together to create the Greater German People's party. Now, with elections approaching, the Greater Germans offered to form a unity slate with the Nazis. Riehl wanted to accept, believing that it offered Austria's Nazis their only chance to enter Parliament at that time. But at the party conference, Hitler strongly spoke out against the idea, calling for the Austrian party to prepare for armed revolution instead.

The leadership council supported Hitler 7-to-1. Riehl, who cast the sole dissenting vote, felt compelled to resign his party chairmanship though he remained a party member.

A few months later Hitler staged his attempt to take over the Bavarian government. That he failed miserably and ended up in jail did not appreciably diminish the respect and allegiance that the Austrian Nazis had earlier shown him. Karl Schulz, Riehl's successor as head of the Austrian Nazis, quickly organized a rally in Vienna to proclaim the Party's diehard loyalty to Hitler. Austrian Nazis smuggled money and newspapers into Germany and gave refuge to Nazi exiles, including Hermann Göring, who spent the following year in Innsbruck recovering from wounds sustained in the failed Putsch. Although discord and dissent would later erupt between the two parties, Austrian Nazism would increasingly come under the influence of the German movement and its Austrian-born leader.

Through 1924 the Austrian Nazis concentrated on building their party and trying to win elections. But in 1925 they turned to more direct and dramatic action.

Not all of these efforts were initially successful. When they attempted to stage an anti-Semitic demonstration in the Burgenland, a group of local Jewish youths armed with staffs showed up and forced them to disperse. But elsewhere they fared better. In late May over one thousand Nazis and other radical rightists, most of them armed, assembled in a wooded area outside of town called Mödling. They subsequently marched to the town's working-class district where some of the marchers seized, beat, and stabbed a Social Democratic town councillor who later died from his wounds.

Arrested, tried, and convicted, the perpetrators received sentences ranging from six months to two years. But despite the shocking leniency of the punishment, the right-wing press expressed outrage at the sentences, saying "Judah has won a victory" and calling the prosecutor "either a Jew or a Jew vassal."

In Vienna, meanwhile, Nazism took its first Jewish life. The victim was Hugo Bettauer, a middle-aged journalist who had converted to Protestantism while still in his teens. In 1922 Bettauer published a satirical novel called *The City Without Jews.* It portrays a Vienna of the future that decides to expel its Jewish citizens. As a result of such action, the city's economy crumbles and its social life deteriorates. (Viennese girls, for example, pine for their Jewish boyfriends who never got drunk and who showered them with presents.) Eventually the desperate city fathers beg the Jews to return.

In many respects Bettauer's novel seems quite prophetic for he not only forecasts the eventual expulsion of the Jews, but even the Nuremberg Laws which would govern it. In his story half-Jews must leave while one-quarter-Jews can remain. On the other hand he proved far less accurate in depicting how quickly and easily the banished Jews would find havens in other countries. (The novel became an immediate best seller, going through several editions. It was also translated into English and later made into a silent film.)

As might be expected, the novel incensed the anti-Semites. But a magazine Bettauer published riled them even more, for in it he ridiculed many traditional institutions and practices while calling for a host of liberal reforms, including legalized abortion. One prominent German Nationalist schoolteacher called for *Lynchjustiz* (lynch law) to silence the controversial journalist.

In May 1925, a week or two before the march on Mödling, a young man named Otto Rothstock walked into Bettauer's office, took out a gun, and killed him. Although Rothstock had acted on his own initiative, he had been a Nazi party member until a month or two before, and had resigned from the Party, so it seems, only to avoid implicating it in his act. Nazi luminary Riehl quickly took over Rothstock's defense.

In a trial that was almost farcical, Riehl easily persuaded the jury to find the young man innocent by virtue of insanity. The judge then sent the defendant to a mental institution which released him twenty months later when its doctors could find no signs of mental illness.

While the Nazis had not planned the Bettauer murder, they were trying to develop opportunities for anti-Jewish violence. Towards this end they had begun hawking their newspaper in the Leopoldstadt in the hope of creating an incident. In August they got what they had been hoping for.

The incident occurred during a rally staged by the Leopoldstadt Anti-Fascist Committee. The Committee had been put together by the district's socialists and communists in May to protest the Nazi provocations. Two young German Nationalists — seemingly middle-class — attended the rally, and seemed to be making fun of the speakers. The crowd grew hostile and the pair fled, but a few young Jews chased after them. One of the pursuers caught one of the German Nationalists — Josef Mohapel — and fatally stabbed him.

The killer, whose name was Seidl, was not at all politically involved. Rather, he was a young hooligan with a criminal record who was known to be violent and unstable. After killing the young German Nationalist, Seidl turned the knife on himself, but was saved from death by a hastily summoned physician.

The anti-Semitic press, including the *Reichspost*, sought to portray the incident as a Jewish pogrom against Christians, and therefore as another illustration of the "Jewish world conspiracy." Thousands of Viennese, including representatives from virtually every Christian and German National group, attended Mohapel's funeral. The *Reichspost* spoke of the funeral procession as consisting of "Christian German Viennese acting in breast-filled harmony."

Seidl, at his trial, showed little awareness of politics or of anything else: he was sentenced to twelve years of hard labor, the heaviest sentence the Austrian Republic would ever hand down for a political killing.

While the Mohapel incident played into the hands of the National Socialists and all anti-Semites, the Nazis had already set their sights on bigger game. The World Zionist Organization had selected Vienna for its 1925 Congress, and the National Socialists, though still quite small in number, decided to disrupt it.

The Nazis distributed anti-Semitic placards and brochures throughout the city calling for a protest demonstration outside the *Konzerthaus* where the Congress was to assemble. Police banned the demonstration, but the Nazis refused to cancel it. When members of the Congress began arriving at the concert hall, they found some ten thousand demonstrators milling about in the late August sunshine eager for action. Soon the action began.

E.G. Gedye, a British journalist whom the London *Times* had recently sent to Vienna as its correspondent, happened to ride past the scene in a taxi at the time. A few days earlier Gedye had written his first piece on Vienna, extolling the city's warm hospitality, tolerance, and charm. The scene before the *Konzerthaus* jolted him out of this vision as he witnessed "organized jeering mobs in the streets and all kinds of physical violence." The mostly young demonstrators were throwing stones and pulling people out of cars. "I myself had to use physical force to avoid being dragged out of my taxicab by crazy youths who clambered over the back armed with walking sticks, convinced that no one could have any business near the Zionist Congress unless he were a member of the hated race."

The "dignified and imperturbed" Zionist Congress delegates, said Gedye, made the young demonstrators look ridiculous. Nevertheless hundreds of police had to fight to clear a way through the angry mobs to allow the attendees to enter the hall, and when this became almost impossible, they charged the demonstrators on horseback to disperse them. The Congress managed to go on but the clashes injured twenty-two policemen along with thirty-three demonstrators.

How did those attending the Congress react to the incident? Meyer Weisgel, who was covering the Congress for the *Jewish Advocate* of Boston, shrugged it off. In a lengthy story on the Congress' proceedings he left the demonstration to his final paragraph. In it he assured his readers that reports about the violence had been greatly exaggerated, for "the spirit that generally prevails" in Vienna was "one of friendliness and sympathy." The riots, he said, only aroused resentment among "the respectable part of the population."

Yet while the conference was going on, the Bishop of Innsbruck was holding a convention of German and Austrian academics in his city and was warning them of the "Jewish world danger." Mass conversions, said the Bishop, were the only way of removing such a curse.

More ominously, two days after the Congress ended and the delegates had left, the leader of Vienna's Christian Social party issued a statement saying that while "native" Austrians did not oppose the national struggle of the Zionist Jews, they were against the subversive and arrogant influence that the Jews exercised over the country's political, economic, cultural, and moral life. He complimented the Nazis on their "success" but said the fight against this detrimental influence should not be handed over to irresponsible groups. The Christian Social party, he said, was determined to carry on the "defensive" struggle against the Jews. The statement indicates that the Christian Socials feared the Nazis might outdo them in Jew-baiting, and were seeking to reassure Viennese Gentiles that the Party still hated and opposed the Jews.

How did the Viennese Jews themselves react to the riots? Apparently they paid them little heed. Of the many former Viennese Jews interviewed for this book, hardly any had even heard of the disorder. (Of course most of those interviewed were children at that time, and a few had not even been born. Still, one might suppose that they would at some time have heard their parents or other adults mentioning the event. Yet hardly any could recall having done so.) As Ashtor says of this decade, "The fire was smoldering beneath the surface and the Jews felt it; but they were neither ready nor able to draw conclusions."

By the mid-1920s it was becoming apparent that Austria's experiment in democracy was floundering. One problem lay in the constitution that saddled the nation with weak governments prone to disruption and obstruction. There was a president but he was not elected by the people and had no power to act decisively in an emergency. Federalism divided the country into nine semi-autonomous provinces while proportional representation encouraged the growth of minor parties, thereby preventing either of the two major ones from obtaining a clear-cut majority.

But a more destructive element lay in the fundamental nature of the two major parties themselves. In essence, both were religious organizations.

The ideology of the Christian Socials derived from the Catholic Church, and Seipel's leadership had accentuated this relationship. As Seipel's biographer von Klemperer has observed, the prelate-turned-politician on several occasions went out of his way to stress the strong interconnection between the Party's principles and the tenets of Catholicism.

The ideology of the Social Democrats was essentially Marxist. Indeed it was probably the most left-wing Social Democratic party in Western Europe. Some even called the Party the Two-and-a-Half International since it seemed to stand halfway between the Second Socialist International and the Third Communist International.

As noted earlier one reason why the Party had taken this tack was its desire to hold down on the growth of the Communist party. In this it had succeeded admirably, for the Communists would never win a single seat in Parliament. But another reason for its doctrinaire approach lay in the influence of its Jewish intellectuals, especially Otto Bauer.

Although Karl Renner continued to be the Party's nominal leader, Bauer was its most dynamic force. And though not an out-and-out extremist, he believed in a dictatorship of the proletariat, considering it necessary not so much to achieve power but to maintain it against counterrevolutionary forces. While Renner would have entered a government dominated by the Christian Socials, Bauer preferred to stay in opposition and wait for the Social Democrats to win a clear mandate. The fact that the Social Democrats ruled Vienna strengthened Bauer's position, for control of the city gave them many opportunities to wield power and dispense patronage and therefore lessened their incentive to move towards the center in order to build or enter a national government.

Bauer and Seipel had both learned the arts of compromise and conciliation as party leaders but they nevertheless took a sacred view of their respective missions. Consequently, the two major parties confronted each other across a chasm that was both wide and deep. Parliamentary interchanges were marked by a minimum of courtesy and a maximum of acrimony. Personal insults including racial slurs were traded back and forth. The whole setup, says von Klemperer, "emphasized division rather than debate, doctrinaire positions rather than the weighing of concrete issues. Parliament in Austria, then, instead of nursing a basic consensus, as it generally does in western democracies, emphasized the divisions in the country and contributed to the destruction of consensus."*

In late 1926 the parties began drawing up their programs in preparation for national elections the following year. The Social Democrats issued their platform in late November. Reflecting Bauer's influence, plus increasing pressure from the Communists who were drawing strength from Soviet Russia's continued existence, the Party's platform bristled with revolutionary phrases. It went farther than previous platforms had gone, and alarmed not just the right but the center. Six weeks later the Christian Social party responded by embracing a program that emphasized its opposition to Marxism and to the "predominance of the decomposing Jewish influence."

The anti-Jewish clause in the Christian Social program was hardly new or noteworthy. Previous party programs had contained even more elaborate anti-Semitic language. But its presence posed a problem for Seipel. Just a little over a year before, he had advised the Archbishop of Vienna to remove such phrases as "the Jewish financial world" and "the Jewish spirit" from a proposed pastoral letter. Seipel told the Archbishop that such sentiments were already implicit elsewhere in the proposed text for the pastoral letter, and that the Church might best leave "this sort of thing," i.e., explicit Jew-baiting, to the politicians. He had also pointed out that the danger came not from capitalism but from its excesses. The real enemy, said Seipel, lay on the left.

The Archbishop had accepted his suggestions and the pastoral letter went out without an explicit denunciation of the Jews. But now the party that was tied to the Church had adopted a still more outspoken anti-Semitic stance.

Seipel's concern stemmed not just from his distaste for vulgar Jew-baiting. He also was aware of the contributions of Jewish businesses to the only major party that admitted the right of businesses to exist, and he did not want to jeopardize their support. Seipel, in fact, even hoped to attract some Jewish votes in the next election, in a desperate effort to win a clear-cut majority. Finally, he did not want to give the impression abroad that the country's governing party was seeking to persecute the Jews.

---

*On a personal level, however, Seipel got along better with the Jewish quasi-Marxist Bauer than he did with the Catholic, and more moderate, Renner. Seipel himself admitted this and it never ceased to puzzle him.

With all these factors evidently in mind, Seipel granted an interview to the Jewish Telegraphic Agency which then (and now) supplied international news to Jewish periodicals around the world. In the interview he claimed that the anti-Semitic statement in the Christian Social program did not refer to "the influence which the Jews exercised in the intellectual and economic sectors," but merely to their involvement in Marxist movements. The leaders and propagandists of Russian Bolshevism, German and Austrian Communism, and even of radical Austrian Socialism were, he said, "mostly Jews." This alone represented the "decomposing Jewish influence" that the Party had in mind. He admitted that the Christian Socials were known as an anti-Semitic party, but he insisted that he, as its leader, would protect the equal rights of all Austrian citizens regardless of their faith.

To his credit Seipel did not issue his statement for Jewish ears alone. He reiterated his commitment to equal rights in subsequent, public speeches. "For me as federal chancellor and as leader of the unity list, there is no Jewish question," he said on one occasion, and he even called the anti-Semitic clause in his party's program "unwise" (*unklug*).

Seipel had until now shown little friendliness to the incipient Nazi movement. He had refused to allow the Nazis to stage a "German Day" in Salzburg in 1924, fearing that their paramilitary formations would provoke a hostile reaction abroad. When the Bavarian government sought to deport Hitler to Austria following his imprisonment for his abortive coup, Seipel had refused to accept the Nazi leader, saying Hitler had forfeited his Austrian citizenship by serving in the German army in the war. The Chancellor did not want such a troublemaker, who was a lapsed Catholic and a German National to boot, back in Austria.

But confronted with a radical program of the Social Democrats, Seipel decided to mobilize all the non-Marxists for the forthcoming elections, and to this end he invited the Nazis to join his unity list. The Nazi party was at this time split between a youthful wing willing to pledge absolute loyalty to Hitler, and a slightly more moderate wing that, while respectful of and deferential to Hitler, still wished to preserve a small measure of autonomy.

The moderates — the term can only be used in a relative sense — still controlled the party machinery and they gladly joined Seipel's unity list. Riehl in fact wound up running from a district that included the Leopoldstadt, an error that caused a great deal of comment until the embarrassed leaders of the unity list shifted him to a less sensitive district. The Nazi party's other wing ran its own candidates who received a mere 27,000 votes.

Seipel's unity slate was not the success he had hoped. The Greater Germans refused to join it, and although their share of the vote dropped by more than half, they still received six percent of the ballots. Minor electoral groups including the Hitler Loyalists, the Jewish Nationalists, and others received three percent, while the Social Democrats increased their share of the vote from 39.5 to 42 percent. So the Christian Social party's unity list missed gaining an absolute majority by one percent. A government with a clear-cut mandate to govern still eluded the splintered nation.

The elections of 1927 had taken place against a tense background produced by a case that was working its way through the Austrian court system. The case stemmed from a clash between the *Heimwehr* and *Schutzbund* in a village in eastern Austria the previous January. During the clash some *Heimwehr* members had fired their rifles, killing an elderly man and an eight-year-old boy who were standing by. Five *Schutzbund* members were wounded.

The three *Heimwehr* members charged with the crime claimed they acted in self-defense, and on July 15 Austria's final court of appeal reached the same conclusion. But while the *Reichspost* broke out with banner headlines in hailing "A Just Verdict," Social Democratic Vienna boiled over with rage. The following day crowds of protesters, responding in part to an inflammatory editorial in the *Arbeiter Zeitung*, began converging on the Palace of Justice. Vienna's Social Democratic Mayor Seitz mounted a fire engine and tried to halt them, but they pushed him aside. Soon they had set the Palace of Justice on fire.

In their efforts to contain the crowds the police had already suffered many injuries. In desperation they had sent for rifles, and once the rifles arrived they began using them. By the time this first police riot in European history ended, four policemen and eighty demonstrators were dead.

The outraged Social Democrats immediately called a general strike. But Seipel, backed up by the *Heimwehr*, stood firm and the strike fizzled out in a few days. The Chancellor attended the funeral of the policemen but ignored the mass funeral of the demonstrators. On the contrary he vowed to show the guilty no clemency, a pledge that earned him the epithet "the prelate without mercy." During the following months 2700 Viennese Catholics formally left the Church. Bauer exacerbated the situation by accusing the Chancellor of wanting to "fertilize with our dead the vineyards of his party and class."

The ugly uprising, along with the radical Social Democratic platform and the bitter political campaign that preceded it, marked the beginning of the end for Austrian democracy. As Clare puts it, "Before 15 July there was a chance, however slight, that Austria's Left and Right might still find the formula for co-existence. After it there was no hope." Austrian fascism was still a mere speck on the horizon, but the increasing turbulence of the country's politics was bringing it closer all the time.

Chapter 17

Jews in the Late 1920s: The Halsman Case

The further hardening of party lines and divisions following the July 1927 riots brought a step-up of racial references and remarks in parliamentary debate. While the Christian Socials and Greater Germans no longer hinted at pogroms, they rarely passed up an opportunity to sneer at the origins of the Jewish Social Democratic deputies. The latter usually counterattacked in the same vein, singling out for scorn the relatively few Christian Socials who had any Jewish forebears and making sport of those Greater Germans with non-German names. (Many Greater Germans as well as many ardent Nazis had Slavic names.)

A parliamentary session in early December 1928 offers a fairly typical example of such interchanges. A Greater German deputy, irate over an attack on his party by Otto Bauer, replied by saying, "What is this impudent Jew talking about in a German parliament?" Later in the same debate, another Greater German deputy, in responding to another Jewish Social Democrat, retorted, "The Christian Socials have nothing to expect from a Jew from Bukovina." A Gentile Social Democrat then replied, "If the Greater Germans want to repudiate someone they always fall back on the place he comes from." "No," protested the Greater German deputy, "it's not the place but his race that I am referring to." The Social Democrat then answered, "Let us not talk about race or I'll have much to say to you about it. So long as Herr Zarboch or Herr Wotawa sit in the ranks of the Greater Germans, I find it hardly fitting for you to raise the subject of race." The newspaper account reports laughter from the

Social Democratic benches in response to the sally. However, it illustrates all too sadly how the Social Democrats were trying to play a game that they could not hope to win.

Outside of Parliament the *Heimwehr* was becoming a political force in its own right. It had gained increased standing during the tensions of 1927 when the government used it to help squash the General Strike. The following year it acquired still more clout when Mussolini, who to some extent had become Austria's big brother, decided to take the *Heimwehr* under his personal protection and supply it with weapons and money.

In response to Mussolini's influence, which certainly coincided with its own natural tendencies, the *Heimwehr* became more, or at least more openly, fascist. Eventually it adopted an oath that repudiated not only the "liberal capitalistic economy" but parliamentary democracy as well. But unlike Italian fascists at the time, the *Heimwehr* also became increasingly anti-Semitic. As one of its leaders said in the spring of 1929, "The Jews must, on account of their race, be regarded as an alien people and be treated accordingly."

Such manifestations of continuing hostility did little to ease the isolation of the Vienna Jews. They continued to consort largely with each other both in Vienna and in the nearby countryside, where most middle- and upper-class Jews spent much of the summer.

In schools an informal segregation reigned especially in those schools with large Jewish enrollments. Ernst Eppler recalls attending a school in the Leopoldstadt that was over fifty percent Jewish. Students sat mixed in class but during recess split into Jewish and non-Jewish groups. Although not averse to copying from Jewish students, who cheerfully let them do so, the Gentiles had already begun to refer to themselves as Aryans, and to refer to the Jews as a parasitical *Gastvolk* (guest people).

The teachers in Eppler's school did little to deter such developments. Despite the school's high concentration of Jewish pupils, all the teachers except for the Jewish religion teacher and the physical education instructor were Gentiles. Nearly all of them were at least somewhat anti-Semitic, Eppler says, and although many tried to conceal it, others did not. One teacher, for example, dismissed the poet Heine as a "Jew who died of syphilis."

But not all Jewish students were willing to accept derogatory remarks and discriminatory treatment. When one Leopoldstadt teacher persisted in denigrating the Jewish girls in her class and in giving them bad grades, they rebelled by refusing to speak in the classroom. The exasperated teacher eventually complained to the principal who investigated. But faced with the girls' steadfast resolution, he finally decided to transfer the teacher to another school. Thus did a group of thirteen-year-old girls offer a lesson to their Jewish parliamentary leaders who, sadly, would not learn this lesson until too late.

In mid-September 1928 newspapers throughout Austria blossomed forth with headlines such as the following: "Dentist Killed in Tyrol! Son Arrested. The Mother an Accomplice? Insurance Motive Investigated." What some would later call the Austrian Dreyfus Case had begun.

The case concerned the death of Max Halsman, a Lithuanian dentist who had been vacationing with his family in the Tyrol. Both Halsman and his twenty-three-year-old son Phillip, an electrical engineer and amateur photographer, loved mountain climbing. They were ascending a mountain trail when Phillip, who had gone ahead while his father had stopped to relieve himself, noticed that the older man was not following. He retraced his steps to find his father's body lying in a brook at the foot of a slope.

Seeking help, the son ran to a nearby inn where the pair had stopped just before beginning their climb. The police arrived and eventually found evidence showing the dentist had been murdered and robbed. (Two similar murder-robberies had previously occurred in the Tyrol and both had gone unsolved.) The authorities did not reveal this evidence to Phillip who continued to believe that his father, who suffered from dizzy spells, had accidentally fallen to his death.

The police asked a detective inspector from Munich who was vacationing in the area at the time to examine the young man. Although there was much blood on the dentist's body, the detective could find no blood on Phillip, not even under his fingernails. For these and other reasons Bavarian police officials concluded that the young man was innocent. But a few discrepancies had surfaced in the confused son's testimony and local tongues had already started to wag. (Very few Jews lived in the Tyrol, and most of what the inhabitants knew about them came from local anti-Semitic pulpits and press.) So Phillip Halsman was ordered to stand trial for the murder of his father.

The prosecution at first sought to establish money as the motive for the slaying, saying the boy and his mother hoped to benefit from the man's life insurance. This aspect of the case collapsed when the defense discovered that the dentist carried no insurance policy, and that his death had left the family a good deal poorer rather than richer.

Faced with a flimsy case, the prosecution and the public seized on any element they could find to fortify it. For example, the son, when asked about the disposition of his father's remains, said he gave instructions to have the body wrapped in a sheet and committed to the ground. Although this was the standard Orthodox instruction, his answer set off cries of outrage in the press and among the populace. To the Tyroleans, who loved big funerals, the young man had disdained to make even a pretense of filial love. Instead he had merely had the old man "dumped."

Given the atmosphere and attitudes surrounding the proceedings, and given the fact that the defense did not know in advance that the prosecution had uncovered evidence showing the man had been murdered, the jury in December voted 9-to-3 to find young Halsman guilty of second degree murder. Since verdicts only required a two-thirds majority to convict, the court sentenced him to ten years at hard labor. But the case had already aroused much controversy, which was further heightened when a prominent professor of law at the University of Vienna reconstructed it and concluded that the son could not possibly have committed the crime. Acting on a defense appeal, the attorney general sent the case back to Innsbruck for retrial.

The second trial did not start until September, and during that time young Halsman remained behind bars. Meanwhile agitation against him continued. As the new trial was getting under way, mass demonstrations in Innsbruck called upon the judge and jury to, in effect, "throw the book" at the defendant. The prelate of the city's cathedral lent his authority to the cause, pointing out from the pulpit how "the greedy, inhuman son did not even have the moral fibre of Judas who at least repented and did away with himself."

In hopes of establishing a motive, the prosecution had originally asked for an expert opinion from the medical faculty of the University of Innsbruck. The opinion had not been fully satisfactory, for while the medical faculty seemed eager to help, they found it difficult to do so. Several defense witnesses had testified to the young man's good character, and although some disagreements between father and son had surfaced during the trial, they hardly sufficed to justify a murder charge. The judge, in instructing the jury at the end of the first trial, had felt compelled to point out that the fact that no motive had been found did not mean that no motive existed.

As the new trial got under way the prosecution requested a second expert opinion from the Innsbruck medical faculty. In their second opinion these "experts" pointed out that while young Halsman seemed to have high moral principles and a good character, he did display a certain insecurity. They then went on to speculate that an Oedipus complex may have caused him to commit patricide.

Since it was Freud who had developed the concept of the Oedipus complex, one of the defense attorneys (a professor of law at the University of Vienna) asked Freud for his comment. Freud repudiated and even ridiculed such a possibility, saying the facts of the case warranted no such speculation. The defense also sought to have a German psychologist testify as to the young man's state of mind, and to have a German chemist testify regarding technical aspects of the case. Both requests were denied by the judge.

At the conclusion of the second trial, the jury voted only 7-to-5 on the murder charge, but voted 8-to-4 to convict the defendant of manslaughter. The judge then sentenced him to four years of hard labor. Halsman reacted by shouting his innocence and accusing the prosecution, the judge, and the jury of being judicial criminals. Three court officers had to hustle the screaming young man from the courtroom.

Following the verdict Halsman, in a fit of despair, went on a hunger strike. His attorneys persuaded him to abandon it although not before it had damaged his health. The attorneys also sent a letter to Austria's president, Wilhelm Miklas, which they released to the press, and filed an appeal to the country's Supreme Court. But the government had just fallen and therefore could take no action, while the Supreme Court, after a hearing, decided to let the conviction stand.

Understandably, the case had all along created anxiety among the Vienna Jews. Many, however, hesitated to speak out lest they give renewed support to charges that Jews band together to protect each other from the workings of justice. Jewish business and professional men discussed the case earnestly in their cafes but quickly became silent or changed the subject when a Gentile approached.

Some Jews, however, together with a few Christians, did rally to Halsman's side, and in the fall of 1929 they held a public demonstration to raise funds and mobilize support for the young man. Sigmund Freud spoke, now over seventy and suffering from the oral cancer that would eventually take his life. At the same time a prominent Jewish attorney, Ernst Ruzicka, had published a book on the case, and two well-known German writers, the Jewish Jakob Wassermann and the non-Jewish Thomas Mann, spoke out in Halsman's behalf.

After the Supreme Court's decision the Halsman supporters realized that with the government still in crisis, only intervention from abroad could win his release. Since fascist Italy had no reputation for justice and England was too far away and uninterested in Austrian affairs, they turned to France.

Berta Zuckerkandl, widow of the famous anatomist, daughter of the former newspaper publisher Moritz Szeps, and a prominent journalist as well as salon hostess in her own right, spearheaded the fight. Her sister had married into the family of Clemenceau, and earlier she had secured a statement of support from the famed French statesman. Clemenceau had since died so Zuckerkandl turned to Maurice Painlevé, the president of the Austrian-French Friendship Society. Acting on her request, Painlevé exacted a promise from Austria's prime minister, Johannes Schober, to release the young man.

In October 1930 Halsman's sentence was commuted to two years, the time already served, and he was freed from prison on the stipulation that he leave Austria immediately and never return. The stipulation, of course, was altogether unnecessary since Austria would be the last country Halsman would ever want to enter again.

Halsman went to France and, adding a French "e" to his first name, became a stunningly successful portrait photographer. When the Germans invaded France ten years later, Albert Einstein, who had sat for Halsman, helped him obtain an emergency visa to America. Here his success continued, and when he and his colleagues formed the American Society of Magazine Photographers after the war, he was chosen as its first president. Some of the leading personalities of the postwar era, including John F. Kennedy, Elizabeth Taylor, and Marilyn Monroe, sat for him. He did more covers for *Life* magazine than any other photographer, over one hundred in all. He also designed two American postage stamps. At his death in 1979 he was widely regarded as the leading portrait photographer of his generation.

Living in Manhattan with his American wife and two daughters, Halsman apparently spoke little about this unpleasant episode for neither his short biography in the *Jewish Encyclopedia* nor his lengthy obituary in the *New York Times* made any mention of it. Curiously enough a similar silence has prevailed in Austria. Until Lucian Meysels published his biography of Berta Zuckerkandl in 1986, most Austrians, including most Austrian Jews, had never heard of what Meysels calls The Austrian Dreyfus Case.

But can the case be compared to the miscarriage of justice that tore France apart for over a decade and created repercussions lasting more than a generation? As Meysels himself observes, it is one thing for a provincial judicial system to railroad a young Lithuanian Jew, and another thing for the French high command to do so to the only Jewish captain on its general staff. But there are other and more disturbing differences as well.

For one thing, the French army did have *some* grounds for suspecting Dreyfus. There was a German spy on the General Staff who had been referred to in some documents as "D." Furthermore, Dreyfus was one of the few officers on the staff who had access to the material involved. Finally, Dreyfus' family came from Alsace, a French border province which Germany had annexed twenty years earlier. Although most Alsatians considered themselves French, they did speak a German dialect amongst themselves and some Frenchmen doubted their loyalty.

Another difference lies in the time the two events occurred. The Dreyfus Case took place in the 1890s, though it extended into the early 1900s. Dreyfus was subsequently cleared, given the Legion of Honor and even returned to the French army as a colonel in World War I. Although anti-Semitism continued as a force in France, it is almost impossible to think of such a case occurring in that country at the time of the Halsman affair. It is, in fact, difficult to think of such an incident happening in Germany at that time.

Finally there are the varying reactions that the two cases engendered within their respective countries. In France numerous non-Jews, including some of the nation's leading writers and politicians, rallied to Dreyfus' side, and the French legal system eventually absolved him. In Austria only a handful of Gentiles spoke out in Halsman's behalf, and it took intervention from abroad simply to get his sentence commuted. In view of what was later to happen in Austria, this may be the most disturbing difference of all.

Vienna's Zionists continued to gain ground in the 1920s, as their organizations proliferated, especially among the young, and their representation in the *Gemeinde* inched up. July 3, the anniversary of Herzl's death, had become an important day in the Jewish community, for several thousand would now march to the Dobling cemetery where Herzl was buried. There, with the members of Kadimah in the lead, they would pass in single file by his grave. (Kadimah was given precedence presumably because it was the first organization to answer his call.)

In the *Gemeinde* elections, young people campaigned vigorously for Zionist candidates, canvassing voters, transporting supporters to the polls and distributing literature to others. Certain changes in the *Gemeinde*'s by-laws helped the Zionists still more. The minimum tax payment for voting in Board elections was reduced to fifty groshen, or less than ten cents, and the requirement of Austrian citizenship was abolished. Other factors aiding the Zionist çause were the growth of Zionism internationally, the continued development of Palestine, and the impact of three of the movement's local leaders: Desider Friedmann, Rabbi Chajes, and Robert Stricker.

Friedmann, like Stricker, had been born and educated in what was now Czechoslovakia, and also like Stricker had been a Zionist since his student days. Friedmann, however, had studied law and had gone on to become one of Vienna's most successful attorneys with several large industrial firms among his clients. He also possessed an urbane and conciliatory manner which made him a good negotiator. His prominence as a lawyer helped give the Zionist movement increased respectability, while his negotiating skills helped it establish a somewhat less acrimonious relationship with the integrationist majority. Following the 1920 elections, Friedmann became the *Gemeinde*'s vice president. (The *Gemeinde*'s president all through the 1920s was Dr. Alois Pick, the last surgeon general of the imperial army and now a professor of medicine at the University.)

Rabbi Chajes was an asset for the Zionists in many ways. Despite the contretemps over his audience with Emperor Karl, he managed to get along quite well with most local Jewish factions, while his reputation as a rabbinical scholar, together with his knowledge of the secular world (including an ability to speak English), gave him international stature. In 1920 he toured the United States speaking at fundraising events for Israel, and in 1921 the World Zionist Organization elected him chairman of its Actions Committee, a post he held for the next four years. When the fifty-one-year-old rabbi died suddenly in

1927, some fifty thousand Vienna Jews turned out on a cold and gloomy December day to attend his funeral. The police had to close the *Ringstrasse* to allow the procession to pass.

Then there was Robert Stricker. Loss of his parliamentary seat in 1920 in no way diminished his zeal or his efforts for the Jewish and Zionist cause. (To him they were both one.) He had long since given up his job on the railroad to become co-owner of a small printing plant. This enabled Stricker to publish his daily Zionist newspaper at cost, and at the same time gave him time to carry on his crusade for Jewish Nationalism both at home and abroad.

Stricker, like Chajes — but unlike Friedmann — had also become a significant figure on the World Zionist scene. The 1921 Congress that elected Chajes chairman of its Actions Committee elected Stricker as the committee's vice president.

It was at that Congress that Stricker nominated Chaim Weizmann, the Polish-born British scientist who had been instrumental in obtaining the Balfour Declaration, to be president of the World Zionist Organization. When Weizmann later indicated a willingness to compromise on the issue of Jewish statehood in Palestine, Stricker became one of Weizmann's fiercest opponents. A subsequent meeting of the Actions Committee in Berlin produced the following interchange between the two:

> Stricker: If you do not believe in Herzl's Jewish state, you should go. You cannot lead if you do not believe.
>
> Weizmann: You dig up Herzl only to oppose . . . .
>
> Stricker: It is you, Weizmann, who must dig him up, because to you he is dead. I do not have to dig him up because to me he still lives!

Stricker soon thereafter resigned from the committee and with some other militant Zionists, including Nahum Goldman, set up a radical faction within the World Zionist Organization. This faction continued to champion the cause of full Jewish statehood in Palestine.

Stricker did not allow his activities abroad to detract him from the cause at home. He remained a member of the *Gemeinde*'s Board of Directors and his voice would often be heard in its deliberations. In a debate on whether to give financial subsidies to Zionist youth groups, a move the integrationists strongly opposed, Stricker called on the integrationists to look at the pictures of former *Gemeinde* leaders which hung on the walls of the meeting room. "Is there any descendant of these honorable men in this chamber?" he asked. "No. Their families and their descendants without exception are baptized, and you find them in the Catholic Church, and that is where you are heading. I vote to support an upright Jewish youth." No integrationist said anything further and the motion carried without a dissenting vote.

But the Zionists did not always get their way. Chajes' logical successor was David Feuchtwang, a district rabbi who supervised Jewish religious instructions in the city schools. But Feuchtwang was also a Zionist and this time the integrationists refused to approve the appointment. For the next six years Feuchtwang exercised the duties of Chief Rabbi but lacked the title.

The *Gemeinde*'s registers for these years also show some troubling trends. The Jewish birthrate had declined forty-five percent from the prewar period. Over one-half of all Jewish families now had either one child or no child at all. Less than a quarter had more than two children. At the same time, the Jewish death rate had risen as the population aged. In 1925 the number of Jewish deaths exceeded the number of births for the first time, and from then on the ratio of deaths to births steadily increased. (The birthrate for Gentiles had also gone down, but only by twelve percent, while the death rate had dropped as well.)

The community was also losing members in a more familiar fashion. In 1923 the number of Jews officially renouncing Judaism reached an all-time high of 1,236. This figure fell to 881 the following year, probably due to the letup in anti-Semitic agitation noted earlier, but the annual number of "dropouts" remained near the 1,000 mark for the rest of the decade. Converts to Judaism, mostly from mixed marriages, averaged slightly less than 300 during these years. The community was losing three members for every one it was gaining.

The Social Democrats bore some responsibility for this trend, for they continued to insist that only class identity, not national identity, counted. Now that they controlled Vienna, they put this principle into practice. Although Bauer and one or two other Jewish leaders had remained on the *Gemeinde*'s rolls, most of the Party's other Jewish officials had left, and they encouraged other Jewish Social Democrats to follow their example. Any Jew wishing to obtain a job or other benefits such as a low-rent apartment from the city would find *Gemeinde* membership a distinct and often determinative handicap.

The Jewish Social Democrats also frowned on institutions that fostered Jewish consciousness. They especially disliked the Jewish private school that changed its name to the Chajes Gymnasium after the Rabbi's death. The city administration lodged frequent complaints against the school, claiming, among other things, that it was overworking its students by requiring them to study Hebrew in addition to the officially required Latin and English. The school usually appealed such complaints to the Minister of Education in the national government and almost always won its case. Thus a Jewish institution had to look to a Christian, and essentially anti-Semitic, bureaucracy to protect it from the hostility of other Jews.

The school itself was not especially religious. The only major change it made in the officially prescribed curriculum was the four additional hours of weekly Hebrew instruction. Still, most of its students came from the recently arrived *Ostjuden*. This was a great disappointment to Chajes, who had been instrumental in its creation, for he had hoped the school would induce many integrationist families to give their children some increased awareness of, and exposure to, their national background. But in this the school apparently failed.

Such developments as the foregoing indicate that in spite of the increased interest in and votes for Zionism, and the continued vitality of the city's Orthodox community, most of Jewish Vienna still did not take its Jewishness very seriously. Integrationism and even assimilationism continued to exert a powerful pull.

As an example of the latter, Joseph Wechsberg tells of his Viennese aunt and uncle who had their daughter baptized so that she could marry a member of the lesser nobility. They then sought to have the marriage performed in one of the city's oldest and most prestigious cathedrals. When Church authorities refused, saying the girl had not been Catholic long enough, the parents made a generous contribution to a Catholic charity. The Church fathers then partially relented, allowing the ceremony to take place in the Votivkirche which, though not very old, was still fairly distinguished.

Hans Ruzicka grew up in Vienna during this time, and recalls two cousins and several friends who eventually converted. But, he points out, not all conversions were the same. Those baptized "lying down," that is as infants, were considered superior to those baptized "standing up," i.e., as adults. One joke of the time, he relates, tells of a Jew who first converts to Protestantism and then converts to Catholicism. When questioned about this, he replies, "If anybody asks me my religion, I can truthfully say Catholic. If he becomes suspicious and asks what my religion was before I became Catholic, I can just as truthfully answer Lutheran."

Ruzicka's father Ernst was the prominent Jewish attorney who wrote a book in defense of Phillip Halsman. But while the older Ruzicka had remained officially a Jew, he had refused to have Hans or his brother circumcised since he regarded the rite as a "barbaric act of mutilation." When Hans attended his first compulsory religious class in school, and the rabbi asked him what he knew about God, the boy replied that God lived in heaven with pearly gates guarded by St. Peter. His answer caused the rabbi to observe that the competition had obviously gotten to him first.

One of Ruzicka's grandmothers was totally assimilated but the other, a Galician, was not. Yet even his Galician grandmother kept her collection box for Jewish charity hidden away lest her maid find it and suspect her of contributing to a conspiratorial Jewish organization. When "the bearded man in the funny hat" came on his monthly rounds to collect its contents, she would leave him standing at the door while she went to fetch it. But when the Sisters of the Poor came to call, she always invited them in and graciously offered them a seat while she went to get her purse.

When we take a closer look at the city's Zionist movement we find its growth, though certainly appreciable, less impressive than it initially appears. Most eligible voters still did not vote in *Gemeinde* elections, and the majority of those who did still voted for integrationist candidates. Adults being solicited by Zionist youth for contributions would sometimes jeer that the youths were only looking for money to buy chocolate. In 1928 Stricker had to close down his daily newspaper and replace it with a weekly which he called *Neue Welt*.

While many new Zionist youth organizations had sprung up, most of them had trouble attracting enough members and soon began raiding members from each other. Moreover, many of these youth groups apparently devoted little attention to anything related to Palestine or, for that matter, anything specifically Jewish. One young Jewish Nationalist of those days reports that when he joined the Zionist Association for Secondary School Students, he found its members preoccupied almost exclusively with playing ping pong.

In 1926 some thirty-nine Jews left Vienna for Palestine. But Vienna was a natural jumping off place for the Holy Land and most, quite possibly all, of these immigrants came from Eastern Europe. Furthermore, only nine left the following year.

One young Viennese who did want to make an *Aliyah* was Josef Toch. In 1928 Toch lost his job, and since such an event was, so he says, almost fatal for a Jew (for Christians did not hire Jews and Jews feared to hire too many), he decided to go to Palestine. When he called the office of the Palestine Agency, a somewhat surprised official referred him to the Zionist youth organization *Hechaluz* (The Pioneers). When he called in person at the *Hechaluz* office, he found it filled with young *Ostjuden*, not one of whom could speak German. When they found that Toch could do so, they immediately embraced him as an honored member, and when they learned he could use a typewriter, they made him editor and virtually sole author of their newsletter. Toch later became a house-to-house fundraiser for the group. Sigmund Freud, who lived in Toch's assigned district, always gave him a generous contribution, and wanted to be informed of the group's activities.

Understandably, most young Viennese Jews, like most of their parents, still hungered for full-scale integration into Viennese life. To this end they joined nearly all organizations that would accept them. They became Pan-Europeans and Esperantists, Boy Scouts and chess players, vegetarians and barefoot walkers. Most of all they became Social Democrats, and while Zionist youths taunted them as assimilationists, they eagerly participated in the Party's various youth organizations. But the integration they hoped to achieve in so doing proved largely illusory. Although the Leopoldstadt was nearly sixty percent Gentile, and nearly all its Gentiles were working-class, the district's Social Democratic Club for students ten years of age and older had only three

Gentile members. These three youths were, in turn, scorned and boycotted by the other Gentile students, although the families of the latter presumably voted Social Democrat.

The situation at the University was hardly better. Kurt Lieber recalls going on a camping trip that the University's Social Democratic students had organized. He and five others were sitting by the lake when one of them said, "Isn't it funny. All six of us here are Jewish." Funny or tragic, such was the situation of the Vienna Jews as the 1930s began.

Part IV

Falling Curtain

There was so much handwriting on the wall,
That even the wall fell down.
　　　　　　　　　　— Christopher Morley

Chapter 18

The Spreading Swastika

By the end of the 1920s the Austrian economy was showing signs of reaching health and stability. Although unemployment stood at twelve percent, production had nearly attained its prewar level and the government in 1929 almost balanced its budget. Then the depression struck.

The collapse started in America and spread rapidly to Europe. It did not, however, affect all the Continent's countries equally. Some suffered much more than others, and the one that suffered the most was Austria. Austria was heavily dependent on exports, which dropped sharply as nation after nation erected tariff barriers. Austria was also heavily dependent on the sale of luxury goods and tourism, expenditures that dried up the fastest in an economic downturn. Austria's fragile economy crumbled.

By 1932 its already high unemployment rate had doubled, while industrial production dropped nearly fifty percent. In some villages children were coming to school barefoot through the snow. In Vienna, on the other hand, snow brought rejoicing since it meant a day's work for those lucky enough to get a job shoveling it away.

Especially battered by the economic crisis were Austria's banks. The country's first major casualty was the *Bodenkreditanstalt*, an agricultural credit institution with branches not only throughout Austria but in some of the secession states such as Czechoslovakia and Hungary. The bank had been under-capitalized and was already in trouble before the depression occurred. The Austrian government had guaranteed some of its loans, and when it started to go under in 1930, Chancellor Johannes Schober, a moderate German Nationalist, sought frantically to save it. He ended up going to Austria's reigning Rothschild, Baron Louis, and begging him to have the Rothschild bank, the *Kreditanstalt*, take it over. According to one report, Baron Louis replied with a sigh, "I will do it but you will regret it."

The Baron did it and both he and Schober regretted it, for within a year the *Kreditanstalt*, Austria's largest and presumably soundest bank, was forced to suspend payments. In desperation the government pumped in treasury funds and the French Rothschild contributed five million dollars to keep the bank going. Baron Louis, an ardent hunter and polo player, sold off some of his rural estates and moved to a somewhat smaller townhouse in Vienna. But the damage had been done. The crippling of the *Kreditanstalt* brought further bankruptcies in its wake.

The severity of the economic crisis revived doubts about Austria's capacity to survive as an independent nation. The concept of *Anschluss* or annexation by Germany, an idea that had never really died (all through the 1920s Austrian schoolchildren had been made to recite "We Austrians Are Germans"), became increasingly attractive. In 1930, while annexation talk was again making the rounds, Schober secretly negotiated a customs union with the German government.

Schober's motives were primarily economic, not political. A customs union would open up a vast market for Austrian goods, an urgent necessity now that rising tariff and import barriers were choking off other outlets. Indeed a customs union does not necessitate any loss of sovereignty. It merely allows goods and currency to travel freely between the two nations involved. But when the two countries disclosed their decision in March 1931, it set off a firestorm, especially in France and the Balkans. France claimed the union violated the Versailles Treaty and got the International Court at the Hague to agree. French banks also called in their short-term loans in Austria, a move that helped precipitate the *Kreditanstalt*'s difficulties a few weeks later. By the fall of 1931 both Germany and Austria had abandoned the customs union idea, but the fact that France and the Balkan states had forced them to do so would not be easily forgotten or forgiven.

In 1932 the loan negotiated by Seipel ten years earlier came due. The lending countries agreed not only to extend it but, in view of Austria's desperate situation, to increase it substantially. But largely at the behest of France, then the Continent's strongest financial power, they strengthened the stipulation requiring Austria to remain a fully independent country.

The customs union fiasco and the new loan arrangements constituted, says Pauley, "a humiliating defeat for the German and Austrian governments. Moderates in the two German-speaking countries had suffered another setback. . . . The Austrians, denied the forbidden fruit once again, wanted it more than ever." Only one group, he says, benefited from the affair: the Nazis.

Austria's political problems during the first two years of the 1930s also furnished the Nazis with a favorable terrain in which to flourish. Seipel had resigned in 1929, partly because of worsening health but partly because he felt that another prime minister might head off the growing hostility between the Social Democrats and the Christian Socials. Since each party had its own army, their mounting rancor threatened the nation with civil war.

As his successor, Johannes Schober adopted a reasonably conciliatory and compromising attitude. But he lacked Seipel's brilliance and initiative, and this, given the still doctrinaire leadership of the Social Democrats, made consensus impossible. In the early fall of 1930 the Republic held what would be its last national election. The balance of power between the parties remained roughly the same, but a new note was provided by the *Heimwehr*, which, although allied with the Christian Socials, ran a slate of candidates on its own. The eight *Heimwehr* members who won took their seats wearing uniforms. For those interested in the preservation of Austrian democracy, it was not an encouraging sight.

As the crisis deepened, fresh efforts were made to bring the two basic parties together. In June of 1931, following the near collapse of the *Kreditanstalt* and the imminent collapse of the customs union proposal, Austria's president, Wilhelm Miklas, asked Seipel to form a grant coalition with the Social Democrats. Although Seipel had reservations about such a move, and was becoming more skeptical of democratic government generally, he agreed to do so. But the Social Democrats scuttled the scheme. As Otto Bauer put it, they would not participate in "administering the affairs of a collapsing capitalism." Another factor deterring them may have been a reluctance to assume any responsibility for the unpopular policies considered necessary to rescue the country's economy. They preferred to stay in opposition while continuing to run Vienna.

The refusal of the Social Democrats to enter a coalition government weakened still further the ability of the country's political system to respond to the economic crisis, and caused many to place less and less confidence in the workings of democracy. Seipel himself had earlier released a plan looking toward the creation of an "authoritarian government." Such a system was looking more and more attractive all the time.

If the first two years of the 1930s offered Austria's Nazis an array of favorable conditions in which to flourish, they were at the outset hardly in a position to take advantage of them. For at the beginning of the decade Austria's Nazi party was in a state of near shambles.

For one thing, the Party, as noted previously, was really two parties. One was led by old-time Nationalist Socialists who, while admirers of Hitler, still wanted to go their own way; the other largely consisted of younger people, many of them students, who were willing to follow the Führer with unquestioning obedience.

But the Party's problems didn't stop there, for even these factions were rent by fissures and feuds based largely on jousts for power. Hitler himself, of course, recognized only the group that declared absolute loyalty to him, and in a few years the other would gradually disappear. But he had become so disgusted at the inability of his own loyalists to unite, that in 1927 he had temporarily dissolved the Vienna branch of the Party, claiming it was too undisciplined and chaotic. He later reestablished it, but at the start of 1930 Vienna's Nazi organization could claim only six hundred members.

Adverse external factors had also plagued the Austrian party. The return of relative prosperity had undercut the appeal of its programs, which were further hurt by the fact that they were imported from Germany and bore little relevance to Austrian conditions. For example, Hitler pounded away at the alleged infamy of Germany paying war reparations to the Allies, but this issue had little application to Austria. Nazi anti-Semitism gave the Party no additional appeal since Austria's existing parties, including even the Social Democrats, had long made anti-Semitism a major component of their own programs. Both Nazi factions lacked funds so that even paying the electricity bills for their headquarters often became a major ordeal. Furthermore, the Catholic Church had little love for a party whose anti-clericalism was quite apparent.

Finally there was the *Heimwehr* and the *Schutzbund* with their uniforms and guns which, along with their parades and drills, offered an outlet for those energies that would otherwise find expression in Nazism. The *Heimwehr*, with its right-wing orientation and bright uniforms, was especially able to deflect many who might have donned the swastika.

But as economic and political conditions continued to deteriorate, the Party began to move ahead. Some other developments also helped. In January 1930 Hitler appointed Alfred Frauenfeld as head of the Vienna branch. Handsome and Nordic-looking — he was one of the few Nazi leaders in either country who actually resembled the idealized image of an Aryan — Frauenfeld was only thirty-one and had been a Nazi party member for only thirty months. But he tackled his task with shrewdness and zeal. Two months after his appointment he brought Goebbels and Göring to Vienna to address a rally in the *Konzerthaus*.

The *Heimwehr*'s failure to win more than eight seats in the September 1930 parliamentary elections also helped the Nazis, but the biggest gain in their fortunes came four days later when Germany held its own parliamentary elections. The German Nazi party, which in the previous national elections had won only two percent of the vote, suddenly achieved nearly nineteen percent, becoming the second largest party in the German parliament.

The election triumph of the German Nazis gave the Austrian Brown Shirts a gigantic boost. Suddenly, National Socialism had become a major political movement. The Party's prestige gained further ground when Seipel gave the German party a quasi-blessing. The old German parties, he said, should bow to the "will of the people" and work with the Nazis. He even called it "undemocratic" to refuse to collaborate with a party that had won nearly one-fifth of the seats in the German parliament. While Seipel's remarks startled the still centrist and essentially democratically-oriented German government, they naturally delighted Austria's Nazis. How could their party be considered anti-clerical and uncivilized when such a distinguished cleric as Seipel had smiled on it? Austrian Nazism was now on its way.

Several developments the following year further played into the Party's hands. The crash of the *Kreditanstalt* and the subsequent scuttling of the customs union not only deepened the economic crisis but whipped up hostility towards the Allies. Hitler's strictures against the peace treaties now took on more weight with the Austrian public.

The *Heimwehr*, which had acted as a brake on the Nazis but which had lost prestige through its poor showing in the 1930 elections, suffered still another setback. Under a new interim leader it attempted to stage a "March on Vienna" similar to Mussolini's March on Rome in 1922. But many *Heimwehr* units refused to participate and the bold move to seize the government fizzled. Denied access to power by either the ballot box or the bullet, many *Heimwehr* members now began responding to the allure of Nazism. The Social Democrats, meanwhile, failed to perceive the shift that was taking place. They continued to direct their fire at the *Heimwehr*, largely ignoring the growing might of the swastika.

Although the Austrian party was attracting members from all sectors of the population, it was attracting more from some sectors than others. While many workers, farmers, big businessmen, and aristocrats still tended to distrust it, the Party was building a base within the middle class among white-collar workers, small shopkeepers, and professionals including doctors, lawyers, and university professors. It was also becoming popular with young people, especially students. In fact the Party's first election victory in Austria came at the Agricultural Institute in Vienna where in the winter of 1931 it captured two-thirds of the seats in the student senate. Six months later the Nazis achieved an absolute majority at the Congress of the German Students Association held in Graz.

But more significant, if less sweeping, election gains were also coming its way. In local elections in Upper Austria in the spring of 1931, the Nazi vote rose thirty-six percent from the previous November. A few months later in a municipal election in Klagenfurt, a provincial capital in southern Austria, the Nazis emerged as the city's second strongest party.

Their surge continued into 1932, helped along by the stiff terms of the new Allied loan. The loan not only extended and strengthened the prohibition against an *Anschluss* with Germany, but also required the dismissal of over eighty thousand civil servants, many of whom, along with their families, now joined the Nazi cause. The Party not only scored impressive increases in local elections in Salzburg and the province of Upper Austria but became a formidable force in supposedly Socialist Vienna. In a spring 1932 municipal election in the Austrian capital, the Party's vote jumped from 27,500 two years earlier to over 201,000, a better than sevenfold increase! More than one out of every six Viennese, and nearly one out of every five Gentile Viennese, had voted Nazi.

But a still more powerful boost from the ballot box came three months later in July 1932 when Germany held new national elections. This time the German Nazis won thirty-seven percent of the vote, becoming their country's largest single party. The Austrian Nazis could joyfully expect further successes for themselves as a spin-off. Control of the country now seemed well within their reach.*

The Social Democrats had continued to show little concern over the growth of the Nazi movement because most of its support was coming from those who had previously backed the Christian Socials and the German Nationals. The sixteen city council seats which the National Socialists won in the 1932 Vienna elections came solely at the expense of the latter two groups. The Social Democrats actually gained an additional seat.

Following the election Otto Bauer wrote, "The Christian Social voter who yesterday voted for the Nazis has not become a German Nationalist. Rather he is annoyed because his party has become so statesman-like that it no more dares to say an anti-Semitic word. Instead it takes money from the Jewish industrialists and gives the people's money to the Jewish bankers."

The statement is noteworthy in more than one respect. It illustrates, first, the point made previously that the Social Democrats were still at this late date

---

*Hitler, officially banned from Austria, was allowed to return to attend the funeral of his beloved niece, Geli Raubal, on September 23, 1931. She had died four days earlier, presumably a suicide, in the Munich apartment in which she and Hitler lived. Hitler did not show up at the funeral but three days later his Mercedes crossed the Austrian border and, closely monitored by the Austrian police, sped to the central cemetery in Vienna. After twenty-five minutes at the cemetery the Mercedes departed for a local hotel. Two and one-half hours later it headed back to Germany. (See *Der Spiegel* of June 8, 1987 for a story on this rather mysterious visit and the rather mysterious relationship between Hitler and his niece which lay behind it.)

not taking Austrian Nazism seriously. It also shows how the Social Democrats' Jewish leaders were still trying to combat the enemy with the enemy's own weapon, anti-Semitism. Finally, Bauer's comment contained a measure of truth. Christian Socials and to a lesser extent German Nationalists were benefiting from contributions from Jewish capitalists. These contributions, which appeared to have increased since 1926 when the Social Democrats adopted their doctrinaire left-wing program, had induced the Christian Socials to tone down their anti-Semitic attacks.

Since 1930 the *Heimwehr* had taken a similar tack, for several of its leaders were now receiving considerable financial help from Jewish businessmen. The Rothschilds, in fact, had rescued the organization's leader, Prince Starhemberg, from personal bankruptcy. Starhemberg had also become friendly with Fritz Mandl, a Jewish munitions maker whose glamorous wife Hedwig Kiesler would later become the American screen star Hedy Lamar.

Another factor which had helped to moderate the anti-Semitism of both the *Heimwehr* and the Christian Socials was the influence of Mussolini. Il Duce was still not pursuing anti-Semitic policies and was not encouraging his allies to do so either. In 1932 he told Starhemberg that he approved of allowing patriotic Jews to join the *Heimwehr*.

But the rapid rise of the Nazi movement in Germany and Austria was prompting all conservative groups to reassess their position. Anti-Semitism had remained deeply imbedded in the consciousness of the entire country, including, as we have seen on numerous occasions, that of the Social Democrats. Now the Nazis were forcing other groups to give it fuller expression.

One of the first responses came, predictably, at the University of Vienna. In the spring of 1930 the Academic Senate with the approval and encouragement of the Minister of Education, adopted an ordinance that would group students according to their "descent." Those with mixed descent would form a group of their own. The measure was, of course, aimed solely at segregating the Jews, but its real significance lay in its refusal to distinguish between professed and non-professed Jews. Christian Jews would be grouped with other Jews since "descent" alone would determine where one belonged. Although the Austrian Supreme Court struck down the ordinance, the Minister of Education, who was also chairman of the Christian Social party, continued to look for a constitutional way of putting it into effect. It marked the first official attempt in either Germany or Austria to implement the basic principle of the later Nuremberg Laws.

At a *Heimwehr* rally five days after the Academic Center's initial action on the ordinance, Starhemberg attacked "those alien, flat-footed parasites from the East who exploit us through an unhealthy economic system." By fall some of the counter-pressures previously mentioned were apparently making themselves felt, because the *Heimwehr*'s journal now called racial considerations irrelevant to the "real battle" between the "patriotic population" and the Socialists. Nevertheless, the Vienna *Heimwehr* distributed an anti-Semitic pamphlet replete with ritual murder and other long-familiar charges, and Starhemberg himself, in castigating Vienna's widely-hated Finance Commissioner Hugo Breitner, referred to him as an "Asiatic" whose "head should roll in the dust." (Of course, Starhemberg's wealthy Jewish supporters also hated Breitner.)

The anti-Semitism of the Austrian Catholic Church had to some degree been held in check by Seipel, whose own anti-Semitism was by Austrian standards relatively moderate. As late as 1931 he had repudiated the "excessive" anti-Semitism of the Nazis. But by 1932, when he gave the German Nazi party his quasi-blessing, he was starting to change. Although wasting away from tuberculosis and diabetes in a Catholic monastery, Seipel gave three interviews to a young Catholic sociologist who afterwards reported, "Much did the Chancellor talk about the Jewish problem and the race question, suggesting a more or less strong antipathy — very surprising to me — against the Jews." In a bedside talk with a friend two months before his death that same year, Seipel said, "We have become soft. . . . Thus Judaism has taken advantage of us. We are too trusting toward the Jews."

Seipel's hardening stance encouraged and was matched by a similar trend throughout the Catholic clergy. At the beginning of 1933, with Hitler's assumption of power imminent and with Austrian Nazism growing apace, the Bishop of Linz issued a pastoral letter saying at the outset, "The Nationalist Socialist race theory is completely incompatible with Christianity and must be decisively rejected. . . ." He then went on, however, to blame nearly all the ills of modern society on the "intense Jewish world spirit" which he claimed was poisoning the souls of the people. The destruction of Jewry's influence, he said, was not only legally justified, but had become "the strict moral duty of every faithful Christian." As one later commentator noted, the Bishop, after shutting the front gate to Nazism, then let it in by the rear door.

Despite these reaffirmations of anti-Semitism, leadership in the fight against the Jews was passing to the Nazis. During the 1930 Christmas season they staged tear gas attacks on Jewish stores and prayer houses. Wall posters began appearing bearing such messages as "If Jewish blood spurts from a German knife, who has anything against it?" Anti-Semitism in Austria had indeed taken on a new and nastier tone.

Once again the University spearheaded this new wave of hate. In November 1930 the Jewish anatomist Julius Tandler wrote the Dean of the Medical School, protesting the disturbances that were wrecking the Anatomical Institute which he headed. But it wasn't only the Medical School that was affected. The entire University was becoming a battleground for it was again becoming increasingly common for Nazis to beat up Jewish students, then toss them down the ramp to the sidewalk where the waiting police would then charge the victims with disturbing the peace. (In all fairness, the police would probably have charged Nazi students with the same offense if any had come within their reach in the same way. Unfortunately few at this time did.)

Outside the University Nazi students seized every opportunity for intimidating Jews. For example, in 1931 Pan-Europa, an organization dedicated to European unity, held an evening discussion on the role of youth and invited youth groups of all kinds to send speakers. Whether or not the Nazis had been invited remains unknown, but they showed up in force, taking over the entire balcony.

Most of the speakers taking part were Jewish, and as each got up to speak, he or she was greeted with hoots and hollers from the balcony. When the obviously Jewish spokesman for Esperanto tried to give the audience a sample of the proposed world language, a Nazi girl shouted "Speak German, Jew, you're not in Palestine." When the equally obvious Jewish representative from the Juvenile Chess Association finished his talk, little of which had been heard through the ongoing uproar, a Nazi shouted "Moishe, go home. The matzoh soup is waiting."

The anxious chairman of the affair, who was also Jewish, decided to place the Zionist speaker last. Fortunately, the speaker, a smart and high-spirited eighteen-year-old named Benno Weiser, had accurately sized up the situation. Discarding his prepared text he addressed himself directly to the balcony. "I come to you not as a liberal, nor as socialist, not as a mason, rotarian, vegetarian, or barefoot walker — but as a Jew, one who is proud of being one, who doesn't pretend to be anything else, and who doesn't give a damn about not being an Aryan."

His remarks produced deafening applause from the largely Jewish audience and a deafening silence from the balcony. The Austrian Nazis were not used to such bold assertions of Jewishness from Vienna Jews.

Weiser then called on the Jews present to leave the problems of European unity to the statesmen and focus instead on the Jewish problem in Austria. And he urged them to ask themselves whether their involvement in the various causes they represented did not represent attempts to avoid the fact that they were Jews. This time the applause was much thinner as many were starting to squirm in discomfort at his words. While his remarks in a sense saved the meeting, his message, unfortunately, went largely unheeded.

Weiser, whose name today is Weiser Varon — he added the Hebrew name when he became an Israeli diplomat in the 1960s — encountered another example of student anti-Semitism the following fall when he showed up to register as a medical student at the University. The Social Democrats had by now finally awakened to the Nazi danger, and a clash between Social Democrats and Nazis in the industrial town of Simmering the previous day had taken three Nazi lives.

Varon felt tension as soon as he entered the building, but although many students were wearing swastikas, he did not connect the strained atmosphere with the previous day's events. Suddenly a pretty girl standing in line ahead of him got out of line, approached him, and took him over to a corner where she quietly suggested that they leave. The young woman, whose name was Lotte Frisch – she would later became an American psychiatrist – sensed the danger and felt it would be safer to go out together.

Her premonition proved correct, for no sooner had they reached the street when they turned and saw two Jewish students with blood streaming down their faces being thrown out the door by a group of uniformed Nazi students shouting "Vengeance for Simmering." Of course, the two students had had no connection with the clash in Simmering, but Nazis were now holding Jews responsible for anything objectionable done by Social Democrats.

Varon by himself then went on to the Institute of Anatomy to register for Dissection, thinking that medical school students, even Nazis, would refrain from such savagery. Furthermore, it was known that the Anatomy Institute was now split into two wings, structurally as well as politically. One wing was presided over by a professor who taught Nazis, the other was headed by Tandler who taught Jews and such other non-Nazi and liberal students as enrolled. Thus the two groups were separated physically as well as politically.

As Varon stood in the lobby looking at the bulletin board, thirty odd students poured out of the Nazi wing and, shouting "Vengeance for Simmering," pounced on a Jewish-looking student coming out of the Tandler wing. Still clad in the white smocks symbolizing their enrollment in a healing profession, they punched and kicked the youth, broke his glasses, and then threw him bleeding down the stairs. Such was the state of medical education at the once prized University of Vienna Medical School as Austria's first republic entered its final phase.

How did the Vienna Jews respond to this new outburst of hostility? For over two years they hardly responded at all. But in July 1932, when Hitler won his plurality in Germany and Austrian Nazis announced a party congress to coincide with the Jewish High Holy Days the following fall, some Jews became conscious of the growing danger.

A group of Jewish war veterans under a former captain and war hero, Siegfried Friedmann, formed the League of Jewish Former Front Fighters. Historian Herbert Rosenkranz says it marked "the first and only successful attempt to unite in a common cause the fragmented and even hostile groups within the Jewish community." Although some Jews made fun of the organization, saying it was only an attempt by some aging veterans to once again play soldier, the League immediately began attracting members. Within a year some eight thousand had joined. Emil Sommer, the hero of the Burgenland who had retired from the army with the rank of general, was asked to be its president.

The League made the protection of synagogues and other Jewish institutions its first order of business. It also began organizing Jewish youth into a movement called *Haganah*, a Hebrew word meaning defense. The veterans sponsored classes in boxing, wrestling, and even judo. But their most effective step, perhaps, was to give young people implements such as large, medieval-like keys, which they could use as weapons but which the police could not officially identify as such.

As a result of these efforts, the High Holy Days passed without widespread Nazi violence. Isolated attacks, however, did occur. One band of Nazis attacked a group of Jews returning from services in the Leopoldstadt, but the young men among them fought back and the surprised Nazis finally departed. No synagogue was bombed or attacked, but an auxiliary prayer room was invaded by Nazis who beat the worshippers with steel rods and destroyed everything they could get their hands on, including the Torah scrolls.

Following the ten-day penitential period, Jewish interest shifted to the upcoming *Gemeinde* elections. In the last election the integrationists had won eighteen seats, the Zionists eleven, and other groups the remaining seven. Although the integrationists had for the first time failed to obtain an absolute majority, they had remained the dominant force. Now the Zionists marshaled their forces. The main Zionist group even produced a traveling musical revue which, combining entertainment with propaganda, toured various Jewish locales. Such aggressive and imaginative campaigning, plus the growing, Nazi-led anti-Semitism, produced a turnout of fifty-one percent, a record for a *Gemeinde* election. It also produced, at long last, a clear-cut if narrow Zionist victory. The five basic Zionist election groups — the word "basic" is used because some of these groups in themselves were coalitions of smaller groups — won twenty-one seats. The union along with two other small integrationist groups won fifteen. Thirty-six years after Herzl had summoned the Jews to consider themselves a people and not just a religion, a majority of his townspeople, or at least a majority of those who cared enough to declare themselves, had finally heeded his call.

The Zionist leaders, along with two to three hundred of their more faithful followers, had gathered in a cafe not far from the *Gemeinde* headquarters to await the election results. When a messenger rushed in with the returns, a shout of jubilation shook the premises. Immediately cries went up for Stricker to speak. But Stricker was now heavily involved in helping Nahum Goldman set up what would become the World Jewish Congress. He also recognized his own limitations. "Tell Friedmann to speak," he said to those around him. "He is the man to lead us in Vienna and he is a good lawyer too. . . . I am not." So Friedmann, a man of moderate height, climbed on top of a table and, having no hat, covered his reddish blond hair with his hand and offered up a prayer of thanksgiving.

Six weeks later, Adolf Hitler, who in the first paragraph of his manifesto *Mein Kampf* had said, "German Austria must return to the Great German motherland," became Chancellor of Germany.

Chapter 19

The End of Austrian Democracy

When Hitler became Germany's chancellor on January 30, 1933, some twenty thousand Viennese gathered before their own city hall to proclaim Hitler as their chancellor too. But they along with six and one-half million other Austrians already had a chancellor. His name was Engelbert Dollfuss.

Dollfuss had come to office the previous May when the country's government had undergone still another breakdown. Although this collapse stemmed from a minor parliamentary imbroglio, no cabinet member except one seemed interested in taking over, for any new chancellor would have to govern with a shaky one-vote majority. He would also have to preside over a disintegrating economy whose rescue, so it was believed, would require painful and highly unpopular measures.

The one cabinet member willing to assume the mantle of leadership was the cabinet's minister of agriculture. Born illegitimate to a peasant mother who would continue working in the fields while her son ran the nation, Dollfuss had studied law in Vienna and economics in Berlin. Entering the army as a private in World War I, he came out a first lieutenant. Soon thereafter he entered Parliament as a Christian Social, and eventually his ambition, intelligence, and rural background made him a logical choice for the agricultural ministry.

At thirty-nine Dollfuss was the youngest government head in Europe. He was also the smallest, for at four feet eleven inches he only came up to the armpit of his closest aide. His height provided Viennese wits with a fresh and rich source of material. The new chancellor, they said, was going to have a postage stamp printed bearing his picture, life-size. Or, the new chancellor had fallen off a ladder while picking a dandelion. Or, Frau Dollfuss had asked him not to wear his army helmet at home for he was scratching up the parquet floors. Yet the jokes soon stopped for Dollfuss displayed a dynamic quality, together with an acute sense of showmanship, which aroused attention both at home and abroad.

Since neither the Social Democrats nor the German Nationals would join his government, he took in the *Heimwehr* and made its leader Prince Starhemberg minister of the interior. With the *Heinwehr* and his own party, the Christian Socials, backing him, he was prepared to confront the Nazis.

Following Hitler's triumph in the July 1932 elections in Germany, the Austrian Nazis began clamoring for new elections in Austria. Dollfuss firmly refused. The Austrian Nazis responded with a wave of two-bit terrorism consisting mostly of tossing crude, homemade bombs designed more to disrupt than destroy. The German Nazis had won many votes by creating such mayhem, and then promising the people they would restore order. The Austrian Nazis were attempting to use the same tactics in their pathway to power. But Dollfuss refused to be intimidated.

Hitler's subsequent appointment as chancellor presented fresh and far more formidable challenges. Germany, with ten times Austria's population, was now ruled by a man who had long pledged himself to unite the two countries. Hitler had evidently not changed his mind for, on the day after his appointment, he issued a message of greeting to his "German brothers in Austria."

His Austro-German "brothers," meanwhile, increasingly responded to his call. One branch of the *Heimwehr* went over completely to the Nazis while the Nazi party's Vienna branch, which had grown from 600 to 40,000 in the previous three years, enrolled another 25,000 members in the next three months. Then in April local Nazis won a startling forty-one percent of the vote in a municipal election in Innsbruck. It was their best showing yet in a major Austrian city.

But Austria's Nazis were not Dollfuss' only political problem. The Social Democrats remained hostile, and their military organization, the *Schutzbund*, clashed repeatedly with the *Heimwehr*. The latter, now in the government, put persistent pressure on Dollfuss to suppress the Social Democrats, and Dollfuss was now heavily dependent on *Heimwehr* support. The new chancellor found himself fighting on two fronts, with the Nazis on his right and the Social Democrats on his left.

In March 1933 a technical foul-up once again produced a parliamentary impasse. Dollfuss seized on the occasion to send the deputies home. They would never convene again, for Dollfuss then invoked certain emergency measures in the country's constitution to govern without them. Then, with the results of the recent Innsbruck election in mind, he canceled all further local elections on the transparently spurious excuse that they would interfere with the summer tourist season. (Elections had never interfered with the tourist season in the past.) Chancellor Dollfuss was well on the way to becoming Dictator Dollfuss.

Moving aggressively on his left, he banned the Communist party and prohibited the Social Democrats from holding their May Day parade, even stationing troops on the *Ringstrasse* to prevent demonstrations. At the same time he continued trying to curb the Nazis. He barred them from wearing their uniforms and insignias and prohibited Frauenfeld, their Viennese leader, from making speechs.

The Nazis responded with increased terrorism. Violence at the universities reached new heights, forcing the government to close several of them in late May. Violence against the Jews also increased. Early in June the Brown Shirts tossed a bomb into a jewelry store in a Vienna suburb, killing its Jewish proprietor. But it was a bomb attack against a police auxiliary group a week later that prompted Dollfuss to take the ultimate step and ban the Nazi party altogether.

The plucky, if power hungry, chancellor had also moved to stir up foreign support. Since the secession states, such as Czechoslovakia and Hungary, were too small and still too hostile to offer opportunities for useful alliances, and since France and Great Britain were too far away and too uninterested, he naturally turned to Italy. When Hitler sent Göring to Rome to sound out Mussolini, Dollfuss hopped on an airplane and followed him. There the Austrian chancellor won Mussolini's backing, for Mussolini wanted no German troops on his northern border. When Hitler subsequently sent one of his cabinet ministers to Vienna to assess the situation, Dollfuss, with amazing cheek, sent a solitary policeman to the airport as his welcoming committee. When the German official subsequently grumbled over his treatment, Dollfuss kicked him out of the country.

But Hitler was also a shrewd, forceful politician and, moreover, had ample resources to respond. Munich radio began broadcasting anti-Dollfuss, pro-Nazi speeches into Austria, and German planes dropped propaganda leaflets along the border. More significantly, Hitler shut off some of Austria's imports to Germany and imposed a substantial fee on Germans wishing to visit the country. The result was a bitter blow for Austrian tourism. Whereas 98,000 German tourists visited Austria in July 1932, only eight came in July 1933. Resort hotels with three hundred rooms were lucky if they could fill five or ten.

Finally, with thousands of Austrian Nazis fleeing to Germany, some of them deported by Dollfuss but most of them departing voluntarily, Hitler organized an Austrian legion with a membership of fifteen thousand. This group drilled and trained while waiting for the chance to strike.

In response to adverse world opinion, Hitler later backed off from some of these measures, such as the airdrops and the radio broadcasts, but he continued to put pressure on the regime. At the same time local Nazis stepped up their terrorism. Bomb explosions became virtually an everyday event.

In September Dollfuss sought to tighten his hold on the country by announcing the formation of the Fatherland Front. It would merge all the country's patriotic groups into one organization under his leadership. When some members of his cabinet disapproved, he dissolved the cabinet and immediately set up a new one, assigning himself most of the portfolios. He was now not only chancellor but minister of foreign affairs, defense, public security, and agriculture. Commented one foreign correspondent, John Gunther, "Vienna went to bed at 10:00 one night in a republic and woke up at 10:00 the next morning in a dictatorship."

Dollfuss followed up this move by holding a huge rally at Vienna's racetrack. Tens of thousands of *Heimwehr* members, army troops, and members of other organizations including the Boy Scouts paraded while shouting "Heil Dollfuss."

Three weeks later a mentally disturbed Nazi fired two bullets at close range into Dollfuss, but the diminutive dictator survived and made a radio speech from his hospital bed. Telegrams, flowers, and gifts of all kinds poured into the chancellery for the man who had become Europe's most popular dictator.

Despite Dollfuss' successes and their own setbacks, Austria's Nazis continued to function. Banned from wearing uniforms, they adopted long white socks as a way of showing their affiliation. Some young people even had their hair cut in such a way as to make a swastika. In Salzburg young men would slink across the border at night for training in Germany, while German agitators would enter as tourists during the day to organize Nazi cells. Those who refused to join were warned they would pay for their refusal later. The police and civil servants felt intimidated. In their propaganda, sometimes smuggled across the border in baby carriages, the Nazis stressed the sanctity of private property to farmers and the sanctity of socialism to workers. In their underground press they referred to themselves as "freedom fighters."

They also continued throwing bombs, and cafes heavily frequented by Jews were popular targets. By the winter of 1934 as many as forty such explosions a day rocked Vienna. It was apparent that though underground, Austria's Nazi movement was not hibernating. On the contrary, it was gathering strength.

The more active members of the Jewish community had been following developments in both Austria and Germany, and the victory of the nationalistic Zionist groups over the integrationists reflected their mounting concern. But the integrationists themselves were showing some awareness of what was occurring. As early as 1931 the Union of German Austrian Jews dropped the German from its name and reverted to its prewar title, the Union of Austrian Jews.

Integrationists were stunned by the Zionist victory in late 1932 despite the fact that Zionist strength had been rising in Vienna since World War I. The Zionists selected Desider Friedmann as the *Gemeinde* president and another Zionist lawyer, Josef Löwenherz, as its vice president. Although oriented like Friedmann towards a policy of compromise and conciliation, Löwenherz (as befits his name, translated as "lion-heart") was more forceful than Friedmann and played a more influential role in the *Gemeinde*'s subsequent history.

The *Gemeinde*'s most pressing problem at this time was financial. Due to the devastating depression, the income of most *Gemeinde* members had shrunk and their tax payments along with it. Many had dropped off the tax rolls altogether and instead were now relying on the *Gemeinde* for assistance. In 1931 the *Gemeinde*'s deficit reached $40,000, a very substantial sum for the Austria of that time.

Hitler's accession to power compounded the problem; almost immediately it produced a stream of immigrants from Germany. Most of these early refugees were intellectuals and artists, for these groups were the first to feel the effects of Nazi policies. (Hitler had hardly been in office six weeks when, for example, he banned the famed German Jewish conductor, Bruno Walter, from conducting a concert.) While some of these immigrants arrived with sufficient resources or contacts to take care of themselves, others did not.

In April 1933 an international group of Jewish organizations held a conference to work out ways to help these refugees. During the ensuing three years the *Gemeinde*, with considerable help from abroad, especially from the Joint Distribution Committee in America, would assist nearly 32,000 impoverished immigrants. Nearly half eventually went on to other countries, but the rest, which included actors, comedians, and others whose profession required the German language, remained in Austria.

The growth of Nazism had caused some Viennese Jews to consider emigration. "In our circles there is already a great deal of trepidation," wrote Freud to his friend Marie Bonaparte. "People feel fear that the national extravaganzas in Germany may spread to our little country. I have even been advised to flee already to Switzerland or France." Still Freud stayed on as did almost all other Austrian Jews. Only in the Tyrol, which had extended its ban on kosher slaughtering to include poultry, and which had organized a boycott on Jewish stores in Innsbruck, did a few younger Jews leave. But nearly all of them came to Vienna.

Looking back on this period, Helen Hilsenrad, a Galician-born Viennese who later fled to America, recalled how Hitler's propaganda was everywhere. "But," she said, "since the process was gradual and did not strike in every quarter at the same time, most of the Jews continued to live as before."

From all we know Dollfuss was not especially anti-Semitic. He socialized with Jews and, when appropriate, drew upon them for help. Once when he wanted to get away from Vienna for a few days, Berta Zuckerkandl loaned him the use of her country house. In addition, Mussolini had initially urged him to reject Hitler's racial nonsense. Following the dissolution of Parliament, his close aide and spokesman, Major Fey of the *Heimwehr*, said the government had no plans for carrying on any radical anti-Semitism.

Many Jews and many Jewish organizations rallied to Dollfuss' side. The League of Jewish Former Front Fighters, though not overly pleased with Fey's limited assurances, joined the Fatherland Front. Karl Kraus, who in recent years had leaned toward the Social Democrats, now threw the weight of his influential journal behind Dollfuss, believing that the dynamic dictator was the only one who could save the nation from Nazism.

But the Catholic Church and Catholic political leaders, fearful of being outdone by the Nazis, continued to increase their anti-Semitic assertions. For example, as soon as Hitler took office his storm troopers launched a series of violent actions against the German Jews. But the negative reactions these incidents created both abroad and among the Germans themselves, led the regime — which in any case had still not consolidated its power — to call a halt. In March Göring even expressed regret over these "few unfortunate incidents" and assured "loyal Jewish citizens" that they had nothing to fear.

The *Reichspost* immediately seized upon Göring's apologetic words to accuse the Nazi regime of "backtracking and reneging" in its war against the Jews. Subsequently the paper saw fit to emphasize that the Nazis had not discovered anti-Semitism and therefore had no business taking credit for it.

Christian Social leaders were also starting to speak out. Dollfuss himself in addressing the Viennese Catholic Men's Association in the spring of 1933 attacked the "Jewish-Marxist spirit." A few months later his vice chancellor, Richard Schmitz, pointed out how "Christian Social anti-Semitism stems from the depth of the national consciousness. Whoever wishes to preserve the German way of life must protect it from becoming flooded by alien nationalities, in this case Jewish." He called Austrian anti-Semitism "practical" and therefore more effective than German anti-Semitism which he termed "radical and verbose."

Schmitz, like most Catholic writers, felt compelled to disavow racial anti-Semitism. However such disavowals were not only becoming more and more hollow — note how he referred to the Jews as an alien nationality — but also more and more absent. Even clerical leaders were increasingly referring to the Jews as a nation with distinct, and distinctly despicable, traits. At a leadership conference of Catholic Action a priest pointed out that even if a Jew converts wholeheartedly to Catholicism, "The aftereffects of his Jewishness are not erased by his baptism. . . . He now belongs to us but not in the same way as other co-believers."

In 1934 Edmund Czermak, chairman of the Christian Social party and Dollfuss' minister of education, published a book on the Jewish question. "We Germans," said Czermak, blithely disregarding the obvious Slavic roots of his own name, "gladly accord full respect to the Jewish people and their national religion." But, he added, "In our national culture they cannot be allowed to have any say except as guests." It should not be forgotten, he warned, that the Jews "have their real homeland in Palestine and give to their guest land only a limited part of their love." He expressed particular disapproval of assimilated Jews, saying that "the religious German must decisively reject baptism as an entrance ticket for the Jews."

As might be expected from what we have seen of their past pronouncements, the Social Democrats in no way attempted to counter such sentiments. The day after Dollfuss attacked the "Jewish Marxist spirit" the *Arbeiter Zeitung* taunted him by citing all the Jews and half-Jews among his supporters. Later when a Christian Social newspaper in Linz complained of the large number of Jews in the Fatherland Front, and called for a quota system to limit them, the Social Democratic newspaper asked, "Is this the thanks which the Fatherland Front Jews received for the piles of money they have contributed?"

Jewish Social Democratic leaders stuck to such tactics even when the anti-Semitism was aimed at them personally. For example, in the course of a bitter parliamentary debate in February 1933, Julius Deutsch, after making a statement on a particular point, said he was willing to take an oath to support it. His opponent derided his offer, saying that the oath of a Jew was worthless. Instead of seizing the occasion to defend his people or even himself, Deutsch merely replied by naming prominent Jews who supported Dollfuss and the Christian Social party.

The number of Jews who had gone over to Dollfuss, however, was undermining the Jewish Social Democrats within their own party. Gentile party members, who had long harbored at best mixed feelings toward the Jews, now became more openly hostile as they saw so many Jews lined up with their enemy. For those few Jews who could discern it, this was scarcely a promising development.

If the Nazis were a thorn in Dollfuss' side, the Social Democrats were yet a bigger one. They did not throw bombs or threaten Austria's independence, but they represented, in a sense, a greater obstacle to his policies. They had a large and well-knit organization which included a trained, volunteer army equipped with rifles and machine guns. Under the Republic's tattered but still not completely torn-up constitution, the Social Democrats continued to rule Vienna. They also controlled the trade unions, with the potential of shutting down the economy through a general strike.

Other factors increased Dollfuss' distrust and dislike of the left-wing party. While many Nazi leaders were, like him, church-going Catholics, the Social Democratic leaders, especially its Jews, were largely hostile to all religion. Bauer himself did little to conceal his personal disdain for Dollfuss whom he regarded as a man motivated essentially by a lust for power. Between the doctrinaire ideologue and the pragmatic opportunist stretched an unbridgeable gulf. Dollfuss had on occasion tried to negotiate with both the Nazis and the Social Democrats, and while neither would agree to his terms, the Social Democrats had proven the most recalcitrant.

But probably the most important factor pushing Dollfuss toward a showdown with the Social Democrats was pressure from Mussolini and the *Heimwehr*. Both were urging him to outlaw the Party and to destroy its already outlawed but still existing citizen army, the *Schutzbund*.

The Dollfuss regime had long attempted to crack down on the *Schutzbund*, sending police to investigate and confiscate its caches of arms. These police raids were provoking increasing, and increasingly bitter, clashes. In February 1934, following an especially violent incident in Linz, Dollfuss outlawed the Party altogether. What followed was a brief but bloody civil war.

Like so many events in Austrian history, it had comic opera overtones. The night the government launched its first moves against the Party, Otto Bauer was at the movies with his wife watching Greta Garbo in *Grand Hotel*. When the Social Democrats decided the next morning to call a general strike, the electrical workers jumped the gun and struck before the designated time. As a result the Social Democrats could not operate their printing presses and therefore could not get the announcement of the strike to their other members. When they subsequently decided to fight, no one at first could find the key to the main municipal arsenal.

But fight they did with such guns and ammunition as they had. Most of the fighting took place in the numerous large housing projects that the Party had erected in Vienna. These projects were well-designed for a defensive battle — some even believed they had been built with that in mind — but the Social Democratic defenders lacked the numbers and weaponry of their attackers.

A particularly fateful step was Dollfuss' decision to use the army's artillery against them. He did so only after several surrender ultimatums had been rejected, and after his commanders had assured him that such a move would bring the revolt to a speedy end and lessen the bloodshed. (Neither the army nor the police had tear gas; the peace treaty had forbidden Austria from having chemical weapons.) As promised, the end came soon after the army cannons began to roar, but the bloodshed was immense. The army fired only half-charged shells, but the death toll ran into the hundreds. Some casualties were women and children who had ignored several calls from the government to evacuate the buildings. What many socialists, perhaps somewhat mistakenly, today regard as their most promising experiment in socialism had been wiped out.

The fall of Vienna placed into the hands of the national government a charming, quirky city with seventeen daily newspapers (London with three times Vienna's population had only nine) and three traffic lights. The national government also gained control of the largest public enterprise in Western Europe. The municipality owned gas works, streetcars, buses and subways, public baths, slaughter houses, and even a department store, along with one-third of all the city's land. It had seventy million dollars in the bank, collected taxes of twenty-five million a year and many millions more in rents, fees, and other revenues, and employed 54,000 people.

Still the government paid a heavy price for outlawing the Party and quashing resistance in the way that it did. The Social Democrats now hated Dollfuss more than ever, and Dollfuss increased this hatred by displaying a vicious and vindictive streak. He hanged eleven Social Democrats and was planning to execute still more when the British ambassador persuaded him to stop.

The Nazis benefited greatly: now the Social Democrats were linked to them by a common status and a common enemy. Some Nazis had even fought with the Social Democrats. While no mass defection of Social Democratic workers into Nazi ranks occurred, some did cross over while many others became much less hostile toward their former foes.

This turn of events hardly helped the Jews. But they suffered still other and more serious consequences from the uprising. With the dissolution of the Social Democrats, the Jews lost the nearest thing they had to a major party. If the Party had done little directly to blunt the thrust of anti-Semitism, it had nevertheless provided them with a mass movement that they could support and even join without fear of being openly treated as a despised or inferior group. It gave them the feeling that they were standing shoulder to shoulder with the Austrian masses. For all its ambivalence and ambiguities regarding the Jewish question, the Party did seem to provide a bulwark against violent anti-Semitism. Now that bulwark was gone.

The way in which it had disappeared hurt the Jews still more. At the beginning of the conflict Bauer went to his prearranged post as head of intelligence. But when messengers stopped returning, he finally gave up and wandered the streets of Vienna in disguise before escaping to Czechoslovakia. Deutsch fought with the defenders and suffered a wound under the eye. Then he too escaped to Czechoslovakia. In Czechoslovakia the two attempted to set up a sort of Social Democratic party in exile in the border city of Brünn. When the Spanish Civil War broke out two years later, Deutsch volunteered his services to the Loyalist government and was put in charge of training German-speaking volunteers for the International Brigade.

The flight of Bauer, Deutsch, and some other Jewish leaders greatly annoyed the Gentile Social Democrats. "Where were the Jewish intellectuals when the workers manned the barricades?" asked one, who then proceeded to answer his own question. "On the train to Prague where they are going to write new pamphlets on the revolutionary struggle."

The not wholly accurate statement showed that many Gentile Social Democrats disliked the Jewish leaders, not only for having fled but also for having been too intellectual, i.e., too theoretical and doctrinaire. Many Social Democrats felt the Party was well rid of its intellectual Jews. The Nazis moved to capitalize on this circumstance as well. Six weeks after the uprising Göring visited Vienna, and in addressing a throng of well-wishers at the railroad station claimed the Austrian capital was no longer a German city because it had become totally Judaized. "The Jews must go," shouted Göring to his wildly cheering supporters. "There must be no more Jews in Vienna."

With the Nazis, the Social Democrats, and the Communists all banned, and other parties merged into the Fatherland Front, Dollfuss moved to legitimize his dictatorship by drawing up a new constitution. At the start of the year Mussolini had suddenly advised him to add a "tinge" of anti-Semitism to his regime in order to take some of the wind out of the Nazi sails. Responding to the suggestion, Dollfuss planned to insert a clause reducing Jewish rights. Some Jewish employees of the Ministry of Justice, however, informed Nahum Goldman of the intended change, and Goldman, unaware that Dollfuss was acting on Mussolini's suggestion, wrote Il Duce asking for his aid. Mussolini then did a turnabout and sent a handwritten letter to Dollfuss urging him not to interfere with or impair the rights of the Jews. Dollfuss promptly canceled his proposed amendment and informed Desider Friedmann, who had also expressed concern, that "no change will be made in the citizenship position of the Jews."

Drafted by a Jewish attorney in the Ministry of Justice and promulgated on May 1, the new constitution transformed the Austrian Republic into a quasi-fascist state modeled along Italian lines. In place of elected bodies there would now be "corporations," that is, appointed bodies representing the country's various economic, social, geographic, and other sectors. Although the document repeatedly emphasized that Austria was a "Christian German state," it stipulated that "all citizens are equal before the law," and that "the enjoyment of civil rights along with the right to public positions, officers, and honors are independent of religious belief."

Vienna's organized Jewish community greeted the document with enthusiastic approval. Moreover they viewed its many clauses favoring the Catholic religion — Dollfuss had earlier signed a concordat with the Vatican — as protecting and furthering Jewish interests. "A constitution adopted in the name of God can not be against the Jews," said the *Gemeinde*'s Zionist president Friedmann, while the integrationist journal, *Die Wahrheit*, maintained that the new constitution, in stressing the obligations of religion and the Christian ethic, conformed to Jewish instruction and morality. The weekly journal of the Orthodox Jews voiced similar sentiments, saying that "What has been created in the name of the Divine Power has stability and can only confer blessings." The periodical of the Jewish Front Fighters cheered the end of Austria's "psuedo-democracy."

Such expressions of support undoubtedly riled the many Social Democratic activists who were still struggling to carry on the Party's activities underground. As for the Nazis, they called the constitution a Jewish plot and, with the help of the monthly subsidy they were now receiving from Hitler, increased their violent actions. All through May and June hardly a day passed without a series of incidents involving terrorism or sabotage.

These machinations came to a head on July 24 when 144 Viennese Nazis disguised as policemen brashly and, as it would turn out, rashly entered the chancellery and attempted to seize the chancellor and his cabinet. Dollfuss had been advised of the plot forty-five minutes before, and most of his cabinet had fled. The *Putschists* managed to seize Dollfuss and shot and killed him, possibly when he tried to escape. But the *Heimwehr* and some loyal elements of the police and the army surrounded the building, and the plot failed.*

Although the tip alerting Dollfuss had come from the Vienna police, the ensuing investigation implicated several high ranking police officials in the coup. Some were executed while others, including the police chief, were sentenced to long jail terms. Dollfuss, who died moaning, "I wanted only peace," became something of a secular saint, receiving what Clare calls the "most pompous and yet somehow the most moving funeral in Austria's history."

---

*This incident also did not lack comic opera elements. The Nazis took Major Fey out onto the balcony of the chancellery and attempted to bargain for his life with the pro-government forces which had assembled below. One *Heimwehr* lieutenant shouted at Fey to jump, saying that he and a few others would catch him. Fey declined but the Nazis in the end surrendered.

The aborted takeover attempt aroused considerable alarm throughout Europe. England and France expressed their concern while Mussolini not only wired the government his support but dispatched several divisions to the Austrian border. Presumably they would have marched in if Hitler had gone to the aid of his Austrian followers.

Hitler seemed somewhat taken aback by the episode or at least by its outcome. He may not have known of the *Putsch* although Munich radio had begun broadcasting reports of Dollfuss' death a day before it occurred. In any case, Hitler at this stage was in no position to challenge world opinion or Mussolini's army. He disavowed the whole episode, replaced his ambassador with the Catholic conservative von Papen, dismissed the leader of the Austrian Nazi party, and ordered his Austrian Brown Shirts to cease their terror campaign. He also eased up on the external pressures he had been putting on the country, though he continued to send the Austrian Nazis $50,000 a month. (This was a truly substantial sum — enough to employ over a thousand workers at above-average salaries at that time.)

While Vienna's Jewish community mourned Dollfuss' death, it took heart from the way the other powers, especially Italy, had responded. Moreover, Dollfuss' successor was his protégé Kurt von Schuschnigg, a cultivated, mild-mannered lawyer who as Minister of Justice under Dolfuss had sought to suppress excessive anti-Semitic rowdyism.

One Jew who was not reassured was Stefan Zweig. Though essentially a non-political person who hardly ever voted, he had sensed danger when the police searched his house following the short-lived civil war of the previous February, and had soon thereafter left for London to stay. In the fall his friend Carl Zuckmayer, an anti-Nazi Gentile writer who had previously fled Germany to become Zweig's neighbor in Salzburg, came to London on a brief business trip. Zweig urged him not to go back to Austria. Said Zweig, "You are returning to a trap and sooner or later it is going to be sprung. There can't be any other outcome."

Chapter 20

Anti-Semitism on "Rubber-Soled Shoes"

Even before the July *Putsch* Austrian public opinion had begun to turn against the Nazis. Their bombs, designed to shake public confidence in the Dollfuss government, had only shaken confidence in the Nazis themselves. These negative feelings intensified when the government in early July raised taxes to pay for the damage that this sabotage had done to public property.

The ill-planned and ill-executed attempted *Putsch*, and Hitler's reactions to it, turned the Nazi retreat into a rout. The government executed the leaders of the would-be takeover and sent many of the movement's activists to a detention camp in Wollendorf. There they joined hundreds of Social Democrats incarcerated since the civil war. Most Nazi weapons were seized. Hitler sent generous sums to help his Austrian followers, but this money took the form of relief payments to families whose breadwinners were locked up or who had otherwise suffered heavy losses. The financially hard-pressed Austrian government actually welcomed such foreign exchange.

The Catholic Church also gradually hardened its stance against the Nazi movement. It did so largely in response to what it could see happening in Germany where Hitler, after signing a concordat with the Vatican, had soon begun to make life difficult for the country's Catholics and their institutions. Catholic youth organizations lost members, church schools shut down, and holy pictures vanished from classroom walls. Most church newspapers also ceased publication. Germany's leading Nazi newspaper, *Der Stuermer*, depicted monasteries as dens of bisexual inequity, and often portrayed priests as lechers who made lewd advances to both young girls and young boys.

In 1935 the German government began putting priests on trial on charges of immorality, smuggling, and treason. A German bishops' conference in August of that year protested against this "war of annihilation" though it diluted the impact of its statement by adding that the Church should stay out of state affairs.

In contrast, the Austrian Catholic Church enjoyed open and outright support from its government. Although the Church would have its differences and its difficulties with Schuschnigg, it benefited from the most privileged position that it had occupied since the 1870s, when Franz Joseph had abolished the old concordat. So when Hitler said, "Austria will be German or it will not be," the chairman of an Austrian Catholic professors' organization replied, "Austria will be Christian or it will not be."

Many other influential groups also stood arrayed against the Nazis. Although in Germany some aristocrats had yielded to Hitler's siren call, most Austrian aristocrats despised this crude upstart and yearned for the return of the Habsburgs. Many of Austria's major capitalists feared the competition from larger, more efficient German firms that an annexation would bring. At the same time, while many individual workers had gone over to the Nazis, many others remained basically sympathetic to the now underground Social Democrats or, in some cases, to the equally underground Communists. Hitler's ruthless suppression of both these parties in Germany assured, or seemed to assure, their continuing hostility to any *Anschluss*.

Perhaps the most damaging blows that the Austrian Nazis suffered during the early years of the Schuschnigg regime were self-inflicted. Hitler's firing of his Austrian commander, a former window-dresser named Habicht, following the July fiasco, left the Nazis without an effective leader. Instead, rival factions within the Party fought furiously over who should rule. At one time there were three claimants for the provincial district leadership of Styria, the Party's stronghold. While fervently embracing the Führer principle of blind obedience in theory, Austria's Brown Shirts seemed incapable of applying it to local practice. It should be added that the only Nazi party that now counted was the faction that had declared unquestioning loyalty to Hitler. The other faction had languished into extinction.

Schuschnigg thus began his reign on a note of strength. He could count on a broad, if somewhat shallow, range of support throughout the country. He could also count on the active support of Mussolini and the passive support of England and France. Important individuals lent their backing as well. Arturo Toscanini, the world-famed, anti-fascist conductor now living in the United States, had turned down Hitler's invitation to conduct at the Bayreuth Festival but accepted a similar invitation to the Salzburg Festival. His gesture was widely interpreted as a political demonstration in favor of Austria's independence. So for the thirty-six-year-old mild-mannered new chancellor, the outlook seemed favorable indeed.

The outlook also seemed favorable for the country's Jews. For the first time since the heyday of Austrian liberalism in the 1870s, they felt they had allies. Leading the list was the Chancellor himself who appointed Friedmann to the National Council, the substitute for Parliament in Austria's now quasi-fascist government. Schuschnigg also appointed two Jews to the Vienna City Council – one, Jakob Ehrlich, to represent the Jewish community itself, and the other, a businessman named Max Eitinger, to represent the city's trade and commerce sector. Solomon Frankfurter, director of the University of Vienna's library and a noted bibliographer, was named to the National Cultural Council. Later Schuschnigg would encourage the appointment of Bruno Walter to conduct the Vienna Opera and would also force Innsbruck Catholics to tone down the anti-Semitic passages in their annual passion play.

The Zionists were especially pleased with the Friedmann and Ehrlich appointments which to them signaled recognition that, as one of their journals put it, "Adherence to Jewry was fully compatible with devotion to the Austrian fatherland." Schuschnigg got along especially well with his fellow lawyer Friedmann who would occasionally go abroad to drum up support for Austria among Jews in other countries.

Another apparent ally was the new head of the Austrian Catholic Church, Theodor Cardinal Innitzer. As a theology professor at the University of Vienna in the 1920s, he had helped poor Jews and even attended a convocation of Kadimah as an honored guest. Serving as the University's rector in 1928-1929, he threatened to close the University for an entire year if attacks on Jewish students did not cease, and for a year they did.

Another ally emerged from within the Catholic community in the person of a thirty-two-year-old army officer's wife, Irene Harand. In 1933, she founded the Harand Movement dedicated to fight "racial hate and human distress." She also started, in collaboration with a Jewish attorney, a weekly paper called *Gerechtigkeit* (righteousness). Although the paper's paid circulation never exceeded 28,000, and although most of its subscribers may have been Jewish, it nevertheless annoyed Hitler's new ambassador von Papen who frequently protested to Schuschnigg about its anti-Nazi contents.

A much more limited and qualified source of support from within the Catholic community came from the former chairman of the Christian Social party, Czermak. In 1934 Czermak, following publication of his book, began discussions with what he called the "true Jews," i.e., the Orthodox. He found them to be a people he could get along with, because they seemed more interested in community and racial solidarity than class warfare. The danger came "not from Jews who recognized their race and religion but from the parasites who have neither national nor religious roots and neither understand nor respect the qualities of their own or their host nation," he said. While Jews in his view were still guests in Austria, at least not all of them were now unwelcome ones.

In addition to several influential individuals, one whole sector of the population — the aristocrats — had become more or less friendly to Jews. Despising Hitler and ardently and actively backing Austrian independence, they had also begun to dislike anti-Semitism, viewing it as crude, vulgar, and lowbrow. Many had also formed close business, cultural, and even social ties with upper-class Jews. The fact that many of these wealthier Jews, remembering the benign reign of Franz Joseph, were themselves staunch monarchists also helped. So from having helped spearhead the advent of racial anti-Semitism in the 1870s and 1880s, the aristocrats now opposed it. Unfortunately for the Jews, however, their new allies were now small in number and limited in influence.

But perhaps the greatest source of succor for the Vienna Jews lay outside the country; specifically, in Rome. When Nahum Goldman called on Mussolini in November 1934 to discuss the situation of the Austrian Jews, he found Il Duce in a most friendly mood. The Italian dictator actually described himself as a Zionist and called Hitler an idiot, a rascal, and an "insufferable talker." He then went on to say, "It is pure folly for the Austrian government, which is in an extremely weak position, to pick any quarrels with the Jews. We cannot permit the Austrian Jews to be attacked. Mr. Schuschnigg will be here next week, sitting in the same chair you are sitting in now, and I shall tell him I do not want to see a Jewish problem created in Austria. . . . You can rely on me."

The next month on the signing of the pact returning the Saar territory to Germany, Mussolini gave an earnest of his feelings toward the Jews. At his insistence the pact included a clause allowing the Jews of the Saar to take all their possessions with them should they choose to emigrate.

The advent of Austrian fascism had ushered in what Weinzierl calls "the final flowering of Austrian Jewish intellectual and artistic activity." To the extent that people still came to Vienna for medical expertise, it was largely Jewish doctors such as Sigmund Freud or ear specialist Heinrich von Neuman who brought them there. If they came for its music, it was largely to attend the Salzburg Festival which Max Reinhardt inaugurated in 1934 or the Viennese opera which had several Jewish singers and which from 1936 on was under the baton of Bruno Walter.

In literature Stefan Zweig and Franz Werfel were the country's two best-known writers. On a less popular level novelist Hermann Broch was attracting much critical esteem for his complex novels; Ernst Waldinger had won a prize from the University of Vienna for his first collection of poetry; and the young Elias Canetti had begun writing the works that would eventually bring him the Nobel Prize. Even Vienna's great Gentile novelist Robert Musil had a Jewish wife and, since his works produced little income, he was financially supported by a special committee of admirers, most of whom were Jews.

In 1930 Karl Landsteiner won the Nobel Prize in medicine for his discovery of blood groups, and in 1936 Oscar Lowi, a professor of pharmacology at the University of Graz, won the same prize for identifying the effects of acetylcholine on the heart and nerves. Austria had now won four Nobel Prizes which, in proportion to its population, was more than that of any other country. And three of these prizes had been won by Jews.

Younger members of the Jewish community continued to gain laurels in sports. Gerda Gottlieb broke the world's record in the women's high jump; Fred Oberländer won the European championship in heavyweight wrestling; Felix Kaspar became a world champion in ice skating; and Gustav Laub became Austria's heavyweight boxing champion. Hakoah walked off with the world table tennis championship in 1936 and won Austria's field hockey championship the following year.

In the 1936 Olympics, Jewish athletes won a gold medal in weight lifting and a silver in kayak racing. Of the fifty-two Olympic medals that Austrians had earned since the Games had begun, Jewish Austrians had won eighteen, or approximately eleven times more than their proportion of the population. They might have garnered one or two additional medals if three of their young women swimmers had not refused to participate in the 1936 Olympiad held in Berlin.

Two older Jews who had earlier achieved laurels as athletes were now scoring successes off the playing field. One was Willi Kurtz who, after a stint as the nation's heavyweight boxing champion, had become Commissioner of Austrian boxing. In his new post he evoked enthusiastic applause from boxing fans for, among other things, making sure that fighters were more evenly matched. But it was Hugo Meisl who had aroused the most widespread acclaim.

In 1910 Meisl had become team captain of the Austrian Soccer League, a position he resumed after World War I in which he had served as an infantry captain. In the last half of the 1920s he helped develop professional soccer in Austria and then coached its national team. Under his leadership it became known as the "Miracle Team" as it piled up one triumph after another in worldwide competitions. By the mid-1930s, Meisl had become a favorite sight at soccer games where, impeccably outfitted in a formal suit, high collar, derby hat, and a gold-headed cane, he would stand on the edge of the playing field directing and encouraging his players on to victory.

Yes, the 1930s did bring forth a new burst of achievement from the Vienna Jews. Yet despite their successes, and despite their new allies, they were now in their worst and weakest position since emancipation from the ghetto.

Early in September 1934, only six weeks after the regime had quashed the Nazi takeover attempt, the Austrian Ministry of Education issued without publicity an edict designed to set up a segregated school system. Those to be segregated would be Jewish pupils, who would henceforth be grouped into their own classes where they would be taught by baptized Jews or by pensioned Christian teachers. Since the official dissolution of the ghetto in 1848, no Austrian government had sought to take such a radical step toward its reestablishment. Nazi Germany in fact had not yet dared to make such a move.

Although the edict caught the Jewish community by surprise, it represented merely the first formal and official step toward implementing a policy initiated during the last days of the Dollfuss regime: removal of Jews from the mainstream of Austrian life.

As noted earlier, Dollfuss had never appeared to be particularly anti-Semitic and Schuschnigg seemed even less so. The new chancellor repeatedly stressed how all groups enjoyed equal rights within the Austrian state. Later he would visit a Zionist camp, write Freud a congratulatory letter on Freud's eightieth birthday, drop in occasionally on the salon that Franz Werfel and his Gentile wife, Alma Mahler, maintained, and spend a long private dinner evening discussing music with Bruno Walter. Yet at the same time Schuschnigg would spur or at least sanction numerous and unprecedented measures to reduce the Jewish presence in Austrian society.

The explanation for such a contradiction between Schuschnigg's personal behavior and his public policies is readily apparent. Austrian Nazism might be in abeyance but it was far from crushed. At the same time Nazism next door was flourishing, and Hitler's growing success in tearing up the Versailles Treaty, in rebuilding the Germany economy, and in instilling cohesion and pride in the German people were all having their effect on Austria. The preservation of Austrian independence was forcing Schuschnigg to do all he could to undermine Nazism's appeal to his own countrymen, and one Nazi policy that exercised enormous appeal to nearly all Austrians was anti-Semitism.

The school segregation edict came to naught; it aroused such open opposition from the *Gemeinde* that enforcement might have endangered Austria's difficult and delicate situation abroad. But the government pressed ahead, or allowed others to press ahead, with more subtle steps to circumscribe and isolate the Jews. As one pro-Nazi newspaper put it, the Austrian government was practicing anti-Semitism on rubber-soled shoes.

Initially these moves coincided with, or were camouflaged by, the crackdown on Social Democrats following the February civil war. For example, when the regime took over the city of Vienna, it removed fifty-eight Social Democratic doctors from the municipal payroll, and all but two of them happened to be Jewish. But it soon became apparent that not only Jews who were Social Democrats were being targeted. Non-Jewish doctors found themselves passed over for promotions to which by seniority they were entitled, and were encouraged or pressured to resign their hospital positions. Medical school graduates applying for internships now had to present both birth and baptismal certificates, a practice that effectively barred Jews from finishing their training at any hospital except the Rothschild Hospital, which could accept only ten or twelve interns a year. The number of Jewish doctors in Vienna dropped beneath the fifty percent mark for the first time in over half a century.

Jewish attorneys, over sixty percent of the Viennese Bar, were more successful in withstanding these trends for they were not as linked to the government through such things as hospital affiliations and medical insurance. But their positions in the Bar Association suffered when the government dissolved the Association and then reconstituted it with only two Jews in place of the previous twelve on the executive committee. Protest at such practices by Jewish lawyers and by Jewish doctors had no effect.

The large number of Jewish attorneys in private practice can be partially explained by their increasing exclusion from the many public service jobs for which a law degree was normally a prerequisite. Indeed, Jews were now being effectively, if unofficially, squeezed out of all civil service positions. By 1937 only 154 of Vienna's 22,600 municipal employees were members of the Jewish *Gemeinde*. When it came to teaching, the informal barriers had become still more powerful; of the city's five thousand teachers only ten were Jewish. Of the Jewish teachers whom the government had discharged only one-fifth had been Social Democrats.

Public service positions were among the most highly prized jobs in depression-racked Vienna and the denial of such jobs to Jewish Austrians, and the ousting of many who already had them, contradicted the excuse given for instituting such exclusionary practices in the free professions. Such steps were often explained as dictated by the need to reduce the number of Jews to their proportionate level. But as Irene Harand sarcastically commented, "We are curious whether the *Herren Antisemiten*, who so vigorously championed the proportional quota system, will champion the entrance of more Jews into government service to give them their proportional numbers."

The drive to exclude Jews touched nearly all areas of Austrian life. When the government reconstituted a major insurance company that had gone bankrupt, it hired back sixty percent of its former Gentile employees but only five percent of its Jews. In effect only those Jews deemed essential to the company's operation were put back on the payroll.

In the press, while few Jewish journalists were fired, most were assigned only to cultural and sports events. Vienna's most promising journalist, the later novelist Hans Habe who had become editor of a daily newspaper at the age of twenty-one, transferred to a German language newspaper in Prague. When the famed *Neue Freie Presse* experienced financial difficulties, the government arranged for its ownership to pass into non-Jewish hands.

Leaders of the Fatherland Front openly promoted boycotts of Jewish merchants and the quasi-official *Reichspost* carried a special page for "Advertisements by Christian Business Firms." In the Boy Scouts Jewish youths were put into their own units but, probably because of the Scouts' international affiliations, a few "show goys" were attached to the Jewish units to make the segregation less obvious.

In the forefront in furthering this new crackdown was the Catholic Church. While Cardinal Innitzer continued to display no hostility to Jews, most Catholic leaders, clerical and lay, had stepped up their attacks. They were concerned among other things with competition from Austria's Protestant churches, which were attracting many Nazis disgruntled with the way the Catholic hierarchy was supporting the Schuschnigg regime. In 1933, Hitler's first year in power, Austria's Protestant churches gained 25,000 new members, five times their recent rate of growth. Although most Austrian Nazis remained, at least loosely, within the Catholic fold, the Church wanted to make sure they would stay there.

Charges against Jews not expressed in respectable Catholic journals since the nineteenth century now began to reappear. An article by one priest in 1934 resurrected Rohling's old claim that the Talmud reviles Christians. Three weeks later the integrationist journal *Die Wahrheit* published an article by a rising young rabbi named Dr. Benjamin Murmelstein that carefully refuted the accusation. Since no non-Jewish periodical picked it up, however, Murmelstein's riposte accomplished little.

In a book published with Church permission, a priest bewailed the fact that "the Protocols of the Elders of Zion are too little known among the clergy and the Catholic intelligentsia." Calling Israel "the handmaiden of Satan," he claimed the Jews were working with the devil in preparing the way for the Anti-Christ. A book by a lay Catholic writer accused the Jews of continuing to practice ritual murder and, when the government decided that this was going too far and confiscated the work, another Catholic writer branded the government's action against such a "scholarly" book as "another instance of the power of the Jews in Austria." (Before the government acted, however, a teacher's magazine had already reprinted a portion of the work.) A minor Catholic poet named Richard von Schaukel assailed Jewish arrogance for distorting "the true face of Austrian art," although a Jewish music teacher, Rosalie Klaar, had set one of Schaukel's poems to music and in so doing had made it the most popular piece he would ever write.

While Catholic anti-Semitism continued officially to hew to a non-racial line — it was usually not Jews *per se* but Jewish materialism, Jewish atheism, Jewish Marxism, Jewish degeneration, etc., that was at fault — the racial anti-Semitism which had long lain under the surface, and which was now being openly pressed by the Nazis, became more and more evident. Although Jewish conversions were still being supported, they had become more and more suspect. One priest mocked assimilationism as mere mimicry while another claimed the Jews lacked "sufficient power of redeeming grace" to overcome their evil inheritance.

Even those priests whose mission it was to encourage such conversions began expressing doubts. In 1936 the Church dedicated a Paulist center in Vienna to encourage and assist conversions. Cardinal Innitzer used the occasion to speak out in behalf of the Jews. "At a time when racial hate and racial deification triumph, it is good to adopt another point of view. Just at this time when the Jews are being denied their basic rights, we should keep in mind God's righteousness and love." The prelate emphasized that "When the Lord said we should all be one, he did not exclude his Jewish brothers." But the priest who was to lead the mission used the occasion to contradict, in effect, his Cardinal and, it would seem, his own mission by saying that Jews who become Catholics bring with them unpleasant traits that make them unfit for a long time to hold positions in the Church. He said he could well understand why some organizations had adopted the Aryan paragraph.

With such sentiments as these emanating from the country's most influential institution, other sectors of Austrian society quickly took up the refrain. The Union of Christian German Physicians spoke out against the "degenerating influence" of the Jews and pledged itself to fight it. The Society of German Austrian Lawyers boycotted an International Lawyers Convention in Vienna in 1936 because so many Jewish attorneys would be speaking. The mayor and vice mayor of Vienna made frequent scornful references to businessmen who were not real Austrians, while business magazines made obliquely negative references to Jews.

Still more outspoken was the Christian Workers Movement whose leader, Leopold Kunschak, so it was once said, believed that "the guilt of a Jew was that he was born a Jew." So actively and ardently did this workers' group attack the Jews that von Papen, Hitler's new ambassador, secretly sought to subsidize it.

In 1935 the government dissolved the Pan-German Union which had become a Nazi front group, but a year and a half later approved its reconstitution as the Pan-Aryan Union. Under its new name the group continued to call on "Aryans of all nations" to unite against the Semitic peril. The Austrian Gymnastics Association warned its members to stay away not only from Jews but from those who may have become infected by the Jewish spirit. Even books "whose contents could Judaize us" should be avoided.

The universities continued to be hotbeds of hate, as they had been under the monarchy and then under the republic, and now under Austria's now quasi-fascist regime. Although all rioting was now suppressed, for the new constitution had ended university immunity from police action, Nazi and other anti-Semitic students began holding events expressly earmarked for Aryans only. The perenially anti-Semitic and increasingly pro-Nazi faculties lent their support by asking Jewish students hard, often impossible questions on oral exams and by trying to intimidate them in other ways. In the Technical School, engineering student Kurt Liebe answered all his professor's questions satisfactorily, and was then asked about something that the course had not covered. When he could not come up with the answer, the professor hesitated for a moment and said, "I will give you a 'satisfactory,' otherwise you will say I am an anti-Semite." This still deprived Liebe of the higher grade which he would otherwise have received.

Benno Weiser Varon, taking his dissection exam at the Medical School a few years later, was asked to describe something that was essentially indescribable. When Varon refused to be intimidated, the instructor finally passed him, but a Jewish female student who had over-prepared for the ordeal was browbeaten into failing. A third and non-Jewish student who was with them passed easily.

Numerous books by professors and dissertations by doctoral candidates written during these years dealt with the Jews and their uniquely dangerous traits. Some of these works cited the *Protocols of the Elders of Zion* as a scholarly reference.

Things were no better in the elementary and secondary schools as the Teachers Association became one of the country's more strident anti-Semitic organizations. Its journal spoke of "the totally demoralizing and corrupting Jewish influence which of necessity springs from the moral and intellectual characteristics of the race." Hans Ruzicka mentions how one of his teachers would adopt a Jewish accent in reading Heine's poems aloud to the class.

During this period Ruzicka tried to join an organization called Sons of Property Owners of the City of Vienna. When he noticed on the application a clause stating that "only those of pure Aryan blood need apply," he called the organization to inquire what it meant. The reply was, "If you have to ask, you obviously don't qualify." (Of course almost no resident of polyglot Vienna could really meet such a standard but apparently not being a Jew sufficed.)

Some stores began to advertise that they would no longer sell to Jews. One day a young blond man entered a large department store and spent an hour with its salespeople trying on suits, hats, and other articles of clothing. When he finished he carried a large armful of his selections to the cashier. After the cashier had carefully wrapped each article and tabulated the final bill, the customer suddenly blurted out, "Oh, I'm sorry. I forgot you don't sell to Jews here." Giving the cashier a courteous greeting he then sauntered out. The young man, Teddy Kollek, left for Israel a few months later where he eventually became mayor of Jerusalem, a post he still holds today.

Jewish-owned newspapers generally ignored domestic anti-Semitism and published only wire service reports on its manifestations in Germany. Most of the Gentile-owned press, however, joined eagerly in the fray. One favorite device was to headline any story that showed a Jew in a bad light. For example, a Jewish businessman who had signed himself as an attorney in a business transaction when he had no law degree became a *cause celebre*. One newspaper accused Jewish doctors of encouraging their Christian patients to have abortions, then illegal in Austria as elsewhere, in order to decrease the number of Aryans in the country. Writes the Christian historian Sylvia Madcregger, "All well-read dailies and weeklies oriented toward Catholic or Nationalist interests maintained a negative attitude toward the Jews. The intensity and approach of their anti-Semitic propaganda varied but all exercised, subtly or openly, an anti-Jewish influence over their readers."

Though the government now exercised substantial control over all areas of life including the press, it suppressed anti-Semitic agitation only when it threatened to produce mob incitement. At the same time Schuschnigg kept his own amicable dealings with Friedmann, his visit to the Zionist camp, his congratulatory birthday letter to Freud, and similar activities out of the newspapers lest the regime appear too friendly to Jews. His minister of education, who also sent Freud a birthday greeting, warned the press that he would confiscate any newspaper that published or even mentioned it.

Were there any gaps in this apparent united front against the Jews in the clerical-fascist state? Yes, some exceptions did exist.

The government actually cultivated Jews who had achieved worldwide renown because they attracted foreign visitors and foreign exchange and also enhanced the country's prestige. More importantly, since these Jews would be welcome almost anywhere, their decision to remain in Austria indicated a belief in Austria's ability to remain independent of Germany. This, it was hoped, would encourage others, both at home and abroad, to believe the same. It was not just Schuschnigg's appreciation of music that induced him to offer Bruno Walter the directorship of the Vienna Opera.

Most monarchists remained well-disposed toward the Jews, and their periodicals sometimes even defended them. A few Catholic priests joined with their Cardinal in repudiating, at least indirectly, anti-Semitism, as did two minor Catholic periodicals. Those priests and nuns who were themselves converts from Judaism usually remained silent on the issue.

Finally there were the Social Democrats. Though officially outlawed they were, like the Nazis, still functioning underground. In October 1934 their now-illegal paper *Arbeiter Zeitung* taunted the regime for squeezing Jewish employees out of government jobs while courting the rich Jews for their money. The paper condemned Jewish capitalists and such Jewish writers as Karl Kraus and Franz Werfel for having become the mainstays of this "dictatorship over the native Austrian people." "Native" in this connection should be read as meaning Gentile.

This stance would characterize the Social Democrats' approach to the Jewish question all through the years of Austrian fascism. In fact the Party's attitude toward the Jews continued to harden, one district leader in Vienna going so far as to order all Jews off his committee, claiming they had ruined the Party. Many Jews continued to belong to and work with the now underground movement, but it was becoming increasingly apparent that if a showdown should come, they would not find their Gentile comrades standing by their side.

Although anti-Semites accused the Jews of profiteering from the ongoing depression, tens of thousands of such "profiteers" were now relying on the *Gemeinde* for supplementary food and other basic necessities. They included bankrupt businessmen, unemployed white-collar and blue-collar workers, and impoverished artists and intellectuals. The *Gemeinde* was also paying for two-thirds of all Jewish burials. At the same time, it was continuing to operate its old-age home, its orphanage, its hospital, and other institutions without any subsidy from the government, although in caring for those who would otherwise use public facilities, it was saving the government money. (With the upsurge in anti-Semitism, most Jews tried to avoid public hospitals and other public institutions where they often received discriminatory treatment.)

In 1933 the *Gemeinde* levied a twenty percent surtax on its taxpayers, but since so many could not pay it, the surtax was made voluntary the following year. By 1936 the number of actual taxpayers had fallen below the number of those receiving assistance: recipients of aid now numbered sixty thousand, or one-third of the city's Jewish population. The result was a severe *Gemeinde* deficit only partially alleviated by help from abroad.

Another and closely related problem confronting the *Gemeinde* was a decline in the Jewish population. For every eight Jews in Vienna in 1923, there were only seven in 1934. For the most part, this continued to reflect a sharp fall in the Jewish birthrate. In 1923 there were 2,733 Jewish births; in 1933 there were only 757. Nearly twenty-eight percent of all Jewish couples now had no children, while an almost equal number had only one child. Many of the other Jewish communities in Austria confronted a similar situation. Of the 161 members of Salzburg's small *Gemeinde*, only fifteen were classified as children or youths.

But a declining and aging Jewish population and its shrinking resource base were overshadowed by another ongoing problem: the bitter divisions within the Jewish community itself. When the government attempted to segregate Jewish children in the fall of 1934, both integrationists and Zionists opposed it, but for almost entirely different reasons. The integrationists rejected segregation because it would widen the differences between Jewish and non-Jewish children. Said the Union, "Children of different beliefs learn to know and respect each other by being in the same classes." The Zionists, on the other hand, welcomed the prospect of all-Jewish schools, and protested only because the segregated Jewish children would be taught by Christians and would not receive a Jewish education. Thus, even when the community's two main components joined to oppose an anti-Semitic measure, they remained essentially at loggerheads.

In their overall reaction to rising racial hate, the two groups continued to bicker. The Zionists called the integrationists *Assimilanten* and castigated them as self-hating Jews who "had gathered their weapons out of the arsenals of the Jew haters." As one Zionist writer put it, "One knows him, this Jewish anti-Semite, who is transported into seventh heaven by a friendly word from a Gentile functionary, and who looks on any feeling of responsibility to the Jewish community as a betrayal of his nationality."

The integrationists claimed the Zionists and other nationalists were playing into the hands of Hitler and other anti-Semites by endorsing the concept of a separate Jewish people. "We do not want to be Austrian Jews but Jewish Austrians," they said, as they accused the nationalists of trying to lead the Jews back into the ghetto.

At the beginning of 1936 the Zionist-controlled *Gemeinde* board appointed Vice President Löwenherz to the well-paid, full-time position of executive director. Robert Stricker, who had become the Austrian president of the newly-formed World Jewish Congress, took Löwenherz's place as vice president. This step, which seemed to cement Zionist control over the *Gemeinde*, incensed the integrationists who, charging "patronage, politics," resigned their seats in the hope of forcing an early election. They also complained to Mayor Richard Schmitz that Zionist rule had resulted in the suppression of the "native-born, religiously-oriented, and fatherland-feeling" part of the membership, and that it was "insupportable that a single group of Jewish national co-religionists who, for the most part, owed their seats to the votes of Jews who were not citizens, should assume responsibility for the welfare of the Viennese Jews."

When Schmitz refused to intervene, the integrationists turned to the courts, filing in succession four petitions, all of which the court rejected, saying it had no authority. The anti-Semitic press meanwhile used the dispute to advantage by pointing out how the Zionist Jews had been accused by their own co-religionists of having no "fatherland (patriotic) feeling."

The death of Chief Rabbi Feuchtwang that summer brought up the question of his successor. This produced further bickering, which was resolved only by the appointment of Israel Taglich to succeed him. Though a Zionist, Taglich was seventy-four and therefore could not be expected to hold the office for too long.

In November the *Gemeinde* held its quadrennial election. This time seventy percent of those elegible cast ballots, shattering the previous turnout record set four years earlier. The Zionists won nineteen, and the integrationists thirteen seats on the board of directors. Other groups won the remaining four. Friedmann and Löwenherz strove to patch up the breach between the two sides, but the basic ethnic, cultural, and socio-economic differences between them, and their basic dislike of each other, did not abate.

In advance of the *Gemeinde* election, the League of Jewish Former Front Fighters had called for a unified slate, pointing out that "the danger which threatens us all does not distinguish between nationally-oriented and non-national Jews." When its words went unheeded, the League resignedly told its members to vote as they pleased.

Soon, however, the League was confronted with a split in its own ranks. Its president, former General Sommer, was an ardent monarchist and, according to one report, had resigned from the army when it offered him a medal following his Bergenland victory, for he would not accept such a decoration from a Republican government. Emperor Karl had died in 1921, but Sommer had maintained contact with Archduke Otto, Karl's eldest son, who was living in Paris and who was eager to assume the throne vacated by his father. Sommer's veterans' group, while sympathetic to a Habsburg restoration, refused to endorse it because "it was a position contrary to that of most Austrians." So Sommer then left the organization to form his own group of monarchist Jewish veterans. What had been one of the more effective organizations in uniting and defending the Vienna Jews had now split into two. (There was also a third organization for disabled Jewish veterans, some of whose members belonged to one of the two other groups.)

Another source of fragmentation was Agudas Israel. Unlike the Zionists or integrationists, this organization of highly Orthodox Jews had welcomed the school segregation edict, believing that it held out the possibility of a true Jewish education for Jewish children. The Orthodox Jews were apparently quite confident that they could persuade the government to change its mind on the question of Christian teachers for such schools, for they were enjoying, or believed they were enjoying, close relations with the quasi-clerical, quasi-fascist regime. They not only supported the government but in the past had openly backed the Christian Social party since it had acknowledged the existence of God, while the Social Democrats had not.

In the fall of 1934, one month after the segregation edict was disclosed, the Orthodox Jews revived their old request to have themselves declared a separate *Gemeinde* with all the authority and responsibility that such a status would confer. The government appointed a university professor named Hohensteiner to investigate the claim.

Professor Hohensteiner submitted a report in June 1935 recommending approval. Noting that the differences separating the Orthodox from other Jews were greater than the differences separating Catholics and Protestants, he said that the law mandating only one Jewish *Gemeinde* for each district "must be regarded as a leftover fossil from the liberal era which has no place in what is now a Christian state." He also taunted the non-Orthodox Jews, saying, "It is a gross contradiction for the present Jewish *Gemeinde*, which is so extremely oriented to freedom and free thought, to insist on a compulsory unification of all Jews within one *Gemeinde*."

Vigorous opposition from both Zionists and integrationists kept the government from implementing the recommendation, but the regime continued to look kindly on the Orthodox Jews, who had so warmly embraced the concept of a clerical state. While continuing to deny any subsidies to the *Gemeinde*'s various social welfare functions, the government began giving money to the Chajes School which, though not technically a religious institution, largely attracted children from Orthodox homes.

In their ongoing feud with both integrationists and Zionists, the Orthodox continued to direct their greatest fire at the latter. "The Jewish nationalists," said their journal in 1935, "have, in a blind rage of destructiveness, oriented all their youth organizations away from and against religion, and have used every means at their disposal to tear out all religious feeling from the hearts of our children." The integrationists, at least, made religion the basis for their Jewish identity and, when they had controlled the *Gemeinde*, had seemed somewhat more responsive to Orthodox demands.

Meanwhile, the presence and power of the Zionists within the Jewish community continued to increase. In 1936 Vienna's most prominent Jew, Sigmund Freud, openly aligned himself with the Zionist cause. He did so when Kadimah wrote him a congratulatory letter on his eightieth birthday, and he replied saying how much he would like the members to consider him as one of their alumni. Soon after, a delegation from Kadimah called on Freud and presented him with the Club's ribbon, which he fastened around his neck.

Most of the Zionist growth, however, was occurring among the young who, with Social Democratic youth organizations now closed down, were joining Zionist groups. Growth among adults was much less impressive as the 1936 *Gemeinde* election results revealed. But the Zionists' most important problem came from within. While the movement in Vienna (as in other countries) had long been divided into a large number of various subgroups and factions, this had not usually prevented them from acting together when it came to key issues. But in the early 1930s a much deeper division arose within the worldwide Zionist movement, and it soon spread to Vienna.

A major split in the World Zionist Organization took place at its 1931 Congress when Vladimir Jabotinsky tore up his membership card and stormed out of the hall. The Russian-born ex-journalist had long been a militant Zionist and something of a militaristic one as well. In World War I he had organized three Jewish brigades in the British army to help liberate Palestine from the Turks. Jabotinsky served with them and in 1918 entered Tel Aviv as a thirty-eight-year-old second lieutenant in General Allenby's army. Two years later he founded the Haganah in Jerusalem to defend Jews against Arab attacks.

Jabotinsky had resigned from the WZO's executive committee in the early 1920s in protest against its willingness to compromise on the issue of Jewish statehood. Now, ten years later, he had made his break complete.

Insisting that no people ever won its freedom without fighting for it, Jabotinsky started organizing self-defense groups among East European Jews, and even made plans for a Jewish naval training academy in Livornio, Italy. As the crisis for the Jews of Europe deepened during the 1930s, he called for the evacuation of one and a half million Jews to Palestine. But since the British Empire had no intention of opening Palestine to massive Jewish immigration, and since the Arabs still constituted ninety percent of Palestine's population, most Zionists considered Jabotinsky a foolish and dangerous fanatic. One prominent Zionist, Ben-Gurion, even called him a Jewish Hitler.

But Jabotinsky's ideas aroused great excitement among younger Jews. His first disciple in Vienna was the later novelist, Arthur Koestler. The Hungarian-born Koestler had recently graduated from the city's university, where he had been a member of a Zionist student organization. Koestler spread Jabotinsky's radical ideas among the students, and many of them responded. Young men from highly integrated and even assimilated families seemed especially interested.

Shortly thereafter, Jabotinsky came to Vienna, bringing with him his basic message: You must put an end to the Diaspora or the Diaspora will put an end to you. His dynamism and charisma overcame his flawed German and enabled him to impress his listeners, many of whom subsequently enlisted in his cause. Jabotinsky's youth organization, formally called Brit Trumpeldor but more popularly Betar, soon had nearly one thousand Viennese members. The response of older Zionists, however, was more limited. Even Robert Stricker, who knew and liked Jabotinsky and who sympathized with his views, declined to join his movement, saying, "I cannot leave the organization founded by Herzl."

Jabotinsky returned frequently to Vienna. It was, after all, the birthplace of Herzl as well as a major jumping-off place to Palestine. But he had also apparently succumbed to its charm. Despite its anti-Semitism, now more rampant than ever, he called Vienna his sweetheart city.

In the spring of 1935 Jabotinsky decided to make his break with mainstream Zionism more definitive by setting up a wholly new organization to be called the New Zionist Organization. But he wanted to hold an international plebiscite to allow his followers to vote on the idea. He came to Vienna, met with some of his mostly young supporters, and asked them if they could host the first Congress of the new organization should the plebiscite carry. They assured him that they could.

Jabotinsky stayed in Vienna for the plebiscite and, after the Sunday morning voting ended, the local Betar held a rally and parade in an open-air stadium. Jabotinsky reviewed the parade from the grandstand. When it suddenly began to rain, and the other spectators fled to the covered section, he rushed down to the field and joined the youngsters, who sang and danced around him in the downpour.

Three months later, on September 7, 1935, the Vienna revisionists hosted the first Congress of the New Zionist Organization at the *Konzerthaus*. The birthplace of Zionism had become the birthplace of its first major offshoot.

The Zionist revisionists, especially their youth and young adult group Betar, quickly became a significant force in the Jewish community. They immediately organized a boycott of German goods, a project that elicited some highly secret support from the Austrian government's Department of Commerce, since such a boycott would help Austrian businesses while saving the government's precious and none-too-plentiful foreign reserves. When the Vienna Betar invited the organization's up-and-coming Polish leader Menachem Begin to deliver a speech, the government proved less cooperative and denied Begin a visa, since it felt his visit might create too much controversy. Yet the regime not only allowed but encouraged Jabotinsky to come to Vienna, and sent one or more official representatives to sit on the stage with him whenever he gave a talk.

But if the government looked favorably on Jabotinsky and his followers, other Vienna Jews, including most Zionists, did not. Jabotinsky's idea that a few million Jews scattered throughout Europe could defy the legalities of the mighty British Empire to obtain refuge in a Jewish state in Palestine seemed not only ridiculous but dangerous to the whole Zionist effort. An additional source of concern was the brown uniforms that his Betar members wore. Jabotinsky had modeled them after the one he had worn in the British army, but they reminded other Jews of Nazi uniforms and strengthened the feeling that revisionism was simply a Jewish form of fascism. Fistfights occasionally broke out between Betar members and other Zionist youth.

So if the revisionists injected new vitality into Vienna's Jewry, they also created still another centrifugal force within an already badly fragmented community. And fragmented it certainly was. Although the city's Jewish population had shrunk to about 175,000, the number of its organizations had grown to about 450, approximately ninety of them temples, synagogues, and prayer houses. The Zionists alone comprised some thirty organizations, including eight separate and at times competing youth groups.

To some extent, all these organizations competed for resources from a dwindling resource base. Even within the organizations themselves, a great deal of factionalism raged. For example, Robert Stricker voted only with great reluctance for Löwenherz's appointment as executive director of the *Gemeinde*, for Löwenherz was a middle-of-the-road Zionist while Stricker, though still a member of the WZO, had joined its more militant wing. At the same time, both men, along with other Zionists, were constantly contending with the integrationists and, to a lesser extent since they were numerically inferior, the Orthodox Jews. "The threat from outside which Austrian anti-Semitism and German national socialism presented did not reduce the divisions within the Jewish community," writes Maderegger. "Rather, it increased them since the various groups mutually accused each other of pursuing policies which furnished fodder to the anti-Semites." The only thing that united the Vienna Jews was their commitment to Austrian independence. Unfortunately, their preoccupation with their own internal disputes, along with their love of Vienna and other factors, prevented them from seeing that the continuation of such independence was becoming less and less likely.

Chapter 21

Countdown

The start of 1935, six months after Dollfuss' death, found his successor Schuschnigg still facing not only a favorable situation at home, with his domestic Nazis divided and discredited, but also an encouraging situation abroad. Shortly after taking office, Schuschnigg had gone to Italy to confer with Mussolini and the talks had gone well. Mussolini had offered to give back the Austrian artillery that Italy had taken in World War I, and to supply Austria with more modern weapons on highly advantageous terms. The two countries signed a pact agreeing to consult frequently on mutual interests.

Austria's relations with other nations also looked promising. Hungary had signed a friendly if rather vague agreement with Austria, while Britain and France especially had indicated an interest in Austria's independence. Meanwhile, Hitler, still remembering the fiasco of the attempted *putsch*, had temporarily relaxed his pressure on the smaller nation. The prospects for Austria's survival as a sovereign country looked bright.

But by the beginning of 1936, a year later, the picture had changed considerably. Mussolini had launched a war against Ethiopia, and this adventure had cost him the friendship of Britain, France, and almost every other nation. Though Austria loyally defended him in the League of Nations, Germany, which had withdrawn from the League, was the only major power to rally to his side. The basis for a fateful partnership had been forged.

It was also becoming apparent that in such a partnership Mussolini would be the junior partner. Not only was Italy smaller and less industrialized than

Germany, but Italian forces, though they had beaten the Ethiopians, had looked less impressive in the field than on the parade ground. Germany's military and political power, on the other hand, was obviously growing. When Hitler in the spring of 1936 marched into the Rhineland, and the French and British did nothing to stop him, the import for Austria was clear. If the Führer could march west with impunity, what would stop him from marching south?

Concerned over the changing power situation (which was also strengthening Austria's domestic Nazi movement), Schuschnigg made another trip to Rome. This time Mussolini, while continuing to assure him of support, urged Schuschnigg to make some conciliatory overtures to his northern neighbor. On his return to Vienna, Schuschnigg almost immediately did so. The result was an agreement in July 1936 in which Germany recognized Austria's status as a sovereign state, while Austria in turn acknowledged itself to be a German nation. More specifically and more importantly, Hitler agreed to end all German trade and travel restrictions against Austria, while Schuschnigg agreed to release Nazis held in the detention camp at Wollendorf and even to take a Nazi or Nazi sympathizer into his cabinet.

While most world leaders and most of the world press greeted the agreement as a sign of easing tension, the consequences for Austria were momentous. Over fifteen thousand unreconstructed Nazis poured out of the Wollendorf camp, their hatred for the regime and their desire to overthrow it only reinforced by confinement. Tens of thousands of tourists streamed over the border from Germany, bringing with them desperately needed foreign exchange but also tales of how Hitler had revived the German economy, restored order in the streets, and rekindled German pride by tearing up the Versailles Treaty. Austrians visiting Germany returned with reports confirming such stories, while a flood of German films, magazines, books, and other materials now poured into Austria to provide added confirmation.

In appointing a Nazi to his cabinet, Schuschnigg chose a well-mannered, somewhat shy lawyer whom he personally knew and liked named Seyss-Inquart, and made him a state counselor. He also appointed a pro-Nazi general as minister without portfolio. Neither of these men, of course, wished to assist the regime to which they now belonged. Seyss-Inquart used his position to help Nazis increase their influence among the Catholic peasantry.

Abroad Mussolini and Hitler drew closer together. Both supported Franco in the Spanish Civil War, which began in the summer of 1936. Both continued to find in each other the only European ally of consequence in an increasingly hostile world. One result of their growing rapprochement was that anti-Semitic diatribes in the Italian press, once only sporadic, were now becoming routine.

In May 1937 Schuschnigg paid what would be his last visit to Mussolini. The Italian dictator repeated his assurances of support, but even his reception of the Austrian chancellor, though perfectly correct, seemed, as Schuschnigg later recalled it, "toned down." In September Mussolini visited Germany, where Hitler accorded him a lavish reception that cemented the bonds between them. Although the Italian dictator later sent the anxious Schuschnigg a message that everything regarding Austria was unchanged, a month afterward he told Hitler's visiting foreign minister that Italy was tired of protecting the Alpine republic. Said Mussolini, "We cannot force independence on Austria."

As his words indicate, Mussolini doubted whether Austria really wanted to remain independent. Schuschnigg was also apparently having doubts, for following the July agreement in 1936 he took steps to show his people that Austria could also defy the peace treaty and, at the same time, maintain its independence. He reintroduced military conscription and imposed a quasi-military discipline in the school system. By winter even women's fashions were showing a military look. Schuschnigg also affirmed Austria's Germanism, even to the point of emulating Hitler in trying to keep non-German words out of the language. To say *Telephon* for *Fernsprecher* became almost, though not quite, as great a sin in Austria as it had become in Germany.

To drum up popular support, Schuschnigg also began making frequent public appearances throughout the country. But several factors curbed his effectiveness. Austria's economy continued to worsen until 1937 when it more or less bottomed out. Some slight improvement was registered that year, but it was too little for any but economists to notice. Another obstacle to Schuschnigg's efforts was his own personality and physiognomy. Though still in his mid-thirties, he lacked any degree of dynamism. This, coupled with his thick eyeglasses, made him a poor substitute for the charismatic Hitler. Writes Pauley, "If his personality made him incapable of being a demagogue, it also prevented him from becoming a real popular leader."

Finally, Schuschnigg was known to be a monarchist and had even removed some restrictions placed upon the Habsburgs. This not only annoyed many Austrians but impaired the country's relations with the secession states as well as with Mussolini and Hitler, all of whom detested the monarchy. Thus, even at the start of 1935 when the prospects for his regime seemed so promising, the Vatican's emissary in Vienna estimated Schuschnigg's base of support as only thirty percent.

Gradually, anti-Schuschnigg jokes began making the rounds. One of them has Schuschnigg asking the mayor of a town he is visiting about the political makeup of the community's inhabitants.

> How many of your people are Christian Socials? About fifty percent. How many are Social Democrats? Some forty percent. Well, then, how many are Nazis? Approximately one hundred percent.

Another joke describes three different brassieres: the Hitler bra for uplifting the masses, the Mussolini bra for holding the masses together, and the Schuschnigg bra for concealing falsies.

With Hitler's power growing apace and Schuschnigg's obviously weakening, Nazi sentiment was rapidly increasing. When Hitler's foreign minister von Neurath came to Vienna in the winter of 1937, mobs shouting "*Heil Deutschland*" and "*Heil Hitler*" so crowded the streets that his car had to move at a walking pace. At a nonpolitical parade of German and Austrian veterans in the Austrian town of Wels the following summer, the spectators spontaneously sang the German rather than the Austrian anthem when the band played the melody common to both national songs.

Austria's Nazis were also growing bolder. They took fewer precautions in hiding their training and drill sessions, though such activities remained officially outlawed. Ever greater numbers of Austrians, especially young Austrians, were wearing the white knee socks which had become the Party's unofficial insignia. More and more swastikas and messages of "*Juden Heraus*" began appearing on the walls and doors of resort communities, and Jewish vacationers were finding more and more of these communities turning them away. One major exception was Salzburg, for its lively and lucrative summer festival drew many Jewish tourists from home and abroad. But Austrians now joked about how Salzburgians spent the winter saying "*Heil Hitler*" and the summer saying "*Heil Cohen*."

Soon Nazi violence began to reappear and, by the end of 1937, bomb explosions and disruptive street demonstrations had become common events. Whenever Austrian police broke up a Nazi demonstration, the German government generally expressed outrage over such "persecution." While much of the violence was not expressly directed at the Jews, some of it was. Jewish cemeteries were vandalized and bombs were thrown at Jewish gathering places. In the streets of Vienna one began to hear the sounds of the "*Horst Wessel*" song, the unofficial Nazi anthem, with its lines:

> Just wait you matzoh-devouring people,
> Soon will come the night of the long knives.

Three days after the 1936 German-Austrian agreement was announced, an unusual notice appeared in the *Neue Freie Presse*. It read:

> The Austrian Consul General in Jerusalem, Dr. Ivo Jorda, will be available to the public requiring information from 10:00 a.m. to 1:00 p.m. at the Federal Chancellery, 1 Balhausplatz, 2nd Floor, Room 63.

Austria, to be sure, was carrying on considerable commerce with Palestine, selling the British Protectorate over a million dollars worth of goods a year. But the notice addressed itself to the "public" and said nothing about trade or business of any kind. The announcement seemed aimed at providing assistance to those thinking of emigrating to Palestine, and in making such an offer it was implicitly encouraging them to do so.

The announcement was an indication of the government's desire to see more and more Jews leave the country. Other hints were dropped as well. The Zionist camp that Schuschnigg chose to visit — he rode over on horseback from his own summer quarters nearby — was set up by the Betar to prepare young Jews for making an *aliyah*.* When Jabotinsky came to town to repeat his call for stepped-up emigration, Schuschnigg often sent the head of the country's department of emigration to represent him. The government's continued campaign to exclude Jews from the civil service, the professions, and other areas constituted still another, and far more forceful, indicator of its intentions in this regard.

Hints from other quarters were also being dropped. A sympathetic mayor of one of the shrinking number of resort communities that still accepted Jews told Helen Hilsenrad and a group of her fellow vacationers, "If I were a Jew, I would flee the country." Stefan Zweig in his repeated visits to Vienna from his new home in London continued to sound the alarm.

Joseph Wechsberg, by then a young attorney in Prague, came to Vienna in late 1935 to see the Opera, for rumors were circulating through Czechoslovakia that Austria would soon go under. He was startled to find uniformed men in attendance who, so he was told, had been instructed to applaud certain mediocre singers of "impeccable" Aryan ancestry. When a Gentile friend told him of his own efforts to obtain an *Ahnenpass*, a genealogical certificate proving Aryan ancestry, Wechsberg was perplexed. "But the Germans are not here," he exclaimed. "Not yet," replied his friend.

Another visitor to Vienna who attended the city's Opera found that the Nazis, in a sense, had already struck. Thomas Mann came to Vienna in the summer of 1936 to read a selection from his new manuscript to his Jewish publishers, the Fischers, who had recently re-established their publishing house in the Austrian capital. Following the reading the group decided to catch the last half of *Tristan and Isolde*. On entering the Opera House they encountered a terrible smell. Nazis had released stink bombs which made the female lead throw up, and forced the rest of the cast to suspend their performance. But the orchestra, under Bruno Walter, continued to play. As Brigitte Fischer later described it, "We found a half-empty opera house almost abandoned by the audience, and in Walter's box his weeping wife. In this weird atmosphere we listened to the conclusion of the opera, conducted by Walter with the last of his strength, but with all the greater devotion."

There were indications of what was coming everywhere. How did the Vienna Jews respond?

---

*The literal translation of *aliyah* is "ascent." As used in this text and in general conversation, it means to emigrate to Palestine and, later, to Israel.

Those who believed most strongly in Jewish emigration to Palestine were the Zionist revisionists, and when Great Britain announced new restrictions on Jewish immigration in 1936, the Vienna Betar decided to defy them. They made contact with some Greek smugglers who had been left with idle ships and crews as a result of America's legalization of liquor. The Greek bootleggers were more than willing to smuggle Jews into Palestine.

In April 1937 a group of sixteen young men left Vienna by train for Athens, where they boarded a ship which surreptitiously but safely landed them in the Holy Land. The venture's success led to a second departure of sixty-eight young people five months later and a third embarkment of 120 youths five months after that. All of them successfully evaded the British blockade.* The first illegal transport consisted mostly of Polish Jews. Of the sixty-eight who comprised the second group, four were Viennese. No reliable figure is available on how many Viennese were in the third group, but of the eighty youths being trained for immigration by the Vienna Betars in early 1938, only ten were Austrians. Former Betar activist Edmund Schechter says he did not know anyone who left Vienna before 1938.

Less militant Zionists were, if anything, showing still less desire to make an *aliyah*. While a few young adults did depart for the Holy Land, most did not. Robert Stricker, in addressing a group of young Zionists, remarked, "There are sixty of us here. If one of us goes to Palestine, that will be a lot."

The integrationists seized on this situation to strike at the Zionists. "They would rather strive for Zion than to have Zion," observed librarian Solomon Frankfurter, while an integrationist joke of the time defined a Zionist as "a Jew who wants to send another Jew to Palestine with the money of a third Jew."

The Vienna Jews were also not hurrying to leave for other lands. In 1936 Manfred Papo, a Sephardic rabbi in his mid-thirties, was offered a congregation in Rio de Janeiro. This was quite an enticement since most rabbis want a congregation, and Papo at the time was teaching religion in the Vienna school system. Moreover, the new post would be in a well-established Sephardic community. Yet he turned it down.

That same year George Clare's father reckoned up his savings and figured he had enough to make a fresh start in another country. His banking and accounting skills were reasonably transferable and he even had a few contacts abroad. Yet he decided to stay. Although Helen Hilsenrad had relatives in America and her husband, the Vienna distributor for Universal Pictures, had business connections there, she gave no thought to immigration. Nor did anyone she knew. Said Hilsenrad years later, "Such blindness was a kind of marvel to be wondered at later."

---

*These figures are taken from Perl, who was actively involved in the operation. Rosenkranz, however, gives fifteen for the first landing, fifty-four for the second, and ninety-six for the third. See bibliography for both sources.

Some elements among the Jewish community's leadership were not totally unaware of the growing danger. Interestingly enough, the integrationists seemed to have more of a sense of what was going on than did the Zionists. Following the July 1936 German-Austrian agreement, the integrationists' union vowed "to be on the alert and to counter the National Socialist poison with all legal means." But the League of Jewish Former Front Fighters merely expressed hope that the ban on intervention into the affairs of other states, which the agreement called for, would be maintained, while the Zionists apparently made no significant comment on the accords at all.

At the headquarters of the *Gemeinde*, however, its now Zionist-oriented officials were stepping up their activities. As early as 1932 Löwenherz had called for a unification of all the Jewish *Gemeinden* in Austria to ensure adequate representation of Jewish interests. In 1935 some twenty-three (out of thirty-four) Jewish *Gemeinden* formed a working association, though each retained its separate official identity.

The new umbrella organization devoted a great deal of effort to the emigration question and held a conference on the subject in November 1937. But the emigrants they had in mind were those from Germany, Poland, and other countries who had fled to Austria and who needed assistance to continue on to Palestine or elsewhere — not Austrian Jews. Although the *Gemeinde* did give some covert assistance to the illegal Betar-sponsored blockade runners, it did almost nothing to help or encourage its own members to emigrate, including those whose poverty was placing a mounting burden on the *Gemeinde*'s resources.

Many factors lay behind the refusal of the Viennese Jews to confront the peril they faced. First, Hitler had somewhat moderated his anti-Semitic policies during this time, in part because of the Olympic Games, in part because the German people showed no real enthusiasm for harsher actions. Although German Jews remained excluded from the professions, the arts, government service, and big business, many small businessmen were still operating. Jews could also frequent most public places without fear of molestation. Consequently, some Austrians believed that even if a Nazi takeover occurred, it would not present any really great new problems. The fact that many heads of families in Austria were war veterans, and that Hitler had so far treated Jewish veterans less severely, only provided further grounds for encouragement.

But most did not really believe that Hitler would come. The growing friction between the Catholic Church and the Nazis in Germany encouraged them to believe that heavily Catholic Austria would successfully resist the Nazi allure. The leading Zionist newspaper hailed the Church as "the most important bulwark of Austrian independence." There was also Mussolini to count on. And then, who knew how long Hitler would last? Like their co-religionists in Germany, many Austrian Jews considered him a temporary phenomenon in the land that had produced such great humanists as Goethe and Schiller. That Germany was also the land that had produced Wagner and other anti-Semites, and that Hitler had restored German pride and, so it seems, filled German pocketbooks, was passed over.

On a more personal level, family ties, especially the well-known attachment of Jewish men to their mothers, kept many from leaving. This was the main reason that Rabbi Papo and George Clare's father gave for remaining in Vienna.

The amiability of most of the Viennese they came into contact with also lulled the Jews into a sense of security. One might hear the *"Horst Wessel"* song echoing in the streets or see the surreptitiously placed wall posters vowing death to the Jews, and still treat such things as manifestations of a fringe movement when Gentile customers and clients still came to Jewish doors, and when Gentile tradesmen, policemen, and their own domestic servants treated Jews with friendly respect.

Finally, of course, there was their intense attachment to Vienna itself, a city which for over a millennium had exerted a powerful hold on the Jews. This loyalty and love remained almost unshakable. So, despite their gradual exclusion from Austria's economic and social life and the growing menace of both foreign and domestic Nazism, the Viennese Jews with very few exceptions elected to stay put. When in late 1937 Zweig returned for what he thought would be his last chance to see his mother, he found better-off Jews inviting each other to full-dress parties and furnishing their homes in style. So unconcerned were they with the future that on the second day of his visit he stopped trying to warn them, seeing that it did no good. "One has often said that the Austrian Jews with all the signs of the coming catastrophe around them behaved like ostriches," writes Tamar Berman. "The German Jews were not free from this, either, but in Austria it took on grotesque proportions."

Hans Ruzicka offers an example of this. A Nazi bully in his high school made a regular practice of tripping Jews on the stairs, stepping on their toes, and spilling their inkwells. Once when the students had been assembled to see a film, he found himself sitting next to the Nazi youth. He asked him why he hated Jews so much, and the young Hitlerite responded with typical Nazi phrases, such as how the Jews were defiling the German nation. At the same time, he assured Ruzicka that he liked him personally.

When the lights went out, Ruzicka suddenly felt the Nazi's arm encircle his shoulder and his hand cup his mouth. At the same time, the young Nazi used his other hand to stub out a lighted cigarette in Ruzicka's palm. On his other side, another student hissed in his ear, "Don't make a sound, Jew-swine. This is only a mild introduction to what we can do to you." When the lights went on he saw another Jewish student with his hand bandaged and his eyes full of tears. He realized he had been part of a well-planned and widespread action.

After school Ruzicka ran to the law offices of his father and grandfather to tell them what had happened. Although both men were prominent attorneys and should have been well attuned to what was going on, both sought to minimize the incident. When Hans persisted, his father, with a shrug of his shoulders, replied, "Accept the fact that these are difficult times and that one must ride out the storm."

In December 1937 Jabotinsky came on what would be his last visit to Vienna. He was scheduled to speak at the *Konzerthaus*, and despite a heavy snowfall the previous day, young Betars came out in force, many dragging their parents to hear him. Clad in a tuxedo and with representatives of the government seated with him on the stage, Jabotinsky held his audience spellbound for four hours. As he ended his speech, he held up a suitcase which he had been concealing behind the speaker's stand, and, with the government's representatives smiling approvingly, he closed his address with these words: "Run, Jews, run."

At the start of 1938 an extremely rare display of northern lights flashed through the skies all over northern Austria. In some communities fire departments turned out, thinking a huge conflagration was in progress. It was said that such a phenomenon had not been seen since 1866 — the year Germany inflicted a humiliating defeat on Austria, permanently reducing her to a secondary and somewhat subservient power.

For those conversant with the country's political situation, the repetition of such a natural phenomenon after seventy-two years seemed more than coincidental. For Germany was once again threatening Austria, and this time it was endangering the country's very existence.

With Mussolini more and more tied to Hitler — the two had signed an Anti-Comintern Pact in the fall of 1937 — Schuschnigg began to look elsewhere for support. He made trips to Hungary, sounded out Czechoslovakia, and appealed to England and France. But from no quarter came any assurances of assistance. Even words of encouragement were becoming scarce.

Czechoslovakia was too concerned with the restless German minority in its own Sudetenland and with Hitler's designs on them and possibly more to wish to get involved with Austria's troubles. Hungary also worried about antagonizing Hitler and its own growing number of domestic Nazis. Furthermore, Hungary had hopes of seizing part of Czechoslovakia for itself should Hitler move against that country. England showed no interest in Austria's plight, especially since the new British ambassador to Vienna seemed to feel that Austria and Germany belonged together. France was concerned since it feared an expanded Germany, but its weak, perpetually changing governments could offer no guarantees. At the beginning of 1938, Austria, a nation with more neighbors than any country in the world, found itself without a single ally.

The first few weeks of 1938 brought little additional comfort. The domestic Nazis became more brazen and disruptive, while Hitler was reliably reported to have said, "I will have Schuschnigg's head." Other reports coming to the Chancellor told of Hitler, ever the frustrated architect, spending hours at his drawing board in Berchtesgarden redesigning the Ringstrasse. Early in February Hitler suddenly reorganized his government, firing his foreign minister, some of his ambassadors, and seventeen of his generals. Many of those dismissed were known to be opposed to the absorption of Austria. Austrian diplomats in Berlin sensed a change of attitude. "They began to treat us like living corpses," one of them later recalled.

For Austria's most endangered subgroup, the Jews, there were more specific signals of approaching trouble. On New Year's Day two newspapers, one of them the *Reichspost* which had become the semi-official organ of the government, called for an end to all Jewish emigration into Austria and for a review of all naturalizations granted since 1918. The announcement surprised Vienna and the following day the city's other newspapers reported on its publication. The government was apparently planning to tighten the vise on the Jews another notch in its ever more desperate attempt to take the wind out of the Nazi sails.

Austria's Nazis meanwhile were doing some vise-tightening of their own. Mobs of teenage boys and girls, and sometimes even younger children, all wearing white socks, roamed the streets molesting anyone who looked Jewish. One such group mistook a party of visiting Italian dignitaries for members of the detested race. On the first Friday evening in February, a group of young Nazis streamed through the Leopoldstadt smashing store windows and throwing a blazing torch into a Jewish prayer house, slightly injuring a few worshippers. (The Nazis were using youngsters for nearly all these provocations, hoping to create an incident should the police react too roughly.)

Hugo Breitner, Vienna's former finance director, correctly read the signs and fled the country, ending up in Claremont, California. But few other Jews followed him. Middle-class Jewish matrons continued to assemble at the Cafe Vindobina for their afternoon bridge games. Better-off Jewish couples continued to frequent the Cabaret Simplicissmus, whose Jewish owners, comedians Karl Farkas and Fritz Gruenbaum (a refugee from Germany), were presenting "Robinson Farkas on Gruenbaum Island" to celebrate the cafe's twenty-fifth anniversary. One is reminded of the words supposedly uttered by a crewman on the Titanic, "The ship is sinking but they're still dancing inside."

The Vienna Jews were, however, showing signs of an increased consciousness of their Jewish identity and of their national culture. In January the Zionists made plans to hold an exhibition and sports festival to celebrate the twentieth year of the *Hechaluz* (Pioneer) movement. The event was intended to call attention to *aliyah* as "the commandment of the hour." On

February 6 all the Zionist youth organizations decided to create a central headquarters organization. The Jewish Cultural Center and the Society of Jewish Sociology and Anthropology each scheduled a series of lectures on various aspects of Jewish history, culture, and thought.

Still, response to these activities, some of which would never take place, remained weak. In early March, N. Tur-Sinai, former president of Vienna's Hebrew Theological School, returned to Vienna to give a lecture and solicit aid for the Hebrew University in Jerusalem, where he now taught. He found it impossible, he later said, "to find real support for the University or indeed any other venture in Palestine." Calling the Viennese Zionists "complacent Zionists," he returned in disgust to Palestine on March 9.

Some of this complacency stemmed from the great faith the Jews continued to place in Schuschnigg, as if the beleagured chancellor could somehow contain Hitler and his swelling numbers of Austrian supporters. When the Nazi leader of Vienna boasted that the Austrian police would never dare prosecute his party for fear of German retaliation, and Schuschnigg replied by ordering a police raid on his headquarters, Sigmund Freud wrote an enthusiastic note to Max Eitinger, the Jewish businessman who represented commerce and trade on the Vienna City Council, complimenting "your worthy, brave government" for "acting more energetically in defense against the Nazis than before." (In the raid the police found various plans for a Nazi takeover of the country.)

But though the Jews believed Schuschnigg would and could stand up to Hitler, Schuschnigg at least knew better. With no sure signs of support from abroad and increasing disruption at home, he reluctantly accepted a proposal to meet with Hitler. The meeting was scheduled for Berchtesgarden on February 12. So full of foreboding was the Austrian chancellor that when his car crossed into Germany on the day of the meeting, he gave orders to close the border if he had not returned by 9:00 that evening.

Schuschnigg succeeded in returning to Austria that evening, but he brought with him what would become his country's death warrant. Hitler had bullied and browbeaten him into signing an agreement that called for Seyss-Inquart to become Minister of Public Security and thereby head of the police. It also called for the release of all remaining Nazis from prison (including one person convicted of plotting to assassinate Schuchnigg himself), the reinstatement of all government officials who had been discharged for being Nazis, and freedom for any Austrian to "profess the Nazi creed." Nazi units were to enter the Fatherland Front. The now 30,000-member Austrian Legion in Germany, a military formation larger than Austria's own standing army, was to return to Austria, though not as a military unit.

Details of the agreement, which leaked out gradually over the next few days, stunned Vienna. Investment capital began moving out of the country, leading to a fall in the stock market and in the Austrian schilling. Local Nazis began drawing up plans for expropriating and apportioning Jewish businesses and property. Said one dispirited aristocrat to Gedye, "Today we are all virtual subjects of Hitler."

The anxiety increased on February 20 when Hitler made a speech that, under the terms of the new agreement, was broadcast on Austrian radio. Although the German leader was supposed to give assurances of his respect for Austrian independence, he did nothing of the kind. Instead, he promised to "protect" the ten million Germans living beyond the borders of the Reich. By this he meant those in Austria and the Sudetenland.

This chain of events momentarily shook many Jews out of their complacency. But their reaction was at first confused and contradictory. The integrationists seized on the occasion to attack the Zionists, saying once again, but in much more dramatic terms, that their insistence on Jewish nationalism was playing into the Nazis' hands. "The political Zionist is an enemy of the Jews," said the integrationist journal on February 18, and to back up its point it referred to an article in a pro-Nazi newspaper some months earlier. This article, in taking note of Jewish nationalism, had said, "If the Jews wish to designate themselves as a particular people, then they must take the consequences of doing so." The integrationist paper then went on to summon all Austrian Jews to assert their Austrian identity. It also appealed to the country's Gentiles. "Christian Austria, be Christian to your Jews. You will have in them your most loyal citizens."

Jewish fears quieted down when a correspondent from the Jewish Telegraphic Agency reported from the Chancellery that the new agreement would produce "no change" in Austria's policy toward the Jews, for the government "steadfastly held to the principle of equal rights for all citizens." *Gemeinde* president Friedmann called on Schuschnigg to obtain similar assurances at first hand. The Zionist paper, ignoring the implicit surrender of Austrian sovereignty in the recent agreement signed with Hitler, now warned against panic or fear. "So long as Dr. von Schuschnigg is at the helm of Austria," said the paper, "no danger threatens the Jews."

On February 24 Schuschnigg replied to Hitler's speech. His own address, under the terms of the February agreement, was broadcast on German radio. He spoke of Austria's economic recovery, which was finally starting to become noticeable, and sought to show how it was based on firmer foundations than Germany's economic revival. He also boldly reasserted Austria's independence, saying that in complying with Germany's demands, the country would go so far but no farther.

In delivering the address in uniform before Austria's appointed Parliament, the normally reserved Chancellor spoke with a fervor and a force that gave his words additional dramatic urgency. It was the best speech he had ever given and provoked a strong reaction throughout the country. In Graz, incensed local Nazis under the leadership of a university professor stormed the city hall and hoisted up the swastika. But in Vienna and in many other areas as well, the speech seemed to mark a turnaround in Austria's gradual dissolution.

Dying people, it is said, sometimes experience a sudden burst of vitality shortly before the end. A similar surge of life now swept through the dying Austrian republic. Pro-government demonstrations, some planned but some spontaneous, began to break out. Austrian symbols and Austrian slogans appeared on walls and pavements, sometimes painted over Nazi ones. The sounds of *"Heil Schuschnigg"* and *"Heil Österreich"* began to compete with and even drown out the shouts of *"Heil Hitler"* and *"Heil Deutschland."*

The sudden apparent turnaround bolstered Jewish confidence. This optimism only increased when, at the end of February, the government signed a new three-year contract with Bruno Walter. If the regime was prepared to continue to have a German-Jewish refugee occupy the most prestigious podium in Vienna, then it was obviously prepared to resist Hitler. In the face of all these seemingly encouraging developments, some Jews who had been preparing to leave started to unpack their bags.

To shore up his domestic support, Schuschnigg now turned to the left and made contact with the still illegal but still functioning Social Democratic party.

Schuschnigg had continued Dollfuss' suppression of the Party largely to appease Mussolini as well as Hitler, for the latter would never have allowed Austria to outlaw the Nazis while permitting the Social Democrats to operate openly. But Schuschnigg, unlike Dollfuss, had no personal animosity toward the Social Democrats or their leaders, and had never treated them too harshly.

The leaders of the Social Democrats, understandably aggrieved at their underground status, had constantly sniped at the Schuschnigg regime. Following the February meeting with Hitler, the Party had issued a statement saying, "The Jesuits, the tradesmen's guilds, the monarchists, and the money Jews are now bankrupt." Still they feared the anti-trade-union Nazis and wanted to regain their legal status. So when Schuschnigg invited them to a meeting on March 4, they showed up. They were impressed with the Chancellor's conciliatory attitude and more and more workers began joining the pro-Schuschnigg, anti-Nazi demonstrators.

The surfacing of the Social Democrats offered little direct opposition to the crackdown on Jews that the Austrian government was pursuing on its own. The Party's leadership was now almost all Gentile, and the Party itself, tinged with anti-Semitism from its very beginning, had become even more so. This can be seen in its statement on the Schuschnigg-Hitler talks when it refers to the "money Jews" when the term "capitalists" would have been more accurate, for presumably the Party was opposed to all capitalists supporting the

Schuschnigg regime, not only those who were Jews. Still, the re-emergence of the Social Democrats may have made some Jews feel more secure.

Despite these encouraging signs, the Austrian crisis deepened. None of the allies or the secession states had publicly protested the latest German-Austrian agreement, although it clearly undermined Austria's sovereignty. (After being appointed Minister of Interior, Seyss-Inquart boarded a train for Berlin, presumably to receive his orders there.) Winston Churchill deplored the "tragedy of Austria" and some French parliamentarians did likewise, but none of these well-wishers held a post in their respective governments.

At home, the police, now under Seyss-Inquart's control, began siding with the Nazis against the government's own supporters. As for Bruno Walter's contract, the government had actually pleaded with him to sign it before he left for a guest tour abroad, for Schuschnigg wanted to show the world that Walter had faith in the country's continued existence. Thus, what the Jews took as a sign of the government's strength was in reality a sign of its weakness.

Schuschnigg was certainly aware of this weakness and in a last ditch gamble to head off the coming catastrophe, he decided to hold a plebiscite. In so doing, he was making use of one of Hitler's favorite devices, for the German dictator had often used plebiscites to confirm his policies and to demonstrate public support. How could he then ignore an Austrian one? Furthermore, Schuschnigg believed that if the Austrians really indicated that they wanted to remain independent, the French at least might come to their aid.

The plebiscite itself, however, posed problems. If the people were asked to vote simply on whether Austria should become part of Germany, they might well vote yes. (American press correspondents in Vienna estimated that the Nazis would win fifty-five to sixty percent of the vote on this particular issue.) Consequently, Schuschnigg framed the plebiscite statement in these words: "For a free and German, independent and social, Christian and united Austria, for freedom and work and for the equality of all those who declare for race and Fatherland." As Pauley writes, "Voting against such a question would be like an American rejecting the Stars and Stripes, apple pie, and motherhood." Only the monarchists, the Jews, and the communists could feel excluded, and the first two groups could be expected to support it in any case. Finally, Schuschnigg set the minimum age for voting at twenty-four. While this was in keeping with the Austrian constitution, it excluded the heaviest pro-Nazi block, young people.

Schuschnigg announced the plebiscite on Wednesday evening, March 10, and scheduled it for the following Sunday. The next day Vienna was ablaze with activity. Fatherland Front supporters painted Austrian symbols and slogans along with "Ja's" over walls and pavements, demonstrators marched through every district proclaiming their loyalty, while government airplanes showered pro-Austrian leaflets on the city. The government-owned radio also pitched in with propaganda broadcasts interspersed with military marches.

This burst of pro-Austrian and pro-government fervor brought a stream of endorsements. Leaders of farmers' associations, veterans' organizations, the Mothers' Protection League, and a host of other groups, including the Protestant Church, pledged their loyalty, until death in some cases, to an independent Austria. The *Gemeinde*, of course, quickly joined in this show of support. By late Thursday it was sending out leaflets urging its members to do all they could to ensure passage of the plebiscite question. *Gemeinde* president Friedmann had earlier the same day called on Schuschnigg, probably at the latter's invitation, and handed him a check for five hundred thousand schillings or roughly $75,000 to help finance the plebiscite campaign. The following morning Friedmann handed another check of three hundred thousand schillings to the secretary of the Fatherland Front.

But as Friedmann was handing over the second check, the fate of Austria and its Jews was already sealed. An enraged Hitler had massed his troops on the Austrian border and sent an ultimatum to Schuschnigg: Resign and allow Seyss-Inquart to form a government or go to war. France was locked in a cabinet crisis, Mussolini refused even to come to the telephone, and no other country was offering a glimmer of support. With Hitler's army at the gates, with no sign of foreign backing, and with his own country divided, Schuschnigg felt he could do nothing else but yield.

By late afternoon, the radio had stopped its propaganda broadcasts and Nazis were pouring into the Chancellery, occupying offices, using the telephones, and otherwise making themselves at home. At 7:15 that evening Schuchnigg made his last radio broadcast. He pointed out that he had refused to shed German blood and so had resigned. The now ex-Chancellor finished his emotional speech by saying, "God protect Austria."*

While Schuchsnigg was speaking, the streets had filled with rampaging Nazis pulling people out of taxicabs and attacking any who looked Jewish or who seemed to be Schuschnigg supporters. Three Catholic youths who had taken part in a Schuschnigg demonstration were severely injured. The Nazis paraded through the Leopoldstadt shouting "Destruction to the Jews" ("*Judah Verrecke*"), but this time they did not destroy any Jewish stores, for they were planning to take these over for themselves.

George Clare spent the evening at home with his parents and another Jewish couple who had come to hear Schuschnigg's speech on the family's radio. The erstwhile Chancellor had hardly finished speaking when a noise from outside brought Clare to the window. He saw a stream of trucks pass the apartment building, each full of brown-shirted men shouting, among other

---

*His friends had a plane warmed up at the airport ready to spirit him out of the country, but Schuschnigg refused to go. He said he must share his nation's fate and ordered his driver to take him home. He would spend most of the war in a concentration camp.

254 VIENNA AND ITS JEWS

things, "*Judah Verrecke.*" Then, looking down, he saw his neighborhood policeman, who had always treated the family with friendly courtesy, now wearing a swastika armband and brutally clubbing a screaming man who was writhing at his feet. The man had shouted an anti-Nazi slogan at one of the trucks.

The visiting couple started to leave. But as they were going out the door, the wife suddenly turned to Clare's mother and said, "Tell me, Stella, what on earth did we talk about before? Maids, children, dresses, food? What world did we think we were living in?"

Part VII

Paradise Lost

It is dangerous to wake up a lion,
And the bite of a tiger is malignant,
But the greatest terror of all,
Is man in his madness.
                    — Schiller

The Germans make good Nazis but lousy anti-Semites.
The Austrians make lousy Nazis, but what first-class
anti-Semites they are!
                    — Alfred Polgar

Chapter 22

The *Blitzverfolgung*

With their assault on Poland in September 1939, the Nazis would give the world an illustration of the *Blitzkrieg* or lightning war. With their annexation of Austria in March 1938, they gave the world an illustration of the *Blitzverfolgung* or lightning persecution.

It began before Schuschnigg had finished his farewell speech, and by the following morning it was in full swing.

The most visible and widespread form that this lightning persecution took was street-cleaning actions. Jews, young and old, rich and poor, religious and nonreligious, were ordered out into the streets to scrub pro-Schuschnigg slogans and symbols from the sidewalks and pavements. But the Nazis added several features to make the work more in keeping with their purposes. The water given the Jews was often mixed with acid, which burned their fingers, and the implements they were given for this "cleansing" were often toothbrushes. Wealthy Jews were ordered to wear their best clothes.

As the Jews bent over their work, storm troopers and Hitler youth stood by to harass and humiliate them in every way possible. In Währing, one of Vienna's wealthier sections, Nazis, after ordering Jewish women to scrub streets in their fur coats, then stood over them and urinated on their heads.

But street-cleaning activities by no means exhausted the persecutors' repertoire. Some Jews were ordered to do knee-bends until they collapsed, others had to carry chairs in and out of cafes until they nearly collapsed, others were forced to clean unwashed toilet bowls, and still others to spit in each other's faces. A visitor walking around Vienna in those early days of the *Anschluss* could also see such sights as the following:

- A group of Orthodox women removing their wigs, a step to them almost the equivalent of taking off their clothes, and then burning the wigs while dancing around in the Tabourstrasse, the main street of the Leopoldstadt;

- A young girl repeatedly bending down and then rising to her feet outside her parents' shop while wearing a placard saying, "Please do not buy from me — I am a Jewish sow.";

- Orthodox Jewish men dancing on torn-up Torah scrolls outside their wrecked temples and prayer halls;

- Hitler youth gleefully cutting off a rabbi's beard;

- Chief Rabbi Taglich, aged seventy-six, and former Surgeon General Pick, aged seventy-seven, on their hands and knees scrubbing the street;

- A blind Jew being pushed from one person to another inside a circle of playful Nazis.

These street incidents subsided a bit after a week or two, but then revived and may have reached new heights during the last days of Passover the following month. With the weather now warmer, a group of Jews were taken to the Prater and made to lie on the ground and eat grass while Nazis stamped on their hands. They were then strapped into the amusement park's giant roller coaster, which was driven at its maximum speed.

Rich and prominent Jews were prime targets for Nazi wrath. The cabarettist Felix Grünbaum was clubbed to death, as was the director of the Scala Theatre, Rudolf Beer. Eighty-two-year-old Solomon Frankfurter, librarian for the University of Vienna, was routed out of his bed and jailed. So were Nobel Prize winner Oscar Lowi and noted ear surgeon Heinrich von Neuman. The latter's arrest even prompted Count Ciano, Mussolini's son-in-law and foreign minister, to protest. "I have telegraphed to Germany to ask for a measure of mercy for von Neuman, the great Viennese Jewish scientist, who has been thrown into prison by the Germans at the age of nearly eighty," wrote Ciano in his diaries. "I hope the Nazis are not being too heavy-handed in Vienna and in Austria in general."

Vienna's most prominent Jew was Sigmund Freud. He was its most protected Jew as well. Ernest Jones, the British physician who headed the International Psychoanalysis Society, and Princess Bonaparte of France rushed to Vienna to help him. Other friends contacted Mussolini as well as Roosevelt in his behalf, and Roosevelt directed the American Chargé d'Affaire in Vienna to intercede in Freud's favor. But after the Gestapo had raided his house three times and forced his younger daughter Anna to come to headquarters for interrogation — she took along Veronal so that she could commit suicide in case she was tortured — Freud decided to emigrate. (Ordered to sign a paper stating that he had been well-treated, Freud wrote, "I am happy to give the Gestapo my best recommendation." This was the form of endorsement used in advertisements for merchandise, but the irony was apparently lost on the Gestapo, who accepted it and let the Freuds go.*)

The reign of terror did not spare the Jews living outside Vienna. Four members of the small Jewish community of Graz were killed in the events of these early days. The country's districts and cities competed with each other in an all-out effort to become *Jüdenrein*, or cleansed of Jews. Linz ordered its six hundred Jews to be out of the city by the end of September. Burgenland's five thousand Jews were told to be out by the end of the month.

In their zeal to carry out their impossibly ambitious directive, the Burgenland Nazis seized the fifty-one Jewish inhabitants of one small village and dumped them, including their eighty-two-year-old rabbi, on a sandbar in the Danube. Their cries of distress aroused Czech residents on the other side of the river, who rescued them. But the Czech government, fearing the Nazis would shove all of Austria's Jews into their territory, sent them on to Hungary, although it allowed the rabbi to stay in the hospital where he had been taken. Hungary sent them all back to Austria.

Although Jews who looked Jewish suffered the most, the Nazis had good records of who was and who was not a member of the cursed race. Efforts to conceal one's national identity usually failed, often with fateful results. A Croatian Jewish woman, married to a non-Jew and working as a floor director in a leading hotel, tried to pass herself off as an "Aryan." When her true ethnic background was discovered, she was beaten to death.

Underscoring this informal anti-Jewish violence were a host of more formal measures. Virtually overnight, Jews were driven out of the professions and from all public and most private employment. They also lost the right to sit on public benches or even to use elevators. (Martin Freud found his mountaineering training a big help during his last few days in the country.) Some sixteen thousand Jewish children were expelled from school, although eventually they were allowed to receive instruction in some unused schools until the end of the year. Children of mixed marriages were allowed to continue in school, but were so isolated and abused, both verbally and sometimes physically, that their lot in many cases was worse than that of the full Jews.

*When they reached London, Anna Freud publicly stated that everyone in Vienna, including the police, "have been very friendly to us." She made the statement only to protect those remaining in the city, including Freud's four elderly sisters, all of whom would later perish in the Holocaust.

On April 1, the new rulers shipped 151 men, most of them strongly identified with the Schuschnigg regime, off to Dachau. Among them were sixty Jews, including such *Gemeinde* leaders as Friedmann, Stricker, and Ehrlich. In late May a larger and exclusively Jewish roundup was held. Some two thousand mostly better-off Jews were seized and taken to various police stations, where they were asked such questions as "Did you during the last five years have an affair with an Aryan girl?", "Do you belong to a Freemason Lodge?", and even "Why were you arrested?" They were then jammed into an ancient empty school in the Leopoldstadt and put to work making straw mattresses.

Three nights later they were lined up two abreast while Gestapo Lieutenant Adolf Eichmann addressed them. "Who volunteers for Dachau?" asked Eichmann in a mocking tone. One elderly man stepped forward. "Why are you volunteering?" queried the bemused Eichmann. "Because I want to get it over with as fast as possible," was the answer. "Well," replied Eichmann, "I would not want you to be lonely. You are all going to Dachau." At this moment, one of the detainees fell into an epileptic fit. Writhing on the floor, he was ordered to get up, and when he did not comply, he was kicked until blood poured out of his mouth and his movements ceased. The others, some clutching small parcels, were then herded onto a wagon for the five-hour trip to the Bavarian concentration camp.

Persecution was not the only thing on the Nazis' minds; plunder was an even greater priority, for the German economy was being stretched and strained in preparation for war. Gold and foreign reserves were nearly depleted.

The Nazis promptly seized Austria's fairly substantial gold and foreign currency reserves and dispatched them to Berlin. They sent the Habsburg crown jewels, however, to Nuremberg, their favorite city. They then set about robbing the Jews.

The Gestapo had arrived in Vienna with a list of two hundred rich Jews, headed by Baron Louis Rothschild. They seized the Baron at the airport as he was boarding a plane, tore up his passport, and imprisoned him in the Hotel Metropole where the Gestapo had set up headquarters. They finally released him after his family had paid a substantial ransom. They also moved against other Jewish businessmen, often making token payments in order to give their actions a guise of legality. When, in ransacking the offices of the *Gemeinde*, they found records of the $120,000 in checks contributed to the Schuschnigg plebescite campaign, they immediately imposed a fine of that amount on the Jewish community at large.

While Nazi officialdom experienced few problems in confiscating the wealth of the rich Jews, it did experience difficulties in dispossessing the lesser ones. The problem was that lower-level Nazis and even street groups disguised as Nazi officials often got there ahead of them. Thus, jewelry, furs, *objets d'art*, and other valuables disappeared before they could be requisitioned by the government. Storm troopers could be seen boasting to prostitutes about the fur coats they had confiscated.

Of Vienna's 146,000 businesses, some 33,000 were Jewish-owned, and many of them were already plundered before the new regime could do so. Trucks rolled up before stores on the Leopoldstadt and uniformed storm troopers loaded them with merchandise as well as household goods, while the police kept the crowds under control. Even the *Gemeinde*'s food supplies for its soup kitchens disappeared.

Aryan "commissioners" were assigned, and in some cases assigned themselves, to most Jewish businesses, but the commissioners, often clerks or manual laborers, usually knew little about business operations. All too many merely helped themselves to the income while ignoring the expenses. Göring accused Austria's Brown Shirts of turning Aryanization into a "charitable operation for incompetent Nazis," and Hitler quickly dispatched a Nazi leader from Germany, Josef Bürckel, to take charge. Bürckel clamped down on the "wild commissioners" and even sent some of them to Dachau. But stealing and cheating at all levels of Austrian Nazism would plague the regime until its end.

As for the Jews, it mattered little whether the government or its individual supporters robbed them. Their total assets, estimated by the Nazis at $1.2 billion at the time of the takeover, rapidly melted away. As the London *Times* observed, "What was once a community outstanding in intellect and culture is being turned into a community of beggars."

How did the Vienna Jews respond to this *Blitzverfolgung*? Few offered outright resistance. One who did was a Jewish athlete who fought so hard against five Gestapo men who were trying to castrate him, that they finally threw him out of the window to his death. Another was a youth who, taken with several other Jews to a bridge where they were all ordered to spit in each others' faces, refused, saying he would rather be shot. He ended up in Dachau. An Orthodox woman at first refused to join the wig-burning dance on the Leopoldstadt, but did so when storm troopers threatened to pour gasoline on her head and set the wig on fire themselves. A department store owner reported for street cleaning wearing his military medals from World War I, plus a Star of David, which was not then required. He was dumped, badly beaten and with many broken bones, at the Rothschild Hospital some hours later.

Robert Stricker and his business partner had a plan for fleeing to Hungary with their families in a well-stocked limousine if the Nazis took over. But when the takeover came, and his partner showed up with the limousine, Stricker refused to go, saying he could not desert his fellow Jews. Sending his daughter to Palestine and his son to America, Stricker stayed on until his arrest and deportation to Dachau.

As the persecutions continued, some displayed considerable courage, or at least willingness to face the worst, for family, friends, and, on a few occasions, for fellow Jews they did not know. A Jewish couple sent their daughter to Palestine but refused to go themselves while their son was in Dachau. A Jewish youth turned down a chance to emigrate for he would not abandon his older sister and brother-in-law who had raised him. Many others who could have left stayed to take care of parents or sick spouses and relatives. And some young Jews would lose their lives helping other Jews to emigrate. During the first years of the *Anschluss*, the Gestapo could find no Viennese Jews to collaborate with it.

In complying with the various humiliations and horrors heaped upon them, some sought to retain a measure of dignity. Bending over his pail, Rabbi Taglich said, "I am scrubbing God's good earth." When taunted with questions as to how he liked his new work, he replied, "What pleases God, pleases me." Few whimpered or whined. As Jews, they had perhaps become inured to the idea that they were at the world's mercy. One of the men who survived the roundup of late May reports the dignified atmosphere in his jail cell while waiting for interrogation. "No one wailed, nobody cried out. One waited for his name to be called and then, without complaint, sometimes even with a little joke, one followed a uniform just as one's father had done."*

Suicide has been a Jewish solution to oppression ever since the days of Masada. Since it was, as we have seen, also a favorite Austrian solution, many Jews chose it. Edward R. Murrow, sent by CBS Radio to cover the *Anschluss*, was sitting in a bar when he observed a Jewish-looking man down several drinks and then take out a razor and slit his throat. The wife of Murrow's colleague, William Shirer, was in the hospital at the time. She reported that a young Jewish mother across the hall had clasped her newborn infant in her arms and jumped out the window, taking both of them to their deaths. Helen Hilsenrad was at the cemetery when she saw four coffins, representing a mother, father, and their two children, carried in. A well-known pediatrician left a note saying, "I have saved the lives of sixty thousand children, but I must now take my own." Assimilated Jews of the upper middle class proved most susceptible to the "Masada solution." "It is quite impossible to convey to anyone in how matter-of-fact a way the Jews of Austria today refer to this way out of their agony," Gedye later reported. "They speak of taking their lives with no more emotion than they had once expressed in talking about taking a short

---

*The Austrian Jewish novelist Jacob Lind, writing of the Holocaust, says that living for generations among people who wished to wipe them out, the Jews were ready to be wiped out. They too believed in the Final Solution.

train ride." A chemist told Gedye that his sale of poisons "in compact form" had quadrupled. Most of the purchasers, however, were buying them as a precautionary measure should greater calamity strike.

According to Jonny Moser, approximately twelve hundred Viennese Jews killed themselves during the Nazi era. This figure, while doubtlessly accurate — Moser is an exceptionally thorough researcher — nevertheless omits the many suicides that took place outside of Austria. It does not include the three Viennese Jews who threw themselves off a refugee ship that had been refused dockage in Helsinki; or the couple who killed themselves in London when they heard that their son, captured while fighting with the French Foreign Legion, had died in a German labor camp; or the doctor who killed himself after successfully emigrating to Shanghai; or the Viennese Jew who, having managed to cross the woods into Czechoslovakia, took poison when he saw Czech guards approaching to shove him back. Nor does the figure include the most famous of Vienna's suicides, that of Stefan Zweig and his wife who, though now safely settled in Brazil, became depressed over events in Europe. These and numerous other extraterritorial suicides should be added to Moser's figures.

Anna Freud had suggested suicide to her father, but he had emphatically rejected the idea, saying it would only please the Nazis. In this the elder Freud was certainly correct. Gedye saw Nazis "gloating over the daily suicide lists," and once, seeing the bodies of a family who had killed themselves being removed from their flat, he noticed that a sign had been put up over the entrance saying, "Neighbors, please copy."

Even their enemies have rarely faulted the Jews for lack of enterprise, and in the turmoil and terror of these early *Anschluss* days, Jewish initiative once again began to stir. The *Gemeinde* may have been looted and laid waste, and its leaders may have been sent to prison or Dachau, but others were ready to carry on.

Some of them were second echelon *Gemeinde* officials. Youth Welfare Director Rosa Rachel Schwarz and First Secretary Ernst Engel, at considerable peril to themselves, secreted some of the funds that the *Gemeinde* had set aside for the Schuschnigg plebescite. They and a few others began holding semi-secret breakfast meetings in the back room of a Jewish-owned tourist bureau or sometimes in the back room of a cafe. Later they moved their "floating *Gemeinde*" to the lobby of the Rothschild Hospital, and began dispensing small amounts of "bread money" to those Jews who had become totally destitute.

But more, much more, was needed, especially to operate the numerous Jewish welfare institutions that were now swamped with demands. One prominent member of the group circulated an appeal through the Jewish community that raised over $62,000 within ten days. Yet even that did not suffice to maintain these facilities, especially with the demands now being put upon them.

In the meantime, the Gestapo had appointed Adolf Eichmann (who had passed himself off to his superiors as an expert on Jewish affairs) to take charge of Jewish emigration. Within ten days the thirty-two-year-old German-born but Austrian-raised lieutenant — he grew up in Hitler's home city of Linz — held two meetings with Jewish leaders. During these sessions he sought to intimidate them with his bullying, threatening manner, while also trying to impress them with his few words of Hebrew and Yiddish and his knowledge of Zionist history.

According to Menachem Menczer, who represented a Zionist youth group at one of these meetings, and is the only person alive today who attended them, Eichmann scorned the Vienna Jews for their lack of support for Palestine. "When he learned the amount of money contributed to Palestine, he professed to be shocked," says Menczer. "That's all for Palestine?" Eichmann asked. "Where have the Jews of Austria spent their money?" Menczer adds, "He talked like a Zionist."

Löwenherz had been imprisoned but not sent to Dachau. Eichmann now decided to release him and make him his administrator for Jewish affairs. This move hardly betokened any affection for Löwenherz, for at their first meeting Eichmann gave his new administrator, who was twenty years older and a war veteran, a box on the ears, and never passed up a chance at later encounters to humiliate him. A younger Zionist named Alois Rothenberg was named by Eichmann to head the Palestine agency.

On May 2 the reconstituted *Gemeinde* opened its doors. Löwenherz was the director assisted by an advisory council. The real director, of course, was Eichmann who a day earlier had boasted in a letter to Berlin, "I have them completely in my power; they don't dare take a single step without asking me first." The only other organizations that the Gestapo allowed to function were the Palestine Agency, which was to incorporate all the Zionist groups, and a Jewish veterans' organization composed of two former veterans' groups. The Nazis were giving the Vienna Jews an organizational unity that they had never come near to achieving on their own.

This new unity was not just organizational. The nearly half-century split between integrationists and nationalists was also fast dissolving, for Hitler was creating more Zionists in Vienna that Herzl had probably ever hoped to do. Some three thousand mostly younger Jewish adults joined the Zionist movement immediately after the *Anschluss* and many more became affiliated with the movement as time went on. On May 20, the *Gemeinde* began publishing a periodical modeled after the *Judische Rundschau* that was issued under Nazi guidance, in Berlin. But the Viennese *Gemeinde* called its publication *Zionistische Rundschau*, and its first number featured an article on immigration that stressed that Jewish settlement in any country other than Palestine could only be considered a temporary move. The new publication also featured on its front page an appeal from Löwenherz and Rabbi Taglich:

> To the Jews of Vienna!
>
> The moment is serious and full of significance; unity and trust in God are the order of the day. What separated us in the past was small and insignificant; what unites us today is great and imperishable.*

The new *Gemeinde* faced some fearful challenges. It had to operate thirteen welfare facilities, oversubscribed with would-be clients. It also had to feed not just the thousands it was feeding before the *Anschluss*, but the tens of thousands of newly impoverished Jews as well. And it had to do all this from a speedily disintegrating resource base.

Fortunately, fellow Jews knew the *Gemeinde*'s anguish and were responding. The Joint Distribution Committee began allocating the first of the $431,000 that it would contribute by the end of the year for Austria's Jewry. The *Jewish Chronicle* of London launched an appeal that brought in over a half million dollars. The Hadassah chapter of New York City rushed a check for $20,000, a sum that represents nearly ten times as much in today's currency. Before the outbreak of war would end their efforts, Jewish relief organizations in America, Britain, and France would pour $4,500,000 depression dollars into Vienna to help save the city's Jews.

Food became their first priority. The Joint Distribution Committee obtained permission from Berlin to operate a large soup kitchen, and within a few weeks it was dispensing meals that people could consume at home. Soon eight thousand Jews, including some who a few weeks earlier had been among the city's wealthiest, were standing in line to pick up their family's daily sustenance. As the impoverization of the community increased, the lines grew longer, but despite the growing strain, and despite frequent Nazi harassment — on two occasions storm troopers descended on the building and threw the food onto the street — the operation continued.

The next order of business was emigration. Eichmann had warned the community leaders at their first meeting of his determination to make Vienna *jüdenrein* as soon as possible, and none doubted his word. By mid-April nearly

---

*Although the *Anschluss* brought some measure of unity to the Jewish community, it by no means ended all discord. Julius Steinfeld, who represented the Orthodox Jews on the *Gemeinde*'s newly appointed advisory board, was frequently at odds with Löwenherz. Steinfeld's son-in-law, New York businessman Charles Richter, believes Löwenherz prevented his father-in-law from getting a visa to America, thereby forcing him to go first to Cuba. Rosenkranz, however, claims there is no basis for such a charge. Even within the mainstream Zionists, disputes persisted. One particularly bothersome one was what criteria should be used in deciding who should have priority in obtaining the few immigration certificates available to Palestine.

fifty thousand Jews had registered at the *Gemeinde* for emigration, while thousands of others were making, or trying to make, arrangements on their own. Löwenherz had secured funds from the Joint Distribution Committee and other Jewish agencies to help finance the exodus, and had worked out an arrangement with the Nazis to supplement those funds with some of the proceeds from confiscated Jewish property.

But formidable problems plagued the emigration effort. For one thing, there were numerous bureaucratic barriers. In order to emigrate, a Jew had to have all his papers in order, and this meant standing endlessly in line at various government agencies, often only to be told that he had everything all wrong and must start again. It was especially important to show that all taxes had been paid, and Nazi officials frequently found that the would-be emigrant owed more taxes than he could possibly pay. Other debts were also discovered. For example, a Jewish landlord had sold a building to a Gentile in 1932, and two years later the Gentile had begun violating the rent control laws by overcharging the tenants. The former Jewish landlord was ordered to pay the fine.

Corruption compounded these problems. When George Clare's father went to get his tax certificate, the official made him first pay for the keep of his insane half-brother, who had been in a public asylum for years. Later, Clare's father found that the same official had forced two other family members to do the same. Fake semi-official travel agencies proliferated and profited by selling phony tickets and bogus visas to despairing Jews.

Eichmann himself was not above such petty crimes. Thus, when Gerson Friedmann of the Palestine Agency's Jerusalem office came to seek a speed-up of emigration approvals, he handed Eichmann a bulky envelope and said, "I know that to do this you have to hire extra clerks. I would be happy to pay their salaries." Eichmann, after inspecting the contents of the envelope, smiled and replied, "Thank you, Herr Friedmann. This will help a great deal."

But the problems of emigrating were picayune compared to the problems of immigrating. Where were the Vienna Jews to go? Palestine seemed the most logical haven, and Jewish hopes for large-scale settlement had been stirred by Britain's offer the previous July to partition the protectorate for a second time and set up, finally, a Jewish state. But the British later began tightening up on immigration, and on the day of the *Anschluss* only sixteen immigration permits were available for Austria's Jews. The Vienna Jews quickly used these up, and the relatively few additional permits that came their way. Since each permit was good for a husband and wife, young Jews frequently married people they hardly knew just to make maximum use of the permits. (Some of these marriages, however, lasted.) But it soon became evident that relatively few Vienna Jews would ever make a British-sanctioned *aliyah*.

The mainstream Zionist agencies were still hoping to persuade the British to ease up; in any case they hesitated to create friction with one of Europe's strongest democracies. Consequently, they frowned on illegal emigration. But the militant Revisionists had no such compunctions and at the end of March Willy Perl, the young lawyer who now headed the Vienna Betar, came to Eichmann with a proposal for smuggling Jews into the British protectorate.

Eichmann considered the idea for a week and then rejected it, saying he would not create any "central headquarters for Jewish criminals" in Palestine. But Perl and an associate went to Berlin and, through various ruses, got permission, as well as foreign currency, to send two thousand Jews illegally to Palestine. They then returned to Vienna and used Berlin's approval to impress Eichmann, who now enthusiastically supported the scheme.

For Perl and his group a series of hair-raising episodes then ensued which, in a work of fiction, would be dismissed as unbelievable, including dealing with Greek smugglers, throwing messages out of basement windows to the feet of passersby, hiding money in cracks in the walls while the Gestapo searched their offices, posing as the British consul while talking in French on the telephone from Vienna to the Greek foreign office, and bribing the janitor of the Greek consulate in Vienna to pose on the telephone as the Greek consul. By June 9, however, arrangements had been made, and 389 mostly young Viennese Jews arrived at the South Railroad Station in the evening to board a train for Athens, where a ship to Palestine awaited.

Eichmann and other Nazi officials showed up to see them off. The well-instructed Betar impressed the Nazis with their military precision as Perl barked out commands in Hebrew. Perl then delivered a speech which Eichmann had previously approved. "You are leaving but you are also coming . . . you leave behind a country and a people that did not want you on your way to your brothers and sisters who are longing for you. A happy homecoming! Happy *aliyah!*" The young people then broke out into "*Hatikvah*" and boarded the train.

But even such feats as these could only rescue a small percentage of the Viennese Jews. Most of them were seeking out other possible havens. Switzerland, Czechoslovakia, and Yugoslavia began closing their borders to Jewish visitors from Austria the very night of the *Anschluss*. A few wiser Jews had taken the train into Germany and from there had made it over the border to France and the Lowlands, using their regular Austrian passports. But those borders soon closed as well. Some immigration to those countries did occur, especially to Holland and Belgium, but they offered no hope for wide-scale entrance.

The United States, which had for so long served as a mecca for European Jews, now seemed to beckon once again. America's Austrian quota was only 1,400, but following the country's amalgamation with Germany, President

Roosevelt combined the Austrian and German quotas, thus providing a possible 27,000 emigration visas. Lines of up to 3,000 formed outside the American consulate. Storm troopers sometimes terrorized the lines, forcing the Jews to run back and forth across the street. One consequence was that a would-be emigrant who had waited all night to be at or near the head of the line often found himself, when the line was finally re-formed, at or near its end. Still, they lined up, waited, and hoped.

But greater obstacles than these awaited them. Many Vienna Jews had been born in parts of the old Empire that now belonged to other countries and thus came under other quotas. Galician-born Jews, for example, came under the Polish quota, which was much smaller and was already heavily oversubscribed. The quota for Romanian Jews was particularly minute.*

Another problem was obtaining sponsors. So few Vienna Jews had emigrated to America in the past that many who now wished to do so could not find relatives or friends to sign affidavits in their behalf. Still, despite such impediments, many managed to leave for the United States.

Great Britain, while imposing a stringent quota on emigration to Palestine, took a fair number of Jews within its own country, many of them to be domestic servants. The Scandinavian governments accepted some, with the Social Democratic government of Sweden providing a sanctuary for many Social Democratic leaders, including the twenty-seven-year-old activist Bruno Kreisky. Many Latin American countries made visas available, although frequently only for a price.

In some instances, bribed foreign consuls such as those of Paraguay and Albania issued visas with the understanding that they were not to be used to emigrate into those countries. Instead, recipients would use the visas to secure a transit visa to another country, and then once there (usually Czechoslovakia) they would try to disappear. In the early days of the *Anschluss*, some Jews with emigration papers but no place to emigrate to joined tourist tours to other lands, such as Italy or Switzerland, and then quietly disappeared during the tour.

Jews abroad sought to help. The former Hakoah members who had stayed in America following their tour in 1925 quickly signed affidavits for their former teammates. Hollywood producer Joseph Pasternak signed so many that the American government refused to let him underwrite any more. A former Viennese physician sent copies of New York City phone books to the *Gemeinde* so that those looking for sponsors could look up possible relatives and friends. The Chief Rabbi of Johannesburg adopted his nephew

---

*A joke circulating within the Jewish community (for even under these conditions jokes continued to circulate) told of a Romanian Jew who applied at the American consulate and was told to come back in the year 2019. The would-be emigrant then asked, "In the morning or the afternoon?"

to expedite the boy's exit. Black sheep and prodigal sons who had left home were now looked to as family saviors. Yet the logjam continued.

Shortly after the *Anschluss*, President Roosevelt called for an international conference to consider help for Nazi victims. Some thirty-two countries responded and in early July their delegates met for a week in the French resort of Evian on the shores of Lake Geneva. But only Holland, Denmark, and Santa Domingo expressed genuine willingness to accept additional Jewish refugees, and the conference ended without any effective action.

The German press chortled over the conference's failure. "They weep crocodile tears over the Jews," observed the leading Nazi newspaper, the *Voelkischer Beobachter*, "but nobody is willing to make any sacrifices for these 'unfortunates,' since everyone knows what the Jew means within a national community. Those countries who themselves refuse to take any Jews merely justify the German Reich's defensive measures against the Jews, measures which in any case are not yet sufficiently far-reaching."

Some believe the Evian fiasco strengthened the hand of the hard-liners within the Nazi party and thus prepared the way for the Final Solution. In Vienna, where hopes for the conference's outcome had been riding high, its failure brought a new wave of suicides. For some Vienna Jews the Final Solution had already arrived.

Still, all was not despair and immobilizing depression. At Evian many countries had complained that the Vienna Jews were mostly white-collar employees, business people, and intellectuals, and their countries needed no more such immigrants. In response, the *Gemeinde* started up Operation *Umschulung* (Retraining) to teach its members new trades. Soon women who, a few months earlier, had had comfortable homes and maids, were learning to stitch corsets while their husbands learned to tap heels onto shoes.

Language courses became particularly popular, and by the end of the summer there were thirteen classes in Spanish alone. During the next three and a half years, over 42,000 Vienna Jews would take one or more of these retraining courses. One result was that the *Gemeinde* soon had sufficient carpenters, mechanics, and other artisans to do all its own repairs — when the materials for such repairs could be obtained.

The Palestine Office began teaching younger Jews agriculture and, for that purpose, managed to rent one or two farms in the countryside. There, insulated to some degree from the torment of Vienna, young people learned how to grow crops and tend livestock with the hope of applying their new skills in Palestine.

While the major Zionist organizations still hesitated to sanction or support illegal immigration, the Revisionist headquarters in London secretly authorized its Vienna youth group to stage further undercover landings. Perl and his associates once again made arrangements with a group of Greek smugglers. The latter were to send a ship to Fiume, Italy, to pick up eight hundred Viennese youth and a group of 220 young Polish Jews sent by the head of the Polish *Betar*, Manachem Begin. In high spirits, over one thousand young people boarded a train in Vienna for Italy.

When the ship failed to appear as scheduled in Fiume, Italian authorities refused to let the train into the country. Perched on a side rail on the Austrian side of the border, the group waited. Several days passed and the young people, crammed in eight to a compartment, were becoming frantic. The train's toilets were discharging onto the ground, creating a dangerous health problem. In Vienna, Eichmann was furious over the delay and threatened to send all eight hundred Viennese youth to Dachau. When Perl hinted that such a step would produce a "Masada solution," Eichmann, fearful of the bad publicity that a mass suicide would create, allowed the train to return to Vienna.

There had already been some suicides among the young people, and for the return to Vienna the *Betar* leaders appointed marshals to prevent more. (As a result, only one additional suicide occurred.) Many of the young people later said their most agonizing moment came when they re-entered their homes and saw the anguished expressions on the faces of their parents. Their mothers and fathers had joyfully seen them off, believing that at least their children would escape: their return was devastating. But the *Betar* in Vienna had learned that because the Danube was an international waterway, no visas were required for those countries through which it flowed. On November 1, the original eight hundred Viennese emigres, plus nearly three hundred more, set sail down the Danube for a port in Rumania where once again a ship was to pick them up. At every docking along the way local Jews turned out to greet the refugees, bringing them food, warm clothing, and in one instance a Torah. This time the ship was there to meet them, and the group made it to the Holy Land.

Many further such efforts would follow, for eventually the regular Jewish agencies, confronted with continued British intransigence on the immigration issue, would support and even stage them. Not all of these ventures would be successful; indeed, some would have tragic results. On one occasion, forty *Betar* activists, having secured the departure of over two thousand fleeing Jews in Rumania, stayed behind to save an additional eight hundred and perished in the attempt. But seventeen thousand European Jews would escape the Holocaust thanks to activities that originated within the Viennese community.*

---

*The full story of this illegal immigration has been told at length elsewhere. From the Viennese standpoint, Perl's own book is probably the best source. I should add that the 220 East European Jews sent by Begin to Fiume were allowed to stay in the country because Poland was then not under Nazi rule. They were eventually rescued; Perl and his group contacted a second group of Greek smugglers, who sent a ship that arrived on September 20. Fiume's few resident Jews plus hundreds of sympathetic Italians, including the local prefect and his wife, showed up at the dock to wish them well.

Emigration to other countries also proceeded as Jews showed similar enterprise in discovering places and procedures that could permit escape. Eichmann, in a sense, assisted them when (acting on a suggestion from Löwenherz) he centralized the entire Jewish emigration effort into one office located in a mansion once owned and occupied by the Rothschilds. Previously a Jew had to go to a dozen or more various offices to obtain all the official permits and papers. Now all could be obtained in one day at a single location. The new system was later adopted in Berlin and elsewhere and greatly boosted Eichmann's career.

A Jew would enter the immigration center in the morning, and after being processed as if on a conveyor belt, would leave in the afternoon stripped of everything he owned, including his dignity, but equipped with a short-term passport and instructions to use it as soon as possible if he wished to escape the concentration camp. It was also customary to leave him with a 10-mark note, worth $2.50, to start his new life. Still, the new office did speed up immigration, with nearly ten thousand Jews leaving Vienna during its first month of operation. Many of them might otherwise not have gotten out in time.

In the meantime, pressures on the Jews remaining in Austria were mounting. During the summer, systematic efforts were made to evict Jews on fourteen days' notice from buildings where non-Jews lived. Teachers were sent into parks and playgrounds to drive out any Jewish youngsters found using these facilities. Virtually the only place where Jews could escape from the oppressive atmosphere of the city was the Jewish cemeteries, which were as yet unmolested.

In August all Jewish adults were ordered to take new middle names, Israel for the men and Sarah for the women. By September, the *Gemeinde* was feeding over half of all Jews remaining in the city. Its old age home had three thousand applicants for its twelve vacancies. Its monthly newspaper filled up with ads from members seeking housing, jobs, and, increasingly, matrimony. The growing shortage of marriage partners for young people was responsible for the growth in matrimonial ads; many of their Jewish cohorts had already left, while contacts with non-Jewish youth had been cut off. By fall, the paper was publishing over fifty such matrimonial ads in each issue as Vienna's remaining Jews sought to get on with the business of life in the midst of deprivation and despair.

Vienna being Vienna, many oddities and ironies occurred during the eight months following the *Anschluss*. One cannot help thinking of them as one reviews the record of those desperate days.

One thinks of Egon Friedell, a cultural critic and historian well-known and respected throughout the German-speaking world. Looking out of his apartment window a few days after the takeover, he saw two SS men enter his building. When he heard a knock on the door a few minutes later, he climbed to the windowsill and, after yelling "Out of my way" to a bewildered passerby, jumped to his death. The SS men were coming to see his maid who was having an affair with one of them.

One thinks of Josef Hilsenrad, in jail on a fraud charge when the *Anschluss* occurred. He thereby escaped humiliation, deprivation, and possible deportation to Dachau. It never occurred to the Nazis to examine the jails, and those Jews serving time continued to receive reasonably decent treatment and food along with other prisoners.

One thinks of Otto Kalir who was allowed to emigrate to New York with his valuable collection of fin-de-siécle paintings because the Nazis considered them decadent and worthless.

One thinks of sign painter Leon Zohn who, barely able to survive in depression-ridden Vienna before the *Anschluss*, now found plenty of work as a consultant since he was one of the few practitioners of his craft who knew how to paint the Hebrew letters that the Nazis had decreed for Jewish businesses.

One thinks also of his daughter Fritzi, whose blond hair and blue eyes caused groups of Jews she did not know to stop talking when they saw her approach lest she turn out to be an Aryan informant.

One thinks of the unidentified Jewish man who, having tried to protect a Jewish woman being beaten by a storm trooper, and having been brought to Gestapo headquarters for doing so, was asked by an official to "help establish law and order in Vienna," and was given a special document authorizing him to do so.

One thinks of the Cafe Kastner where as late as August 1938 Nazi party members with swastikas in their lapels could be seen playing cards with Jewish customers.

One thinks of former General Sommer who, arrested more as a monarchist than as a Jew on the first day of the *Anschluss*, was released from jail in August only to find that his physician son-in-law had just been sent to Buchenwald. Sommer then decided to write to General von Brauschitsch, the commander-in-chief of the German army, requesting an interview. His wife and daughter thought he was crazy for doing so, but von Brauschitsch replied, granting his request. So Sommer, a man whom the lowliest Nazi in Vienna could abuse at will, traveled to Berlin where the head of the German army greeted him courteously and, after hearing his plea, told him, "Your son-in-law will be on his way home before you get back to Vienna."

But this brings us to the final irony. Although Sommer saw to it that his daughter and son-in-law left the country, he declined to go himself, believing that the current oppression could not last. He was by no means alone in

The festive opening of the Fourteenth International Zionist Congress in Vienna's Concert Hall, August 1925. *"Wiener Bilder," August 23, 1925.*

Mounted police disperse a Nazi-sponsored demonstration against the holding of the 1925 World Zionist Congress, Vienna. *"Wiener Bilder," August 23, 1925.*

Members of the militant faction of the Zionist movement on a pilgrimage to Theodor Herzl's tomb, Vienna, 1930. Left to right: Saul Macover, Meir Grossman, Zeev Jabotinsky, Robert Stricker, Leopold Sitzmann, Fritz Richter. *Courtesy of William Stricker, New York City.*

Right, Stefan Zweig, 1881–1942. *Austrian National Library.*

Below, Robert Stricker, 1929. *William Stricker, New York City.*

Robert Stricker and his wife, Paula, in Basel, Switzerland, during the 1931 Zionist World Congress. *Courtesy of William Stricker, New York City.*

Seventh class of the Zwei Peres Chajes Gymnasium in the Castillenzgasse, 1931. The school was 12 years old that year—many of the students shown later perished in the Holocaust. *Permission of Leo Glueckselig, New York City (in back row, clowning, with girl's arms around him).*

Aron Menczer (front) with members of Zionist youth group. *Courtesy of Jacob Metzer.*

Aron Menczer surrounded by "his kids" (Menczer is third from left, front row). Probably a birthday or Hanukka celebration. *Courtesy of Jacob Metzer, The Hebrew University of Jerusalem, Israel.*

Above, Dr. Josef Lowenherz, 1936. *Austrian National Library.* Right, an anti-Semitic poster, Vienna, March 1938. Across the chest of the large figure with swastika tie, it says, "Fight against the Jewish spirit and the betrayal of the people." Below, "Jews are becoming adjusted to being non-Jews—this was not meant to be." *Austrian National Library.*

Jewish scholars (Rabbi Murmelstein, later administrator of Theresienstadt, stands in back row on right). This picture was "posed by order of the S.S." Vienna, 1938. *Documentation Center of the Austrian Resistance.*

Three Viennese Jews are forced to scrub Schuschnigg campaign
slogans from the street in Vienna. *Documentation Center of the
Austrian Resistance, Vienna.*

The window sign tells us that the owner of this bookshop, "Is in Dachau!!!"
Yivo Institute for Jewish Research, New York City.

Vienna, March 1938. A young man is forced to paint "Jew" on the wall of an apartment building, supervised by an Austrian Nazi party member. *Institute of Contemporary History, Vienna.*

thinking so. Rumors of Hitler's impending demise circulated freely through the Jewish community, a favorite one being that Hitler had cancer of the mouth and would soon die. Others simply believed that Allied pressure would force Hitler out of office, or at least make him ease up on his policies.

Whatever the reason or rationale, many Jews refused to abandon Vienna. Helen Hilsenrad met a woman, while they were both standing in the *Gemeinde*'s food lines, whose entire family had affidavits of support from relatives in the United States. Yet they were in no hurry to leave, she said, for her husband was certain that Hitler's end was fast approaching. William Geisler recalls that all twenty-nine members of his family could have emigrated, for they had relatives in the United States, Great Britain, and Australia. Yet only nine chose to do so. The rest believed that it would all blow over.

Many elderly Jews thought themselves immune from Nazi terror. What would Hitler want with us old people, they frequently said. One grandmother claimed that "Hitler is only against the Polish Jews, and I am a Viennese." Freud's four sisters all refused to emigrate. So, initially, did Freud himself. Martin Freud believes that only after the third Gestapo raid, and the summoning of Anna to Gestapo headquarters for interrogation, did his father make up his mind to go. Even then, says the younger Freud, "he left with great reluctance and only after strong persuasion."

The fierce attachment of so many Jews to a city that had through the years, and most especially in recent months, demonstrated its equally fierce hate for them, remains the greatest, and grimmest, irony of all.

Chapter 23

A Closing Circle

If Vienna Jews could still view the future optimistically six months after the *Anschluss*, they could point to one encouraging development. The random street violence which marked the initial weeks of the takeover had died down. Pressures on Jews had increased, but were now taking the form of official harassment rather than outright terrorism. For example, the raids on synagogues which reached a highpoint during Passover virtually ended. No longer need Orthodox women stand sentinel outside synagogues and prayer houses on Saturday ready to give a warning signal to their men praying within should a band of storm troopers or Hitler Youth show up.

On September 2 several thousand Jews jammed the city's largest synagogue to say goodbye to four hundred young people who were soon to set out for Palestine. A highlight of the joyous event was the presentation to the young emigrants of the Torah scrolls from twelve soon-to-be-shut-down synagogues. The recipients carried the scrolls triumphantly up and down the aisles preparatory to carrying them to the Holy Land. It would be the last truly festive occasion of the Vienna Jews.

A few weeks later, France and Britain shocked the Jews, and much of the rest of the world as well, by yielding to Hitler at Munich and accepting Hitler's dismembering of Czechoslovakia. By early October the first Jewish refugees from the now German-occupied Sudetenland arrived in Vienna. About the same time, Vienna held its first blackout exercises, and local Nazis, emboldened by Hitler's triumph at Munich and the earlier failure of the Evian conference, seized on the occasion to pounce once again on the Jews. So many people with broken arms and legs, smashed-up faces, and other injuries were brought to the Rothschild Hospital that they were put first in the corridors and then, when these filled up, on the lawn.

On Rosh Hashanah Eve, Nazis stormed synagogues in the Leopoldstadt, pushing, cuffing, and driving out the worshippers. Then, on Yom Kippur Eve in early October, they rounded up a group of Jews and carted them off to the Danube Canal, where boats were supposedly waiting to take them to Palestine. Of course, no such boats existed and Berlin, when informed by Jewish leaders of what had happened, said it was a mistake. Those caught up in the exercise, however, had to wait in the *Gemeinde* for two days before their house keys were returned.

On October 6, Nazis set fire to three synagogues, one of them the largest in the Leopoldstadt. Five days later they raided a youth center, beating the youngsters so severely that some had to be hospitalized. Moshe Auerbach, an emissary of the Jewish agency in Palestine who arrived in Vienna at about this time, reported back, "What most characterizes the situation of the Jewish masses here is their bewilderment, despair prompted by the feeling of their inability to find a way out, and above all, fear that any day may bring new persecutions."

These fears proved well-founded when, two weeks later, Nazis throughout the Reich staged their first, nationwide pogrom: *Kristallnacht*, or the Night of Broken Glass.

Seizing upon the shooting of a minor German embassy official in Paris by a desperate seventeen-year-old Polish Jew as an excuse, Nazi mobs raged through Vienna destroying temples, plundering Jewish businesses and homes, and seizing Jews. Men standing in line at the immigration office were herded into a cellar and beaten mercilessly. Then, with heads still bleeding, they were dumped into trucks and shipped to Dachau. Another group were rounded up and jammed into a room so tightly that no one could move. Kept there all day and night without food and hardly enough air to breathe, a few became so desperate they jumped out of the window to their deaths.

The pogrom brought the first mass arrest of Jewish women. For them the Nazis had other things in mind.

Nazi doctrine strictly forbade sexual contact with Jews, and as a result, rape had not figured heavily in the *Blitzverfolgung*. But frustrated Nazis continually looked for ways to sexually exploit Jewish women. For example, they had earlier forced women in the Leopoldstadt to stand naked for blood tests supposedly being done for medical research.

On *Kristallnacht* they went further. In one place of detention storm troopers forced Jewish women to disrobe and participate in lesbian orgies with prostitutes while their Nazi captors watched. In another detention center they ordered some two hundred Jewish women to strip and then dance with high-kicking legs. When one refused, they tied her down spread out on a table and forced the other women to spit in her face.

The terror did not spare those few Jews still living in the provinces. In Innsbruck the Brown Shirts beat four prominent Jews to death. One middle-aged couple were thrown into the river — this was only a few weeks before ski season — and when they managed to make it to shore, the man was arrested.

In Graz, Jews were routed from their beds and forced to hit each other about the head with stones. They were then taken to Dachau, and made to walk through rows of club-wielding SS men to a room outfitted for torture. They stood there for four hours before the SS men entered, took a young Jew who was not quite normal and, making him stand on a platform, gave him a prayerbook and told him to recite prayers. But the young man could not read Hebrew.

In Linz, the storm troopers went too far and began raping Jewish women. The Gestapo intervened and two Austrian storm troopers received four-year prison sentences for racial pollution.

Kristallnacht left Austria with only one functioning Jewish house of worship, the temple next to *Gemeinde* headquarters. All others, with one exception, were destroyed. (The exception was a temple in the ninth district that the Nazis intended to take over for their own purposes.) In Vienna over four thousand Jewish businesses were looted and two thousand Jewish dwellings were "Aryanized." The *Gemeinde*'s food supplies were thrown into the street and contaminated by glass from the shattered windows. Fortunately, *Gemeinde* officials had prudently stockpiled some spare food at a secret site, but it was a week before feeding operations could be resumed.

On the day following *Kristallnacht* a Viennese Gestapo unit boasted in its official report that it had completed its work "thoroughly and rapidly" and that "the event paralyzed the Jews to such a degree that they could not even exhibit their customary outbursts of despair. It may be stated with certainty that after today's events the Jews have lost every vestige of desire to carry on."

The events also gave substance to the fears expressed by a Zionist official who had visited Vienna shortly after the *Anschluss*. At that time, he reported finding the city's Jews "living not only in a fool's Paradise but a veritable Hell" and warned that "the policy may aim at a complete annihilation of Austrian Jewry."

With the memory of *Kristallnacht* seared into their minds, and its scars often imprinted on their bodies as well, and with the regime's mounting threats and harassments to spur them on, Jews throughout the Reich now began a frantic dash for the exits. Fortunately, their brethren from Britain, France, and America could offer financial assistance. Fortunately also, the pogrom's barbarism had finally shocked some other countries into opening their doors a bit wider.

The country that responded most generously was Great Britain. The British offered to take five thousand Jewish children for three years, and by December 10 the first trainload of seven hundred youngsters from Vienna was en route to London. They and those that followed readily found homes with British families, many of them Gentiles. Thereafter, Britain began taking one thousand Jewish children a month, about one-quarter of them from Austria.

Another country of refuge was Holland. Officially, the Dutch closed their frontiers to Jewish immigration in mid-December, but in practice they turned away no child who arrived at their borders without parents. Consequently, Jewish parents could place their children in groups aboard Holland-bound trains with reasonable assurances that they would be taken in and cared for. (Unfortunately, the Dutch kept the children together, which made it easier for the Nazis to seize and deport them later when Holland was occupied.)

Belgium and the Scandinavian countries also bent their immigration rules when it came to younger refugees. Belgium, in fact, would eventually take in four times as many Austrian Jews as Holland.

Saving adults was much more difficult for many of the most eligible had already left. Those who remained had fewer contacts and other resources to draw upon. Some were physically impaired, others possessed insufficient or the wrong kinds of skills, and nearly all were desperately poor. Yet they tackled their problems with enterprise if not always good sense. A group of Jewish war veterans managed to procure some agricultural equipment and began training themselves and their families to become farmers. A group of physically disabled Jews formed the "Self-help Organization of Jewish Cripples" and calling themselves willing and capable workers, asked the *Gemeinde* to help them emigrate. A group of disabled war veterans who were also musicians organized an orchestra, hoping to emigrate as a group. One hundred Jewish musicians who had formed an orchestra sought to emigrate to China, and when this plan fell through, boarded a ship in Hamburg for Trinidad. They had no landing permit for the Caribbean colony and their ultimate fate remains unknown.

No avenue of escape went untried. When Britain announced that it would accept a certain number of Jewish women to work as housemaids but required them to be single, the *Gemeinde*'s rabbinical office began issuing instant divorces to any woman needing one for that purpose. (It was thought that if one member of the family could get out, then he or she could help the others follow.) When it became known that Japan was maintaining occupied Shanghai as an open city, one thousand German and Austrian Jews a month began pouring into the Chinese metropolis. Michael Blumenthal, one of these Jews, later became U.S. Secretary of the Treasury. When South American consular officials indicated that sufficient money under the table would secure a precious bona fide visa, many Jews, often with the help of Jewish relief agencies, found ways of scraping together the needed sums.

Illegal border crossings did not figure greatly in the plans of most Jews. It was difficult just to get to the borders and, without expert assistance, almost impossible to cross them. Still, some made it through and those who succeeded in getting to England were usually allowed to stay. Among them were eight young couples from the Leopoldstadt who worked their way through the Lowland countries and then, by means of a clandestine boat trip, landed on the English shore. By September 1939, some 3,500 Jews, one-quarter of them Austrian, were lodged in a former British military camp in Kent.

Illegal immigration offered at this time the only route to Palestine, for the British government in July had suspended all legal immigration for six months. In response, some mainstream Zionist leaders had established the Mossad le Aliya Bet, and following *Kristallnacht*, its Vienna office organized and sent 386 German and Austrian Jews to Italy and Yugoslavia to board a ship for an unsanctioned landing in the Holy Land. The mission succeeded, and preparations had begun for a second one when a Nazi newspaper publicized it. The alarmed British then put pressure on Yugoslavia to halt all further such transits.

In May 1939 the British issued a new White Paper which stated that they would admit fifteen thousand Jews a year to Palestine for the next five years, after which all further immigration would require Arab consent. This move convinced many Zionist leaders, including Ben Gurion, to start supporting illegal immigration. Gradually, many regular Jewish organizations, including eventually the Joint Distribution Committee, began secretly supporting it as well.

Since most such immigration efforts used the Danube, Vienna played a prominent role. Nevertheless, although most Viennese Jews were now eager to make an *aliyah*, only five percent would succeed in doing so. Underground journeys to the Promised Land were difficult to execute. Many of the ships went aground or suffered some other mishap, and many of those vessels that did get to Palestine were seized by the British and turned away. Moreover, space on the ships was scarce. Not only were German and Polish Jews also struggling to flee, but Hitler's occupation of Czechoslovakia in the spring of 1939 brought 120,000 more Jews into the Nazi orbit. The already narrow pipelines to freedom were becoming increasingly clogged.

The May 1939 census revealed that 84,000 Jews had left Austria. Through the next four months immigration efforts continued for the 114,000 who remained. The outbreak of war in September closed off Great Britain and France. It also ended the contributions of their relief agencies. Now the Joint Distribution Committee had to shoulder singlehandedly the task of supporting and, if possible, saving the remaining Vienna Jews.

With Eichmann's permission Löwenherz traveled abroad, first to Amsterdam, later to Lisbon, trying to open up new routes to safety or to enlarge those that existed. But possible places of refuge were shrinking all the time. In the spring of 1940 the Germans invaded Denmark and Norway, and a month later overran Holland, Belgium, and France. Russia began denying travel visas to fleeing Jews, thereby effectively sealing off Shanghai. The German attack on the Balkans and then Russia in the spring of 1941 further tightened the cordon. In August 1941 the Nazis, perhaps because of their pressing need for manpower, forbade any further emigration by Jewish men under the age of forty-five.

In early November 1941, one month before America's entry into the war, the gates slammed shut. Eichmann, who had been relentlessly pressing the Jews to leave, would not permit any further departures. Diplomatic representatives from Uruguay and Venezuela sought to intervene in particular cases, usually in vain. The Argentine consul made his Jewish mistress his secretary, but the move failed to exempt her from the new restrictions. While a few more would manage to slip out, usually via small ships to Lisbon, nearly all the more than 44,000 Jews still left in Vienna, almost half of them over sixty years of age, were trapped. The exodus had ended.

Britain, which had prevented so many Jews from going to Palestine, took in 31,000 Austrian Jews, more than any other country.* America came next, with over 28,000; then China, with 18,000. Only 9,000 made it to Palestine. Of the smaller countries, Belgium led the list; well over 4,000 Jews were admitted. Last was Canada. With a population of 7,000,000 and a land area greater than that of the United States, Canada accepted only eighty-two Austrian Jews. Australia and New Zealand took in about 1,900.

The compatibility in aims between the Jews and their greatest immediate enemy, Eichmann, was another irony. As more and more Jews made it to safety, or what they thought was safety, Eichmann's fortunes rose: within three years the once obscure Gestapo lieutenant had become a colonel in charge of Jewish emigration throughout the Reich. Of course, he owed much of his success to Löwenherz's suggestion that a centralized processing center for Jewish emigration be established.

But the final irony is once again the grimmest one. Some 17,000 Jews who found their way to other European lands came under Nazi control again when the war spread to these countries. All their enterprising efforts went for naught — most of them suffered the same fate as their fellow Jews left behind in Vienna.

---

*A major reason for Britain's restriction of emigration to Palestine was to insure Arab support in the event of war with Germany. The British could, of course, count on Jewish support in any case.

The aftermath of *Kristallnacht* brought no surcease but rather a step-up in anti-Jewish regulations. Many of these new measures simply formalized practices that had already become routine in Austria. For example, the explusion of all Jewish children from public schools on November 15 affected only children in Germany proper, for in Austria they had been turned out of classes almost from the first day of Nazi rule. But other post-*Kristallnacht* measures brought new restrictions for all Jews under the Nazi yoke.

Berlin now empowered all district leaders to restrict Jews from certain streets and areas and even to relocate them into specific districts. Jewish war veterans lost the right to wear their military uniforms and Jewish attorneys were forbidden to advise Jews on legal matters. Along with other Jewish professionals, they had lost their right to practice their profession since the first days of the *Anschluss*, but just as doctors had been allowed as "medical assistants" to treat Jews, Jewish attorneys as "legal assistants" had been allowed to advise them.

A series of harsh economic measures completed the impoverization of Jews throughout the Third Reich. In December all remaining Jewish businesses were confiscated — almost none were left in Austria, but some still existed in Germany — and two months later Jews were ordered to hand over all gold, silver, and any other valuables. Some gave away their jewelry and silver to Christian friends or used them for barter in order to keep them from falling into Gestapo hands.

To complete its confiscation of Jewish wealth, the government imposed a fine of $300,000 on all Jews throughout greater Germany. Soon the *Gemeinde*, with funds from the Jewish relief agencies, was feeding almost the entire community. It also doubled the number of places in its homes for the aged, although another three thousand still remained on the waiting lists. As a Gestapo report in the first quarter of 1939 expressed it, "The loss of every economic basis has also brought for the Jews in *Ostmark* [the new name for Austria] a pervasive worsening of their condition. The social restructuring is continually producing increased proletarianization."

At the same time, the regime kept up a drumfire of hate propaganda against the remaining Jews. As early as the summer of 1938 it mounted an exhibit entitled "The Eternal Jew," which 350,000 Viennese attended. School-children were taken in groups. A flood of posters and films depicted the Jews in the worst possible light. Viennese policemen were required to see *"Jew Süss,"* one of the more notorious feature films starring the well-known German actor, Werner Kraus. In May 1939, Jews were paraded through the streets with placards in retaliation for French and British "encirclement" of Germany.

The outbreak of war in September 1939 produced a further worsening of conditions. Many Viennese blamed the Jews for the war, holding them especially responsible for Britain's hostility toward Germany. Jews walking the streets were frequently insulted and sometimes beaten, while at night their homes were ransacked. Löwenherz warned them to remain as inconspicuous as possible, especially when it came to walking in the *Wienerwald* (Vienna Wood), which, since it was not officially designated a park, was still legally open to them. The *Gemeinde* director also appealed to the Nazi authorities, who promised to speak to the police.

The spontaneous attacks diminished, but the government increased its own pressures. More and more Jews were evicted from buildings where Aryans also lived and were forced to move in with other Jews. Soon two and sometimes three families were sharing a single flat. Making this enforced togetherness more onerous were decrees forbidding Jews to be out after 9:00 p.m. in the summer and after 8:00 p.m. in the winter. All radios were also confiscated. Food rationing for the general population was accompanied by special, much more limited rations for Jews. Soon they were allowed to buy only unrationed food, such as potatoes, and could only make such purchases between 12:00 and 1:00 p.m. By that time, any unrationed, unspoiled food was generally gone.

The war also brought a cutback in help from abroad. It not only ended relief efforts by the French and British agencies but forced the Joint Distribution Committee to reduce its contributions as well; the American relief agency now had to help the nearly three million Polish Jews who had fallen into Nazi hands. But while the Joint Distribution Committee reduced its $100,000 a month subsidy to the *Gemeinde*, it continued to provide food as well as money for special emigration efforts. From September 1 to December 1, over five thousand more Jews emigrated, about one-half of them to the United States. The reduction in the number of Jews left in Vienna did not make the cutbacks in aid much easier to absorb, for the remaining Jews, two-thirds of whom were now over sixty, needed more help than ever.

The elderly were not the *Gemeinde*'s only charges. It was also caring for over 2,300 children. Many had lost their parents through deportation to concentration camps, suicide, or death from various illnesses which had now become more deadly because of the malnourished state of the community and its lack of medical care. Some of these children had become separated from their parents in illegal border crossings. In some cases, parents who could leave but could not take their children with them handed them over to the *Gemeinde*, intending to send for them later. In only a few cases had there been outright abandonment.

At an earlier stage of the *Anschluss* most Jewish parents had rejected offers to give up their children for adoption abroad. But as the situation steadily deteriorated, their sentiments started to shift. When word went out in the fall of 1940 that two wealthy American women, each hoping to adopt a child, were at the *Gemeinde*, the building was soon mobbed with young mothers frantically offering their babies in the hope of ensuring the children's survival. For survival for any Jews remaining in Vienna was beginning to look increasingly doubtful.

The Nazis had introduced forced labor for Jewish men in early 1939. Most of the work sites were in and around Vienna, but a few men had been sent to Germany. Their employers, greatly pleased with their willingness and ability to work, asked for more of them. But few additional working-age men were available. The men were given one day off a week to work on their emigration problems.

With the outbreak of war, the Nazi need for labor mounted, and by the winter of 1939 Jewish men as old as seventy, and even pregnant women, were shoveling snow and performing similar tasks. In the spring of 1940 two summer labor camps were set up outside Vienna for fifty Jewish teenage boys, while a group of Jewish girls were sent to Germany to work in the harvest. All of them had volunteered for such work, but most soon regretted having done so, for they toiled sixty-hour weeks with little food and under difficult living conditions. Their employers paid them the minimum wage but then collected it again for their room and board. The work projects were only intended to last the summer and all were returned to Vienna in the fall.

The *Gemeinde* staff itself had encouraged the young people to volunteer; it wanted to save them from idleness which could lead to trouble. It also hoped that the work would teach them some manual skills, show the regime that young workers could be useful, and help to ensure their future.

The *Gemeinde* sought to keep some educational, Zionist, and even cultural activities going. It operated a school where Hebrew, Jewish history, and other subjects were taught in addition to regular subjects. In the summer of 1938, it had also operated an agricultural camp, and two such camps the following summer. In September 1940 the *Gemeinde* managed to stage a Youth Aliyah exhibition, and the following May discreetly arranged a series of late afternoon concerts. But the widening of the war with the attack on Russia brought an end to most of these efforts. By the fall of 1941 the *Gemeinde* no longer had the resources to educate the less than nine hundred Jewish children and youth still left in Vienna.

The attack on Russia brought further restrictions. Previously, Jews could take streetcars but had to stand if Aryans wanted the seats. Now they could use public transportation only if they lived four miles from their places of work, and then had to stand on the rear platform. Certain streetcar lines were completely forbidden, as was all movement in the inner city.

The Jewish blind or deaf had already lost their invalid badges, but now they and all other Jews acquired a new sign of impaired status. On September 1 the regime ordered all Jews over six years of age to wear a yellow star. The stars had to be of a certain size, well-sewn, and conspicuously displayed. The *Gemeinde* worked day and night to get them ready in time. Some war veterans took to wearing their military decorations with their stars in an effort to ease the stigma, but stopped doing so when infuriated Nazis began arresting them.

Earlier experiences had already taught the Jews to take all official measures seriously. Shortly after *Kristallnacht*, for example, a retired engineer had refused to cooperate with a surly finance official seeking an additional tax payment. "What do you want from me, a seventy-eight-year-old man? I will sell everything. You can't do anything to me," he had shouted. Afterwards, according to a Gestapo report, he had had "the impudence" to complain of the official to the finance office. The man was promptly arrested and packed off to a concentration camp.

Most violations of the early ordinances had involved less outright defiance. Thus, a seventy-one-year-old man was jailed for ten days for visiting a park, while a couple in their late sixties were arrested for taking seats on the streetcar while Aryan passengers were standing. (This was before the decree requiring Jews to keep to the rear platform.) In just a single two-month period, September and October 1940, the Gestapo processed over 1,300 incidents involving Jews. Most were denunciations of Jews by Gentiles for such crimes as going to the movies or being out after curfew.

The yellow star greatly reduced the stream of such complaints: now the Jews were openly branded and few indeed would dare to do what they were not allowed to do. Still, a few elderly people sometimes became confused and wandered into public parks or into stores after hours, or in some way violated one or more of the now 250 anti-Jewish regulations on the books.

The stars exposed the Jews to all kinds of unpleasantness even when they were not violating any ordinances. Ditta Jeglinsky Lowy was walking on the street when a storm trooper came up to her and bellowed, "Hopefully all of you will soon be burned." She was about thirteen at the time.

On another occasion she and a girlfriend decided to see a movie, now illegal for Jews. Holding school books over their chests to conceal their stars, they purchased tickets and entered the theater. Suddenly, in the midst of the film the lights went on as the Nazis took up a collection for *Winterhilfe.* The terrified girls managed to cover up their stars in time and escaped unscathed, but they never tried going to a movie again. Despite her youth, Ditta was working full-time in a leather goods factory. The entire work force, at least in her department, consisted of Jews. The work itself was not overly onerous and the employees received a small stipend for their labor. (Otherwise, of course, they could not have survived to work.) She also had a boyfriend who lived in the Leopoldstadt, and since Jews were not allowed out after 8:00 p.m., they would usually stay over at each other's homes when they saw each other.

Menashe Mautner, the *Gemeinde*'s senior social worker, has left a written account of his experiences in the city during this time. Once he was assisting home an older man just released from the hospital. While they were waiting for a streetcar, the man, still in a weakened condition, sat down on a bench. An SS man, seeing the violation, jumped over the track, gave the older man a box on the ears, and shouted, "Soon we will be getting rid of all of you for good."

On another occasion, Mautner himself took a seat in a streetcar section reserved for special groups, including disabled veterans. When passengers protested, he quickly quieted them by pointing out that he was a disabled veteran with an artificial leg. On still another occasion, he was going home when he slipped and fell on some ice. For three hours he lay on the ground imploring passersby to help him get up. None would do so. Eventually he managed to get up on his own but fractured his wrist in the process.

But if passersby were loath to render aid to anyone wearing a star, they remained ready to denounce them even for activities not officially proscribed. Gestapo reports even note the arrest of a sixty-six-year-old Jewish man in late 1941 for collecting cigarette butts on the street. "His behavior and disgusting appearance stirred up displeasure in the passersby." The incident occurred a few days before Christmas.

Chapter 24

Deportation and Destruction

The specter of the concentration camp haunted the Vienna Jews from the very beginning of the *Anschluss*. Their fears were certainly well-founded: by the end of the year nearly ten thousand of them had been sent to Dachau or Buchenwald. The camps had not yet acquired quite the image of horror they later assumed. For one thing, no children, women, or elderly men were sent to the camps. For another, they were not yet known as extermination facilities. While many prisoners died, and urns containing their ashes were sent back to their families with bills for cremation expenses, most internees continued to survive. Even releases from the camps were then quite common.

Eichmann frequently used the threat of stopping such releases to pressure Jews into emigrating. The Nazis even brought back Friedmann and Stricker — the outspoken Ehrlich had been beaten to death — but kept the two Zionist leaders under close surveillance and refused to let them emigrate. Both bore visible signs of their rough treatment. Stricker for a long time was unable to move without assistance.*

---

*During Stricker's stay in Dachau, a German guard once stuck a revolver in his mouth. Stricker reacted by laughing. "Why do you laugh? Don't you know I can kill you?" said the guard. "Yes, but you are not such a coward that you would shoot an unarmed man who cannot defend himself," responded Stricker. The guard then withdrew the revolver and walked away. One of Stricker's fellow inmates later related this incident to Rabbi Stephen Wise of New York City, who in turn related it in a letter to Stricker's son William.

But following *Kristallnacht* signs began to appear that the Nazis had more vicious plans in mind. Josef Meisels, a young social worker at the Jewish home for waifs and strays, was accompanying his charges to their special school when an anxious SS man approached him with a strange request. The SS man's adopted five-year-old daughter had been found to be Jewish and had been taken to the home. His wife and his other children were crying every night because they missed the little girl. But the SS man's request was not for special treatment for his former daughter. Rather, he beseeched Meisels to help the little girl get to Palestine. "I now think," says Meisels, "that he knew or had some idea of what was coming."*

During the following year other signs appeared of what might be in the offing. The government dissolved all Jewish agencies except the *Gemeinde*, saying it needed to centralize Jewish matters to facilitate emigration. This move would also, however, facilitate deportation. A woman fumbling for her papers at the emigration office in the summer of 1939 was told, "Hurry up, Jewess. When war breaks out all the Jews here will be killed."

The outbreak of war in September brought immediate indications of the change in policy. Within two weeks the Nazis sent over one thousand Jewish men to Buchenwald, among them one hundred over the age of seventy-four. Although not executed, these new internees were so badly mistreated that by Christmas about one-third were dead.

The number of urns coming back to Vienna now became so great that mothers and wives who had been anxiously hoping to hear from their loved ones now hoped just as anxiously not to, since the only communication they were likely to receive would be the funeral urn. Indeed, it was not unusual for a woman, when asked about her deported family member, to reply, "God be thanked, I have heard nothing." The city's already high rate of Jewish interments reached such a level that authorities had to limit them to five or six a day, for the cries of the mourners were disturbing the general public.

The speedy German occupation of Poland opened up new territories and inspired the Nazis with new ideas on how to get rid of Vienna's remaining Jews. On October 10 Eichmann directed Löwenherz to prepare a list of one to two thousand able-bodied men for "colonization" work in the area south of Lublin. Craftsmen such as carpenters were especially wanted. Löwenherz, like nearly everyone else, believed what Eichmann said regarding the mission, and actually the Nazis apparently did intend at the time to set up a functioning Jewish colony there.

The *Gemeinde* sent out a letter to those selected, ordering them to report for colonization work in Poland, and stressed that "all concerned should take

---

*There was, of course, nothing that Meisels could do to fulfill the request. The little girl soon became ill and died.

builders' tools with them, such as mallets, saws, planes, hammers, and nails."
According to a Gestapo report, "The rest of the population knows hardly
anything at all about this operation."

Two transports containing in all about 1,600 men left Vienna during the
last ten days of October. The men had been told that their wives and children
would follow them, but when they reached their destination, some three
hundred were selected out, while the rest were forced to swim the Sam River
to the Russian zone. The Russians reluctantly accepted them but sent back
word not to send any more. They then dispatched most of the Jews to labor
camps in Siberia.

The Joint Distribution Committee, acting at the suggestion of
Löwenherz, refused to transfer any more foreign exchange to Vienna unless
the deportations ceased. This resolute gesture, in addition to the failure of the
original colonization plan, the refusal of the Russians to accept further Jews,
and the army's need for all available trains, brought the deportations to a
temporary halt. But in February 1941 some five thousand more Jews were sent
to Poland, and in October 1941, with previously Russian-occupied Poland and
much of eastern Russia now in German hands, deportation on a massive scale
got under way. By July 1 of 1942, over 25,000 Jews had been removed from
Vienna.

Although Austria now had a concentration camp of its own at
Mauthausen outside Linz, relatively few Austrian Jews ended up there. Instead,
they were at this time sent to Riga, Minsk, the Lodz ghetto, and other locations
in the East. Most of them suffered the same fate as other Jews caught up in
the Holocaust.

The beginning of the mass deportations produced a spirited discussion among
the community's leaders as to whether they should assist the operation. But
only the head of the Disabled War Veterans, an engineer named Siegfried
Kolisch, opposed cooperating, and even he eventually came to agree with the
others that in helping carry out such activities they could protect the weak or
deserving while providing some comfort and assistance to those selected.
Although as early as September 1941 some news of the killing of Jews had
reached Vienna – a letter from a soldier at the eastern front which told of
shooting one thousand Jews had been displayed in a shop window – most
officials believed that the deported Jews were being put to work. When a year
later a messenger from Poland brought a report on what was happening in
Auschwitz, the *Gemeinde* leaders dismissed it as *unmöglich* (impossible).

Of course it was convenient for them to discredit such reports and to go
on preparing the deportation lists. Any resistance would have put its leaders
on a train to the East. As it was, not only they but also their immediate families
were allowed to stay in Vienna. Nevertheless, they did have reason to disbelieve

such reports. Mass executions not only seemed barbaric but also illogical. The regime now needed every bit of manpower it could get: why should it want to destroy whatever labor the Jews could provide? Had not the Nazis, in clamping down on emigration in the second half of 1941, first decreed an absolute prohibition on the departure of men under forty-five?

Rumors, however, continued to mount and in 1943 Löwenherz called unannounced at the office of Vienna's Jewish commissioner, Karl Ebener. The *Gemeinde* director, so Ebener later testified, seemed "an utterly broken man" and asked for a meeting with Huber, Ebener's supervisor. "I asked him what he wanted and he told me that he had heard reports that Jews were being put to death and he wanted to make sure that that was in fact the case. I thought he might have a bad time of it and that he might conceivably be charged with spreading enemy radio reports, but Löwenherz said that that was all the same to him."

Ebener took Löwenherz to Huber, who telephoned Berlin and then reported to them that such "empty, evil rumors" had no foundation. Löwenherz, said Huber, "was visibly relieved."

Those who would judge the *Gemeinde* director harshly for his role in the deportations should keep in mind not only his earlier and quite effective efforts in facilitating emigration, but his willingness to place himself in peril to check on these reports at this time. As for arranging the deportations, the *Gemeinde* to a slight extent did manage to affect the process. Löwenherz was able to delay deportations of the waifs and orphans (he had hoped, of course, to hold off their deportation indefinitely). A few of the most elderly or ill were allowed to remain. But for the most part, *Gemeinde* officials could do little to save anyone. Even their earnest efforts to ease the pain of departure were frequently thwarted. When Mautner called to say goodbye to his two nieces, he found them locked up in their building. When he yelled up to their window, the elder shouted back, "Goodbye forever, Uncle."

Even though most deportees did not know they faced outright extermination, they reacted to their selection with desperation and despair. Some, especially assimilated Jews, committed suicide. Others, seeking to escape, wandered helplessly around the streets for days until hunger finally drove them to the *Gemeinde* for food. A few who had secreted some money or valuables held out longer by buying food on the black market. A very few managed to buy themselves a hiding place. One young Jew held off the SS with a revolver until, overcome with teargas, he shot his parents and himself. His brother was then seized and tortured to death for his crime.

To help with the deportations the SS organized a JUPO or Jewish police force. Only six Jews joined it. The leader was Wilhelm Reisz, an intelligent and well-educated youth with something of a religious background. But Reisz was also violent and unstable, in part at least because several members of his family had committed suicide, while his brother had been beaten to death before his eyes. As JUPO head, he behaved so brutally that many Jews feared him more than they did the SS. After an *Aktion*, Reisz and his Aryan wife would hold a drinking bout with his SS superior.

A group of much less willing collaborators were some young women who, brought to the collection center, were asked to help make a movie with the assurance that they would be spared deportation. They naturally agreed.

The motion picture was to be entitled *How Jews Lived Before 1938*, and was designed to depict Jews as a lewd and orgy-loving people. Its major scene was a wedding in which the young women had to march naked to the *mikvah* or ritual bath. Then, with the cameras grinding away, they were forced to sit on the knees of old and sick Jewish men who had been taken out of the old age home for this purpose. *Gemeinde* staff members were also compelled to assist as actors, extras, or in operating the lights.

The film was never shown and in all likelihood was simply a pretext for ogling naked Jewish girls as well as for terrorizing them and other Jews. The Nazis also never had any intention of keeping their promises to the girls, who were immediately whisked from the filming site back to the deportation center. Most of them were in such a state of shock from the experience that they could not even speak. Only one, a social worker who played the bride in the mock wedding scene, survived the Holocaust and lives today in Israel.

At the deportation center Jews would encounter either Alois or Anton Brunner. These two unrelated men successively headed Jewish deportation during these years.

Alois, the first to hold this position, freely whipped and kicked his victims, but before hitting one with his fist he would put on a white glove to protect himself from pollution. Jews manifesting any resistance were not only beaten but were sent off without their coats and luggage.

Once while riding with a group as transport commander in mid-winter, Brunner noticed the former financial manipulator, Sigmund Bosel. He had the now elderly and ill man chained to the floor of the train, and then began berating him for his misdeeds. Bosel, still wearing his pajamas, begged for mercy, but Brunner kept on until, finally tiring of the game, he took out his revolver and shot him.

Brunner's successor, Anton, known as Brunner II, was an intelligent man with a Catholic education who hitherto had been known for his polite manner. His new position transformed him into a raging animal. He tore up letters of protection, one of them reportedly from Göring himself, and found ways of sending off disabled and decorated war veterans, partners in mixed marriages, foreign Jews, and others who were supposed to be spared. He beat bloody an Orthodox Jew who took off his hat but not his small yarmulke, ripped the earrings out of the pierced ears of a woman, poured a bucket of cold water over an elderly woman who clung to her handbag, and tore the gold dentures from the mouth of an elderly man. When the man pleaded that he could not eat without them, Brunner laughingly replied that he would no longer need them. (All valuables disappeared unrecorded into his desk drawer.)

Brunner II deliberately broke up families, sending their members on different trains. He even separated the sick from healthy relatives: children with scarlet fever would be sent on one train and their mothers on another.

At the ghettos or camps to which they were sent, the accomplishments of the Vienna Jews continued to stand out. The more than thirty Viennese musicians, actors, singers, and painters who came to the Lodz ghetto contributed greatly, according to the Lodz chronicles, to the ghetto's cultural life. On December 3, 1941 the pianist Leopold Birkenfeld gave a concert which, said the chronicles, "literally enchanted the audience."

Even at the concentration camps, before they became death camps, the esprit and elan of the Vienna Jews made themselves felt. The satirist Fritz Löhner Beda, who was among the group of one thousand sent to Buchenwald in the fall of 1938, organized a song competition among the inmates. He then submitted under another name the entry that won first prize. It ended with these words: "Whatever our fate, we still say 'yes' to life." Both Beda and Birkenfeld died in the ovens of Auschwitz.

By late spring 1942 Vienna's Jewish population was down to 22,000, a little over one-tenth its pre-*Anschluss* figure. Most of those still left were residents of old age homes and other institutions, severely disabled and/or highly decorated and/or high-ranking war veterans, Jewish partners in mixed marriages, certain prominent or privileged Jews, and *Gemeinde* employees and their near relatives. But Hitler was pressing for the removal of all Jews from Vienna, and the deportation trains once again began chugging to the East.

This time, however, many of these trains were heading for Theresienstadt, a small Czech town that the Nazis had evacuated the previous year to create a new Jewish ghetto. It was decided to resettle about 14,000 of Vienna's remaining Jews there.

The first trainload consisted mostly of the elderly, the ill, disabled war veterans, and those Jewish partners whose mixed marriages had ended through death or divorce. Then in September 1942, most of the city's prominent Jews, including Friedmann and Stricker, received their deportation notices. So did many *Gemeinde* employees and their families. So also did Aron Menczer.

We now meet a young man who was perhaps the greatest hero of the Vienna Holocaust. Aron Menczer was one of six brothers, all of them staunch Zionists. (Their Galician-born father had attended Herzl's funeral.) One brother, Mordecai, had emigrated to Israel in the early 1930s, while another,

Menachem, had, as we have seen, represented Zionist youth at one of Eichmann's first meetings with the leaders of the Jewish community.

Aron, age twenty when the *Anschluss* came, was also a Zionist youth leader and in that capacity was soon helping younger Jews to emigrate. Following *Kristallnacht* he escorted a group of teenagers to Palestine. Helly Frost Barzilay, who was one of the group, remembers him as a good-looking, dynamic, and charismatic young man who, at the same time, was intensely kind and thoughtful. Virtually everyone else who knew him and who still is alive today speaks of him in similar terms.

Hardly had Aron launched his charges safely in Palestine, when he made plans to return to Vienna. His brother Mordecai desperately tried to talk him out of returning and even hid his passport. But Aron was insistent. As long as Jewish children remain in Vienna, he said, my place is there. Finally, Mordecai relented, returned the passport, and Aron left.

Back in Vienna he resumed his youth work and in the summer of 1939 headed an agricultural training project that the *Gemeinde* operated for young people at an open portion of one of its cemeteries. In August Eichmann allowed him to attend a Zionist youth congress in Geneva. After the congress ended, a friend followed him to the airport, begging him not to return again to Vienna, but Aron insisted on doing so, saying, "I cannot desert the young. What must be must be."

The following month Aron became director of the Youth Aliyah school which the *Gemeinde*, with Nazi permission, had established. Despite the increasingly stringent conditions, he managed to organize cultural activities, Sabbath meetings, a Herzl memorial service, and even the Youth Aliyah exhibit. When the regime called for fifty male youths to work in the labor camps and one hundred girls for harvest work in Germany in the spring of 1940, Aron arranged for two hundred young volunteers to march into the courtyard of Gestapo headquarters clad in white blouses and blue pants or skirts, singing Zionist songs.

When the Youth Aliyah school was shut down and most of its members sent to labor camps in Waidhofen and Doppl the following summer, Aron eventually joined the group at Doppl and found ways of maintaining contact with those in Waidhofen. When the camps were closed down in the late summer of 1942, and the young people were returned to Vienna for deportation, he organized them into two groups for farewell get-togethers. At each gathering Aron, standing before a portrait of Herzl, gave a short talk on Zionism in Vienna, reconciled leaders of various factions within the groups, and then asked them all to take a special Zionist oath he had drafted. It ran as follows:

> I vow on my honor to strive at all times for the preservation of my people, to be ready to give assistance, to be faithful to Judah and to Zion, and to attempt to strengthen my people's faith in a Jewish homeland.

Aron was ordered to report on September 22 for transportation to Theresienstadt two days later. Stricker, Friedmann, and their wives, along with various *Gemeinde* employees including Mautner, were scheduled to go on the same train. Aron's young followers accompanied him to the deportation center, impressed and heartened by his fresh, energetic, and confidant manner.

As Stricker and Friedmann unbuckled their knapsacks for inspection, the young Zionists spontaneously broke out into "Hatikvah." Their singing so impressed the inspecting SS officer that he stopped working until they finished. A former Aliyah school official, also present for deportation, turned to Mautner and, in a voice brimming with emotion, exclaimed, "Look, Mautner, at Hitler's inferior race."*

With the remaining mass transportations the following month, the authorities dissolved the *Gemeinde* and replaced it with a Council of Elders. Löwenherz remained as the Council's director, along with 334 of the *Gemeinde*'s 1,676 staff members and volunteers. The rest had all been sent to Theresienstadt. Among them was Rabbi Benjamin Murmelstein, who had been working with Löwenherz but who would now become Theresienstadt's Jewish administrator.

Approximately 6,200 or over two-thirds of the 8,300 Jews still left in Vienna owed their right to remain to their Aryan spouses. But marriage to non-Jews did not by any means automatically spare a Jew from deportation. Most of those allowed to stay were Christian or *konfessionslos* Jews. Moreover, four thousand of them were women, for in Nazi eyes it was apparently less reprehensible for a Jewish woman to be married to an Aryan man than the other way around. Twenty-two hundred families fell into the latter category.

Foreign Jews, Council employees, Jews performing especially important work, and a few privileged cases made up the rest. Among the latter were the Jewish daughter-in-law and the two half-Jewish grandchildren of the German composer Richard Strauss, who had accepted an invitation to move to Vienna from Munich.

Life for most of these remaining Jews was difficult indeed. They were forbidden milk, meat, and many other foods. Despite the high proportion of older people and women, seventy percent, including 1,065 who were over sixty-five, had to work six-day weeks. They were forbidden access to all publications except the Viennese edition of the *Nachrichtenblatt*, a weekly news sheet issued first by the *Gemeinde* itself and then by the Council of Elders until its publication

*The young people, most of whom had just been discharged from the labor camps, would soon be deported to far worse places than Theresienstadt. The only one known to be alive today is Martin Vogel, a half-Jew whose Aryan father managed to keep him in Vienna.

was suspended in January 1943. During its final three months of publication, it carried 502 obituaries for a population of a little over 8,000.

All remaining Jews were closely watched, and any stepping out of line, such as accompanying an Aryan partner to a movie, was usually quickly reported. Aryan partners were continually pressured to divorce their Jewish mates, but, to their credit, only ten percent did so. Still, as a result of denunciations, divorces, and other factors, deportation trains continued to run to Theresienstadt and to the extermination camps. Such deportations, and a continued high death rate within the community itself, shrank the Jewish population still more. By the time of its liberation in the spring of 1945, the Viennese Jewish community counted only 5,815 members, approximately three percent of its prewar population.

What happened to the others? In all, 67,601 Austrian Jews were sent to concentration camps or ghettos. Nearly one-quarter of them had been picked up in other European countries to which they had fled. Of them all, only 2,142 were still alive at the war's end. Nevertheless, thanks in part to Eichmann's brutal but effective expulsion techniques, about two-thirds of all of Austria's Jews survived the Holocaust.

Theresienstadt was established in November 1941 as a "model" ghetto. Here, forty miles from Prague, German, Austrian, and Czech Jews designated as privileged because of their age or status were to live out their remaining years in comparative comfort. The ghetto's population consisted of the elderly, former leaders and employees of Jewish *Gemeinden* and their families, selected war veterans, prominent scientists, artists, and intellectuals, and the offspring and relatives of famous Jews. Among the latter was the son of operetta composer Oscar Strauss and the youngest sister of Ludwig Wittgenstein.

Theresienstadt residents were allowed facilities and activities unheard of elsewhere in the Reich. There was a nursery, an infirmary, a bandstand, and for a while even a coffee house. The ghetto's residents put on concerts, poetry readings, and lectures. They could also attend either Jewish or Christian religious services. (From one-fifth to one-quarter of Theresienstadt's Jews were Christian converts.) Theresienstadt's residents could often obtain the best of medical and dental care, for here were some of the best Jewish doctors and dentists in all of greater Germany.

The model ghetto made a strongly favorable impression on Swiss Red Cross officials who superficially inspected it in June 1944. A week or two later, the Nazis appointed Kurt Gerron, a Jewish film director who had been sent to the ghetto, to make a film entitled *The Führer Presents a City to the Jews.*

But there was another side to Theresienstadt, a side that the Swiss Red Cross did not see and that Gerron did not dare film.

Theresienstadt was only five-eighths of a mile square and had only 219 houses plus a military barracks. Before its conversion to a ghetto it had housed some six thousand people. But by the late fall of 1942, a year after its transformation, the population had grown to nearly sixty thousand. People slept anywhere they could, including eighteen who bunked down in the kitchen. They were actually the more fortunate ones since the kitchen was the warmest room in the entire colony.

The intense congestion combined with steadily declining food rations and steadily deteriorating sanitary and other living conditions, along with arduous work schedules, made the population susceptible to illnesses. Even children's diseases would sweep through the community, taking many lives. By war's end some 32,000 residents, about one-fifth of them from Vienna, had died from hunger and disease.

But the community's own death toll did not suffice to reduce the overcrowding, which grew worse as more and more Jews arrived. So the Nazis began running a shuttle train to Auschwitz. Residents lived in constant terror of deportation, especially after one deportee left a note on the train describing what he saw when he arrived at the extermination camp.

As the war worsened, the deportations accelerated, and by the time the community was liberated over one-half of all those sent to Theresienstadt had been shipped to Poland. The more prominent were in no way spared. Stricker and Friedmann, along with their wives, were sent to their deaths in the fall of 1944, as was K.S. Friedländer, a former Austrian field marshal. Aron Menczer, who had worked with the young children of Theresienstadt, and who had become their idol, accompanied a group of one thousand youngsters into the Auschwitz gas ovens one year earlier.*

But if it was in Theresienstadt that Vienna's greatest hero fulfilled his final mission, it was also here that the man many consider to be its greatest anti-hero played out his last role. This was Benjamin Murmelstein.

Murmelstein had been one of the city's more distinguished rabbis. In 1934 he wrote a repudiation of charges regarding the Talmud for the integrationist journal. He was also the author of a well-received essay on Maimonides and of a two-volume work on Jewish history. He had taught in a rabbinical seminary and his congregation included some of the city's more prominent Jews.

But many of his rabbinical colleagues had long disliked and distrusted Murmelstein, and the *Anschluss* proved their doubts about him correct. Having lost most of his congregation, Murmelstein joined the staff of the *Gemeinde*, and almost overnight the rabbinical scholar became an all-too-able administrator. He developed a good working relationship with Eichmann and

*There is some question as to whether Aron knew that the group of children he was escorting, who had been brought to the camp from Bialystock, were destined for extermination. Earlier there had been talk of sending them to Switzerland as part of an exchange arrangement. Dr. Kurt Wiegel, who now heads the orthopedics department in a hospital outside Tel Aviv, but who as a youngster knew Aron at Theresienstadt, says Aron was aware that they were not going to Switzerland but apparently did not know for sure that they were going to Auschwitz. He describes Aron Menczer as "a great leader and a good friend."

other Nazis and zealousy discharged their assignments. Asked once to prepare a list of one thousand Jews for deportation, he proudly announced that he had two thousand ready to go. Löwenherz and other *Gemeinde* staff members detested but also feared him.

Appointed Jewish administrator at Theresienstadt, Murmelstein developed a close and cordial relationship with the ghetto's SS commander, Karl Rahm. Rahm also came from Vienna and the two conversed freely in Viennese dialect. As Rahm's chief Jewish aide, Murmelstein carried out his work rigorously and ruthlessly.

The short, barrel-shaped, thirty-eight-year-old rabbi was allowed to live with his attractive Hungarian Jewish wife and their young son in an apartment of their own. But since his sexual needs exceeded the bonds of marriage, he frequently required the ghetto's more appealing female residents to go to bed with him if they wished to escape deportation. Because of these and other practices, his fellow inmates soon began referring to him as "Murmelschwein."

Murmelstein realized the precariousness of his own position and constantly carried poison with him should it suddenly change. But he managed to maintain a good relationship with Rahm and in the winter of 1945 this enabled Murmelstein to save the lives of most of Theresienstadt's remaining inmates.

Rahm had put some eighty male inmates to work building a "vegetable warehouse," but the Jewish engineer in charge of the project noticed certain peculiarities, such as the fact that the "ventilating" pipes led inside rather than outside. Concluding that the "warehouse" was really to be a gas chamber, he contacted Murmelstein who persuaded Rahm to cancel the undertaking.

In the spring, however, the Commandant began draining a duck pond just outside the town, fostering fears that he was preparing a grave for mass executions. Fortunately, the impending arrival of the Russians directed his attention elsewhere.

In early May the Russians liberated Theresienstadt and the International Red Cross took over its operation. They found some 16,000 emaciated and bedraggled inhabitants, all that were left of the 141,000 "privileged" Jews who had been sent there. Among the oldest was Ditta Lowy's eighty-eight-year-old grandmother, who had been sent there along with her daughter and granddaughter because her other daughter had been the chief nurse at the Jewish home for the aged in Vienna. Another elderly Viennese who had survived Theresienstadt was General Sommer.

At the other end of the age spectrum there was Jona Jakob Spiegel. His mother had been deported directly from Vienna to her death at Auschwitz, while he, as an eight-month-old baby, had been brought to Theresienstadt. Although without relatives or family friends, he had received adequate care from the adults and was three years old when the Russians arrived. Now in his late forties and living in London, he is the youngest survivor of the destruction of the Vienna Jews.

Chapter 25

"The Righteous Are Too Few"

Were the Austrians more zealous Nazis than the Germans? Were they more ardent and active anti-Semites? To what extent did they participate in the Holocaust? Much of the material previously examined touches on these questions, but now we must deal with them directly.

Most of us have seen newsreels of Hitler's rallies and remember all too well the thousands upon thousands of ecstatic Germans raising their right arms and shouting "*Sieg Heil.*" While the Nazis in Germany's last free election received only about one-third of the vote, few would dispute that from the mid-1930s to the turning point of the war they would have swept any fair and free election.

Yet the emotional appeal that Nazism exercised over the Germans appears almost mild compared to the reaction that, intially at least, it evoked in Austria. No sooner had the Schuschnigg government collapsed on that fateful Friday in March, when the dam broke.

To the British correspondent Gedye, the "Brown Flood" transformed Vienna into an "indescribable witches' Sabbath" with mobs of men and women milling about hysterically shrieking the name of their new "Führer." To the anti-Nazi playwright Zuckmayer, it was as if "the netherworld had opened its gates and vomited forth the lowest, filthiest, most horrible demons it contained . . . a torrent of envy, jealousy, bitterness, blind, malignant craving for revenge. All better instincts were silenced." Zuckmayer had witnessed the coming of Nazism in Germany, but never in that country had he seen anything remotely resembling what he saw in Austria.

Hitler's arrival in Austria three days later evoked another storm of pro-Nazi sentiment. The greeting his former countrymen gave him "mocked all description," according to a Swiss correspondent, while the *Times* of London noted how "few conquerors in history have had such a reception. No adjective suffices to describe the jubilation. . . . There are no signs of a people bowing unwillingly to the foreign yoke." According to William Shirer, who had earlier covered the rise of Nazism in Germany, "The Brown Shirts at Nuremberg had never bellowed the Nazi slogans with such mania." The half-million people who jammed the Heldenplatz to greet Hitler's entry into Vienna remain today, nearly fifty years later, the greatest number of Austrians ever to come together in one place.

The *Anschluss* was not Germany's first annexation. Hitler had taken over the Saar in 1935 following a plebiscite, and the Rhineland in 1936 following a military invasion. Since each of these territories had long been part of Germany but had been under hostile French administrations since World War I, one might expect the rejoicing of their inhabitants to exceed by far that of the Austrians. Yet the opposite was the case. As Göring privately remarked after the Austrian takeover, "Our last march, the reoccupation of the Rhineland, is completely eclipsed by this event — especially as far as the joy of the people is concerned. . . . The Führer is deeply moved."

So deeply moved was the Führer that he ended the puppet state created by his Austrian followers and decided instead to make Austria part of the Reich. As Fest notes, "The elemental delirium seemed to permit no alternative."

To give the move a stamp of legitimacy, Hitler scheduled a plebiscite of his own for April 10. Both Germans and Austrians were to vote on whether to combine their countries into one. In Austria, 4,270,000 voted "*Ja*" while less than 12,000 voted "*Nein*," giving the proposed annexation a majority of 99.75 percent.

The result, to be sure, requires some readjustment. No Jews or leading anti-Nazis could vote. Moreover, the balloting was not completely secret. Visiting one polling station in Vienna, Shirer observed a fairly wide slit in the ballot booth which enabled the election officials to see how the voter voted. Still, the size of the turnout and the low number of invalid ballots leave little doubt that even a properly conducted election would have produced a substantial pro-Nazi majority. After the war, Socialist leader Karl Renner estimated that two-thirds of the Austrian people had voted "from the heart."

The last days of the Schuschnigg regime had seen an outburst of public support for the embattled Chancellor. Even some of his opponents had expected his plebiscite for Austrian independence to carry. Yet, a month later, all this support had apparently melted away. What produced such a sudden turnaround in popular sentiment?

Part of the answer lies in the fact that the turnaround was not all that great. Austria had all along harbored far more Nazis than had seemed evident on the surface. Once Hitler marched in, they came out of the closet in droves. Many had even held leading positions in the Fatherland Front and other pro-Schuschnigg organizations. In one Viennese high school, to take just one example, the teacher who chaired the school's Fatherland Front organization and the school secretary who assisted her turned out to have been long-time Nazi party members.

The Nazis had even penetrated, if not permeated, the highest levels of Schuschnigg's own government. Schuschnigg had long suspected such linkages, but only when Hitler made his foreign minister and close confidante, Guido Schmidt, the director-general of Austria's largest steelworks, and gave Schuschnigg's bodyguard, a Viennese plainclothes policeman who had become his constant companion, a high position in the Gestapo, did the fallen Chancellor realize the extent to which he had been betrayed.

But the tens of thousands of underground Nazis who bobbed to the surface cannot in themselves explain the sea of swastikas that greeted Hitler on his return to Austria. Plainly, what had happened was the fastest and fullest mass conversion in history. Virtually overnight, millions of Austrians who had previously supported their country's independence had executed a 180-degree turn. Fairly typical was the Salzburg tobacconist who a few weeks before the *Anschluss* had screamed "Loyalty to Austria" as a Fatherland Front parade streamed by. But when the German soldiers marched in, she knelt on the street in reverence and the following day began cramming cigarettes into the pockets of German soldiers, calling them "German brothers."

In Vienna, Ernst Ruzicka, seeing his janitor with a swastika in his lapel, mused, "These are the people who cheered the Emperor and then cursed him, who welcomed democracy after the Emperor was dethroned, and then cheered [Dollfuss'] fascism when that system came to power. Today he is a Nazi, tomorrow he will be something else."

The Austrian press of that period offers another striking example of this overnight flipflop. The Friday, March 11 edition of the semi-official *Reichspost* spilled over with endorsements of Schuschnigg's plebiscite by various organizations, including the *Reichspost* itself. But two days later, the newspaper carried a front-page editorial that, under the title, "Toward Fulfillment," began, "The storm of great historical events blows the spirit of spring through our homeland" for "thanks to the genius and determination of Adolf Hitler, the hour of all-German unity has arrived." The rest of the paper describes Hitler's triumphant reception in Linz and reports warm messages of welcome, many from organizations that a few days before had with equal enthusiasm supported Schuschnigg.

Karl Renner was one prominent anti-Nazi Austrian who joined the ranks of Hitler's well-wishers soon after the *Anschluss*. In a newspaper interview shortly before the plebiscite the Social Democratic leader suddenly, and surprisingly, called for a "*Ja*" vote for "our Führer Adolf Hitler."

The cause and conditions of Renner's about-face have spawned considerable speculation. But according to Professor Radomir Luza, who after the war interviewed an individual whom Renner consulted at the time, the Social Democratic leader acted entirely on his own initiative. In fact he sought permission from the Nazi authorities to issue an outright appeal to his old comrades to vote for the annexation. Gauleiter Bürckel referred the request to Rudolf Hess, Hitler's then deputy. Hess agreed but ruled out a direct appeal, suggesting the newspaper interview instead.

Two rationales have been advanced to explain why the sixty-eight-year-old Renner made such a move. One theory is that since the Social Democrats had long supported the *Anschluss*, they should therefore not oppose it simply because it was being done under the wrong government. As Renner himself later explained, "Systems change but states endure." Such an explanation, however, overlooks the fact that the Social Democrats in 1933 had officially renounced their support for the *Anschluss* after they had seen what Hitler was doing to their German comrades.

Another reason that has been offered is that Renner was trying to save those comrades, Jewish and non-Jewish, who had been arrested. But at least two Austrian historians believe he acted only to save himself, for unlike most Social Democratic leaders, Renner spent the remainder of the Hitler period living quietly and comfortably in retirement.

The response of two key sectors of the population — the Catholic Church and the intellectual/cultural elite — to the *Anschluss* is especially noteworthy. The Church's reaction to, and its relationship with, Hitler will be examined in the next two chapters. Let us now examine how Austria's non-Jewish intellectuals and artists responded to his New Order.

For the most part, they welcomed it as warmly as anyone else, if not more so. Only a handful emigrated, the most noteworthy being Robert Musil, who fled to Switzerland with his Jewish wife. The rest stayed, and all but a few enthusiastically cooperated with their new rulers. The members of the Vienna Philharmonic smilingly displayed their swastika armbands while posing for a group picture, and Goebbels on his two visits to Vienna pronounced himself well pleased with their responses to him personally. Austrian film studios ground out pro-Nazi and anti-Semitic films, while Austrian writers kept the printing presses running. After the war, the Allies would ban 1,606 works of Austrian authors for containing pro-Nazi sentiments.

Many Austrian professors had already been Nazis or Nazi sympathizers, and the *Anschluss* caused most of the rest to join them. Comparatively few

Gentile professors lost their positions for lack of loyalty to the regime, and almost none emigrated. The later Nobel Laureate, physician/biologist Konrad Lorenz, wrote a "scientific" article supporting Nazi racial theories. Proportionately, Party membership among university professors and other intellectuals greatly exceeded Party membership among Austrians generally, although the latter also enrolled in substantial numbers.

This contrasts with what occurred in Germany, where Hitler's assumption of power produced a substantial outflow of non-Jewish artistic and scientific talent. Such writers as Thomas Mann, Bertolt Brecht, and Erich Maria Remarque quickly left the country. So did conductors Hermann Scherchen and Fritz Busch, architect Walter Gropius, and numerous others. When Goebbels offered Stefan Georg, Germany's leading poet, the presidency of the Academy of Poets, Georg sent a Jewish friend to relay his rejection. He then left for Switzerland. When Goebbels told motion picture director Fritz Lang that the Führer believed that Lang could make *the* film on National Socialism, Lang responded by departing for Hollywood where, only with difficulty, was he able to pursue his career.

Even some who stayed proved less than cordial to the regime. The artist Käthe Kollwitz remained an outspoken critic until she died, and only her extensive reputation saved her from the concentration camp. Wilhelm Furtwängler, conductor of the Berlin Philharmonic, openly spoke out against Hitler's initial purge of Jewish musicians, and although he later reached a *modus vivendi* with the Nazis, their relationship remained less than friendly. The regime much preferred the Austrian conductor, Herbert von Karajan, who had joined the Nazi party in Salzburg in 1933, a few weeks after Hitler came to power. Embarking subsequently on a career in Germany, von Karajan became a particular favorite of Göring.

With the *Anschluss*, Austrians from all walks of life sought to follow von Karajan's example, and eventually one out of ten Austrians became members of the Nazi party. In Germany less than one out of fourteen took this step.

Two further factors make this difference in Party enrollments more significant. First, Austria had a substantially larger proportion of Jews, as well as Catholic priests, nuns, and monks, all of whom, for quite different reasons, could not become Party members. Factoring out these non-eligibles widens still more the gap between Austrian and German Party membership. The second factor is that Nazi rule in Germany lasted twelve years; in Austria, only seven. Consequently, Austrians had less oportunity to join the Party. Yet, as the figures show, proportionately many more of them did so.*

*The latest figures on Austrian Nazi party membership released in the fall of 1986 by Professor Gerhard Boetz showed that one out of every four adult males in Austria joined the Party. Boetz's research also reveals that most pre-*Anschluss* Nazis were fully employed white-collar workers and professionals. Although unemployment has often been advanced as the reason for Austria's warm embrace of Nazism, apparently it played little role in inducing Austrians to join the Party.

When the Nazis took over Germany in 1933, they unleashed many of the same or similar outrages against Jews committed by their Austrian counterparts five years later. In Germany, Jews were paraded with placards around their necks, rabbis were forced to dance, Jewish-owned stores were destroyed, and many Jews were shipped off to concentration camps. Yet differences between the German and Austrian Nazi approach to the Jews are strikingly apparent.

To begin with, the scope and intensity of the German Nazi crackdown on Jews never neared that of the Austrians. In Germany such incidents tended not only to be isolated and sporadic, but soon began to peter out. By 1935 only one Jew still remained in Dachau. Moreover, the subsequent annexations of the Saar and the Rhineland brought no noticeable outbreaks against the Jews living in those areas. While these Jews did lose most of their rights and eventually most of their property, prior to *Kristallnacht* they were not subjected to wide-scale humiliation and physical harm.

The annexation of Austria was quite different. In Vienna even the Jewish wife of the American minister feared to venture out in the street. "What one saw in Vienna was almost unbelievable," writes William Shirer. "The Viennese, usually so soft and sentimental, were behaving worse than the Germans, especially toward the Jews. I had never seen quite such humiliating scenes in Berlin or Nuremberg. Or such Nazi sadism."

Shirer's verdict is confirmed by many others, including, albeit from a very different perspective, the SS. Six weeks after the takeover, the official SS journal, *Das Schwarze Korps*, remarked how "the Viennese have managed to do overnight what we have failed to achieve in the slow-moving, ponderous north up to this day. In Austria, a boycott of the Jews does not need organizing — the people themselves have initiated it."

So great was the anti-Semitic fury of the Austrian Nazis that it often undermined the designs of their own leaders. Eichmann found his plans for speeded-up emigration frequently frustrated by such acts as the destruction of the *Gemeinde*'s card index or the arrest of people whom he had processed for emigration. In some instances such zeal produced events that, in another context, would seem comic. When a directive went out to all communities to cleanse themselves of Jews as soon as possible, one Alpine village that had none telegraphed back, "Impossible to obey order; please send us Jews."

If the indignities and injuries that the Austrian Nazis inflicted on their Jewish countrymen in 1938 were more wanton and widespread than those that occurred in Germany in 1933, then the most important reason for the difference probably lies in the differing reactions of the Austrian and German publics. While anti-Semitism among the Germans was certainly extensive, it was not, except for a relatively small number, very intense. Fest claims that the typical German was only a lukewarm anti-Semite, and although this may sound ridiculous in view of the Holocaust, evidence exists to bear him out. Even after years of subjecting the Germans to constant anti-Semitic propaganda, Hitler complained that they were still "insufficiently enlightened about racial matters," and so the SS "has had to carry the main burden."

Grunberger, after an exhaustive study of records and interviews with Jewish survivors, concludes that the average German did not share the obsessive anti-Semitism of the Nazi leadership, but rather maintained an attitude best described as indifferent. Their limited anti-Semitism, combined with their almost innate love of legality and order, made most, though certainly not all, Germans look with disfavor and even disgust on the street violence against Jews which accompanied Hitler's assumption of power. Moreover, when the Nazis organized a boycott of Jewish stores for April 1, 1933, it failed miserably. In at least one district, purchases at Jewish stores actually increased.

Such an attitude represents a far cry from the reaction of the Austrian public, who gathered to watch with amusement, or at least quiet interest, the most obnoxious outrages, including the urinating on the heads of Jewish women in Währing. "It is not so much all the brutalities of the Austrian Nazis which I have witnessed or verified from the victims which blurs the image of the Viennese I thought I knew," said Gedye. "It is the heartless, grinning, soberly dressed crowds . . . fighting one another to get closer to the elevating spectacle of an ashen-faced Jewish surgeon on his hands and knees before half a dozen young hooligans with swastika armbands and dogwhips that sticks in my mind."

After describing how the surgeon was made to scrub the street with a solution mixed with acid which burned his hands, Gedye continues, "And the Viennese — not uniformed Nazis or a raging mob, but the Viennese little man and his wife — just grinned approval at the glorious fun. That is the picture that I have somehow to reconcile with that of the softhearted, oversentimental folk whom I thought I knew so well."

The German soldiers who marched into Austria took no part in these street scenes, while a few of their officers openly showed distaste. When a guide escorting two officers around Vienna pointed to a street-cleaning action, and remarked, "See how our Führer has found work for the Jews," one of the officers replied, "That's not work, it's a *Schweinerei* [obscenity]." On another occasion two other officers went up to two elderly Jews scrubbing the pavement and, kicking over their buckets, told them they could go. The officers then cursed the Austrian storm troopers supervising them.

When Austrian Nazis crammed eighty Jews into a miserably small cell — their offense was that they had been reluctant to shine the shoes of Gentile bystanders before a cafe — a German officer transferred twenty of them to another jail to relieve the insufferable overcrowding. When a sixty-five-year-old woman with heart disease broke down while street scrubbing, a car carrying German soldiers stopped and took her home.

This last incident is notable for another reason. Shortly before the car appeared, the woman's sixteen-year-old grandson had pleaded with the Nazis to let him take his grandmother's place. His plea had evoked the following response from a woman spectator: "Congratulations, Franky. That's interesting. That shows real class." The onlooker evidently knew the family and was observing the scene without too much concern.

This attitude on the part of those they had known and trusted marks another difference between German and Austrian treatment of Jews. During Hitler's long rise to power, Germans who joined or even sympathized with his movement did not usually hide the fact from any Jews they might happen to know. Those who continued to maintain contact with Jews usually did so in the honest, if foolish, belief that anti-Semitism was merely one of Hitler's election ploys and would not play a significant role in his government. Hitler actually toned down anti-Semitic propaganda during his last two campaigns, although he never abandoned it.

When Hitler came to power, most Gentiles distanced themselves from Jews they had known but did not actively turn on them. In Vienna they often did. In the few days they were allowed to attend school after the *Anschluss*, Jewish students were surprised to hear teachers who had always been friendly suddenly spout anti-Semitic diatribes. Their fathers and mothers were equally startled to see once friendly neighbors and once loyal maids become not just indifferent but hostile. A barber giving a haircut to a long-standing Jewish customer sliced off a piece of his ear. When the Jew bemoaned the fact to his doctor, the doctor said, "You should be glad the barber did not cut off the whole ear."

Their Gentile erstwhile associates could also be quite greedy. A day or two after the *Anschluss*, a group of vendors at the open-air market, describing themselves as men of "Nationalist Socialist conviction," appropriated the stalls of their thirty Jewish colleagues. Neighbors sometimes did not behave much better. "Frequently," writes Perl, "after a Jew had been arrested the neighbors broke into his home and searched it on their own initiative, helping themselves to whatever they liked." Some maids, writes Rosenkranz, demanded jewelry and silkwares from their Jewish employers under threat of calling the storm troopers. Others, after agreeing to hide valuables in their rooms in exchange for a handsome present, then informed their boyfriends, who would break in and ransack the place.

When the Klaars returned from Berlin where they had gone to arrange their emigration, they found that their maid, who had earlier been given their double bed, had appropriated many other items as well. She threatened to denounce their teenage son for having forced her to submit to "racial pollution," a charge that would send him to Dachau, unless they left that evening. As they were going out the door, she smilingly informed them that her Communist boyfriend had now joined the SS.

Still more surprising, and saddening, to many Jews was the discovery that many they had known, liked, and trusted had actually been Nazi party members all along. On the Friday afternoon of Schuschnigg's resignation, Paula Wessly and Attila Höbigger, Vienna's most illustrious husband-and-wife acting team, began rehearsals of a play by Zuckmayer under the direction of the Jewish director, Ernst Lothar. The next day Zuckmayer and Lothar learned that the couple were long-time Nazis. (Höbigger did give Lothar some assistance later in emigrating.) The surgeon who had operated on Freud and who gave him his medical certificate for emigration also turned out to be a Nazi.

At the University, two young assistant professors, one Jewish, one Gentile, had been close friends and constant companions for years. After the *Anschluss*, the Jew discovered that his Gentile friend had for some time been a member of the Nazi party. But his surprise was probably less than that of the Jewish woman whose Gentile husband on the day of the *Anschluss* suddenly put on his Nazi uniform, which he had apparently owned for some years, and threw her out of their home.

Many years before, Robert Musil had called attention to his people's penchant for doing one thing while saying another. The *Anschluss* taught the Jews, along with Chancellor Schuschnigg, just how accurate his observation was.

Some wise and well-off Vienna Jews escaped the terror of the first days of the *Anschluss* by simply boarding the train for Berlin and staying comfortably and securely in hotels. That Berlin, the capital of Nazism, could provide a safer haven from Nazi terror than Vienna seems incredible, but many Austrian Jews subsequently found it to be so. We have already seen how General Sommer and Betar leader Willi Perl received civil and even courteous treatment in their respective missions to the city. As emigration increased, more and more Jews found it necessary to go to Berlin, since the German capital was now Austria's capital as well. Most of them were amazed at the contrast in the way they were treated there as compared to Vienna.

The Klaars, for example, on arriving in Berlin, found they could register at a decent hotel without so much as a raised eyebrow. They passed through the hotel's beer cellar, eliciting no insults or dirty looks even when they brushed past a table of uniformed Nazis. (Clare makes it clear in his book that all the family looked Jewish.)

Later, in visiting relatives in Berlin, George was dumbfounded when his cousin asked him if he wanted to see a show, a movie, or simply drive around in his car. In Vienna, Jews no longer went to movies or shows and their cars had long been confiscated. On Berlin's main shopping street, only one store carried the message that Jewish customers were not wanted. The German secretary for the British firm that was helping the Klaars to emigrate showed genuine sympathy for their plight and did all she could to assist them. "With every additional day," writes Clare, "my impression grew stronger, and it was shared by my parents, that after Nazi Vienna one felt in Berlin almost as if one had emigrated and escaped from Hitler's rule."

Of course, cosmopolitan and left-wing Berlin had never been a Nazi stronghold, but the situation elsewhere in Germany was apparently not very different. Benno Weiser Varon, passing through the western part of Germany in September 1938 on his way to Holland, does not recall "a single derogatory remark or unfriendly gesture," though he was easily distinguishable as a Jew. "Even the Gestapo man whose advice I asked — for I had official permission for my transit — was friendly and helpful. It struck me that his anti-Semitism must have been impersonal. That of the Austrians was quite different."

In the eastern part of the country, some Jews in Stettin, sheltering a group of Austrian Jews who were trying to emigrate to Latvia, hardly a hospitable or even safe sanctuary for Jews in any case, could not understand the desperate desire of their Viennese co-religionists to emigrate at any price.

A few weeks later, the Nazis staged *Kristallnacht*. While *Kristallnacht* set a new high in anti-Semitic savagery throughout the Reich, its fury in Austria surpassed the level reached in Germany. Innsbruck alone, with 130 Jews, accounted for over ten percent of all Jews killed outright during the eruption. (The official figure, reported by Gestapo chief Heydrich to Göring, listed thirty-five Jewish dead.) "Compared to Crystal Night in Vienna," says Simon Wiesenthal, "the one in Berlin was a pleasant Christmas festival."

The reactions of the German and Austrian publics were also different. A report of the American consul in Leipzig, Germany, for example, speaks of the Nazis throwing Jews into a small stream and then "commanding horrified spectators to spit at them, defile them with mud, and jeer at their plight." In Baden-Baden, where all the Jewish men were rounded up and marched to the synagogue, one of the marchers later reported, "I saw people crying while watching from behind their curtains." Many non-Jews, he says, deeply resented the round-up. In Dusseldorf a Nazi woman felt compelled to apologize to her fellow-passengers on a streetcar the following day.

In Berlin George Clare, who spent the evening quietly with his mother in their Jewish pension, recalls walking into a hat shop the following morning. All three salesgirls were busy with customers, but "as I came in, one of the saleswomen looked up, saw me, recognized my Jewishness — of that I am certain — left the customer she had been speaking to and immediately attended to me. Neither the customer so abruptly abandoned nor anyone else in the shop said one word." His mother had a similar experience at the hairdresser's, and before she left, the beautician said, "Madame, I want to apologize to you for the terrible thing that happened last night. Believe me, we didn't want this."

In Vienna things transpired differently. Unlike Leipzig, there were apparently few "horrified" spectators who needed "commanding" to join in the melee. On the contrary, according to one Gestapo report, "We could scarcely hold back the crowds from mishandling the Jews. Frequently several broke through the barriers and beat the Jews. There were frequent cries such as, 'Beat them to death, the dogs,' and 'teach them to work in Dachau.'" Sympathy for the Jews, says the report, "was almost nonexistent, and the very few who voiced it were set upon by the mob." At least one Gestapo official complained of the rough way Vienna's Hitler Youth handled the Jews.

One later Gestapo report from Vienna does mention a negative reaction on the part of those not connected with the Nazi party. But it blames this reaction on the pogrom's undisciplined character. Had the operation been carried out on the basis of some law or regulation, then, says the report, such feelings would not have arisen. Undoubtedly, the fact that in Austria the pogrom seemed to get out of hand and degenerate into a wild mob action threatening law and order greatly contributed to whatever uneasiness the public subsequently manifested. The only expressions of remorse mentioned by Rosenkranz came in Innsbruck, where a few Gentile women expressed sympathy to the community's rabbi over the outrages.

Fest, in calling attention to the wave of revulsion in Germany over *Kristallnacht*, claims the pogrom "was only successful in Austria." This may be overstating the case, but a distinct difference in the degree to which it was accepted, or not accepted, by Austrians and Germans does seem apparent.

Following *Kristallnacht*, differences between German and Austrian treatment of the Jews narrowed considerably as ruthless persecution became the order of the day throughout the Reich. Yet such differences did not by any means disappear.

Five months after the pogrom, district leaders throughout the Reich received authorization to evict and concentrate Jews within their jurisdictions. This authority was vigorously applied in Austria but not in Germany. "It is notable," writes Rosenkranz, "that in Berlin the first attempt at evicting and resettling Jews took place only in the middle of 1941, and then only to a moderate extent." Moreover, he says, "the initiative was not well received by the Gentile population, although many were certainly ready to take advantage of the empty dwellings." A report in September of that year, he states, shows the majority of Berlin Jews still living without subtenants. He also notes that the Berlin Jewish *Gemeinde* was still receiving food susidies from the German government, while the Viennese *Gemeinde* was receiving none.

Rosenkranz also points to the differences in the content of the two journals being published by the two *Gemeinden* following the pogrom. "While a tone of panic pervades the Viennese edition, the Berlin journal announces

Jewish programs of plays, concerts, films, etc., in an effort to overcome the shock of *Kristallnacht* and restore people to a normal intellectual and everyday life." The head of the Jewish Cultural League in Berlin visited Vienna with the aim of helping the Jews create a similar league, but he found them too demoralized to do so.

The daily activities of the heads of the Berlin and Viennese *Gemeinden* also present a contrast. In Berlin, Rabbi Leo Baeck had taken over this position, having refused to emigrate while there was still work to be done in assisting Jews. But he was not entirely cut off from outside support. A complete stranger once stuffed chocolate in his pocket, while on another occasion an equally unknown man handed him some ration cards, saying, "You dropped these."

A German nobleman offered to hide a manuscript Baeck was writing and ten Stuttgart industrialists came to his apartment to tell him they had pleaded with Hitler to be allowed to keep their Jewish workers. "We are certain we can shield a thousand Jews from Nazi atrocities," they told him. Baeck himself reported, through a mail drop that a Gentile well-wisher was helping him maintain in Switzerland, that "there are Christians hiding Jews in attics and cellars. Many people help."

As we follow Rosenkranz's detailed account of Löwenherz's activities in Vienna, we see no signs of such outside support. No Gentile hands him ration cards or offers any assistance or even any sympathy. He and his fellow *Gemeinde* employees seemed totally isolated and cut off from the non-Jewish community.

In January 1939, Eichmann brought a group of officials handling Jewish emigration in Berlin to Vienna to show them how his successful centralized operation worked. The visitors from Germany, says Rosenkranz, "were horrified over the slave-driving methods and intimidation which Eichmann had imposed on officials of the Viennese *Gemeinde*." Later, when the deportation started, Wilhelm Reisz and two other members of his six-man JUPO (Jewish Police) went to Berlin to show officials there how to conduct a deportation raid. On his return, Reisz said, "The Viennese are not well regarded and the raid went badly because the local population resisted it. The SS had to take it over."

A diary kept by Ulrich von Hassel (who, according to Reitlinger, maintained the best private information network in Nazi Germany) also records German resistance to the deportations. On November 1, 1941 von Hassel wrote that the population had registered such disgust over deportations that Nazi party leaders distributed pamphlets blaming the Jews for Germany's problems and warning that sympathy for the Jews was treason to the Reich. (A month before, when the Jewish star was decreed, a few Germans began wearing them in sympathy but, says Retilinger, "the police soon took care of that.")

Goebbels' diaries disclose two later instances of German resistance to the deportations. In an entry on March 6, 1943 Goebbels notes that "Unfortunately, there have been a number of regrettable scenes at the Jewish Home for the Aged where a large number of people gathered and even took sides with the Jews." In another entry five days later he reports, with obvious vexation, that many German businessmen had alerted their Jewish employees of impending deportations, and as a consequence "we failed to lay our hands on about four thousand Jews who are now wandering about the streets and are naturally quite a public danger."

Most Germans, of course, did not openly oppose the deportations but watched in silence as the Jews were taken in open trucks to deportation centers. In Vienna, however, onlookers on occasion jeered at the deported Jews. It should also be noted that the deportations proceeded at a much more rapid pace in Vienna than in Berlin. From October, 1941 to June, 1942, some sixty percent of Vienna's remaining Jewish population, but only thirty percent of Berlin's, was dispatched to the east.

It was in Berlin that the only organized protest against the deportations occurred. When in 1943 the authorities sent off a group of Jewish men married to Gentile women, the women assembled in the street outside of Gestapo headquarters in a futile effort to prevent the deportation trucks from leaving. Vienna had almost as many mixed marriages as Berlin, but in Vienna no such gesture took place.

The Austrian National Socialist Women's Association certainly offered no encouragement to those involved in such marriages. On the contrary, when the authorities ordered a Jewish star to appear on all dwellings occupied by Jews, the Nazi women's group in Vienna pressured to have the star put on those occupied by mixed couples as well.

When it came to the treatment of children, Vienna's Nazi women showed no softening in their attitude. Some months after the *Anschluss* their association decided to take over a Jewish infant and toddlers home for its own purposes. They demanded that all the youngsters be evacuated by the evening of the same day the notice of the takeover was given. Löwenherz managed to get a twenty-four-hour delay and transferred the children temporarily to the infirmary of a home for older children, hoping desperately that no epidemic or wave of illness would break out among the older children before he could find permanent quarters to lodge the younger ones.

Only one prominent Nazi woman in Vienna appears to have made any effort to ease the plight of the Jews. This was Henrietta von Schirach, wife of the city's appointed mayor. On a visit to Berchtesgaden with her husband Baldur, she asked Hitler if he could not alleviate their condition. The Führer promptly told her to mind her own business. Frau von Schirach was German.*

We now come to the question of how extensive, and how intensive, was Austria's involvement in the Holocaust. To begin, how much did the Austrians know about the Holocaust?

Some time after the mass extermination of Jews began in Poland, the soap rumor made its appearance. According to this rumor, fat from the bodies of dead Jews was being used to make soap. The story spread through those areas of Poland around the extermination camps, and many Poles stopped buying soap as a result.

The rumor also circulated extensively in Austria. Charlotte Teuber, currently a professor of political science at the University of Vienna, says that "in those days there were two kinds of soap. One irritated the skin. The other was given out only to pregnant women, to hospital patients, and to other medical patients on prescription. Rumor had it that the better kind was 'made out of Jews' and had become known as 'Jews' soap.'" Apparently the Austrians had fewer scruples about this soap than the Poles, for Professor Teuber adds that "everyone did all they could to get a bar of it."

The soap rumor never acquired the currency in Germany that it did in Austria. Most Germans, in fact, never heard it. How does one explain why it was so prevalent in one section of the Reich and not another?

Before answering this question we should note that the Nazis made every effort to suppress awareness of the mass exterminations, to the point of lying about them even to their own leaders. On October 10, 1942 Berlin sent out a memo to all district and section chiefs telling them that the Jews being sent to the east were being employed in work camps. Any rumors to the contrary, said the directive, should be immediately suppressed. Little outright mention would ever be made of the exterminations in official documents, including personal correspondence between those handling them. Consequently, although most Germans suspected, or certainly should have suspected, that the deported Jews faced a very grim future, relatively few seemed to have known about the mass shootings and the gas chambers.

Now a belief in the soap rumor presupposes an awareness that Jews were being exterminated *en masse*, and if the rumor circulated much more extensively in Austria than in Germany, many more Austrians must have known or believed that such exterminations were taking place. This could mean

*Her compassion, however, was in no sense shared by her equally German husband, who repeatedly pressed for further deportations.

that relatively more Austrians than Germans were involved in the actual killings, or that those who were involved were more inclined to inform the folks back home. Actually, both of these suppositions are correct.

In 1985 Nazi hunter Simon Wiesenthal published an excerpt from a letter written by a seventeen-year-old Austrian kindergarten assistant working in Poland during the Holocaust. The letter is addressed to a girlfriend in Linz, and in it the teenager says, "Today six thousand Jews will be knocked off close by (they will get to the Kingdom of Israel). I just saw how they were bundled off in trucks."

The flippant tone with which this youngster, who had chosen a nurturing profession, speaks of such an event is certainly disturbing. Still, it is only an individual case and on that account not too much can be read into it. Far more significant is the openness with which she writes of it to her girlfriend. If many such letters were streaming back into Austria from the east, then the Austrians should have acquired a greater awareness of what was going on.

That Austrians associated with the extermination effort would feel quite free to write home about it can also be seen in a previously mentioned letter. It will be recalled that Mautner once spoke to Löwenherz about a letter that a Viennese merchant had posted on his shop window. In it the merchant's son told of helping to carry out a mass shooting of Jews on the Eastern Front. (This was apparently before mass exterminations in an organized sense had begun.) That the merchant would proudly display such a letter to the public seems in itself indicative of the freedom with which Holocaust-involved Austrians believed they could tell the people at home about what was going on.

But just how many Austrians were in a position to impart such information? Here we have more comprehensive and definitive data to work with.

At the outset, we should note that Austria made up eight and a half percent, or about one-twelfth, of the population of what was now Greater Germany. Yet Austrians made up between thirteen and fourteen percent of the SS. In actual figures, the combined SS at its height had slightly more than 1,100,000 members, of whom 150,000 were Austrians. However, the SS included about 200,000 non-Aryans who were accepted into its ranks. Consequently, it appears that an Austrian was almost twice as likely to join the SS as was a German. To put it differently, Germans outnumbered Austrians in the SS less than 6-to-1, while they outnumbered them in Greater Germany by 11-to-1.

Many Austrian SS men rose to high positions. The most famous, of course, was Eichmann who, though born in Germany, grew up in Hitler's hometown of Linz. About seventy percent of Eichmann's staff, including his transportation chief Franz Novak, were also Austrians.

Other Austrians commanded the SS units in the Warsaw, Riga, and Vilna ghettos, and in the district of Galicia. SS units in Holland, various sections of Russia, and much if not most of the Balkans were also headed by Austrians.* The SS chose the medical school of the University of Graz to serve as its medical research institute, and sent the school interesting research objects, such as skeletons of prisoners who had been subjected to medical experiments.

Many Austrians also rose to high positions in the Gestapo. The most prominent was the lawyer Ernst Kaltenbrunner, who in 1942 became head of the *Sicherheitsdienst*, the most feared of the Gestapo's two main branches. Under his command Gestapo atrocities against the Jews reached their highest point.

When the Nazis launched their war against Russia and Russian-occupied Poland, they set up extermination squads to destroy resisters and other unwanted people, including many of the vast numbers of Jews who now fell into their hands. Despite being heavily outnumbered in the German Reich, more Austrians than Germans, says Wiesenthal, served on some of these squads.

The diary of an Austrian SS man has come to light in which he describes the shooting of some Viennese Jews who had been deported to the east before the gas chambers were fully in place. The victims, he notes, died with remarkable courage, still dreaming of Vienna. As to his own reactions, he writes, "Actually, I felt nothing at all. No sympathy. Nothing."

Most regular army commanders sought to distance themselves from the extermination effort, a practice that greatly vexed Hitler and his Gestapo chief Himmler. But there were exceptions, and perhaps the most outstanding was the army's highest ranking Austrian general, Alexander Löhr. As commander of the occupation troops in the Balkans, Löhr vigorously uprooted Greek, Slovakian, and Yugoslavian Jews and sent them north to their deaths. He also killed thousands of Yugoslavs in reprisal for partisan attacks, prompting the Yugoslavs after the war to execute him as a war criminal. He was one of the few regular German army generals to meet such a fate.

Yugoslavia also listed as war criminals some 2,500 other Austrian officers in the German army. One was First Lieutenant Kurt Waldheim, currently Austria's president, who was an intelligence officer on Löhr's staff. Another, much less known today but more important at the time, was Franz Böhm, the former chief of staff of the Austrian army. Böhm was put in charge of Serbia and he apparently discharged one aspect of his mission without *schlamperei*, for, says Hilberg, "In Serbia there was less delay in the killing operations than almost anywhere else, for here the German machine of destruction worked with particularly dedicated zeal and feverish endeavor to 'solve the Jewish problem.'"

---

*The SS General Otto Skorzeny, one of Hitler's favorites, was also Austrian. Though Skorzeny was known mostly for such daring escapes as the rescue of Mussolini, Reitlinger says he played a role in the deportation of the Hungarian Jews.

When the Nazis turned to gas to carry out mass exterminations they first used specially made vans built by Sauer, an Austrian firm. The SS never liked the gas vans which frequently developed mechanical troubles. But Austrian engineers soon developed the gas chamber which was first tried out in Austria itself. The test site was Hartheim Castle near Linz, where thousands of physically and mentally impaired Austrians were killed. These Austrian engineers later helped install the gas chambers in the extermination camps and kept them in good repair all during the war.

Turning to the death camps themselves, we find that forty percent of the staff members, according to Wiesenthal, were Austrians. This means that on a proportional basis Austrians outnumbered Germans by almost five to one. As with the SS and Gestapo, a substantial number of Austrians served in high positions at these camps.

Foremost among them was Odilo Globocnik, who exercised overall supervision over Treblinka, Sobibor, and Belzec. In this capacity he headed *Aktion Reinhard*, which took the lives of nearly 1.9 million Jews. Globocnik's personal staff, including his chief of staff and adjutants, consisted mostly of Austrians. Apparently they did their work well, for Goebbels praises Globocnik in his diaries for the effective and inconspicuous way he was discharging his delicate assignment.

The commandant of Treblinka itself, the biggest and worst of the three camps, was also Austrian, as were two-thirds to three-quarters of his staff. Other concentration camps headed by Austrians included Plaszow where thirty thousand Jews died, and Theresienstadt where more than thirty thousand Jews died, although Theresienstadt was not technically a concentration camp.*

We now come to Austria's own concentration camp, Mauthausen. Though its commandant was from Munich and its twenty-nine guards included many non-Austrians, the ninety-four civilian employees were mostly from the surrounding area.

Like all camps directed and operated within the Reich itself, Mauthausen was not designed as an extermination camp. It was built around a set of quarries only seventeen miles from Linz, and its inmates were to mine the granite that these quarries contained. Yet, when the Gestapo in 1941 classified all concentration camps located inside the Reich according to the severity of their conditions, Mauthausen, and Mauthausen alone, received the highest classification for harshness. The camp was intended for those for whom there was no prospect of being returned to society, and its mortality rate was more than three times that of other camps situated within the Reich.

*At Ravensbruck, a concentration camp for women, an Austrian midwife was in charge of drowning the babies of pregnant inmates. She was not a staff member but an inmate herself, who ironically had been sent there for practicing abortions.

Although many of Mauthausen's inmates died from exhaustion and disease, others perished through more deliberate means. When an inmate became too weak to work, or offended a guard in any way, in winter authorities would stand him against the wall and pour cold water over him until he froze to death. Other methods of execution were to push inmates from one of the 103 steps that they had to climb in carrying rocks from the quarry, or to order them to run to the barbed wire and then shoot them as escapees.

At one of Mauthausen's satellite camps the staff concocted a "death bath": those earmarked for execution were put into a large vat and doused with cold water for one-half hour or more. SS guards stood around the bath with oxtail whips, beating back anyone trying to get out. As the water mounted higher, those not already frozen were drowned.

A research study of all concentration camps carried out by the University of Stuttgart concluded its report on Mauthausen by saying that "deliberate extermination played a more significant role in this camp than in other concentration camps located in Germany and Austria."

The civilian staff, reported Stuttgart researcher Gisela Raditsch, at one time protested the pushing of inmates off the quarry steps, but only because "the scraps of brains and flesh stick to the rocks and present an ugly sight." In one instance, a nearby farmer's wife complained of repeatedly seeing prisoners shot and left to lie half dead for hours when the shots had failed to kill them outright. She asked that in the future "such cruel events not take place or at least not have to be witnessed by the population." In noting that Mauthausen was surrounded by farms and was only four miles from a town, the Stuttgart researcher concluded that "the later, oft-raised claim that people had no idea of what was transpiring in the concentration camps shows itself in the case of Mauthausen to be unsustainable."

Mauthausen was originally intended for hardened criminals, and in its early days living conditions in the camp were not so severe. But as Jews began arriving in late 1941, the situation rapidly worsened. By the end of the war, 119,000 prisoners had perished at Mauthausen, 39,000, or more than one-third of them, Jews.

Many of Mauthausen's Jewish victims came from Holland where Seyss-Inquart had become Hitler's chief administrator. Seyss-Inquart's entire staff was so heavily Austrian that the Dutch referred to his headquarters as the "Danube Club." The "Danube Club" would send 110,000 Jews to their deaths.

In the face of such facts as these, Simon Wiesenthal holds the Austrians responsible for 3,000,000 Jewish deaths, or well over half of those killed in the Holocaust.* Precise figures on this point are difficult, perhaps impossible, to state, but based on the evidence one fact seems clear. Although tens of

---

*In the most recent edition of his definitive work, *The Destruction of European Jews*, Professor Raul Hilberg puts the total number of Jewish deaths from the Holocaust at 5,100,000.

thousands of Germans energetically and often enthusiastically participated in the slaughter of Jews, the Holocaust from Hitler on down was even more of an Austrian phenomenon than a German one.

Were there no sympathetic or empathetic responses from the Austrian population to the lot of their Jewish fellow citizens? Yes, there were. Most Austrian refugees can recall at least one instance of Gentile aid or at least sympathy. Although some maids turned on their Jewish employers, others stood by them, sometimes at some danger or at least inconvenience to themselves. In a few instances, landlords went through the legal route in evicting their Jewish tenants to allow them more time to find other accommodations. Some Gentiles made food purchases for Jews they knew, and some Gentile shopkeepers allowed Jews themselves to buy fruit and other forbidden foods.

Even professed Nazis could at times bend to help or at least not hurt a Jewish acquaintance. William Geisler recalls a Nazi schoolmate crossing the street to avoid having to encounter and thereby abuse him. Helen Hilsenrad mentions how a Nazi storm trooper signaled an escape route to a Jewish man he knew who had been seized in a random roundup. George Clare remembers how the leader of the Nazi boys in his class said that they should always regard the Jewish boys in their class as friends.

Most of these Gentile acts of kindness involved Jews who were personal friends or at least acquaintances. But there are a few reported instances of sympathy shown to strangers. An Aryan commissioner left the Jewish businessman to whom he was assigned because he could not bear to see the man, now earning about two shillings a day, desperately running around trying to raise the ten shillings needed to pay the commissioner's wage. A youth who grabbed a Jewish man and made him wash windows also gave him a cigarette and apologized, saying he was required to do what he did. Viennese policemen sometimes allowed concentration camp deportees to see family members, and a few constables even shared their box lunches with the men who usually had to go without food for several days while awaiting shipment to Dachau.

Some of these good deeds were risky. A shopkeeper sold food to Jews outside the proscribed hours, explaining when he was arrested that they were, after all, human beings too. A seventy-three-year-old master carpenter who found living quarters for a Jewish woman was sent to Dachau. Clare reports that a Gentile friend called on him the second Sunday after the *Anschluss* and invited him out for a walk, an invitation that exposed his friend to possible unpleasantness since Clare looked Jewish.

Real heroes and heroines are, of course, rare among all peoples and certainly Austrian Gentiles produced a reasonable number. Leading the list is Anton Schmidt, an army sergeant stationed in Vilna. Schmidt worked day and night to save Jews. He smuggled food and medicines into the Vilna ghetto and smuggled Jewish escapees out of it, hiding them in freight trains. If the escapees had any money, he used it to bribe guards. He also acted as a courier between Jewish partisans hidden in the woods and their families in the ghetto, and toward the end even supplied weapons to the partisans. Asked by one Jew if he wasn't taking too many risks, Schmidt replied, "Everyone must croak some day. If I can choose to die as a killer or a helper, then I choose to die as a helper."

As seemed inevitable, Schmidt was eventually caught and executed in the spring of 1942. In his last letter to his wife and daughter he wrote, "I have only acted as a human being and indeed wanted to cause no one harm."

Another Austrian who paid with his life for helping Jews was a Viennese-born police sergeant who, before being shot as a traitor in 1944, escorted as many as four thousand Jews from the Cracow ghetto to comparative safety. The safety was furnished by another Austrian hero, businessman Julius Madritsch, who sheltered the Jews in two clothing factories that he had opened in occupied Poland. Though Madritsch had no need for most of them as workers, he pretended that he did and thereby prevented their deportation to Auschwitz.

Still another hero was Ewald Kleisinger, an Austrian army officer in Warsaw, who hid three escapees from the ghetto uprising in his room. He then sent them with forged papers to his parents in Vienna, who sheltered them until the liberation.

By 1970 over fifty Austrians had been memorialized as righteous Gentiles in Yad Vashem in Jerusalem, and several more have been identified since. (In the fall of 1955 three Austrians, two women and a male civil servant, were honored by the president of Austria and the Israeli ambassador for having protected Jews. And in 1985, five more Austrians, four of them women, were similarly cited.) As late as the summer of 1986 it was learned that a retired high-ranking civil servant in Innsbruck had, at some risk, protected a Jewish woman and her daughter while he was serving as a young officer in Yugoslavia. He was discovered by the daughter, who had been trying to find him ever since the war ended.

Initially, it was believed that only 219 Austrian Jews had survived the war in hiding, but the figure has since risen to nearly 700. This places it at only a little under the official number who survived in Germany, which in 1939 had a Jewish population twice as great.

Yet in making comparisons, we must take certain other factors into account. In Austria, a much more diligent search has been made for such survivors. Erica Weinzierl devoted several years to this pursuit, even enlisting the cooperation of Austrian television and radio in asking for reports on those who helped Jews. Not only has no equally extensive effort been launched in

Germany, but the continued Soviet control of East Germany has discouraged such investigation. Moise Bejske, an Israeli judge who chairs the Claims Committee of Yad Vashem, believes that as many as one thousand Jews may have survived the Nazi era in hiding in Berlin alone. Furthermore, there was at least one extensive network involving businessmen, priests, and others that until 1944 smuggled dozens of Jews out of the country. Nothing of this kind ever existed in Austria.

Other factors also make Austria's overall record somewhat less impressive than it might otherwise seem. Many "U-Boats" (underground survivors) owed their survival to marriage into Christian families or to their having converted to Christianity before the *Anschluss*. Many others survived by giving money and jewelry to their Gentile protectors.

A popular joke in Austria during the 1960s points up this latter motive: Two friends meet on the street and the first, noticing the other's expensive new clothes, asks him where he has gotten the money for such raiment. "Oh, I have a Jew hidden in the basement," is the reply. "But the war has been over for twenty years," says the first. The second then responds in a sarcastic tone, "I should tell him?"

Though neither family relationships nor financial contributions played any role in the cases of the heroes and heroines cited above, nor in dozens of other cases as well, still Weinzierl admits that such relationships and contributions loom large in the overall picture. Moreover, she deplores the all-too-frequent disclosures that prevented the toll of survivors from being higher. "The continued betrayals and denunciations of U-Boats and political underground resisters," she writes, "is not to be attributed primarily to National Socialist fanaticism, but to that specific Viennese characteristic which Arthur Schnitzler has identified as 'disinterested meanness.'" Consequently, she has given her book on the Austrian response to the Holocaust the title that, translated, has been used for this chapter: *Zu Wenig Gerechte* (Too Few Righteous, or Decent, People).

Other Austrian Gentile historians more than share Weinzierl's concern over the reaction of their countrymen to the persecution of Jews. "The resistance of the Austrians against the arrest and deportation of their Jewish fellow-citizens was shockingly minute," writes Maderegger. Karl Stadler, after noting the loss to Austria's cultural and economic life from the Holocaust, goes on to say, "But far more worrying is the thought that a crime of such magnitude could be perpetuated against so little opposition." Walter Maass perhaps sums up the situation when he says, "The story of the Final Solution in Austria is certainly a gloomy one and has not ceased to trouble the conscience of Austrian writers and historians to this day. Even if it is true that the long economic crisis from 1929 to 1938 greatly contributed to Hitler's success, the question remains: Why was Austrian soil so fertile for his particularly virulent brand of anti-Semitism?

Chapter 26

Silent Pulpits

In earlier chapters we saw how Austria's Catholic Church had been the biggest bulwark of the Dollfuss-Schuschnigg regime. We also saw how its leader, Cardinal Innitzer, demonstrated his personal sympathy and support for the country's Jews on many occasions. The *Anschluss* brought a speedy and sweeping reappraisal in the positions of both the Church and its leading prelate.

Hitler had no sooner crossed the border when Innitzer sent him a message of welcome. At the same time, the Cardinal publicly called on the faithful to give their new rulers full obedience and to offer thanks in their Sunday prayers for the absence of bloodshed during the "great political upheaval" that the nation had undergone. Innitzer followed up these gestures by ordering Vienna's churches to be festooned with swastikas and their bells to be rung on Hitler's triumphant entry into the city.

The day after Hitler's arrival in Vienna, Cardinal Innitzer called on him at his hotel. The Cardinal gave the Hitler salute to members of the Führer's entourage in the lobby, and in his meeting he assured Hitler that Austria's Catholics would be his most loyal followers as long as he granted the Church and its organizations the rights that he had formally accorded the German Church in a concordat signed some years before. Hitler quickly agreed, and although he had repeatedly, and increasingly, violated such pledges in Germany, Innitzer took his promises at face value. The Cardinal, who a few weeks earlier had so strongly supported Austria's independence, emerged from the meeting strongly supporting its demise.

Three days later, Austria's Catholic Episcopate issued a statement praising the accomplishments of National Socialism and urging approval of annexation. Two letters from Innitzer to Gauleiter Bürckel to that effect, each signed with the salutation *Heil Hitler*, were subsequently released to the press. On March 27 Austria's bishops published a letter saying, "We joyfully recognize that the National Socialist movement has produced and is producing outstanding achievements. . . . On plebiscite day it will be our self-evident duty as bishops, and our national duty as Germans, to declare ourselves in support of the Reich. We expect all faithful Catholics to acknowledge what they owe their nation."

The fervor with which Austria's Catholic clergy flung themselves into the arms, or rather at the feet, of Hitler astonished and annoyed many of their German colleagues. It also alarmed the Vatican. The latter summoned Innitzer to Rome and had him sign a statement modifying his endorsement and pointing out that it was not in any case binding on the faithful. Still, as the subsequent plebiscite results show, Austrian Nazism had received a powerful boost from the organization that up to now had constituted its most formidable foe.

Although the Church started out more than willing to cooperate with the new regime, it faced at the outset a particular problem as far as the government's Jewish policies were concerned. What should it do about its thousands of Jewish Catholics?

The *Anschluss* brought all of Austria's Jews under the so-called Nuremberg Laws. These laws classified as "full Jews" all those who had at least three Jewish grandparents. Also classified as full Jews were those who had only two Jewish grandparents but who were registered as or married to a Jew as of September 15, 1935, the date when the laws were promulgated. Those with two Jewish grandparents but not a member of a Jewish community or married to a Jew were designated as *Mischlinge* (mixed breeds) of the first degree, while those with only one Jewish grandparent became mixed breeds of the second degree.

The Nuremberg Laws made thirty thousand Viennese who no longer considered themselves Jews into Jews once again. The *Gemeinde* lost no time in extending to them a hand of reconciliation. "Assimilation has become impossible," it said in the second edition of its new newspaper. "Now has come the time to return. Everyone is welcome regardless of their earlier views and opinions."

Many of those who had simply become *konfessionslos* did return. But many of those who had converted to Catholicism held quite sincerely to their Catholic beliefs. A few had even become priests and nuns.

To compound the problem further, over seventeen hundred Jews converted to Catholicism during the first five months following the *Anschluss*. Most were former Catholic women who had converted to Judaism to marry Jewish men and who now rushed back to the Church in the hope of saving not only themselves but their families. But a few were probably born Jews who had either acted out of misguided expediency (because such a conversion would not do them any good under the Nuremberg Laws), or possibly out of genuine conviction, since it must have seemed to many Jews during that period that God had abandoned his supposedly Chosen People.

Eichmann reacted to this stream of conversions by closing down the Paulus Mission. He even arrested one priest who had performed eighty baptisms. At the same time, however, he told the *Gemeinde* not to handle Christian Jews but to let their own religious organizations deal with them. This sometimes presented complicated problems, such as the case of a Jewish woman who, though married to a Christian man, had never renounced Judaism. She was the mother of six children and pregnant with a seventh. Eichmann assigned the mother to the *Gemeinde* and the children to a Christian facility.

What were these Christian facilities? For the Catholic Jews, Cardinal Innitzer eventually set up a mission in his own residence. Its primary task was to help them emigrate. To secure funds, he wrote what he called "begging letters" to the Vatican and various Catholic bishops abroad.

While the response to his letters fell well below the Cardinal's expectations, in part no doubt because of the continuing depression, he did secure $30,000 in cash or pledges. Its utilization often led to some complicated arrangements. For example, Innitzer once borrowed $3,500 from the Joint Distribution Committee which, after he had written several imploring letters to Rome, the Church paid back in New York. But his effort was late in getting started, and when the Gestapo began closing down emigration, some of the money set aside for this purpose was apparently lost. In all, only 150 Catholic Jews, one of them a priest, made their way to safety through Church financing.

The Catholic Jews remaining in Vienna also required assistance and this too produced unique problems. Sick Christian Jews were barred from Aryan hospitals while the Rothschild Hospital could only take professed Jews. The Church eventually found a woman doctor to treat Catholic Jews for a modest fee. In cases of death, Catholic Jews were not allowed burial in a Christian cemetery, and the Church paid the *Gemeinde* for their burial. Operating on a monthly budget of less than $2,000, the Cardinal's assistance center did what it could for its non-Aryan members.

The "Yellow Star" edict and the ban on appearing at public gatherings created fresh dilemmas for the Church, for if fully enforced such measures would bar Jews from attending church services. Shortly after the issuance of the "Yellow Star" edict, Cardinal Innitzer sent a letter to the church deans (*Dechanten*) of Vienna urging them to let Christian love guide their actions toward their Jewish parishioners. He also urged them to make no separation during masses between Aryan and non-Aryan worshippers and to pray for Catholic Jews. But two weeks later he sent out a directive canceling the first letter and substituting a shorter one which said simply that "non-Aryan Catholics can take part in the mass."

When the Nazis began deporting Catholic Jews along with other Jews, the Church's concern increased, especially when such actions affected Jewish nuns and priests. Innitzer joined some German bishops in asking priests to offer prayers for the Christian deportees, and some members of the clergy sent them food packages. In very few instances, however, was any attempt made to hide baptized Jews from the authorities. Consequently, most Catholic Jews who did not emigrate were deported. In the Lodz ghetto the first Christmas Eve services for Catholic Jews were conducted by Sister Maria Regina Fuhrman, a Viennese Jewish nun with a master's degree in theology.

When the Nazis began deporting Jewish partners of mixed marriages, Cardinal Innitzer joined with some German Catholic leaders in contacting the Vatican, which in turn pleaded with Berlin. Hitler, beginning to feel the losses on his Eastern Front and needing to ensure unity within the Reich, grudgingly agreed to suspend the program. Hence, a few thousand Jewish partners in mixed marriages were saved. Most of these Jews, of course, were converted Christians or, at the very least, *konfessionslos*.

If the efforts of the Austrian Church in behalf of its Jewish members were relatively modest, its efforts in behalf of non-Christian Jews were nearly nonexistent. Judging from the numerous photos and reports of the early days of the *Anschluss*, no Catholic clergyman took part in or observed the public outrages against the Jews. Judging from the same evidence, not one priest ever sought to remonstrate or even plead with the terrorizers, many of whom were teenagers.

Twenty years after the war ended, Weinzierl sent out a questionnaire to 2,700 priests over the age of sixty, asking them if they knew of help given to Jews either by themselves or other Catholics. Only 327 priests (twelve percent) responded, and only thirty-one or just over one percent of those polled, responded affirmatively. In most cases the help was given to Christian Jews and was relatively minor. One priest mentioned how generously Jewish businessmen before the *Anschluss* had helped the poor in his parish, but described himself as a staunch anti-Semite nevertheless.

The lower clergy did provide a few conspicuous examples of sacrifice and risk when it came to helping Jews. A Leopoldstadt priest hid sixteen Jews, while a village pastor, Father Alexander Seewald, pointed out in his post-

Kristallnacht sermon that Jesus was a Jew and "therefore the descent of a human being can never be a crime." Arrested two weeks later, Father Seewald spent the rest of the war in a concentration camp.

The hierarchy of the Austrian Church manifested no public and, as far as can be learned, no private concern over what was happening to non-Christian Jews. The Church was starting to have problems of its own with the regime, and presumably did not want to make them worse. Still, in Germany at least two bishops, one of them the Cardinal Archbishop of Berlin, publicly spoke out against the deportations. But in Austria, as Stadler has put it, "One looks in vain for protest against the humiliation, persecution, and destruction of Jews."*

If Catholic efforts to protect Catholic Jews were limited, then Protestant attempts to assist Protestant Jews were almost non-existent. A handful of the country's Protestant pastors, including a theology professor who had been a confirmed anti-Semite, did render some aid, but most ministers discouraged their Jewish parishioners from even coming to church. The presiding bishop of the country's evangelical church asked a foreign church organization to take care of the spiritual needs of the country's Protestant Jews, saying that his own pastors no longer dared to do so. Nonspiritual needs were apparently not even mentioned.

The foreign church organization contacted by the bishop was a mission set up by Swedish Lutherans in Austria some years before. Although not expressly created to aid Jews, it became one of two main assistance centers for Austria's Jewish Protestants. By the time the Nazis closed it at the end of 1941, it had helped three thousand Protestant Jews and their often Gentile spouses to emigrate to Scandinavia. Only thirty, or one percent of this number, represented post-*Anschluss* converts for the mission required a year of instruction and observation before it would approve a conversion.

The second source of assistance to the Protestant Jews was a mission set up by a Dutch Quaker named Frank van Gheel Gildemeester. He had originally

*The Catholic Church in Austria also kept silent over the Nazis' euthanasia program, although one of its main centers of operation was at Hartheim Castle, only seventeen miles from Linz. Here, where the regime's first gas chamber was put into operation, some thirty thousand insane, crippled, or hopelessly ill people were killed. Maas believes the surrounding villages must have learned about it because of the ghastly odor from the ovens and the bones and ashes dropped from trucks carting away the residue. Protest from German clergy over euthanasia centers in that country finally forced Hitler, at least ostensibly, to suspend the program.

Maas also wonders about Austria's doctors, many of whom must have known about and some of whom must have participated in the euthanasia program. To my knowledge, not one Austrian doctor has ever been punished for such participation, although as late as May 1987 West Germany sent two elderly physicians to prison for their role in such killings.

intended to help all Jews, but Eichmann told him only to assist Protestants and the *konfessionslos*. Much of the money he received for this purpose came from a Quaker industrialist in Philadelphia named Robert Yarnell. But Gildemeester also worked with Eichmann in taking the property of rich Jews and using a certain percentage of it to help poorer Jews emigrate. Gildemeester's mission, says Rosenkranz, assisted in one way or another about five thousand Protestant or *konfessionslos* Jews.

In Germany the Protestants had set up their own mission years before to help their admittedly much larger number of Jewish members. Several thousand Protestant pastors, led by Martin Niemoeller, who ended in a concentration camp, and Dietrich Bonhoeffer, who ended on the gallows, openly opposed discriminatory laws against Jews and other Nazi policies. Although the majority of Germany's Protestant ministers accepted and in many instances approved of the Nazi regime, an appreciable minority, ranging from twelve to thirty-five percent, continually opposed it at great personal risk. The deportation of Jews in Germany prompted a few Protestant bishops to speak out. Among them was the head of the Evangelical church in Württemberg, who wrote the government, saying, "There must be an end to putting to death members of other nations and races."

No such voices were raised in Protestant Austria, and no Martin Niemoellers or Dietrich Bonhoeffers emerged from its ranks. Instead, Pastor Johannes Iverson, the last head of the Swedish mission, later expressed shock over the deep hatred of the Viennese for the Jews. It was not confined, he said, to a small group but was widespread. As he wrote on returning to his native Gotheberg, the leading people of Vienna believed that "the Jews must be destroyed. One must fumigate them the way one fumigates lice." The most educated, reasonable, and "well-meaning" people in Vienna, he said, could not understand his helping Jews. "You help Jews?" they had asked him in amazement. "That can't be true. That is simply not possible."*

*The June/July 1987 issue of *Illustrierte Neue Welt* carries an article by Pastor Göte Hedenquist who headed the Austrian mission until September 1939. In it he mentions going to Venice to receive a check from Joseph Hoffman-Cohn, the chairman of the American Board of Mission to the Jews. This money, he says, enabled them to keep feeding Vienna's Protestant Jews. He also writes, "In my memory I see the children behind the closed windows of a train looking out at their parents and siblings standing on the platform. Since such departures were closely monitored by the Gestapo, the parents did not dare to get too close. The parents also struggled to hold back their tears until after the train had left. They then wandered back to their empty apartments, their sole consolation being that their children would now be safe."

Chapter 27

Birth of "The First Victim"

The excitement and exhilaration that swept Gentile Vienna during the early days of the *Anschluss* soon diminished, but it did not immediately disappear. For the Nazi takeover brought a stream of benefits that for several weeks maintained Vienna in a state of semi-euphoria.

Many of these benefits stemmed from the *Blitzverfolgung* (Lightning Persecution). Gentile businessmen and professionals no longer needed to worry about Jewish competition, while customers of Jewish merchants and wholesalers and clients of Jewish doctors, dentists, and lawyers, no longer needed to worry about paying their bills. For many Viennese the *Anschluss* marked a sort of Jubilee Day, with all debts now erased. Adults entered Jewish-owned toy shops and candy shops with their children and, after allowing the youngsters to pick out what they wanted, left without paying. Jewish property, plundered by the Nazis or sold by hastily departing Jews, flooded the market at bargain prices. Jewish emigration, suicides, and arrests made many more dwellings available in housing-short Vienna. Finally, there were the ongoing street humiliations and harassments of Jews to provide amusement and distraction.

A more significant blessing brought by the *Anschluss* was the sudden availability of employment. To some extent, this too resulted from the *Blitzverfolgung*, as tens of thousands of Jewish workers lost their jobs. Thousands of positions became vacant in the textile industry alone, a situation that created a crisis since not enough qualified Gentiles were available to fill these places.

329

Highly prized positions in the civil service opened up as the Nazis began dismissing and imprisoning Gentile civil servants who had become too closely identified with the Schuschnigg government. The new regime was at first helped in cleansing itself of such people by numerous denunciations from those who hoped to take their places. The stream of such denunciations reached such massive proportions, however, that Bürckel finally forbade denouncers from applying for the positions of those they had denounced. He also imposed heavy penalties for false denunciations. The purging of the civil service continued only slightly abated. Employment was created for many by this and by growth in the number of government positions generally, because a police state requires a much more extensive governmental apparatus.

But the greatest source of new employment was Germany's war economy, to which the Austrian economy was now joined. Government contracts linked directly or indirectly with rearmament accelerated Austria's industrial development, with beneficial spillover effects on its service sector. In addition, some 100,000 skilled workers found employment in Germany itself. Unemployment, which had stood at nearly 400,000 at the time of the *Anschluss*, dropped to less than 100,000 within a year, and six months later had gone down to 32,000, an overall decrease of over ninety percent.

Many Austrians attributed the beneficial boom to the elimination of the Jews from economic influence. They soon discovered differently, however, as some of the negative effects of Hitler's rearmament program appeared.

In Germany Hitler had also created many jobs, and had raised the real (inflation-adjusted) *weekly* earnings of the average worker. But he had done so only by increasing the tempo of work and by lengthening the work week, to fifty-five and, in some key industries, sixty hours. Inflation-adjusted *hourly* wages actually declined.

The average German with his zest for work adapted to the new conditions quite easily. A German, it has been said, does not labor to live but lives to labor. The average Austrian did not. "You have to prove to the world that you are not easygoing," said Göring as he opened a steelworks in Austria that had been renamed after him. "An eight-hour day is not enough. Work! Work!" But his hearers did not readily heed this exhortation. Eventually the government even had to forbid Austrians from taking their bicycles with them when they went to Germany to work for too many, appalled at the rigorous work schedules in Germany, had used the bicycles to flee back to Austria.

A still greater source of disillusionment and discontent were the shortages that the armaments program was producing. Germany had already begun to feel such shortages by the time the *Anschluss* had occurred. One example: by the evening of the day the Germans marched into Linz, all underpants in the city were sold out. Other Austrian communities experienced similar runs on various goods now in short supply in Germany. German tourists poured into

Austria to take advantage of the sumptuous meals and consumer goods no longer available in the Reich proper. But soon, of course, such items were no longer available in Austria either. It took less than a month for the whipped cream which had made Viennese coffee so famous to disappear, even from the city's best hotel restaurants.

By fall, pressing supply scarcities had spread to more mundane foodstuffs, and at the Vienna open air market half a dozen saleswomen paraded around the square with empty baskets, sarcastically shouting the slogan, "We thank our Führer." Prices were rising and black marketeering was becoming rampant.

The outbreak of war in 1939 intensified all these problems. The standard work week lengthened to sixty hours and shortages of basic foods became commonplace. Although the regime would maintain caloric consumption at a fairly high level, and make white flour and milk available until the last months of the war, many goods, including anything resembling real coffee, all but disappeared.

The war imposed other sacrifices that upset the Austrians still more. The drafting of over a million men, 173,000 of whom would die in battle, the blackouts, and, toward the end, the air raids were not what they had in mind when they so lustily cheered the coming of Hitler and the end of Austria's nationhood.

Many Austrians, including some long-time *Anschluss* advocates, now discovered that they missed being Austrians. The Germans at first made Austria into a province which they called *Ostmark*, a name that bore no historical association with Austria. Later, *Ostmark* was dissolved into simply the Alpine and Danube districts of Germany. With all of Austria's gold now in Berlin and its crown jewels in Nuremberg, and with Vienna reduced to a provincial capital, little remained to show that a nation had once existed.

To reinforce this loss of national identity, Berlin appointed mostly Germans to rule the region. (Leading Austrian Nazis were usually given high posts elsewhere.) This practice also rankled the Austrians, especially since the German officials lived so lavishly. Vienna's new mayor, Baldur von Schirach, employed seventeen chambermaids at his sumptuous mansion.

Many of the German officials felt, and expressed, contempt for Austrians, whom they regarded as lazy, sloppy, and only opportunistic Nazis. This annoyed the Austrians who, for their part, believed that they were being forced to bear the main burden of the war. Under German rule the well-known Viennese tendency to carp and complain appears to have reached its greatest flowering.

Another source of tension lay in the regime's attitude toward the Catholic Church. Hitler of course never intended to keep the promises he made to Cardinal Innitzer, any more than he had kept similar promises made to the Church in Germany. But the suddenness and sharpness of his crackdown on

332 VIENNA AND ITS JEWS

the Austrian Church surprised almost everyone. Within six months he had closed down two of Austria's four theological seminaries, along with 1,400 Church schools. He had also forbidden 150 priests to teach religion, instituted a compulsory civil ceremony for marriage, liberalized divorce, and began to seize Church property.

Many local Nazis whose relations with the Church had become embittered during the Dollfuss-Schuschnigg years of clerical fascism apparently abetted the crackdown. One observer recalls seeing a poster, affixed to the wall of a church, that bore the following message:

> Stand the Jews and priests againt the wall,
> So you serve your Fatherland.

At a religious festival in St. Stephen's Cathedral on October 7, Cardinal Innitzer finally spoke out, telling the packed gathering, "There is a cross over Austria, but it is not the cross of Christ." (The word for swastika in German is *Hakenkreuz* or "hooked cross.") Some eight thousand Catholic youths seized on the Cardinal's outburst to demonstrate outside the cathedral carrying signs reading, "We thank our Cardinal" and "Jesus Christ is our Führer."

The next night Hitler Youth, aided by storm troopers, stormed the Cardinal's palace, breaking windows, ripping up paintings, plundering valuables, and tossing a curate out the window. The regime followed this up by staging a massive anti-Church rally six days later and by imposing a special tax on Church membership.

Protestant groups at first fared better under the Nazis, but eventually they too began to feel the lash as the regime closed down or took over their schools and other institutions. Jehovah's Witnesses and Seventh Day Adventists were especially singled out for ruthless suppression, and many were shipped to concentration camps and even executed. Says Pauley, "By the fall of 1938 the Germans had managed to alienate virtually every social and political group in Austria."

In October 1943, the foreign ministers of Great Britain, Soviet Russia, and America met in Moscow to discuss a variety of matters. In the course of these talks they touched briefly on Austria and, with apparently little difficulty, composed and issued a communique that stated, "Austria, the first free country to fall victim of Hitlerite aggression, shall be liberated from German domination." From the time of the *Anschluss* on, Western journalists had frequently referred to the "rape" of Austria because they wanted to stir up anti-Nazi sentiment in the free world. Now the Allies had given Austria the status of victim.

This designation seems puzzling in view of the warmth with which the country had welcomed Hitler and the zeal with which it had, at least at the beginning, put his policies into practice. With a million Austrians fighting in the Nazi armies, and with only ten thousand Austrians, most of them Jews, fighting in the Allied armies, why did the Allies so suddenly and completely absolve Austria of complicity in Nazism's misdeeds?

Several reasons have been suggested to explain this action. They include the not entirely frivolous suggestion advanced by a senior American diplomat that it was because Roosevelt and Churchill in their youth had spent happy summers in Austria and felt that such a jolly people couldn't be real Nazis. But the most likely reason was the desire of the Allies to stimulate Austrian resistance, for the Moscow declaration went on to say that the Austrians "have a responsibility which they cannot evade, and in the final settlement account will inevitably be taken of the part they play in resisting the German invaders."

As it so happens, resistance groups had already begun to form in Austria. As early as 1940, a Catholic priest, Karl Roman Scholz, began organizing an "Austrian Freedom Movement." Not long afterward, a Protestant teacher named Otto Haas started an underground organization with two other teachers. Austrian Communists who had fled to Moscow were infiltrated back into the country to work with whatever Communists remained, as well as with left-wing Socialists. They largely confined their efforts to carrying out minor acts of sabotage.

In southern Austria, monarchists joined with Slovene partisans backed by Tito to set up an anti-fascist movement. Toward the end of the war, small, scattered groups of partisans emerged in certain Alpine regions.

But the Austrian resistance managed to inflict only minor damage on the war effort. The Nazis had taken over the country one and a half years before the war and had ample time to arrest those likely to cause trouble. Most Austrian young men who would normally have been the backbone of such resistance were away at the front. Austrians and Germans spoke a common language. All these factors hampered such resistance efforts. Denunciations and betrayals, though certainly not uncommon in underground movements in other Nazi-occupied countries, were perhaps even more common in Austria. Nearly all the embryonic resistance movements were soon betrayed, and over 36,000 Austrians, about one half of one percent of the population, were either executed outright or otherwise died in concentration camps.

Another and possibly more critical cause of Austria's relatively feeble resistance effort lay in its inability to generate real popular support until the final days. Carping and complaining may have begun early but, as Maas points out, "A large percentage of the population only turned against the Nazis when it became clear they were losing the war. Even then many remained inactive, and restricted their opposition to cautious grumbling, listening to foreign broadcasts, and dealing on the black market."

Another Austrian Gentile writer, Professor Jürgen Koppensteiner, goes even further in this assessment. Noting that most Austrians reacted to the worsening conditions of the war with jokes critical of the regime, he concludes that, "There was scarcely any active resistance."

By the fall of 1944 it had become evident to almost everyone that Hitler's days were numbered. The July 20 plot against him may have misfired, but the Allies were bearing down. Paris had been liberated and Rumania had crossed over to the Allied camp. Conditions in Vienna were so bad that even the Burg Theater closed down and its actors and actresses were put to work sewing and tailoring uniforms. Air raids pounded the city mercilessly.

Disenchantment with the regime now turned increasingly into open defiance. Austrian soldiers began deserting in droves and soon some forty thousand were hiding in Vienna alone. The Viennese themselves grew so antagonistic that SS men feared to go into some districts without revolvers in their hands. Housewives leaned out of their windows to shout insults at ordinary soldiers.

Under these conditions a more unified and broad-based resistance movement began to emerge. Formed in the fall of 1944, it called itself O5, the O standing for the first letter of *Oesterreich*, the German name for Austria, and the 5 standing for the fifth letter of the alphabet, E, which is the name's second letter. Seven days before Christmas, and with the Nazi regime approaching its end, a group of political leaders met in the apartment of a former Christian Social parliamentarian and set up the Provisional Austrian National Committee. By spring the Committee had representatives from all major political groups in Austria, including the Communists.

The membership and activities of the O5 movement grew rapidly as the war's misery increased and its increasingly inevitable end approached. Soon many army officers joined it.

When Russian troops approached Vienna in April 1945, Hitler dispatched tanks and SS troops to defend the city to the last. His long-standing love-hate relationship with Vienna apparently survived to the very end, for he needed the tanks to defend Berlin. The Provisional Austrian National Committee sent a sergeant major through the Russian lines with the German plans for Vienna's defense. They hoped by so doing to save the city from destruction. Although this move, like so many resistance efforts in the past, was betrayed from within, and three army officers involved were publicly hanged from street lampposts, the sergeant himself got through. Vienna was therefore spared the heavy damage that otherwise would have occurred.

As the Russians swept into the city from the west, the last remaining SS troops retreated across the Danube canal into the Leopoldstadt. (A Swiss newspaper observed the irony of the Jew haters now being cooped up in the former Jewish ghetto.) They soon abandoned the Leopoldstadt too, but not before they had discovered nine Jews who had survived for months by hiding in a cellar. The SS men quickly lined up the group — including an eighty-two-year-old woman — against a wall, and machine-gunned them down.

But Jews had now begun arriving in Austria. Some were former Austrians who had joined the British army and who were now being parachuted into the country to prepare the way for the Allied advance from the west. Many had achieved officer rank and all had assumed British names to prevent their being summarily shot as traitors should they be captured.

A colonel and a captain landed in Vienna to make contact with the resistance. A lieutenant colonel landed in southern Austria, where he persuaded the commander of a German airfield to surrender his facility intact. A grandson of Sigmund Freud also parachuted in and won a medal for hunting down the scientist who prepared the poison gas for the extermination chambers.* Another Austrian Jew who entered with the British army was Richard Berger, whose father, the former Zionist leader of Innsbruck, had been beaten to death on *Kristallnacht*. Young Berger managed to track down his father's killer in Klagenfurt some one hundred miles away and, restraining his desire to exact justice on the spot, turned him over to the authorities for punishment.

But not all Jews entering Austria during these final months were wearing uniforms. Some were hardly wearing anything at all.

In the summer of 1944 Eichmann drove thousands of Jews from Hungary and other parts of the east into Austria to prevent their liberation by the Russians. As they straggled through one Austrian town, an alpine community named Eisenerz, a crowd emerging from a movie threw stones at them and one survivor even recalls shots being fired. Those who did not perish during the march ended up working in small factories in and around Vienna or on a "wall" the Nazis were trying to erect to hold the Russian advance. Given starvation rations and mercilessly worked, they died by the hundreds.

At the beginning of April, thirteen hundred of these Jews were marched to an annex of Mauthausen. Some six hundred or nearly half died en route.

At Mauthausen itself, executions of inmates accelerated as the war drew to a close. About thirty thousand were murdered or died from disease and exhaustion in the camp during the final four months of its existence. Jews and gypsies made up the largest proportion of the dead.

---

*Many other Austrian Jews serving with the British armies were also decorated. Among them was a Captain Kennedy who received both a Military Cross and another military medal for, among other things, leading a commando raid into Germany. Many Austrian Jews also served with distinction in the American army. One of them was the former journalist and later novelist, Hans Habe, who rose from private to major, winning a Bronze Star for valor in the process.

On May 1 the camp took the last thirty thousand of its inmates, Jews and non-Jews, and marched them to Ebensee. Some Austrians, motivated by compassion or influenced simply by the impending arrival of the Allied armies, put out bowls of water for the corpse-like figures, and a few even tossed apples to them. At Ebensee the men, mustering their remaining strength, refused an order to march into a tunnel because they realized that their overseers planned to blow it up and bury them within it. The overseers, nervous over the nearness of the Allies (sounds of Allied gunfire could already be heard in the distance), decided to let them live and ran off to save themselves.

In Vienna the fortunes of war had produced no halt in the city's efforts to cleanse itself of as many of its remaining Jews as possible. On April 14, just hours before the Red Army entered the city, the authorities dispatched a trainload of 109 Jews to Theresienstadt. It was the Nazi regime's last deportation of Jews to the east. So, in a sense, the Holocaust ended in Vienna where, in another sense, it had begun nearly forty years before when a young would-be art student, who had come to the city with no pronounced prejudices against Jews, had departed for Germany having during his Vienna sojourn become, as he himself later put it, "an absolute anti-Semite."

Part VIII

Postwar Vienna: Dream and Reality II

*I asked an acquaintance who had returned
from the U.S. . . . . and had married a Viennese
Gentile, how he felt as a Jew living in Vienna.
He answered in his wife's presence, "Oh, it's
very simple. All you have to do is close both
eyes and ears."*
        — Benno Weiser Varon in 1955

Prelude

Rebirth of a Community and a Country

Most of Vienna's exiled Jews created rewarding lives and successful careers for themselves in their adopted homelands. They became prominent musicians and conductors, writers and journalists, psychiatrists and psychologists, motion picture producers and performers, businessmen and financiers, statesmen and diplomats. An exceptionally high number entered academic life, and as late as the 1980s more professors at the Hebrew University in Jerusalem had been born in Vienna than in any other city. Scattered and dispersed, Vienna's transplanted Jewry flourished anew.*

Many of these expatriates displayed exceptional ingenuity in utilizing new languages. Actor Oskar Karlweis went first to France, where he was soon acting and even improvising in perfect French. He then went to New York where he played long, demanding roles in English. Benno Weiser Varon, after less than two years in Ecuador, became that country's first syndicated columnist. Most spectacular of all, perhaps, was the career of Rudolph Flesh, a young lawyer who, within five years after coming to America, earned a Ph.D. in Library Science from Columbia. He then went on to write over ten popular books on

*A partial listing of the better known emigrees in America includes conductors Erich Leinsdorf and Julius Rudel, composer Frederick Loewe of *My Fair Lady* fame, novelist Frederic Morton, singer-actress Martha Schlamme, economist and Federal Reserve Board chairman Arthur Burns, financier Felix Rohatyn, psychiatrists Helen Deutsch and Viktor Frankl, psychologists Anna Freud and Bruno Bettelheim, motion picture producer Otto Preminger, art dealer Otto Kalir who discovered Grandma Moses, and Henry Grunewald who became editor-in-chief of *Time*.

the teaching and usage of English, including such best sellers as *Why Johnny Can't Read* and *The Art of Readable Writing.*

One might also note the case of chemical engineer Max Wang who earned a degree in foreign languages at Loyola University at the age of eighty-nine.

Even in sports Vienna's Jews continued to acquire laurels. In 1941 an older Gerda Gottlieb broke the American high-jumping record for women, while in 1951 a much older Fred Oberlander became Canada's heavyweight wrestling champion. The following year the now American Richard Berman won his seventh world table tennis championship.

In 1959 former Hakoah members from all over the world gathered in Jerusalem to celebrate the fiftieth anniversary of the founding of their team. But the only group of exiles who made an effort to stick together as a group were the Orthodox Jews of the *Schiffschul.* They established Congregation Adas Yereim in Brooklyn, New York which soon became noted in the Orthodox world through its publications and other activities.

Only a few Jews showed any interest in returning to Vienna. Some had held such positions as teachers of religion for Jewish pupils in the Austrian school system and could therefore regain their jobs with full pension credit for the years in exile. Some had not managed to create satisfactory lives for themselves abroad. Many who had fled to Shanghai fell into this category. Finally, some were simply homesick.

Among the more notable returnees was cafe owner and comedian Karl Farkas, the surviving member of the comedy team that had operated and performed at Vienna's most sophisticated nightclub. In lieu of compensation the Austrian government gave him the honorary title of Professor. Farkas could frequently be seen sitting at Sacher's showing obvious delight at hearing the waiters address him as "Herr Professor."

Not all who returned, however, had such a happy time of it. Doctor Paul Klaar, a former police surgeon and decorated World War I veteran, had during the *Anschluss* worked first as a "medical assistant" certifying Jews for Theresienstadt and had then been deported to Theresienstadt himself. Although he was made chief surgeon of the Vienna police and was given the title of Imperial Counselor on his return, he tried three times to commit suicide before walking into the path of an oncoming train and dying of his injuries.

Two other Theresienstadt survivors, General Sommer and his wife, went at first to Danvers, Massachusetts to join their married daughter. But the old general longed for Vienna and so the couple applied for and received the first two passports issued by the new Austrian government. Sadly, a crippling stroke ended his hopes and soon thereafter his life. His ashes were brought back to Vienna and given a state funeral with "military honors."

The son of Joseph and Sophie Löwenherz returned as an officer in the American army to bring his exhausted parents to his new homeland. But first there was a barrier to surmount: the Russians had accused the elder Löwenherz of collaboration with the Nazis. Fortunately, several Jews, including some who had come back from concentration camps, spoke out in his defense and the charges were dropped. Löwenherz and his wife then left for New York City, where he lived until his death in 1956.*

Löwenherz was not the only *Gemeinde* functionary to face collaboration charges. The Czechs arrested Rabbi Murmelstein, but released him after an investigation. Murmelstein stayed on in Prague to become the star witness at the trial of Karl Rahm, who was sentenced to death. The Rabbi then went to Italy hoping to obtain a teaching position at a rabbinical seminary. When this project fell through, he became a traveling salesman for an Italian furniture firm. Though partially invalided from a heart condition in the early 1980s, he observed his eighty-second birthday in Rome in June 1987.**

JUPO head Wilhelm Reisz was arrested in Vienna and sentenced to five years in prison. Although the sentence was not a long one, and he would still have been a young man after serving it, Reisz hanged himself in his jail cell shortly after his trial ended.

Most of the other *Gemeinde* officials and employees, including those sent to Theresienstadt, left for other countries, the majority going to Israel. Their desire to depart was not only understandable but fortunate, for newer and fresher energies were needed as the *Gemeinde* now entered the busiest phase of its history.

From 1945 to 1953 some 170,000 Holocaust survivors from central and Eastern Europe streamed into Vienna. Most of them were heading elsewhere, primarily Israel, but almost all had to spend some time in Vienna while making preparations for continuing their journey. With help from Allied and Jewish relief organizations the *Gemeinde* took care of them while helping them make arrangements to reach their ultimate destinations.

---

*During his ten years in New York, so William Stricker tells me, Löwenherz continually felt the need to justify his actions whenever he met former Viennese Jews. However, Herbert Rosenkranz and Jonny Moser, the two foremost historians of the Viennese Holocaust, view Löwenherz as a decent man whose effective methods during the early years of the *Anschluss* saved thousands of Jews. Stricker himself also returned to Vienna as an American army officer but for him there were no parents to bring back.

**Murmelstein was contacted by the Israeli police in 1962 who thought of using him as a witness in the Eichmann trial. He prepared a long deposition for the trial, and when he was not called, reworked it into a book which he published in Italy. In 1977 Claude Lanzman filmed ten hours of interviews with Murmelstein but decided not to use any of this footage for his film *Shoah*.

Murmelstein has also been extensively interviewed by Professor Leonard Ehrlich of the philosophy department of the University of Massachusetts at Amherst and by Ehrlich's wife Edith. They are preparing a manuscript that will examine the Rabbi's dilemma in a deeper context than has been possible here.

Some of the new arrivals decided to stay in Vienna. Along with the few returnees and the still fewer number of *professed* Jews who had never left (most of Vienna's five thousand surviving Jews were converted or *konfessionslos* Jews who quickly resumed their non-Jewish status now that the Nuremberg laws no longer operated), they formed a new Jewish community of about twelve thousand. As such, they stood ready to participate in Austria's rebirth.

But what kind of Austria would it be?

Chapter 28

Remembering to Forget

Following Kurt Waldheim's controversial but successful campaign for the Austrian presidency in 1986, the French newspaper *Le Monde* published a cartoon showing Freud sitting by his empty couch reading the election returns. The caption has the psychoanalyst saying, "Amazing. Millions of amnesiacs and not a single patient."

The real Freud, however, might not have found Austrian amnesia so amazing — since forgetting the unpleasant and ignoring the inconvenient are long-established, deeply ingrained Viennese traditions. As we have seen, the most famous line in the city's most famous operetta views such a practice as the key to happiness: "Happy is the one who forgets about what cannot be changed." Consequently, many Austrians after the war quickly began to erase all embarrassing and encumbering memories. As the Austro-American novelist Ingeborg Lauterstein puts it, they decided to remember to forget.

Remembering to forget took many forms, from scratching out the once proud inscription "Nazi Party Member" from the tombstones of dead relatives to omitting sensitive facts from personal resumes and records. If Waldheim aroused much censure abroad for having left out of his biography all references to his Nazi student affiliations and his service on General Löhr's staff, he drew far less criticism within Austria itself. He was far from being the only Austrian to suffer from that selective loss of memory which some have now dubbed Waldheimer's Disease.

Historians themselves, especially during the first few decades after the war, seemed to suffer from this malady. In 1969 Hanns Leo Mikoletzky published his massive *Österreichische Zeit-Geschichte* (Austrian Contemporary History), a work that won him the Cross of Honor for Science and Art along with the directorship of the National Archives. In the four hundred pages he devotes to the interwar years, he makes only one brief reference to the Jews. In the surprisingly scant forty pages he devotes to the entire Nazi period, he does earmark three and a half pages for the Jews, implying for the most part that their persecution was strictly a German phenomenon. A biographical essay by another professor on Leopold Kunschak praises the Christian Social labor leader as "the democratic conscience of the first republic," leaving out all mention of Kunschak's frequent calls for pogroms against the Jews. When Rosenkranz's book on the Jewish persecution in Austria came out in 1978, it received highly favorable reviews in two or three rather obscure journals but the rest of the Austrian media ignored it. When a Protestant minister from America, the Reverend James R. Lyons, visited Vienna in 1986, he was startled to find the city's bookstores bare of material on the Nazi era.

Not until 1981 would a book appear on the development of Austrian Nazism. It was the work of an American historian, Bruce Pauley, and was published in English. As another historian, John Bunzel, put it, "The uncovering of the past [in Austria] has always been a greater crime than the misdeeds of Hitler himself."

Those who taught history quite naturally took the same tack as those who wrote it. As a result, the war years and even the interwar years often received short shrift in the classroom. Vienna journalist Peter Czernin says his high school history course jumped from 1918 to 1945, omitting the intervening years completely.

Such a situation quite naturally has affected Austria's postwar literature. Although none of Austria's more important postwar novelists shows any Nazi sympathies, none has written much about the country's Nazi past. As a result, no significant literature of the war has emerged in Austria as it has in Germany with the novels of Günter Grass, Heinrich Böll, and others.

The government itself has quite often fostered such inattention to the country's past. When a prominent Austrian Nazi after the war wrote a 363-page manuscript showing that eighty percent of his countrymen had supported the Nazi regime, the chancellor of the new government arranged to have it suppressed, saying it might "arouse a violent controversy."

Since Germany decided to maintain its concentration camps as reminders of the past, Austria has done the same with Mauthausen, and annually brings school children to visit it. But the memorial plaque at the former concentration camp that lists the nationalities of those who died there makes no mention of Jews. When special exercises were held at Mauthausen in 1985 to commemorate the fortieth year of its liberation, one popular Viennese paper covered the event in five lines, while another ignored it completely.

With their media, their historians, and their government urging them to remember to forget, few Austrians had trouble doing so. Weiser Varon, returning for a visit in the summer of 1955, found that while the German tourists he met freely expressed distress over what had happened to the Jews, not one Austrian did so. Instead, his former math teacher, in commenting on the return of a Jewish composer and musician from America, said, "He should have stayed there." A woman school teacher, when told that Varon had emigrated in September 1938, replied, "How clever of you." A former neighbor who had taken over his father's store, described in detail how much she and her family had suffered during the war. "Isn't it funny?" she asked rhetorically. "We who stayed behind were bombed and those who left now want restitution."

A British army officer who served in the occupation of both Germany and Austria after the war later compared the attitudes of the two peoples. "Most Germans," he wrote, "though making excuses for their personal support of the Nazi regime, nevertheless accepted a kind of generalized national responsibility for their past. This the Austrians emphatically failed to do. They seem to have mislaid the Hitler years."

Remembering to forget characterized and underscored postwar Austria's approach to its many remaining Nazis and to its few remaining Jews. Consider the way the country has resolved or failed to resolve some of the issues that each group has presented.

In its first statement, issued before the war had ended, the provisional Austrian government said, "Those who out of contempt for democracy and democratic freedom erected and maintained a regime of violence, denunciation, persecution, and suppression, which brought this country into a misadventurous war and then abandoned it to devastation, should count on no clemency. They will be dealt with according to the same harsh laws which they have applied against others."

Initially the government, with the Allies looking over its shoulder, appeared ready to back up these strong words with equally strong action. It passed a severe War Crimes Law, set up "People's Courts," and instituted proceedings against 130,000 accused war criminals. But when the proceedings ended, only 13,000 or ten percent had been found guilty. Of these, forty-three received the maximum penalty, death, but only thirty were actually executed.

Most of the others received light sentences which in many cases were later shortened still more. One who drew a life sentence was released in three years. By 1954 only fifty Austrian war criminals remained in Austria's prisons.*

The government classified another 400,000 Austrians as minor offenders. As such, they lost their positions and voting rights, but generally escaped prosecution. Then, in 1948, the government gave a blanket absolution to all minor offenders, removing virtually all their disabilities. According to a poll that year, only two percent of Austria's ex-Nazis now felt that overcoming their Nazi past was their biggest problem. Writes the Gentile Austrian historian Dieter Stiefel, "From 1947/1948 denazification largely came to an end. They could resume their professions and even their former positions without having lost that much." As a result, he says, "A fundamental confrontation with fascism failed to occur."

Austria's universities posed especially difficult denazification problems, for nearly all their professors had some Nazi background. One-half to two-thirds of all professors were therefore suspended or pensioned. But a large though not precisely known number of those not pensioned soon returned. Moreover, others managed to retain their positions all through the purge. When the Allies ordered the dismissal of one outspoken Nazi professor at the Institute for World Trade in Vienna, the accused professor's colleagues elected him Rector. Comments Steifel, "a not untypical story."

Denazification in the cultural world was even weaker. Indeed, except for the banning by the Allies of pro-Nazi books, films, and other materials, it hardly occurred. Former Nazi von Karajan took over the podium of the Vienna State Opera to conduct an orchestra consisting largely of former Nazis and Nazi sympathizers. Little turnover occurred in Austria's theater as well.

In 1948 postwar Austria's struggling film industry released its first notable film, *The Angel with the Trumpet*. It starred the Nazi acting couple, Attila Höbigger and Paula Wessely. Its director was Karl Hartl who, shortly after the *Anschluss*, had been personally appointed by Goebbels to be production chief of the Vienna Film Industry. Although Hartl and the Höbiggers had been busy making anti-Semitic films just a few years earlier, their new film depicted a Jewish family sympathetically. Their fast turnaround apparently bothered no one.

*One of those who was executed was Anton Brunner, the notorious Brunner II. His predecessor, Alois Brunner, or Brunner I, escaped to Syria where, under the name of George Fischer, he remains to this day. Some Austrian war criminals, such as Globocnik and his chief of staff, committed suicide, the latter in the courtroom during his trial. Austria's two most prominent Nazis, Seyss-Inquart and Kaltenbrunner, were tried and executed at Nuremberg. General Böhm was also arraigned at Nuremberg but committed suicide in jail before his trial.

With the signing of the Austrian peace treaty in 1955 and the subsequent departure of the Allies, Austria's former Nazis became much bolder. They and their sympathizers had created the League of Independents under the leadership of a non-Nazi in 1948. Now they renamed their organization the Austrian Freedom Party and chose Anton Reinthaller, a former member of Seyss-Inquart's short-lived Nazi cabinet to head it. When Reinthaller died two years later, they elected a former SS lieutenant, Frederick Peter, to take his place.

The Party fared rather poorly in the parliamentary elections that year, since the two major postwar parties, the People's Party and the Socialist party, were also bidding for Nazi support and by now had moved several ex-Nazis into lower-echelon leadership positions. Still, the twelve seats (out of 165) that the Freedom Party won represented twelve seats more than its German counterpart, the national Democratic party, would ever obtain in any postwar election in Germany.

Austria's new constitution, drawn up under Allied supervision, expressly prohibited all pro-Nazi, militaristic, and racist organizations, but ex-Nazis and pro-Nazis now became more open in their activities. Austria, in fact, became a favorite conference site for pro-Nazi organizations as well as a favorite haven for ex-Nazis from Germany and elsewhere. Among the latter was a Belgian SS general named von Werbelen, who had been sentenced to death in absentia in his own country, but who had found sanctuary in Austria. When the Austrian government, acting under persistent and insistent pressure from Belgium and other countries, finally brought von Werbelen to trial, the jury acquitted him.

In other trials Austrian juries acquitted two Polish brothers accused of helping slaughter twelve thousand Jews in their home city of Stanislaus, and former SS commander Franz Maurer, who had once been known as the "Hangman of Vilna." In both cases, courtroom spectators burst into applause when the verdicts were announced.

Especially noteworthy is the case of Franz Novak, Eichmann's transportation chief, who had sent 1.7 million Jews to the extermination camps. With the Allies gone, Novak, who had been living under an assumed name in Vienna, came out of hiding. Soon he was enjoying a dual career as the manager of a printing plant and as a high-level functionary of an SS veterans organization.

In 1960, however, West Germany's War Crimes Prosecution Office issued a warrant for Novak's arrest, and this action embarrassed the Austrian government into bringing him to trial. In 1964 a bare majority of an eight-member jury found him guilty of "public violence" and sentenced him to eight years in prison, but the presiding judge, who had been a public prosecutor under the Nazis, set aside the verdict and released him.*

Novak's acquittal set off protests within as well as outside of Austria. A few weeks afterward, as Austria prepared to celebrate the tenth anniversary of Allied withdrawal and Austrian independence, Vienna's Chief Rabbi Chaim Eisenberg declined an invitation to represent the Jewish community at the fete. In his telegram to the government he said, "You may celebrate. We shall mourn." On the day of the celebration virtually the entire Jewish community turned out for a memorial service at the city's only surviving synagogue.

The fact that Novak had first been indicted in West Germany illustrates the varying responses between the two countries to their war criminals. While West Germany in the 1960s expanded the staff of its office handling such cases to over one hundred, Austria reduced the staff of its office from ten to six. When West Germany worked out an agreement with Austria to take depositions of witnesses in Austrian courts, a move that would greatly facilitate prosecutions of war criminals in West Germany, Austria's Minister of Justice quashed the move.

In 1966 Simon Wiesenthal sent a letter and a thirty-page memorandum to the Austrian government detailing Austrian participation in the Holocaust and calling attention to the hundreds of Austrian perpetrators who were living openly in the country. He asked for their prosecution, under Austria's own War Crimes Act. The letter has never been answered.**

About a month after the war ended, the Allies set up a displaced persons camp in Salzburg. It primarily housed Jewish survivors of the Holocaust. Salzburg residents soon began referring to the camp as "New Palestine" and to its inmates as "Hitler's unfinished business." At about this time, Austria's new coalition government passed, as one of its first measures, a relief act for those who had spent time in the concentration camps. But the relief was to go only to those imprisoned for political reasons. Since Jews were regarded as racial victims, they were automatically excluded.

---

*In defending himself at the trial, Novak said that he understood that Jews were only to be exterminated through hard work under unbearable conditions and not through mass executions. He found this justified, he said, for it was not right for Jews to survive while Germans were being killed at the front. He freely admitted experiencing a "feeling of joy" in carrying out his duties.

**In recalling the era in an interview twenty years later, Wiesenthal pointed out how "West Germany usually had about twelve attorneys traveling to Israel and other countries looking for information," while Austria, claiming it had little money for such activity, "sent at most an attorney to Israel now and then to leaf through some files." Wiesenthal made it clear that while he has not always been pleased with the intensity of West Germany's activity in this area, he does regard it on the whole as a serious effort. Austria's exertions he took far less seriously.

Howard Sachar goes even further in endorsing West Germany's prosecution of war criminals, saying the agency entrusted with this mission "worked tenaciously to bring the crimes of Germany's past to light and judgment."

These two unconnected events, one at the official level, one at the popular level, would set the tone for Austria's postwar approach toward the Jews.

At the political level the policies of both of Austria's major postwar parties toward the Jews were influenced not just by lingering anti-Semitism but by their eagerness to win the support of the country's substantial number of leftover Nazis, along with their families, friends, and allies. Although the conservative People's Party was the more logical place for ex-Nazis to turn, the Socialist party did what it could to attract them to its ranks. For example, it discouraged its former Jewish leaders from returning to Austria, making an exception only for those who had formed useful connections with Socialist parties abroad. Still, the People's Party proved somewhat more successful than the Socialist party in wooing such voters.

As the 1949 parliamentary elections loomed, the Socialist Minister of Interior in the coalition government authorized the formation of the League of Independents, hoping that it would attract right-wing votes that might otherwise go to the People's Party. The latter responded by stepping up its solicitation of ex-Nazi support. One of its election posters showed an appealing young man labeled People's Party extending a hand to a former Nazi who, in addition to having a millstone around his neck, is being pelted by mud from two rowdies. Both rowdies had disturbingly long, hooked noses.

In 1947 the Austrian government, giving in to pressure from the Allies and from former Jewish concentration camp returnees, modified its original relief act to include Jewish concentration camp victims. But when in 1951 Israel asked West Germany and East Germany for $1.5 billion in compensation for German Jews, the issue of restitution flared up again.

East Germany dismissed the request out of hand but West Germany, after several months of negotiations, agreed to pay $822 million. West Germany refused, however, to make any payments to Austrian Jews, saying that was Austria's concern.

A committee for Jewish claims against Austria was organized to undertake similar negotiations with the Austrian government. These negotiations dragged on for nine years, with Austria at first refusing even to discuss the subject and then finding one reason after another to postpone or drag out the talks. Eventually, faced with pressure from the American and British governments, hostile editorials in the world press, and telegrams from American labor organizations to its Socialist vice-chancellor, the coalition government agreed to pay $6 million in compensation plus an additional ten percent to cover administrative costs. Although this represented less than one percent of the figure agreed to by West Germany, the claims committee, exhausted by nearly a decade of haggling, agreed.

Gustav Jellinek, who served on the claims committee, later described the differences in the negotiations between the two countries. "The West German government . . . from the very beginning, was ready to work with the claims committee to reach a settlement quickly, since the entire West German Parliament backed them up. The Austrian government was from the very beginning determined to concede nothing. They refused to work with us and tried to sabotage our efforts. And the entire Austrian Parliament backed them up."

That Austria's Parliament truly represented the attitude of the Austrian people in this respect is borne out by a succession of public opinion polls since the war. With ninety-five percent of the country's Jews expelled or exterminated, anti-Semitic sentiment in Austria still runs high. A poll by Dr. Hildegard Weiss of the University of Vienna's Sociological Institute in 1984 showed eighty-five percent of the population admitting to some degree of anti-Semitism. While thirty-five percent described their anti-Semitism as "not strong," that still left half the population feeling otherwise. Some twenty percent, in fact, told her interviewers they could see some positive elements in Auschwitz.

What has particularly troubled many well-meaning Austrians is the existence of anti-Jewish feeling among young people born after the war. In the 1960s Professor Kurt Schubert, a Catholic Talmudist and chairman of Judaic Studies at the University of Vienna, sorrowfully described it as the one common denominator among Austria's highly variegated youth. One pro-Nazi student organization whose meetings were frequently punctuated with cries of "Up with Auschwitz," won thirty percent of the vote in student elections in Vienna in the mid-1960s. By 1970 its support had slipped substantially, but as late as 1980 ten percent of all students in Austria still described themselves as anti-Semitic.

In 1986 one recent Ph.D. told the New York Times critic Bernard Holland that the last war was really a Jewish conspiracy, citing the names of Eisenhower and Roosevelt as "irrefutable proof." Says Holland, "A wartime residue of propaganda seems to have slipped permanently into the public consciousness."

One final incident is worth noting. In 1948 a Jewish dentist with his wife and baby daughter fled to Vienna from Budapest. The family eventually found an apartment in the inner city. They soon noticed, however, that a music teacher who lived in the same building would never return their greeting and would never ride in the elevator if any of them were using it.

By 1986 the dentist had died, his widow had become partially crippled, and his daughter had become a prominent journalist. But the now elderly music teacher was still refusing to say hello to either mother or daughter and was still huffing and puffing his way up the stairs to avoid sharing the same elevator. As an old song has it, "*Wien bleibt Wien*" (Vienna remains Vienna).

*   *   *

In 1970 Bruno Kreisky, Jewish by birth and even by appearance, became postwar Austria's first Socialist chancellor. He governed the country for the next thirteen years, enjoying considerable popular support during most of that period. How does one explain the Kreisky phenomenon in light of the country's persistent and still quite pervasive anti-Semitism?

The son of a small clothing manufacturer, Kreisky joined the Socialist party as a teenager and became one of its most active and ambitious young members. In 1935 the twenty-four-year-old lawyer was arrested by the Schuschnigg government and sentenced to a short term in prison. Three years later he was arrested again, this time by the Gestapo, but was released under the stipulation that he leave the country immediately.

His strong Socialist background enabled him to emigrate to Sweden, where he quickly formed ties with the governing Social Democratic party. He also formed ties with a wealthy Gentile Swedish heiress whom he married. These two accomplishments overrode the disadvantages of his Jewishness and made him a natural choice to become First Secretary of Austria's legation in Stockholm after the war.

By 1953 Kreisky had worked his way back to Vienna to become Secretary of State for Foreign Affairs and three years later was awarded a seat in Parliament. He was articulate, witty, highly pragmatic, and fluent in English. His background in both Parliament and foreign affairs, plus his political astuteness, made him a good choice for foreign minister in the coalition government in 1959. (At this point, his Jewishness may also have helped, for Austria's recalcitrance in the Jewish compensation issue was creating image problems for the country.) In 1963 his fellow Socialists chose him as party chairman and as such he successfully led the Party into the 1970 elections.

But if Kreisky had become Austria's first Jewish chancellor, he soon showed that he was a Jew of a certain kind; one not unknown in Vienna's past.

Not long after Kreisky took office, Nazi hunter Simon Wiesenthal disclosed that the Chancellor had appointed four ex-Nazi party members, one of them a former SS officer, to his cabinet. Then, a year or two later, when Kreisky began holding talks with Friedrich Peter with the idea of bringing Peter's Freedom Party into his government, Wiesenthal revealed that Peter was a former SS lieutenant who had served on an extermination squad which murdered ten thousand people, two thousand of them Jews.

These disclosures incensed Kreisky, who called Wiesenthal's documentation center a political Mafia using Nazi methods in an effort to undermine him. He also said that since Wiesenthal himself had spent the Nazi years in various concentration camps, he must have had an "understanding" with the Nazis to have survived. Nevertheless, Kreisky abandoned his plan to bring Peter and his neo-Nazis into the government.

By now it had become evident how Kreisky had managed to become Chancellor. Many ex-Nazis and their still numerous sympathizers had voted for him and his party, foreseeing quite accurately that a Jewish chancellor could more easily and more completely give them respectability and, more importantly, access to power. As the Catholic psychiatrist Wilfried Daim put it, Kreisky could provide them with absolution from a past that they no longer wished to acknowledge.

Under Kreisky, Austria's always half-hearted prosecution of war criminals came to an abrupt end. In 1974 his Socialist government introduced a new criminal code which, in the words of Howard Sachar, "all but foreclosed the possibility of future trials" for war crimes. The bill quickly passed through Parliament. The small office handling such cases was abolished the following year when the last such trial ever to be held in Austria ended.

But Kreisky's attitude toward ex-Nazis proved less disturbing to many Jews than his attitude toward Israel. At first, Zionists throughout the world hailed his election, for not only was the new chancellor Jewish, but his only brother lived in Tel Aviv. An incident that occurred three years after he took office, however, made them reconsider.

Some years before, the Jewish Agency had rented a castle in western Austria to temporarily house Jewish refugees from Eastern Europe, pending their eventual emigration to Israel or elsewhere. Then, in 1973, Arab terrorists held up a train coming from Czechoslovakia and seized three Soviet Jewish passengers and a Czech customs official as hostages. Kreisky immediately offered to close down the refugee center to obtain their release.

The French newspaper Le Monde called his move "capitulation," President Nixon asked him to reconsider, and Israeli Premier Golda Meir rushed to Vienna to plead with him not to make such a concession. But Kreisky stood firm, while his defense minister told Parliament that the adverse publicity was coming from newspapers "which are in Jewish hands."

From then on, Kreisky pursued an increasingly pro-Arab, anti-Israeli policy. He brought PLO leader Arafat to Vienna and made him what the Viennese call "salonfähig" (literally, suitable for the salon, or, more figuratively, eminently respectable). Western Europe's only Jewish prime minister also became its only government leader to invite Libya's Colonel Khadafy for a visit. Khadafy accepted and received red carpet treatment. Vienna remains today the only West European capital to have royally received these two archfoes of the Jewish state.

But while Kreisky was praising Khadafy as a patriot, he was calling Menachem Begin, Israel's new prime minister, a terrorist and "a little Polish lawyer or whatever he is." If such words seemed to smack of Jewish anti-Semitism, then Kreisky supplied further substantiation for such a surmise by saying, "The Ostjuden are alienated from normal ways of thinking" and then going on to generalize that "the suspicion that Jews are intelligent is false . . . there are clever people among them but in general they act in a wrong way." Kreisky has also been quoted as saying, "If the Jews are a people, then they are an unattractive people." He has never denied saying this.

Kreisky explains his actions and attitudes by echoing the prewar Socialist argument that socialism offers the best solution to the Jews while Zionism only encourages anti-Semitism. The argument seems outmoded to most Jews, who wonder if even Kreisky really believes it. Many do concede that the haste of certain Jewish leaders to "claim" him probably exacerbated his inherent distaste for his Jewish identity. But that distaste appears to have been there all along. He has never been to Israel, even to visit his brother, who has since died.

Among other things, Kreisky broke the postwar taboo on telling anti-Semitic jokes by publicly telling a few himself. It is no wonder, then, that he also became the butt of many such witticisms. One of them perhaps sums him up as well as any scholarly diagnosis: There is only one person now left in Austria who doesn't know Kreisky is a Jew: Kreisky.

Chapter 29

The City Without Jews

In his 1923 novel, *The City Without Jews*, Hugo Bettauer depicted a Vienna without Jews as a Vienna devoid of vitality and heading toward economic ruin. But anti-Semites of that period customarily envisioned a Jew-free Vienna as an economically flourishing city which had finally rid itself of corruption, filth, and material values. Which of these past visions best matches present-day reality?

When it comes to corruption, none of Europe's smaller countries seems to have equaled Austria's record, for since the war, but especially perhaps in recent years, Austria and its capital have been rocked with one scandal after another. The Viennese themselves say that the country is so corrupt that you have to stand in line at the newspapers with your scandal and even then they may turn you away for lack of space. Before the Waldheim campaign, in fact, people amused themselves by betting on how much money had disappeared that week from the federal treasury. (During the Waldheim campaign, they began betting on what countries would allow Waldheim to visit them if he were elected. According to the *New Yorker*'s Jane Kramer, Bulgaria led the list, followed by Greece, Libya, and Syria.) Bosel and Castiglioni may be gone, but Vienna remains Vienna.

What was probably the country's greatest scandal broke in the summer of 1985 when it became clear that numerous wine growers and/or dealers had added a chemical used in certain kinds of anti-freeze to their product. The additive, which can cause brain and kidney damage, was used to increase the

357

quantity and sweeten the taste of a wine output that a series of poor harvests had made too meager and too sour.

What bothered many Austrians was the government's slowness in acting. As one newspaper pointed out, the pronounced discrepancy between the low supply of wine predicted on the basis of crop figures, and the much larger amount that reached the market, should have aroused immediate attention. Yet the government moved only after many suspicious reports had already leaked out and foreign importers had become alarmed.

Among those expressing concern over the country's level of postwar public morality is Vienna's current Archbishop, Alfons Cardinal Stickler, who speaks sadly of "the different kind of life that exists in Austria where almost every week brings a new scandal." Adds the prelate, "Who knows how many conspiracies are hidden from view that could break out any day?"

At lower levels *Protektion* continues to play a significant role in Austrian life. Political connections can help considerably in securing a good job, including a university professorship or even a good apartment. Low-numbered license plates are sought in the belief that they can help in problems with the police. While such phenomena are hardly unknown in the United States, they are not that common in Western Europe.

The numerous sidewalk prostitutes and their pimps who once made Vienna the vice capital of central Europe have, to a great extent, vanished, as they have from so many other European cities. But a certain subterranean sleaziness remains. In the summer of 1985, for example, Ken Russell's film *Crimes of Passion* (which depicts a fashion designer who moonlights as a prostitute) opened in Vienna to considerable critical acclaim. Scenes from the film, accompanied by laudatory comments, were even shown on Austrian television. Yet in the United States this essentially pornographic film was shown only on cable television, where it was dismissed by the *New York Times* as "real schlock." One might also add that the Austrian government puts out tourist brochures carrying advertisements from "Escort Services" openly hinting at prostitution. (How else can one interpret an advertisement that offers an "escort" for at-home service?)

But if the "city without Jews" has not realized the dream of the anti-Semites, it also does not seem to have fulfilled Bettauer's prophecy of economic and cultural calamity. Vienna today gives the appearance of a reasonably prosperous capital of a reasonably prosperous country. Moreover, its numerous theaters, concert halls, bookstores, newspapers, and magazines attest to a lively cultural life as well.

While such an impression is not wholly false, it is also not wholly true. Vienna's serious theater offers mostly foreign or prewar plays — Arthur Schnitzler has been a constant favorite -- while its feeble postwar motion picture industry has produced only two internationally recognized films in forty years (*The Angel with the Trumpet*, mentioned earlier, and *38*, which received an Oscar nomination in 1986).

The Viennese still take their music seriously and their orchestras continue to command respect. But during the past forty years the city has nurtured few notable composers or conductors. Since the departure of von Karajan from the State Opera in 1964, the conductor whose work on that podium has won the most critical acclaim has been Leonard Bernstein. In fact, the Opera asked Bernstein to conduct its 100th Anniversary performance in 1959.*

In literature, three Austrian novelists have achieved substantial recognition outside the German-speaking world: Jakov Lind, Peter Handke, and Thomas Bernhard. But Lind is Jewish and neither he nor Handke now live in Austria. Bernhard can best be described as an anti-Austrian Austrian. In fact, as a result of several lawsuits, he no longer allows his books to be published in his native country.

Intellectually and scientifically the city without Jews also seems a pale shadow of its former self. Virtually no one comes to Vienna to consult its doctors, scientists, and scholars, for the city is no longer a major center for any branch of learning. Nor does its daily press elicit any esteem within or outside the country. Finally, as Vienna's sportswriters have glumly admitted, no soccer team has come near to equaling the resplendent record of the great teams coached by Hugo Meisl.

In the early 1970s historian Elizabeth Barker compared Vienna to "a camel living on its richly stored cultural hump." Some fifteen years later journalist Jane Kramer described the city as an "imperial ghost town," and quoted one foreign diplomat as saying, "Postwar Austria is like an opera sung by understudies."

Vienna's and Austria's economic success may also be somewhat less than what meets the eye. In 1983 the country ranked twentieth in per capita gross national product, putting it near the bottom of the list among industrial nations. Vienna has lost over twenty percent of its prewar population, while Munich, the nearest major city both culturally and geographically, has doubled in size.

Much of the prosperity that postwar Austria has achieved comes from tourists visiting Vienna for its past, and the Tyrol for its natural splendor and its good and relatively inexpensive skiing. Another boost has come from the

---

*Bernstein has enjoyed conducting the orchestra, and the orchestra has enjoyed working under him. His visits boosted their records sales. However, one story I heard in Vienna says that when one of its musicians sought to reassure Bernstein that the orchestra's reputation for being anti-Semitic was unfounded since it had three Jewish members, Bernstein reportedly replied, "That's the difference between Vienna and New York. In New York we don't know how many Jews we have."

United Nations, which has made Vienna the headquarters for some of its agencies. Vienna now ranks third after New York and Geneva as a center for U.N. activity.

A still bigger economic boost has come from the Arabs. Thanks to the opening created by Kreisky and zealously exploited by his successors, Austria does a thriving business with the Arab world. Austrian-made armaments are especially in demand. Although the country's state-owned Voerst steelworks is a notorious money loser, its military products division earned over $30 million in profits in 1985, principally through supplying arms to Libya. Thus, in a rather perverse way, the Jews have unintentionally contributed to Austria's prosperity by allowing the country to capitalize on its anti-Jewish and, more specifically, anti-Israel policies.

Arabs certainly seem to find Vienna attractive and congenial. In the spring of 1986 the Union of Arab Bankers held a conference in the city, and the eighty delegates told the local press how much they enjoyed visiting Vienna and doing business with its bankers.

A few months earlier, Palestinian gunmen had shot up Vienna's airport, killing some and wounding others. A similar raid had occurred simultaneously at Rome's airport. But while Italy soon discovered and disclosed signs of Libyan involvement, Austria's interior minister, Karl Blecha, could find no indication of Libyan involvement in Vienna. (Both Austria and Italy do a thriving business with Libya.) Said *The New York Times*, "Mr. Blecha avoided mentioning that the terrorists were traveling on Tunisian passports that Tunisia said had been confiscated from its nationals working in Libya."

A few years earlier, Palestinians had also bombed Vienna's only synagogue during a bar mitzvah service. The bodyguard of a wealthy attendee shot and killed the driver of the getaway car, and the terrorists were captured and sent to prison. But no arrests have yet been made in the 1986 bombing of a Leopoldstadt apartment building which housed several Orthodox Jewish families. No one was injured in this incident and it is not clear whether it was the work of Arab or local terrorists. But the city now stations policemen, sometimes armed with submachine guns, around various Jewish offices and institutions. Commented Austrian television in the fall of 1986, "The newly erected centers of Jewish life in Vienna look like fortresses."

Although present-day Austro-Jewish relations reflect the deep roots of a long and troubled history, it would be a mistake, and a grievous one, to conclude that nothing has changed. Austria's attitudes and policies toward the Jews and their new homeland may bear the imprint of the past, but they differ in one or two important respects from those of the prewar era.

The most significant difference is the emergence of a sizable number of Austrian Gentiles who deplore their country's deeply entrenched anti-Semitism and who are struggling to change it. They may be only a minority, but they are not a negligible one. Moreover, they are growing in number.

After the war, Viktor Matejka, a Catholic anti-Nazi who spent several years in Dachau, became Vienna's first city councilor for education and culture. Matejka proposed buying Arnold Schönberg's former house and inviting the composer back from California to occupy it. The proposal was, of course, never accepted and no invitation to return was ever issued to Schönberg or any other exiled Jew. Still, an attempt had been made and some Austrian Gentiles had supported it.

Since then, there have always been Austrians ready to reach out to Jews and to speak out against their enemies. Overt and organized expressions of anti-Semitism have almost always aroused counterprotests from concerned Gentiles.

During the Waldheim presidential campaign, some young Austrians passed out anti-Waldheim leaflets on the streets of Vienna despite frequent taunts from passersby that they were being paid by the World Jewish Congress to do so. Many older Austrians wrote anti-Waldheim letters to their local newspapers, and when these letters went unpublished, they sent them to the *Gemeinde*. (Only one daily paper of general circulation opposed Waldheim's election. This was the conservative *Salzburger Nachrichten*.)

Who are these Austrians who are trying to change their country's long-standing anti-Semitic position? Many are devout Catholics. In fact, Vienna's Jews frequently tell a questioner that they have better contacts with well-educated, devout Catholics, both clergy and laypeople, than with any other sector of the population.

Such sympathy and support from Catholic quarters have on many occasions been voiced publicly. When the jury acquitted two Polish-born brothers, Wilhelm and Johann Mauer, on trial for slaughtering Jews, Austria's most widely read Catholic paper *Kleine Zeitung* called the verdict a scandal. It then went on to explain why. "Forty witnesses have heavily incriminated the accused, but the jurors did not believe these witnesses because these witnesses were Jews. That is what we mean when we speak of a scandal." Very likely such clerical condemnation helped prod the judge to reject the verdict and to order a new trial. (At the second trial the brothers were convicted and given prison sentences of eight and ten years.)

The acquittal of Franz Novak by the presiding judge also evoked clerical censure. The distinguished Catholic journal *Furche* questioned "the moral legitimacy of a judge administering the law in the name of a republic whose advocates he had once sent to the gallows." (The judge, it will be recalled, had been a prosecutor under the Nazis.) Vienna's then Archbishop, Cardinal Koenig, in castigating the judge's decision, expressed concern for the "dangerous Austrian mentality" that permitted such a judicial travesty.

In March 1986 a group of Austrian Catholics, led by a Monsignor who teaches theology and a police inspector who heads a prominent organization of laymen, made a pilgrimage to Israel. At Yad Vashem they laid a wreath on, and said a prayer at, the memorial stone to the dead at Mauthausen. Said one of the delegation's leaders, "Our task in Austria, dear friends, is to conquer once and for all every bit of anti-Semitism."

Another group that has moved to the forefront in fighting for better Austro-Jewish relations are the intellectuals. Like the Austrian Catholic Church, Austria's postwar intelligentsia, or at least many of its younger members, have done an about-face since the days when they often spearheaded attacks against Jews. When two older Austrian social scientists told an international conference on fascism held in Norway in 1985 that only ten percent of their countrymen were now anti-Semites, three of their younger colleagues promptly and sharply questioned this finding and the research on which it was based. Said one of the three, Brigitta Galanda, "Authoritarian, racist, and anti-Semitic tendencies are much more extensively present in the population than has been maintained."

In 1987 the Austrian National Bank, sensitive to the bad publicity Austria had received in the Waldheim campaign the previous year, rather exuberantly released a study showing that only seven percent of all Austrians were now anti-Semites. Both the Jewish and academic communities reacted with scorn. Said sociologist Bernd Marin, "This political misuse of opinion research will cause immense damage to our reputation as Austrians, scholars, and democrats."

The naysayers were proven right a few weeks later when the United States put Waldheim on its list of those forbidden entry to the country for complicity in war crimes. This step unleashed a new wave of hostility toward the Austrian Jews. As the German magazine *Der Spiegel* reported, "Not only are insults daily occurances but brutal attacks are increasing. Jews have been thrown out of cabs by cab drivers and have been spat upon on public streets." Three drunken youths seized Rabbi Jacob Biederman with the intent of beating him but he managed to escape. Biederman shrugged off the incident as "nothing special."

Confronted with such an outburst of anti-Semitism, some of Austria's leading historians hastily staged, at their own expense, a symposium entitled, "Contemporary Austrian History in Crisis." A badly shaken Erika Weinzierl told the gathering, "I have devoted a quarter century of my scholarly life to research and adult education and look at the results."

Turning to the arts, we find further signs of change. By the mid-1960s, Viennese audiences were fervently applauding Schnitzler's most outspoken play on anti-Semitism, *Professor Bernardi*. Twenty years later they were ready to applaud a combined Austrian-Israeli production of *Ghetto*, Joshua Sobol's play about the Vilna ghetto, which features an Austrian SS officer as its major villain.

Skeptics, of course, might argue that the intellectuals and artists are only responding to current international trends that have made anti-Semitism unfashionable. They might also point out that such sentiments could turn around if Jewish artists and professionals ever again became numerous enough in Austria to compete extensively with Gentiles for acting roles, university appointments, and other professional positions. But most skeptics would concede that a welcome and quite fundamental change has occurred.

By the mid-1980s the government itself had begun to encourage such a change. It commissioned a film of Mauthausen and a school text on Jewish history, the first volume of which appeared in the midst of the Waldheim campaign. From 1982 to 1986 the government disbanded five organizations and forbade or limited thirty events believed to have pro-Nazi overtones. When neo-Nazis began distributing anti-Semitic literature outside Vienna's public schools and youth centers in 1985, Parliament responded to a request from the Jewish community and unanimously enacted legislation to facilitate the prosecution of those involved.

At the local level, Salzburg has named a street after Stefan Zweig and a group of the city's youth renovated and repaired the city's Jewish cemetery. Vienna has named a small park after Sigmund Freud, and, according to the *Gemeinde*'s present director Fritz Hodek, a Gentile who converted to Judaism, the city has also contributed quite generously to the maintenance of various Jewish institutions. (Cemetery upkeep is a particularly burdensome problem since Vienna's Jewish dead now vastly outnumber the living and many of the relatives who would otherwise care for the graves disappeared during the Holocaust.)

A measure of expediency may underlie such endeavors, for Austrian authorities remain continually conscious of world opinion, including the feelings of Jewish tourists. Furthermore, their efforts do not begin to match those undertaken in Germany where state and local governments, says Howard Sachar, have competed with each other in building magnificent synagogues, Jewish schools, and other facilities. Still, one cannot deny the crucial role that government aid has played in the survival of Jewish life in Austria.

And Jewish life has survived. The Jewish community puts on lectures, exhibitions, and concerts, many with Zionist themes. It operates a home for the elderly, a cultural center, and a variety of institutions for children and youths. In 1984 its younger adults, determined that Vienna should not become a Jewish cemetery, started a day school which, within two years, enrolled 180 pupils.

A variety of less official agencies supplement these activities. They include a B'nai B'rith lodge, the Jewish Welcome Service run by Mauthausen survivor Leon Zelman, and the Friends of the Weizmann Institute, which now even has a chapter in Innsbruck. Reading the reports of such activities in the *Illustrierte Neue Welt*, Vienna's Jewish monthly, one gets the impression of a revived and robust Jewish community in action.

Reports of the accomplishments of individual Jews tend to fortify this impression. As the fiftieth anniversary of the *Anschluss* approached, Jews in Vienna held positions as Director of the Austrian Tourist Bureau, Honorary Chairman of the Austrian Society of Friends of Children, and Deputy Chief Editor of one of Austria's two major news weeklies, *Wochenpost*. (The other news weekly is *Profil*, which published the first revelations of Waldheim's Nazi past.) Many Jews had become successful musicians, actors and actresses, documentary film makers, and television reporters. Austria's representative in the 1985 European song contest was the talented, attractive Timma Brauer, who was born in Israel and who spends part of each year there.

But any impression of a thriving Jewish community must be tempered by a look at the statistics. While West Germany's small Jewish population is growing, Austria's much smaller population is declining. From 11,224 in 1954 it has steadily dwindled to 6,200 by 1986, or under one tenth of a percent of the population of 7.6 million. Further and substantial shrinkage seems inevitable, for of those remaining nearly two-thirds are over sixty years of age. These are, to be sure, only official figures. To their number one could add the several thousand "closet Jews" who do not appear on the *Gemeinde*'s rolls. But such Jews cannot be considered members of the community, and most of them eventually emigrate or intermarry.

Intermarriage or emigration also threatens the acknowledged Jews since such a small and aged community offers its young people sharply reduced opportunities for finding mates. A recent advertisement in the *Gemeinde*'s magazine illustrates this problem. It says, "I am seeking for my sixteen-year-old daughter a nice-appearing and well-behaved young man for leisure-time activities."

This Jewish mother may have found an escort for her daughter. Many Jews who began thinking about emigration during the Waldheim campaign may change their minds, and the new Jewish school will probably grow as it adds a new class each year. Moreover, a number of Jews may continue to hold prominent positions in Austrian society. But few would speak of a revival of past glories, for with twenty-five deaths versus only five births a month the trend line is all too clear. Vienna's once illustrious Jewish community is gone, and there will never be another.

Epilogue

The Answers

There is a time to question oneself and a time to act; there is a time to build and a time to rebuild. Whatever he chooses to do, the Jew becomes a spokesman for all Jews, dead and yet to be born, for all the beings who live through him and inside him.

— Elie Wiesel

The fact of Jewishness has been nothing but an evergrowing goodness to me, and it seems clear to me now that it can be, at least for me, nothing but a fruitful and inexhaustible inheritance.

— Delmore Schwartz

As many travelers to Israel know, El Al's nonstop flight from Tel Aviv to New York leaves on Fridays at 1:00 a.m. Such a departure time eliminates the possibility of its crews having to work or its passengers having to ride on the Sabbath. This schedule also allows the American visitor to spend a last full day in Israel without paying for a night's lodging. On the other hand, he or she is likely to be half asleep when the boarding light at Ben Gurion airport finally flashes.

Certainly this was true of the flight that left on January 23, 1987. Most of its passengers tumbled into their seats and soon fell asleep. But some did not, and I was one of them.

This had been my first trip to Israel, and as the plane taxied down the runway, memories of my eventful visit flashed through my mind.

I remember walking with Menachem Menczer, one of the three surviving brothers of Aron Menczer, through the grounds of his thriving kibbutz near the Golan Heights and, the next day, spending an evening at the Jerusalem home of his nephew, Professor Jacob Metzer, talking with Israel's last ambassador to Austria, Michel Elizur.

I remember interviewing Dr. Raphael Gat, who is writing a complete account of the Austrian Holocaust for Yad Vashem, at a cafe in Tel Aviv; then going on to another cafe to interview Max Diamant, a former Zionist youth leader in Vienna who spent time in the Doppl labor camp; and then hopping a bus to the home of retired Professor Ben Shimron, who has written a monograph on the Chajes Gymnasium and who is himself a rich source of information about pre-*Anschluss* Vienna. And, of course, how can I ever forget the amiable, animated plumber from Afghanistan who sat next to me on the bus back to Jerusalem, and who mustered his few words of English to urge me to make an *aliyah*.

Finally, I remember the colorful, evocative sights and sounds of Jerusalem, interlaced with informative trips to Yad Vashem which for me were highlighted by interviews with historian Herbert Rosenkranz, now a member of its staff.

Yes, I had much to remember and much to rejoice about as well. For I had the answers to my questions.

Actually, I had the answers before I went to Israel and my trip only amplified and confirmed them. Were the Austrians more anti-Semitic than the Germans? Surely, the answer to that has long been apparent. As the Austrian Jewish writer Friedrich Torberg said after the war, "I consider anti-Semitism an integral part of Austrian existence . . . the last [Austrian] anti-Semite will die only when the last Jew dies."

Israel itself offered further proof of the difference between German and Austrian attitudes. In Israel I first heard of Germany's Atonement Movement, which brought hundreds of young Germans, but no Austrians, to the country to work in nursing homes and other institutions. There I saw scores of German tourists but almost no Austrians, and read about a visiting soccer team made up of German mayors which a much younger Israeli team had, rather ungraciously, shut out 9-to-0. There I heard Raphael Gat point out how protests in Berlin had prevented thousands of Jews from being deported. "There were people in Germany who spoke out but not in Austria," he observed. And, he added, "In Germany anti-Semitism was more of an intellectual position. In Austria it was a way of life."

One final incident reported by Rosenkranz is of interest here. During the early days of the *Anschluss* many Jews began frequenting a cafe opposite the Hotel Metropole which the Gestapo had taken for its local headquarters. The cafe's Gentile proprietor said he would protect his Jewish customers, though he did not say just how he would do so. A much more important reason for the cafe's new popularity among Jews was its proximity to Gestapo headquarters. Vienna is the only city in the history of the Holocaust where Jews actually looked to the Gestapo to protect them from the populace.

Now the second question: Did the Vienna Jews passionately love this city that so passionately hated them? Here, too, the answer seemed already apparent. Recall that from 1934 to 1938 Viennese Jews faced not only the threat of Hitler but growing suppression and oppression from Austria's own quasi-official anti-Semitic policy. One might suppose that at least young Jews, denied vocational and other opportunities, would have departed in droves. Yet, with very few exceptions, they and their elders refused to leave.

Even after the *Anschluss*, and the *Blitzverfolgung* which followed it, many continued to cling to the city. Kurt Stadler quotes a Jewish woman saying in September 1939, "Thank God for the war. Things will be better for us; we can stay after all." The deportations themselves failed to snuff out Jewish feeling for the city. Louis Lowy, a Czech Jew who was in Theresienstadt almost from the first day it opened, says he was struck by the strong and strange attachment that deportees from Vienna retained for their city. "The Viennese Jews had a love for Vienna which none of the German or Czech Jews had for their particular cities," he says. Today, almost a half century later, such feelings have still not completely faded. Says Rosenkranz, "I still love Vienna although I hate the Viennese." Says Weiser Varon, "I am no longer an Austrian, but I will always be a Viennese."

But now comes the more difficult question: What made the Jews so ardently love a city that so ardently hated them? What produced what is undoubtedly the most unrequited love affair in urban history?

We must first list Vienna's genuine charm, composed in part of its physical appeal, cultural attractions, leisurely pace, and the outwardly amiable manner of its people. Since these qualities have enchanted so many people over so many years, why should they not have exerted a similar effect on the Jews? Vienna had offered the Jews numerous opportunities to capitalize on their abilities and achieve their ambitions, for the city's economic centrality and its many cultural institutions, combined with the easygoing or lazy (the choice of adjective depends on one's personal perspective) nature of its inhabitants, opened up numerous avenues for advancement.

Finally, Vienna's polyglot population and central location between East and West gave it a cosmopolitan ambience that facilitated, or seemed to facilitate, integration and even assimilation. As Zweig noted, nowhere was it easier to be a European.

Another Viennese quality, however, proved still more seductive and, in the end, more destructive to the Jews. It has been mentioned before, but its importance requires reiteration.

The Viennese, as the best of their own writers has observed, had a remarkable facility for acting one way while thinking another. In everyday personal relations their attitudes were often disguised. A Jew would frequently find his corner policeman, neighborhood tradesman, and his own clients or customers quite friendly, and this naturally deceived him into thinking that all was well. There might be hostile posters on the wall and hostile headlines in the paper, there might be "incidents" of hooliganism and worse, but how could he really feel endangered when his daily contacts with Gentiles were so pleasant? Jewish women, in particular, were often shielded from the venom that lay beneath the Viennese veneer. Many of them would undoubtedly have agreed with Hilde Wang Massler when she says, "My life up to the *Anschluss* was one happy memory."

Certain other factors encouraged such self-deception. The Social Democrats regularly polled forty percent or more of the vote nationwide and well over fifty percent in Vienna itself. Of course, without the Jews, the Social Democrats might have polled only a little over one-third of the vote nationally and might never have secured a majority in Vienna. Furthermore, the Social Democrats themselves, including their Jewish leaders, were hardly free from anti-Semitism. But it was easy to disregard such things, especially if one were not overly interested in politics anyway, as was the case with many of Vienna's Jews. Freud, for example, never bothered to vote until he was fifty-two, and rarely read a newspaper.

So most Jews voted for the Social Democrats and then went about their business, believing that all was or would be well. As Clare points out, "Every Jewish Social Democrat sensed a protective wall of non-Jewish Social Democrats around him." When the confrontation with open and violent anti-Semitism came, threatening Jewish freedom and survival, that protective wall proved no protection at all.

Another factor that may have fostered a false sense of security was the Lueger phenomenon. Because Jewish life continued to thrive during Lueger's reign as mayor, and because anti-Semitism even ebbed during his years in office,* many Austrian Jews may have been lulled into the belief that they had little to fear: I believe they failed to see that Lueger only deflected Vienna's virulent hatred toward the Jews. Lueger needed the support of the wealthier Jews and of their powerful ally, Emperor Franz Joseph, to carry out his ambitious programs. He achieved this support by talking one way while acting in another.

---

*This at least is the impression of Professor Shimron.

Vienna's Austro-Germans recognized and applauded his adroit utilization of what had already become a standard Viennese pattern of behavior. They could especially appreciate such a strategem since it produced a sharp growth in city jobs and services that primarily benefited them. But though Lueger kept Jew-hatred under control, he in no way reduced it. On the contrary, his frequent anti-Semitic pronouncements only enhanced its respectability and increased its latent force.

But what had made Jew-hatred so powerful in Austria to begin with?

Some of the answers were already supplied in Chapter Three. It will be recalled that Austria had a much higher percentage of Jews than any other West European country. When Hitler came to power, Austria had proportionately more than three times as many Jews as Germany, four times as many as England, over five times as many as France, and twenty times as many as Italy. Only Holland, with a Jewish population of 2.2 percent, came close to equaling Austria's Jewish percentage. Moreover, over nine-tenths of Austria's Jews were clustered in the country's major city which made them a more conspicuous presence.

In his memoirs, the German-Jewish writer Jakob Wassermann points up this fact. Writes Wassermann, "One circumstance puzzled me before I had been long in Vienna. In Germany I had associated with Jews scarcely at all; only now and then did one appear in my circle and no special stress was laid by either himself or others on the fact that he was Jewish. Here, however, all whom I came into professional or social contact with were Jews." Adds Wassermann, "I soon realized that all public life was dominated by Jews."

It will also be recalled that Austria's over ninety percent Catholicism contributed to anti-Semitism in two ways. The Church was, first of all, more avowedly and uniformly hostile to the Jews than were the Protestant churches. Secondly, Catholicism was less compatible with capitalism. By putting a damper on the entrepreneurial energies of the Gentile populations, it enabled Austria's proportionately large number of Jews to play a more dominant economic role. It also enabled them to exercise more influence in other areas of Austrian life as well.

Various fortuitous factors also contributed to Austria's anti-Semitism. The influx of the *Ostjuden* during World War I, the country's ambivalent attitude toward its own capital city, the left-wing, nearly revolutionary, stance of the Social Democrats in the 1920s — these and many other developments fostered *Judenhetze*.

But though such circumstances may explain much of Austria's anti-Semitism, they do not explain it all. While they may explain why Austrian Nazis might want to urinate on the heads of wealthy Jewish women in Während, they do not explain why other Nazis took such delight in tormenting poor Orthodox Jews in the Leopoldstadt, and why so many other Austrians found it so amusing to watch them do so. They do not explain why so many Austrians served in the SS and in the concentration camps even though other jobs were abundantly available. They do not explain why so many remained so eager to abuse and denounce Jews long after most Jews had fled and those remaining had been reduced to a bare, borderline existence.

We now enter the tricky and rather treacherous territory of the basic Austrian mentality. Here we, or at least I, cannot come up with definitive and comprehensive answers. But some parts of the puzzle can be pointed out.

Austrian writer Albert Fuchs once described his countrymen's favorable characteristics as amiability, lightheartedness, and verbal dexterity (*Zungenfertigkeit*). Their defects he denoted as superficiality, lack of principles, and brutality.

Fuchs, it is true, was Jewish, but many non-Jewish Austrians appeared to agree with him. Hermann Bahr once said that the typical Viennese does not abuse someone because he dislikes him but because he finds abusing someone pleasurable. Professor Jürgen Koppensteiner, who now teaches in the United States, finds in the average Austrian "a large amount of aggressiveness, sentimentality, melancholy, and depression." Robert Musil's observation of Austrian two-facedness has been frequently cited. Thomas Bernhard claims that in his native Salzburg "the confidence trick has been developed into a fine art" and that "National Socialism could easily supersede Catholicism overnight." He gives no indication of finding the rest of his country any different.

Let us begin by looking at the question of aggressiveness or brutality. We have, of course, seen numerous instances of this, but one can find examples of similar behavior in other lands, including Israel. What does seem more distinctive to Austria is the pervasiveness of that quality that Schnitzler called "a disinterested meanness." The Catholic historian Weinzierl has indicated that she agrees with such an assessment of her fellow Austrians. So does an Anglo-Saxon American woman married to an Austrian who tells me how her sister-in-law laughed when her son burned his fingers, and who, on a trip to America, laughed when they saw an older woman fall on some ice. This American regards her sister-in-law's reactions as typically Viennese.

At times such disinterested meanness shades into a callousness that can be cruel or have cruel effects. It was surprising for an American to read in the Austrian magazine *Profil* in the spring of 1986 that most Austrian hospitals only allow parents to visit their hospitalized child once a week. Why? Because, as one hospital administrator puts it, "The children get all stirred up and cry when the mother leaves." Dr. Hans Czermack, a leading pediatrician who is trying to change this policy, claims that thirty percent of all Austrian children are behaviorally damaged, many from hospital stays. He refers to Austria as an "underdeveloped country."

If a remarkable number of Austrians exhibit a certain callousness bordering on cruelty, one should hesitate to brand it aggressiveness. On the contrary, a certain passivity seems to characterize much Austrian behavior. We saw in Chapter Two how Golo Mann noticed such a passive streak in the Revolution of 1848. It also seems evident in the *Blitzvervolgung* as numerous Viennese gathered with complacency, if not amusement, to watch the terrorizing of Jews, some of whom had been their friends and neighbors.

In his memoirs, Hjalmar Schacht, Hitler's financial wizard before they broke in 1939, recalls an incident that underscores this aspect of Austrian character. In 1921 when Schacht was campaigning for a new Centrist party which he and others had organized in Germany, Schacht said he addressed about fifty campaign rallies on the Party's behalf. Although many were stormy affairs, only on one occasion was he prevented from speaking. "It happened in Vienna before a packed house," Schacht said. "Spread about in the front row were some fifty rowdies who set up such howls and catcalls that I had to abandon my speech. . . . Behind them were three thousand citizens who had come to hear about the German Democratic party. Those three thousand allowed themselves to be terrorized instead of throwing them out."

A more distinctive and in many ways more troublesome trait is what Fuchs calls a lack of principle and what Bernhard sees as a propensity for the "confidence trick." Here, too, the Austrians scarcely stand alone, but here, too, evidence suggests that they are more disposed to duplicity than many other Europeans. Numerous instances of this have been cited, especially as it affected the Jews. Lueger's celebrated but cynical one-liner — "I determine just who is a Jew" — carries with it a connotation that no merit lies in consistency of principle.

The revelations in the spring of 1986 regarding two of Austria's most famous citizens, Kurt Waldheim and Herbert von Karajan, present a case in point. Waldheim was found to have lied about his Nazi affiliations as a student and, more significantly, about his involvement in deportations and reprisals as a member of General Löhr's staff in the Balkans. Von Karajan, who had always maintained that he joined the Nazi party in 1935 in order to keep his job with a German orchestra, was found to have actually joined the Party in 1933, only ten weeks after Hitler's assumption of power and while the young conductor was still in Austria. Yet the Austrian press, with very few exceptions, reacted by rallying to Waldheim's side while ignoring completely the new revelations about von Karajan. One sometimes gets the impression that in Austria naked opportunism is not just a tolerable vice but an admired virtue.*

*Such behavior patterns apparently enter into Austrian business practices as well. Benjamin M. Andersen, who edited the *Chase Economic Bulletin* during the interwar years, was in Vienna in 1929 when he heard that the *Bodenkreditanstalt* was in trouble. Said Andersen twenty years

But the Waldheim and von Karajan episodes illustrate a further and more significant aspect of Austrian behavior. Peter Czernin, the enterprising *Profil* reporter who first investigated the Waldheim affair, says that Waldheim refused to admit anything unfavorable about his past even when incontrovertible evidence was placed before him. "He even rejected his own picture," says Czernin. Biographer Roger Vaughn found von Karajan refusing to admit to Nazi party membership in 1933 even when confronted with xeroxes of his own party cards which showed the date.

The really remarkable thing about these incidents is that the reactions of both men seem in a peculiar way to be sincere. They actually appear to believe their own denials and grow furious when others do not. In other words, they behave as if the embarrassing evidence was about someone else, not them.

Professor Reinhold Knoll, a sociologist at the University of Vienna, also has something of interest to report on this point. Knoll's father was one of the few professors at the University whose anti-Nazi views cost him his position following the *Anschluss*. With the end of the war, the older Knoll was given back his professorship and put in charge of a committee formed to investigate those professors incriminated by Nazi involvement.

In looking over his father's notes of the various cases the committee handled, the younger Knoll says that many of those incriminated spoke of their past activities as if they were speaking of someone else. It appears that, like Waldheim and von Karajan, not only could they not accept any real responsibility for their acts, but they could not admit *even to themselves* that they had committed them. (In a sense, Kreisky behaves the same way when he talks about the Jews as if he were talking about another people, not his own.)

Something does seem sadly amiss with what is sometimes called the "Austrian soul." Conductor George Szell refers to Vienna as a "luscious dessert with an unsavory filling." His late colleague, Bruno Walter, could not understand how the "home of music" could also be the home of "so much hate and so many hateful activities." "A psychologically oriented research investigation," wrote Walter in his memoirs, "may some day trace Austria's downfall to that national dualism, or at least to the irreconcilability of high cultural inclinations and deeply barbarous tendencies."

---

later, "The one case in which a banker has deliberately lied to me regarding credit information came when I went to an important official of another Vienna bank who owed me the truth with respect to such matters, and received from him the unqualified assurance that the *Bodenkreditanstalt* was perfectly safe and sound." Five months later it collapsed.

An American businessman who managed a factory on the Austrian border in the early 1970s tells me he experienced similar problems. Austrian businessmen and even bankers, he says, would say things they did not really mean or that weren't even true. If one signed an agreement with them, one could never be quite sure they took it seriously. Doing business with Austrians, he says, is unlike doing business anywhere else.

While the investigation that Walter suggests obviously lies well beyond the scope of this book, one factor that might figure in such an inquiry deserves attention.

People with low self-esteem generally harbor far more prejudice against others than those who feel good about themselves. (A study demonstrating this was reported in the September 1986 issue of *Psychology Today*.) At the beginning of this book, the low self-esteem of the average turn-of-the-century Austrian was noted. That Austria today still has a high suicide rate, coupled with a high rate of auto deaths, indicates that such feelings may not yet have disappeared.

This lack of self-esteem obviously played a role in the development of Austria's anti-Semitism. Moreover, many Viennese Jews may have exacerbated it by their own negative feelings about themselves *as Jews*. For while a person of low self-esteem will tend to feel negatively about others in general, he will especially despise anyone suffering from the same malady. No one incurs less respect than a person who fails to respect himself; the fact that so many Jews failed to respect their own Jewishness, and instead strove to identify with the Austro-Germans, may well have caused the Austro-Germans, plagued as they were with their own self-doubts, to despise Jews all the more.

But why should the Austro-Germans have had such negative feelings about themselves in the first place? I cannot hope to answer that question, but I would like to point to one possible element — the lack of a sure sense of national identity.

No country in history ever surrendered its independence so quickly, so completely, and so enthusiastically as did Austria in 1938. More than thirty years after the war, a 1976 poll still found less than half of Austria's population willing to affirm Austria's status as an independent nation. (By 1985 the figure had risen to about two-thirds.) Ever since the Empire began to disintegrate, the Austro-Germans have felt the pull of their northern neighbor, and though many Austrians actually dislike Germans, many at the same time wish to identify with them.

To add a further component to this complex problem, relatively few Austro-Germans are Germans in any realistic sense of the word. One has only to glance at the vast number of Slavic, Hungarian, and even Italian names in the Vienna phone book to grasp the dimensions of this problem. What's more, many of those with German names actually come from non-German stock. Waldheim's family name was originally Watzlawik, as befits its Czech origin. Even the Schwarzenbergs, one of Austria's noblest families, were originally Czech, while the first Baron von Karajan, great-grandfather of the present conductor, was Greek.

The Aryan concept was ludicrous enough in Germany where, according to the German historian Walter Goerlitz, even the average Prussian aristocrat was one-quarter Polish. In Austria the concept was farcical, for the Germans of Austria may well be the least "racially pure" people in Europe. Their insecure ethnic identity may not only have helped make them arch anti-Semites — the most fervent Nazis often had Slavic names — but coupled with Austria's insecure sense of nationhood, may have contributed to their apparent doubts about their own self-worth.

Of course, such speculation, if true, can provide only part of the solution to the mystery of Austrian behavior. But before leaving this subject to those better equipped to deal with it, I should like to remind the forty-three percent of Austria's population who, according to one opinion poll, still regard the Jews as a "guest people," that Jews were living in Austria when many of *their* own forebears were living elsewhere.

But what does the story of Vienna and its Jews have to teach us about the Jews themselves? Actually, a good deal, though most Jews have long since learned its lessons. One of the first lessons that springs to mind is another paradox: The less Jewish a Jew becomes, the more may *his very Jewishness* imperil him.

For one thing, he loses the self-respect without which, as we have seen, he can never hope to gain the respect of others. For another, he loses the institutions and sense of community that he will desperately need should danger strike. The Jewish community cannot hope to protect itself unless it is first a community.

During the Holocaust, many Nazi leaders, believing their own propaganda about Jewish conspiracies, were surprised to find that the Jews did not even have a communication network. Erich von dem Bach, the SS commander for central Russia, told Allied interrogators after the war, "In reality the Jews had no organization at all. If they had had some sort of organization, they could have been saved by the millions; instead they were taken completely by surprise."

Some Polish and Russian villages did have fairly cohesive Jewish communities, and this is probably why they were the only ones to offer any organized resistance to the Nazis. Such resistance did not and could not accomplish much, but in alerting the community to Nazi moves and, in a few cases, burning down the community when the Nazis moved to evacuate it, it did enable a few Jews to escape execution. The Viennese Jews who had fought so gallantly for Austria in World War I organized virtually no resistance to the Nazis at all.

But perhaps the real protective role of unifying institutions, and the sense of community which alone can build and maintain them, is preventive. Had the Viennese Jews been cohesively organized before the *Anschluss*, they might well have been able to conciliate or at least moderate the hostility of some of their enemies. Representatives of a unified Jewish community, for example, might have negotiated a better understanding with leaders of the Catholic Church. Since the Jews posed no real threat to the Church, and since they did have something to offer it, even if it were only financial assistance to the Church's many hard-pressed charities, an improved relationship might have resulted. The attempt itself would perhaps have favorably impressed some church leaders. (Many better-off Jews did contribute to Catholic causes, but done on an individual basis such contributions could, and did, accomplish little.)

The critical role of Jewish institutions can also be seen in the help that came from abroad once the terror started. One fears to contemplate what might have occurred if the Joint Distribution Committee and other organizations had not quickly moved into Vienna to dispense aid. All too often, many of us grew tired of the frequent pleas for funds. Sometimes we make fun of those Jewish organizations that superficially seem more like social gatherings than anything else. But when the need has been there, whether in Vienna in 1938 or in Israel in 1948, their help has been indispensable.

Of course, adherence to and support for Jewish organizations does not preclude in any way involvement in non-Jewish ones. We of the Diaspora remain loyal citizens of our various countries and participate fully in those activities that concern us individually as citizens. We may be Democrats or Republicans, radicals or conservatives, world federalists, nationalists, or isolationists. But those who believe that support for broad-based political activity eliminates the need for specific Jewish activity should look carefully at the Viennese experience. A large number of Viennese Jews believed that socialism alone would solve, indeed eliminate, the Jewish problem. It did not, nor has it ever done so. Nor, for that matter, has any other cherished, all-embracing "ism".

In his perceptive novel, *The Road to the Open*, Arthur Schnitzler has one Jew say to a left-wing friend, "Who created the liberal movement in Austria? The Jews. Who betrayed and abandoned the Jews? The liberals. Who created the German Nationalist Movement in Austria? The Jews. Who left the Jews in the lurch and indeed despised them as dogs? The German nationals. And just the same thing will happen with the socialists and communists. Once the dinner is ready to be served, they will chase you from the table."

Schnitzler's admonition has proven true. Indeed, the most conspicuous manifestations of anti-Semitism today are coming from the Left, largely, though by no means exclusively, in the form of anti-Zionism. At the same time, of course, plenty of anti-Semitism remains on the Right, especially the Far Right. Consequently, whatever our other causes and concerns, Jews should support, and support vigorously, Jewish institutions, Jewish communities, and Jewish life.

Our plane lands at Kennedy airport and bleary-eyed we stumble out into the early morning cold. My journey to a vital part of the Jewish present in Israel is over and my journey into the Jewish past in Vienna is also drawing to a close. Most of my research and much of my writing has already been done.

But in another sense, the journey has just begun, for I know I will make many more trips to Israel and I will write other books on Jewish subjects. For in this, my first foray into Jewish history, I have found more than just the answers to my questions. I have also found a part of myself.

Notes

The following notes provide annotation only for those quotations and other major points of interest whose sources cannot be readily traced from the text itself to the bibliography. Most of the sources cited are only briefly identified, and the reader should consult the bibliography for the full references.

Chapter 1.

Although I have drawn heavily on Zweig in this chapter, Schorske, Morton, Johnson and Marek have also supplied useful information. Marek has been especially helpful in depicting the lighter side of Viennese life. Several other authors have furnished occasional tidbits. Thus, Martin Freud describes walking with his father on the Ringstrasse, Drucker tell of tipping customs and of how the title "von" was awarded, and Crankshaw mentions the Opera's special stall for army officers. I remember reading the story of Dr. Schmecktgut in Robert Ripley's *Believe It or Not* as a child and have never forgotten it. Harry Zohn, who is a musician as well as a Germanist and Herzl scholar, told me that Vienna has generated more songs about itself than all the world's other major cities combined.

Chapter 2.

Although Schorske's stimulating book is better known and certainly a must for anyone wishing to understand the Vienna of this period, I found Johnston's book, which won the 1971 Austrian History Prize, more helpful for my purposes. The quotations from Musil and Adler, the material on dueling, on Austrian technological and other achievements, and much of the information on Austria's political, economic and social problems have come from Johnston's valuable work.

Marek and Zweig have also continued to be good sources. Marek supplies a good, if somewhat superficial, outline of the developing political situation. The stabbing of the war minister in 1848 and Golo Mann's observation on Viennese behavior during this time are taken from Marek, as is material on dueling, the role of the army, attitudes toward food, and quotes from Viennese writers on Viennese grumbling and self-deprecation. Zweig comments on the tax situation ("small tips to the state"), describes the problem of sex, Austrian conservatism, how the army had more great bandmasters than generals, etc.

Prince Rudolf's statement on the army's role in holding the Empire together comes from Morton, along with material on Vienna's pagentry, Franz Joseph's many titles, etc. The quotations from Kuernsberger and Bahr are from Grunwald, along with the story of the war minister's cousin who was sworn in by error. Funder describes Catholic grievances and relates the story of a popular priest who did not believe in preaching to women. Funder also reports the studies showing the low earnings level and high tuberculosis rate among Vienna's tradesmen, as well as much material on the ethnic rivalries within the Empire.

Many of the above sources, especially Marek and Crankshaw, also provided a framework for viewing Austria's economic problems, but on this point I have found the articles by Jacob, Meisel and Sandgruber particularly helpful. Feis presents figures on the movement of foreign capital into Austria, while Mitchell presents other economic data plus figures on Austria's infant mortality rate. Hawlik's first chapter has also been used.

Freud's statement on women, together with the attitudes of his colleagues and Viennese society generally toward him, are from Clark, but Drucker also offers an interesting contribution. Drucker also supplies the story of Gertrude Bien and other items on the position of women and on the ambiguous attitude of the Viennese toward sexuality and morality. Mahler's statement to his wife about her composing music, or rather about her not composing music, is from Monson.

Chapters 3 and 4

Stadler, Mahler, and the book edited by Ben-Sasson have been the principal sources for the capsule history of the Viennese Jews up to 1800. They, along with Johnston, continue to provide material for the nineteenth century but now many other works come into play. Grunwald has been especially valuable. Franz Joseph's rejection of re-ghettoization of the Jews, the quotes from the field marshall on Israelite officers, from Hermann Bahr on Galician Jews, from the Rabbi (Mannheimer) at the funeral of the rebels of 1848, Grillparzer's poem on Jewish emancipation, the hesitation of liberal Jews to establish a new Temple in 1826, and most of the material regarding Jews in Parliament avoiding their Jewishness comes from Grunwald, including the quote of the Jewish parliamentarian who refused to let his German heart be torn out of his bosum.

Bloch supplies the anecdote on the Jewish child in the Christian school — he is the Galician rabbi quoted on this point — as well as material on Jewish Germanism and on Baron Rothschild's non-Jewish staff and soirees. The quote from Baron Hirsch is from Bermant along with material on Jews in Austrian journalism. Bihl also has a good deal of material on Jewish participation in journalism and in other areas of Austrian life including the military. Drucker covers some of the same ground in the interesting essay on Freud in his own book, and is also the source for all my information on Schwarzwald whom he knew.

Bihl documents the pro-Germanism of Jews living in the outlying provinces but I have drawn on Pawel for the situation in Prague, including his account of the "December Storm" of 1899. Both Gold and Goldhammer provide data and description on Jewish growth in Vienna, with the latter also giving some figures on Jewish assimilation.

Tur-Sinai's article in *Fraenkel* (1967) includes his quoted remarks. All the quotations from Martin Freud are from his article in the same book. Many other essays from *Fraenkel* were also used in these two chapters, including Mandell's, which contains the quotation from Liszt on hearing Sulzer's choir, and Rabbi Willman's which describes Güdemann's threat to resign over the prayer book issue. The dispute between the Orthodox and the integrationists is also reported in many other works, including Rozenblit, Grunwald, and various essays in Fraenkel, but the most detailed account, and the only one which mentions the *Schiffschul,* is in Richter. The description by a contemporary writer of Mannheimer preaching and Sulzer singing will be found in Pick's essay in Lohrmann. This essay also gives an account of the founding and development of the Vienna *Gemeinde.*

Other sources include Johnston who, among other things, describes Otto Weinniger, points to the gradual disappearance of Hebrew instruction, and recounts the joke of the strangers on the train. Hawlik provides the quote from Felix Braun and the one from Mahler about his fears that his Jewishness may block his upward path; Janik and Toulmin describe Karl Wittgenstein. (I might add that Freud's younger brother Alexander, though he lacked a university education, became Austria's foremost expert on transportation and as such played a key role in the country's economic development.) The statement from the wealthy Galicians on the proposed new temple and the one by the Zionist writer Isador-Shalit on why the Jews sought to be Germans are quoted by Rozenblit, while the quotes from and about Karl Kraus are from Wistrich supplemented by material from Johnston, Schorske, and others. Pope Pius VII's statement rejecting liberalism is from Stewart.

Prelude and Chapter 5

The emergence of racial anti-Judaism has been chronicled in many works including the first chapter of Bracher, and Arendt's short book. One factor often neglected in such summaries, however, is the less than successful effort by the Catholic Church to shift its investments into manufacturing and finance. Dedijer, however, devotes some attention to this important aspect of Catholic anti-Semitism.

As to the emergence of anti-Semitism in Austria, Schubert, Pauley, Grunwald, Morton, Rozenblit, Hawlik, Fuchs, and Jonny Moser's articles in *Traum und Wirklichkeit* and in Lohrmann have all been used in Chapter 5. Needless to say they overlap in content considerably. Other sources include Sandgruber, who describes the anti-Jewish cartoons after the stock market crash; Funder who describes Jewish money lending and who offers a sympathetic view of the anti-Semites (though he ignores their more extreme outpourings); and Stewart who points out how the "Jewish Baron" had become a stock figure in political cartoons.

The quote on "arrogant, insolent Jews" is from Pulzer; Vogelsang's statement about not reviling the religion of the Jews appears in Moser's article in Lohrmann; and the incident regarding the outburst at the meeting of the Medical School's charitable association is recounted in Schnitzler's memoirs.

Chapter 6

Bloch's autobiography is the best source of the events he was involved in, and although it is, like most memoirs, somewhat self-serving, its facts are in no way disputed by the accounts of his activities in Schubert, Grunwald, Rozenblit, Gold, and others. Grunwald, for example, mentions how Jewish leaders blocked Bloch's appointment to a professorship.

The founding of the Union is also described by Bloch as well as by Rozenblit, with the former giving Zins' statement expressing the need for, and goal of, the Union and the latter giving his statement emphasizing Jewish Germanism. The previous attempt to form a multi-ethnic party is described by Grunwald but Bloch contributes the comment from Fischof on its failure. Grunwald is also the source of Kaufmann's statement and of the agreement by Jewish city councilors not to appear in public life as Jews.

Gold describes the founding of Kadimah and gives its call to arms ("Ethnic Comrades!" etc.); Martin Freud in his article in Fraenkel (1967) notes the flocking of Jewish students to the German Liberal Students Association; Schnitzler, among others, presents the Waidhofer resolution and the Jewish zeal for learning fencing which prompted it; and Meysels reports the incident regarding Zuckerkandl. Wistrich, Pauley, Pulzer, and Moser's articles in Lohrmann and in *Traum und Wirklichkeit* also provided useful information for this chapter.

Chapter 7

Description of the measures and antics of the anti-Semites in Parliament in the 1880s, and the formation of the Pan-German and Christian Social parties can be found in Schubert, Pauley, Hawlik, Pulzer's article in Fraenkel, Morton, the articles by Moser in *Traum und Wirklichkeit*, and Lohrmann, and in Grunwald who reports the incident, "Business Before Pleasure." The material on Prince Rudolf comes primarily from Morton, while Dedijer points out the anti-Semitism of Rudolf's successor, Franz Ferdinand. (According to Dedijer, Franz Ferdinand's hostility was directed at the integrated and assimilated Jews, for the Archduke respected the Orthodox Jews.)

The incidents of attempted entrapment of Jews plus the kidnappings of Jewish children in Galicia come from Bloch, as does the material concerning Dr. Schwarz's child, Archbishop Kohn, and Schneider's encounter with the tailor at Lemberg. The puppet skit is mentioned by Beckermann in her own essay in her book.

The most complete account of the founding of the "Defense Against Anti-Semitism" Society is in Moser's article in Lohrmann. Wistrich provides the most complete account of the Socialist Party's attitude toward the Jews, but the quote from Karl Kautsky comes from Pulzer's article while the baiting of Viktor Adler in the provincial legislature is from Simon.

Bloch's battles in Parliament and with Father Deckert are reported in detail in his memoirs, but the Deckert affair is also reported in Grunwald, Wistrich, Moser, and many others. Nothing which they write contradicts Block's own account which is accompanied by lengthy transcripts of the trial proceedings.

Chapter 8.

Pauley outlines von Schönerer's rise and fall but other previously mentioned writers supply many interesting details. Jenks, for example, gives his statement, "Our anti-Semitism is not directed against the religion of the Jew. . ."; Moser in *Traum und Wirklichkeit* supplies his statement on "Semitic overlordship in money and word"; and Morton provides a detailed account of the drunken incident in 1888 which brought a temporary end to von Schönerer's career.

The early chapters of Hawlik chronicle Lueger's rise to power while Funder, who witnessed this rise to power, supplies valuable supplementary material including crowd reactions, etc. The quotation, "Give to Rothschild," is from him. Other sources are Wistrich for Lueger's statement on Fischof, Bloch on Fischhof's admonition to him about Lueger, Fuchs on rising church attendance resulting from the political use of the pulpit, Pulzer who provides the excerpt from the letter of Christian Socials to Pope Leo XIII disavowing racial social anti-Semitism, and Morton who tells of the harassment of Liberal voters at the polls. Herzl's experiences and reflections are from his diaries. I should point out that Hawlik and Funder leave out much of Lueger's anti-Semitic activity and so I have also drawn upon Wistrich, Pauley, Jenks, and other previously mentioned authorities on this period. A forthcoming biography of Lueger by Richard Geehr should prove especially informative, while the most definitive work yet published on the early years of Lueger's party is that of Boyer.

Chapter 9.

The basic material on Lueger's activities as mayor, along with Freud's statement to Fliess on the Emperor's veto, comes from Hawlik. Other sources besides those mentioned in the text include Marek for Franz Joseph's "You may count on it. . ."; Herzl's diaries for his statement to Badeni; Isaiah Berlin for Lueger's sneering reference to science; and Richard Geehr who has told me of Lueger's subsidies to the Aryan theater and his public espousal on two occasions, once before and once after his election as mayor, of the ritual murder myth.

Fuchs was my best source for Father Scheicher, and Moser in *Traum und Wirklichkeit* for Houston Chamberlain. Weinzierl mentions Rome's admonitions to the CSU regarding racial anti-Semitism.

Mahler's statement on his homelessness can be found in *Traum und Wirklichkeit*, while Monson and Walter are further sources on his troubles in Vienna. The Hilsner case is covered by several writers, with Grunwald supplying the quotation from Masaryk. Von Schönerer's later political career is described by Stadler, Pauley, and others.

Most of Hitler's biographers, but most notably Jenks, describe Hitler's numerous positive contacts with Jews before and during his Vienna years. Stadler points out the way statements from von Schönerer's newspaper appear later in *Mein Kampf.*

Chapter 10.

For source material on pre-Herzl Zionism see Gold and Rozenblit or, for that matter, almost any biography of Herzl. The two biographies I have drawn upon to summarize his life are those of Cohen and Stewart. Herzl's diaries have also been consulted.

Most of the quotes about Herzl from his fellow Viennese Jews (including the stanza of verse) come from Zohn's 1985 paper, although Zohn's own interesting comment on Herzl comes from the essay on the Jewish leader in his 1986 book. Other sources are Cohen for the statement by Lord Rothschild; Zweig for the reaction of theater audiences and "The King has arrived"; Rozenblit for Shalit's "Herr Doktor, what you have written. . ." and for the statement by a "later Zionist" on the "ostrich policy"; and Wistrich who, along with Zohn, provides material on the reaction of Karl Kraus. Fraenkel's own essay on Herzl and Güdemann in his 1967 book is also informative. (Martin Freud in his essay in the same book says he only knew Herzl as a journalist and as the father of his sister's school friend, although, as Clark points out, Sigmund Freud sent Herzl a copy of his book on dreams with a message of praise for his good work.)

Chapter 11.

The principal source for the activities of both the integrationists and Zionists (including the battles between them) covered in this chapter is Rozenblit. She also briefly discusses the emergence of Jewish nationalism in eastern Austria, but most of my material on this development, and the court battles it engendered, comes from Stourzh. The quote from the University's rector on the 'foolish fanaticism' of Zionist students also comes from Stourzh's lengthy and detailed article.

Stadler and Marek, among others, tell of the growth of Austrian socialism while Wistrich, Bermant and Rozenblit, among others, point out Jewish involvement in the movement. But see also entries 177-187 in the catalogue section of Lohrmann for further material on Bauer and Adler.

For Schweitzer's promotion see Rubin, for the deaths of Zuckerkandl and Mahler see Meysels, for the development of orthodoxy see Richter, for Barany's work and its recognition see Helmut Leitner's article in Lohrmann, and for Jews in sports see Hans Morgenstern's article in Lohrmann as well as Juhn's essay in Fraenkel (1967).

Chapter 12.

Marek mentions the jokes about Franz Ferdinand while Cowles describes Vienna's jubiliation on going to war, and Zweig describes the justification given by the intellectuals who joined in. Martin Freud describes his military career in his book. The advancement of Jewish professional officers comes mostly from Rubin, but Mrs. Ellen Sommer Taxer has filled in some of the details about her father. Hilde Spiel's essay in Fraenkel (1967) tells about Eugenia Schwarzwald although Drucker also supplies material on this remarkable woman.

For Poale Zion's anti-war activity see Beckermann's essay in her own book and also entries 158-165 in the catalogue section of Lohrmann. Mannes Sperber's experience comes from his essay in Beckermann, while Gstein provides figures on Jewish burials and housing. Zweig describes the bartering for food that went on between city dwellers and farmers. Both Moser in *Austriaca* and Spira describe the problems of the *Ostjuden*, and both quote the statement by Joseph Roth on their plight. For the material on Stricker see Fraenkel's 1950 book.

Chapters 13 and 14

All standard histories of Austria describe the painful transition from once-proud Empire to war-ravaged Republic, but I found Pauley, Barker, and von Klemperer especially helpful, with the latter supplying the quotes from Seipel on Jews. Zweig gives a graphic portrayal of the effects of the inflation, while Wechsberg mentions the sudden desire of performers to play in the provinces and Mrs. Massler tells of using the blank side of paper currency for school work.

Moser's articles in *Austriaca* and in Lohrmann, especially the former, provide much of the material on postwar anti-Semitism, but Spira's book has also been helpful. Pulzer's article in Fraenkel documents the formation of the Greater German People's Party, the Christian Social election manifests of December 1918, the Party's 1920 election poster of the Jewish snake, and the fear of the University rector over "Levantization." Von Klemperer recounts Seitz's attack on Seipel and also describes the Social Democrats' ambitious programs in Vienna. The *Traum und Wirklichkeit* program book contains further material about these municipal undertakings which prompted one London newspaper, *The Spectator*, to call Vienna the "miracle of Europe." For more on Breitner, see entry 184 in the catalogue section of Lohrmann.

Schubert discusses *The Protocols* and their impact on Central Europe and on the Jews themselves. Schuschnigg (1971) documents the close involvement of the Jews with the Social Democrats as does Fischer, who supplies the quote "the Jews in the Vienna headquarters." Both Berman and Weinzierl mention the "racial" census effort. Helen Hilsenrad reports the mistaken beating by anti-Semites of a Roman Catholic priest on the Franz Joseph Kai (she and her fiancee were the couple who escaped), while the August/September 1986 issue of *Illustrierte Neue Welt* published a piece describing Einstein's visit to Vienna.

Chapter 15.

For Schnitzler and Zweig's achievements see Zohn's essay in Fraenkel and for the achievements of Jewish athletes see Morgenstern's article in Lohrmann. Sommer's Burgenland success comes from Rubin and from Taxer. Beckermann reports on the 120 Jewish organizations, while Richter describes the expanded activities of the Schiffschul.

My chief source of information about Rabbi Chajes is Professor Ben Shimron, but Moser in *Austriaca* describes Chajes' interview with Karl and its controversial aftermath, entry 152 in Lohrmann gives some of the Rabbi's background, and Fraenkel's own essay in his 1967 book touches on Güdemann's role in Chajes' appointment.

Although Fraenkel's 1950 book, supplemented by some telephone conversations with William Stricker, provides most of the material on Robert Stricker, Moser in *Austriaca* briefly describes the formation and activities of the Jewish National Party, quotes the Union's prediction of its repudiation at the polls and gives his own comments on the party. Entries 166-170 in Lohrmann describe, and reproduce in part, the party's election materials while Simon provides the most complete tally of how it fared at the polls.

Hilsenrad describes the mood of Vienna as the economy started to revive. Canetti (1982) offers a portrait of Karl Kraus and his followers, and Schechter tells of Hakoah's triumphs, although the incident "Hurray for Mr. Jew" is from Friederich Torberg's essay in Beckermann.

Chapter 16.

Most of the material on the origins and early activities of the National Socialist Party in Austria comes from Pauley, although Fest also provides some interesting data including the chillingly prescient statement from Richard Jung, "This Hitler will some day be our greatest." Botz describes the Moedling incident and the killing of Mohapel, while Bettauer's assassination is covered most completely by Hall but also by Pauley, Moser, and many others. The breaking up of the Nazi rally in the Bergenland by Jewish youths was told to me by Moser who comes from that province.

Pauley, Gedje and Moser are my chief sources on the 1925 Zionist Congress incident, with Moser supplying the statement of the CSU leader complimenting the Nazis. Weisgal's report is in *The Jewish Advocate* of August 27, 1925. Von Klemperer is my primarily source for the sharpening rift between the two major parties and for most of the statements by Seipel, although Seipel's claim that "for me there is no Jewish question" and his semi-disavowal of the anti-Semitic portions of his party's program comes from Moser in *Austriaca*. All of these writers, along with Canetti and Clare, describe the storming of the Palace of Justice and its aftermath, but figures on the number of dead vary slightly from one to the other.

Chapter 17.

The parliamentary interchanges are from Spira. Von Klemperer mentions the *Heimwehr*'s growing attachment to fascism and its repudiation of the "liberal capitalist economy." Ernst Epier tells of his school days in Beckermann, while Esther Menczer tells in an interview of the silent resistance of the thirteen-year-old girls, of whom she was one, against their anti-Semitic teacher.

My primary but by no means exclusive source for the Halsman case is the short book published by the *Österreichischen Liga für Menschenrechte*. Other material comes from Ross (Ruzicka) and Meysels, as well as from various newspaper clippings unearthed by my research assistant, Gwen Moser, plus the June 1979 obituary of Halsman in *The New York Times*. I should point out that although there is no question of Halsman's innocence (indeed Hans Ruzicka returned to Austria in the 1960s and got the Austrian government to officially acknowledge it), the case is somewhat complex and confusing and discrepancies appear between the three accounts of it from which I draw.

As to the growth of Zionism, Schechter describes the annual march to Herzl's grave, while Kollek tells of young people campaigning for the movement. Maderegger reports the change in the *Gemeinde*'s requirements for voting.

William Stickler describes Friedmann, and Shimron continues to be my main authority on Chajes and the Chajes gymnasium, although the information on the Rabbi's funeral comes from Ashtor. All the material on Robert Stickler during this period, including his interchange with Weizmann and his short speech to the *Gemeinde*'s board of directors, comes from Fraenkel (1950). The information on Jewish births, conversions, etc., comes from figures in a 1936 *Gemeinde* report which the present executive director Dr. Hodek kindly made available to me.

Marek in Beckermann tells of Zionist youth groups raiding each other and the prediliction of his own group for ping pong. Berman gives the figures on *Alliyah*, Toch tells of his adventures in Beckermann, while Epier in the same book mentions the three lonely Gentile members of the Leopoldstadt Social Democratic youth group.

Chapter 18.

Pauley supplies figures on the Depression in Austria and chronicles the growth of Austrian Nazism. For the failure of the Customs Union and the ensuing failure of the Kreditanstalt, however, I have drawn also on Anderson who recounts these events from an economist's point of view, and from Wechsberg who describes the encounter betwen Schober and Baron Louis. Seipel's activities and all of his statements come from von Klemperer. The *Heimwehr*'s attitude toward the Jews and the statements of Starhemberg about them are from Spira, who is also the source for Otto Bauer's comment on "The Christian Social voter who yesterday. . ." The University's attempt to segregate Jewish students is described by Moser in his article in Lohrmann and also by Mikoletzky, while the statement by the Bishop of Linz can be found in Spira along with his comment about letting Nazism in by the back door. The pan-Europa meeting is described in Varon's 1984 article and his experience at the Medical School in his 1974 article, which also gives some information on the League of Jewish Front Fighters. Other sources for the League are Rosenkranz, Maderegger, Weinzierl, Hilsenrad, and Ellen Sommer Taxer. Both Moser, in *Austriaca*, and Maderegger give tallies on the *Gemeinde* vote in 1932, but the descriptions of the scene in the nearby cafe and Stricker's statement, "Tell Friedmann to speak. . ." are from Fraenkel (1950).

Chapter 19.

Pauley provides a useful outline of political events, especially those concerning the Nazis, during this period, while Maderegger chronicles the increase in anti-Semitism and the Jewish response to it as well as to the new Dollfuss constitution. Other sources include Gunther's *Vanity Fair* article on Dollfuss's height, background, and his actions as chancellor prior to the civil war; Spira for the statements by Czermak, Schmitz and the *Arbeiter Zeitung* as well as for the interchange between Deutsch and a hostile parliamentarian; Rosenkranz for "the after effects of his Jewishness. . ."; Moser in *Austriaca* for Fey's assurances and the response of Jewish Front fighters as well as for the Union's name change; Levin for Hitler's subsidy to Austrian Nazis; Zweig for young Nazis slinking across the border and Nazi intimidation of Austrian civil servants; Meysels for Dollfuss and Zuckerkandl; Mikoletzky for Hitler's greeting to "the German brother people in Austria" and for general background; Schubert for tourist hotels with only five or ten rooms rented (interview); Clark for the quote from Freud; Michaelis for Mussolini, Goldman and the new constitution; Clare for the "Heil Dollfuss" parade in which he took part as a Boy Scout; and Tartakower's article in Fraenkel on the international conference at, and the pledge of outside aid for, the Vienna *Gemeinde*.

The description of the civil war is based primarily on accounts in Pauley, Gedje, Clare, and Gunther's novel. (Though fiction, Gunther's book is quite factual in recounting actual events and in giving actual figures such as Vienna's land ownership, bank accounts, traffic lights, etc.) Schwarz's article in Fraenkel (1967) supplies the statement "Where were the Jewish intellectuals . . ." while Zweig's admonition to Zuckmeyer is related in Zuckmeyer.

Chapter 20.

This chapter draws heavily on Maderegger, and most of the expressions of anti-Semitism and many of the Jewish responses to it come from her scholarly book. Other sources, besides those indicated in the text itself, include Pauley on problems of Austrian Nazis, Prittie and Lewy on persecution of the Catholic Church in Germany, Weinzierl on Innitzer's and Harrand's pro-Jewish activities, Stadler on German subsidies to Kunschak, Michaelis on Mussolini's assurances to Goldman, and Moser (interview) on Schuschnigg toning down the Passion Play in Innsbruck.

Leitner and Morgenstern, in their respective articles in Lohrmann, describe Jewish accomplishments in medicine and in sports, but the May 13, 1935 issue of *Box Ring* offers further material on Willi Kurtz while Schechter describes Hugo Meisl on the soccer field. The sports department of the *Boston Herald* kindly computed for me the total number of Austria's pre-war Olympic medals.

Other sources include Clare for "show goys" in the Boy Scouts and for Shaukel's poem that was made into music; Schuschnigg (1971) for Czermak's statement on the "true Jews"; Walter for his dinner with Schuschnigg; Bentwich in Fraenkel (1967) on the school segregation edict and Leftwich in the same book on the transfer of the *Neue Freie Presse* to Gentiles; Gstein on the insurance company dismissals and on destitute Jews needing *Gemeinde* assistance; Spira for the *Arbeiter Zeitung* statement; Rosenkranz (1978) for the Union's efforts to block Löwenherz's appointment and for figures on declining Jewish population (on this last point also see Berman and the *Gemeinde*'s report for 1936). In interviews, Papo and Meisels have told me of life in the University, Varon has pointed out the poor prospects for medical students, and William Stricker has explained his father's reluctance to support Löwenherz.

The founding of the New Zionist Organization is mentioned by Maderegger, Penkower, and others, but I have found Schechter's book the most useful, for he describes the role of Koestler, the invitation to Begin, the rally on plebiscite day, and many other details. However, Perl mentions the boycott of German goods while Eliahu Fried has told me of the fist fights with other Zionist youths.

Chapter 21.

Schuschnigg in his 1946 book provides interesting and informative accounts of his meetings with Mussolini and Hitler, and of his other foreign policy efforts. Pauley outlines the Chancellor's growing problems with domestic as well as German Nazism, including the two anti-Schuschnigg jokes.

Other sources are Clare for interpretation of the 1936 accords, the newspaper announcement about the consul-general from Jerusalem, the New Year's Day newspaper stories calling for a halt to immigration, the statement from an Austrian diplomat, "They began to treat us like living corpses," and for the general mood of the last days including the show at Cafe Simplicissimus, mistaken molesting of Italian dignataries, etc.; Gedye for material on Schuschnigg's base of support, his meeting with Hitler (Gedye's is probably the best account) Schuschnigg's last-minute overtures to labor leaders, etc.; Maderegger for the Zionist paper calling the Catholic Church "the most important bulwark. . .". Sigmund Freud's congratulatory note to Eitinger; the *Juedische Presse*'s warning against panic; and *Die Wahrheit*'s "Hear, Jews of Austria, you are Austrians!" Moser supplies a useful summary of organized responses to the developing crisis including the statements of the Union and the Front. Fighters following the 1936 accords, the Jewish Telegraphic Agency's reassuring report following the Schuschnigg-Hitler meeting, and the checks from Friedmann for the Schuschnigg plebiscite, etc.

Perl and Rosenkranz, along with von Weisl in Fraenkel (1967), describe the Betar's blockade running. Rosenkranz (1978) and Moser cover the *Gemeinde*'s activities. Rosenkranz also describes the Zionist and cultural events in the winter of 1938 and gives a breakdown on Jewish organizations at that time. Also see von Papen for Austrian responses to the Wels parade and von Neurath's visit; Spira for the statement of the Social Democrats following the Hitler-Schuschniggg meeting; Karner for an overview of the Austrian economy; Weinzierl on Nazis beating Catholic youths; Zuckmeyer on Northern Lights and Nazi use of children for provocative demonstrations; Ashtor for statements by Stricker and Frankfurter; and Tur-Sinai's article in Fraenkel (1967) for his statement on Vienna's "complacent Zionists."

Mrs. Papo has told me of her husband's reasons for not leaving Vienna and, together with Mrs. Korelek, has described the replacement of Latin-rooted words with German ones. They also told me the anti-Zionist joke that was so popular with the integrationists. Eliahu Fried has described Schuschnigg's visit to the Betar camp — he was at the camp at the time — and also Jabotinsky's last Vienna speech. (Fried says that his father, whom he had taken to the talk, commented afterward, "He [Jabotinsky] certainly knows how to speak but of course what he said is all nonsense.")

Chapter 22.

Rosenkranz's book has been the most important source of material for this chapter. Much of the terrorization of the Jews and the Jewish efforts to cope with it comes from his work. English readers will find in his lengthy article in Fraenkel (1967) a good summary of these events, while his article for the Yad Vashem proceedings gives a fuller picture of Löwenherz and more explicitly credits him with the suggestion of the centralized emigration operation which expedited the departure of Jews.

Gedye, Hilsenrad, Varon, Levin, Shirer, and Bentwich also contribute to the picture of the *Blizverfolgung,* as does Lauterstein, who in *The Water Castle*, mentions the urinating on the heads of the Jewish women in Währing. (Although the book is a novel, Mrs. Lauterstein has told me that the incident actually occurred. She was living in Währing as a young girl at the time.) Lauterstein along with Weinzierl mentions the treatment of half-Jewish school children and Weinzierl also gives the total figures on the *Joint*'s expenditures in Vienna, although Rosenkranz, Levin, and others describe its activities more fully.

Rosenkranz and Gedye describe the plundering of Jews while Reitlinger and Luza give Göring's reaction. Gedye supplies the quotation from the London *Times* on the Jewish community's impoverization. Perl is the main source for the emigration activities he was involved in, and though his description of these events may at times seem self-glamorizing, briefer accounts in Penkhower, Levin, and others tend to bear him out. Perl also supplies information on the Gestapo's May roundup including the questions asked of the Jews and the scene involving Eichmann prior to the dispatch of rounded-up Jews to Dachau.

Moser gives the full figures on Jewish suicides in his contribution to *Wien 1938* published by the *Verein für Geschichte der Stadt Wien*. Levin describes the scene between Eichmann and Gerson Friedmann, supplies the quotation from Eichmann's letter to his superiors, and mentions the Jewish man asked by the Gestapo to help establish law and order in Vienna. Hans Habe in his novel on the Evian conference quotes the Nazi newspapers gloating over its failure, while Hilsenrad describes the reaction of the Vienna Jews, Ernst Epier quotes his grandmother on Hitler only hating the Polish Jews, and Bentwich describes the *Gemeinde*'s newspaper, including its advertisements. Peters and Martin Freud recount the Freud family's experiences with the Gestapo.

In terms of interviews and correspondence, I am grateful to Harry Chameides for information on Jews joining tourist tours to get out of Vienna (his own mother used such a strategy to escape); to Rhoda Kalman for describing her mother's experience in buying a bogus South American visa to get a travel visa; and to William Geisler, Mrs. Ellen Sommer Taxer, and Harry and Fritzi Zohn for the material on their families used at the end of the chapter. Friedel's suicide is covered by Meysels in his book, and Meysels has confirmed to me that the critic really did shout "Out of my way" before leaping to his death.

Chapter 23.

Rosenkranz provides the most detailed description of the deteriorating conditions, emigration procedures and other actions taken by the *Gemeinde* to cope with the situation, and the horrors of *Kristallnacht*. Mautner's experiences come from his book. Hilsenrad describes the storming of the synagogue on Rosh Hashonah, the jamming of the men into the room on *Kristallnacht* and the suicides which resulted, the granting of instant divorces, and the young mothers offering their babies for adoption. She also describes the Zionist youth farm which she visited, and the retraining programs in which she participated. (She learned to make corsets, but when she came to America she found that here they made them quite differently and all her training was useless.)

Other sources include Weinzierl for denunciations of Jews including the incidents of elderly Jews being arrested, the Gestapo report on Jewish proletarianization, the exhibition "The Eternal Jew," and supplementary material on emigration, *Kristallnacht,* etc.; Penkower for formation of Mossad le Aliya Bet and its activities, the actions of the British regarding emigration to Palestine and the responses of leading Zionists and Zionist agencies to them and the quote from the Zionist official on the Vienna Jews living in a "Fool's Paradise" and "veritable hell"; Levin for the quote from Auerbach, the quote from the post-*Kristallnacht* Gestapo report on Jewish despair and Jewish conditions and activities generally; Perl for illegal emigration; and the *Illustrierte Neue Welt* of August 1986 for the report of the eight couples from the Leopoldstadt getting to England. I also had helpful interviews with Ditta Lowy, Joseph Meisels, and William Geisler. (The latter told me of the Nazis leaving the temple in the Ninth District untouched during *Kristallnacht,* thus correcting published accounts which maintain that all temples but the main one were destroyed.)

Chapter 24.

Rosenkranz's book describes the deportations including the activities of the JUPO and the two Brunners, the making of the lewd film, and the role of Aron Menczer. However, the statement, "Look, Mautner, at Hitler's inferior people" comes from a footnote in his article in Fraenkel (1967). Rabbi Wise's letter to William Stricker is reprinted in Fraenkel's 1950 book which also describes the condition of Robert Stricker and of Friedmann on their release; Hilsenrad describes the reaction of Jews to the urns from the concentration camps ("God be thanked, I have heard nothing!"); Levin reprints in English the first deportation announcement issued by the *Gemeinde* while Stadler quotes the Gestapo report, "The rest of the population knows hardly anything . . ."; Penkower reports the messenger from Poland and the *Gemeinde*'s reaction to his message ("Unmöglich"); Hilberg gives an account of Löwenherz's later call on Ebener, an event which, curiously, is not in Rosenkranz's book; Gilbert describes the shooting of Bosel, Beda's song contest at Buchenwald, and the cultural activities of the Vienna Jews in the Lodz ghetto, the latter account taken from the Lodz chronicle; Vogel gives the fullest account of Aron Menczer's last days in Vienna; while Moser reports on mass shootings of Vienna Jews in Riga and Minsk and adds to Rosenkranz's description of the lot of those Jews still in Vienna once the mass deportations ended.

In interviews, Max Diamant tells of life at the Doppel work camp and Aron Menczer's stay there; Ditta Lowy tells of the harsh conditions confronting the girls working in Germany — she did not volunteer but talked later with some who did – and Joseph Meisels recounts the incident involving the SS man's adopted daughter. Hilly Frost Barzilay has described in a letter to the author the trip to Israel which Aron Menczer conducted.

The section on Theresienstadt is based on written accounts in Reitlinger, Rosenkranz, Hilberg, Gilbert, and Spies and on interviews with Sidoni Korelek, who was Murmelstein's secretary, Lisa Gidron, Kurt Wiegel, Ditta and Louis Lowy, and Leonard and Edith Ehrlich. The Ehrlichs were not in Theresienstadt themselves but, in addition to extensive interviews with Murmelstein, they have also interviewed the engineer assigned to build the projected gas chamber.

Chapter 25.

Göring's comment "Our last march . . ." plus the promotions of Guido Smith and Schuschnigg's own bodyguard are in Schuschnigg (1946); the teacher and school secretary as secret Nazi's comes from Papo (interview); the incident of the Salzburg tobacconist comes from Zuckmeyer; Ruzicka's comment is in Ross; Renner's "from the heart" comes from Mikoletzky who is one of the two historians who dispute Renner's excuse for the plebecite endorsement. (The other is Josef Buttinger whom Mikoletzky quotes to this effect. However, as the text indicates, Luza has come up with the most complete account of Renner's action); von Papen and Fest note Hitler's original plan for a puppet state; Haffner mentions the exodus of German writers; Vaughan recounts von Karajan's Nazi history; Lang told of Goebbels' offer to him in a filmed interview which has been shown on various occasions; Botz's research on Austrian Nazi party membership was reported in the November 1986 issue of *Illustrierte Neue Welt*; and Varon's statement on "rape of Austria" comes from his 1955 article.

Gilbert discusses the quieting down of Nazi attacks on Jews in Germany, and Fest and Haffner point out the failure of the April 1, 1934 boycott. Fest provides the quote from Hitler, while the quote from *Das Schwarze Korps* comes from Grunberger. Martin Freud mentions the telegram "Please send us Jews," and Levin mentions Eichmann's frustrations with Austrian Nazis. The two incidents of German officers repudiating street incidents are from Gedye, while the stories of Germans shifting Jews to a less crowded cell and of picking up the ailing Jewish woman are from Rosenkranz. Max Alter tells of once-friendly teachers suddenly spouting anti-Semitism and Rosenkranz reports the ear slicing incident. Other sources are Gedye for the open-air market expropriations, Zuckmeyer for the play rehearsal with Hörbigger and Wessley, Massler for the incident of the two young professors, and Hilsenrad for the story of the Jewish woman and her closet Nazi husband.

Varon's statement on passing through Germany is from his 1955 article; the Jews passing through Stettin is from Rosenkranz; the Wiesenthal comment on *Kristallnacht* is from *Der Spiegel*; Perl quotes the American Consul's report from Leipzig; Gilbert gives the reaction in Baden-Baden; and Engelman the reaction in Dusseldorf. Weinzierl quotes the Gestapo report, "We could scarcely hold back the crowd . . ." while both she and Levin cite the Gestapo report on the population's subsequent uneasiness over "illegality." For Baeck's experiences see Neuemark; for Reisz's comment on his trip to Berlin and for the actions of the Nazi women's organization see Rosenkranz; for the demonstration of Aryan wives in Berlin see Weinzierl; and for Henrietta von Shirach's effort see Hilberg. See Hilberg for the soap rumor; Meissl for Teuber's statement (it appears on the back of the book under *Zeitzeugen*); the Wiesenthal Center's Information Bulletin 26 (January 31, 1987) for the quote from the kindergarden assistant; Luza for the number of Austrians in the SS; and Krausnick for the overall figures on the SS. Most of the material on Austrian participation in the Holocaust comes from Wiesenthal's memorandum and letter, but the quote from the SS man's diary comes from Weinzierl while Hilberg describes Loehr's record along with Böhme's. Maas, who spent the war years in Holland, mentions the "Danube Club," Gilbert points up the role of the Sauer factory, and Wiesthal in an interview spoke of how assiduously the Austrian engineer kept the gas ovens in repair. Although most of the data on Mauthausen comes from Raditsch, Maas also discusses the camp while Eckstein provides figures on its Jewish inmates and gives the camp's Gestapo classification for harshness.

In addition to those cited in the text, Rosenkranz and Maas give instances of individual acts of kindness. Weinzierl recounts the stories of the Austrian heroes but English readers will find an abbreviated account in Maas. The report on the latest "*Gerechte*," the retired Innsbruck civil servant, comes from the August/September 1986 issue of the *Illustrierte Neue Welt*. For Judge Bejske's observation see Meyer, and for the network that smuggled out Jews see Engelmann who spent the last months of the war in Dachau as a result of his participation in it. The joke about the Jew hidden in the basement was told me by Varon.

Chapter 26.

The response of Cardinal Innitzer and the Austrian Catholic Church to the *Anschluss* comes principally from Lewy, Prittie and the March 13 edition of the *Reichspost*, with von Papen supplying some additional details about the Cardinal's call on Hitler. Prittie and Lewy also report the negative reaction from German Catholic Church leaders and the Vatican. Both Rosenkranz and

Weinzierl describe the Church's attitudes and actions toward its Jewish parishioners, with Weinzierl furnishing more details on the Church's efforts. Maas offers English readers a summary of these activities. For German Catholic Church leaders speaking out against deportations, see Gilbert and Prittie. The quote from the *Gemeinde*'s newspapers saying "Assimilation has become impossible," is found in Rosenkranz, while the story of Sister Fuhrman comes from Gilbert.

Most of the material concerning Protestant responses in Austria to the Nazi persecutions comes from Rosenkranz, although Weinzierl mentions the theology professor who helped Jews. She also supplies the statement from Pastor Ivarsson. The data on German Protestants comes from Bracher, Prittie, and Gilbert, with the latter furnishing the quote from the Bishop of Würtemberg.

Chapter 27.

See Karner for falling unemployment figures; Rosenkranz for the impact on the textile industry; Gedye for Austrians resisting German work standards and Göring's exhortation, "You have to prove to the world . . ."; Gedye and Mikoletzsky on shortages; Mikoletzky on denuncations by eager job seekers, and Bürckel's response; and Pauley, Barker, Maas, and others on Austria's loss of national identity.

Luza chronicles the crackdown on the Catholic Church but the poster affixed to the wall of the Leopoldstadt Church is from Kalman (interview). Pauley, Weinzierl, Maas, Barker, and Stadler, supplemented by Schubert (interview), describe Catholic responses and the resulting raid on the Chancellery.

See Barker, Pauley, Weinzierl and Maas for the Allied foreign ministers' statement, the rise in Austrian disgruntlement, and the emergence of Austrian resistance, but see a review of three books about Austria in the October 9, 1986 *New York Review of Books* for Roosevelt and Churchill regarding Austrians as a "jolly people." See Mikoletzky on the closing of the Burg Theater and food rations; Maas for a complete breakdown of Austrian war dead; Gilbert, Rosenkranz, and Hilberg for the driving of Hungarian Jews into Austria (the Eisenerz stone-throwing is in Hilberg); Volume I of *Wiederstand und Verfolgung in Oberösterreich*, published by the Documentation Center for the Austrian Resistance in Vienna, for the water and apples given to prisoners marching to Gunskirchen; Bentwick in Fraenkel (1967) for Jewish soldiers parachuting into Austria; and Gilbert for Eichmann's last deportation.

Prelude and Chapter 28

Sources for the Prelude include Zuckmeyer for Oscar Karweis; *The New York Times* of October 7, 1986 (obituary page) for Rudolph Flesh; Harry Zohn (interview) for most of the other prominent exiles; Ashtor for professors at Hebrew University; Morgenstern in Lohrmann for athletic accomplishments; Juhn in Fraenkel (1967) for the Hakoah reunion, Charles Richter (interview) for Adas Yereim; Clare for Dr. Paul Klaar; Taxer (interview) for General Sommer; Hodek, Rosenkranz and William Stricker (interviews) for Löwenherz; Leonard and Edith Ehlich (interviews) for Murmelstein; Rosenkranz (1978) for Reisz; and Moser as well as Tartakower in Fraenkel (1967) for rebirth of the *Gemeinde*.

Sources for Chapter 28 include Lauterstein (1985) for "Remembering to Forget"; Bernhard for erasing party membership from tombstones; Pollak for the essay on Kunschak; Pauley for the ex-Nazi's suppressed manuscript (its title, he says, is *Hauptman Leopold* or *Captain Leopold*); Kramer for Czernin's school experience; Varon (1985) for remembering Mauthausen and (1955) for reactions on his return visit; *Der Spiegel* of April 14, 1986 for the quote from Bünzel; and Rathkolb's essay in Meissl for the British officer's observation, " . . . mislaid the Hitler years." (It is quoted in English.)

Stiefel provides the first statement of the provisional Austrian government along with the most complete account of its initial prosecution of Nazis, but see Rathkob in Meissl for the poll of ex-Nazis, Weinzil in Meissl on the dismissal of professors, Vaughan for von Karajan, and Holzbauer for "Angel with a Trumpet." For English readers, Barker gives a good description of Austrian politics in the 40s and 50s, while Lindvai and Sacher furnish details on the more important trials of ex-Nazis. See the former for Novak's statement and the latter for Rabbi Eisenberg's telegram.

See Teuber for the Salzburg displaced persons camp; Moser for the relief act for concentration camp returnees; Spira and Braunthal for Socialists discouraging Jewish leaders from returning; Spira for the People's Party election poster; Jellinek's article in Fraenkel (1967) for compensation proceedings and his comment about them; Kramer for Weiss's opinion poll; Lindvai for pro-Nazi student organization; and *The New York Times*, September 18, 1986, for Holland's article. The story of the music teacher who won't ride in the same elevator with his Jewish neighbors was told to me by Halpert.

The material on Kreisky comes principally from Spira, who supplies all the Kreisky quotes as well as the one from Daim, and from interviews with Schubert, Papo, and Halpert. The anti-Kreisky joke was told me by Mahum Gross.

Chapter 29.

See Kramer for Austrian jokes on scandals; the March 30, 1986 *Kurier* for Cardinal Stickler's statement; and the August 3/4, 1985 *Salzburger Nachrichten* for "Der Skandal liegt nicht nur beim Wein" by Viktor Herman, an interesting article which assesses the wine scandal within the context of contemporary Austrian culture. See Peyser on Bernstein's success with the Vienna State Opera, although the story in the footnote was told me by an Austrian journalist; Koppensteiner for Austria's economic status and the role of politics in getting apartments; *Die Presse* of March 28, 1986 for separate stories on the Arab bankers' convention and on Austria's armaments business; the Sunday *New York Times* of January 12, 1986 for comment on Blecha's absolution of Libya; and *ORF* of October 10, 1986 for the comment, "The newly erected centers of Jewish life . . ."

Harry Chameides told me of Matjeka's proposal while Halpert, among others, mentioned the good contact Jews now enjoy with devout Catholics. Both Spira and Stiefel describe anti-Fascist demonstrations. The statements from Catholic sources condemning the conduct and/or outcomes of the war criminals' trials come from Lindvai, while the *Illustrierte Neue Welt* of April 1986 describes the Catholic pilgrimage to Yad Vashem. *Die Presse* of July 5, 1985 reported the results of the opinion poll released at the conference in Norway and on July 27/28 published Galande's reply in its Letters column. The *Illustrierte Neue Welt* published in March 1987 the National Bank's poll and Marin's response, and in May it reported on the hastily-called symposium and gave Weinzierl's statement. For *Der Spiegel*'s account of the Austrian response to the Waldheim ban see "Österreich's Juden haben wieder Angst" in its July 6, 1987 issue. *Die Gemeinde* of March 7, 1987 contains letters from anti-anti-Semitic Austrians, a story on Timma Brauer, and the advertisement by the Jewish mother, while the December 1986 *Illustrierte Neue Welt* published a summary of Jewish life and activities in contemporary Vienna.

Epilogue.

See Gstein for Torberg's statement on Austrian anti-Semitism; Spiel for Bahr's opinion on Austrian abusiveness; *Profil* of April 1, 1986 for Dr. Cermack's condemnation of hospital regulations regarding children; Kramer for Peter Czernin's experience with Waldheim; Meissl for Knoll's essay regarding his father's experience with de-Nazification; Bernard Holland's "Through Vienna's Glass Darkly" in the September 18, 1986 issue of *The New York Times* for Szell's opinion of Vienna; *Die Presse* of July 5, 1985 for the poll on Austrian attitudes toward Austria's independent existence; and Hilberg for von dem Bach's statement on Jews' lack of organization. Other helpful interviews were with Rosenkranz, Varon, and Massler.

Bibliography

Anderson, Benjamin M. *Economics and the Public Welfare.* Indianapolis, 1972.

Arendt, Hannah. *Antisemitism.* New York, 1968. (Although published separately, this is part of her larger work, *The Origins of Totalitarianism.*)

Ashtor, Eliahu. "Viennese Jewry in the 1920's." In *Kurt Grunwald at Eighty.* Jerusalem, 1981.

Barker, Elizabeth. *Austria 1918-1972.* Coral Gables, 1973.

Beckermann, Ruth (editor). *Die Mazzesinsel.* Vienna and Munich, 1984.

Ben-Sasson, H. H. (editor). *A History of the Jewish People.* London, 1976.

Berlin, Isaiah. *Personal Impressions.* New York, 1981.

Berman, Tamar. *Productivierungsmythen und Antisemitismus: Ein Soziologische Studie.* Vienna, 1973.

Bermant, Chaim. *The Jews.* New York, 1977.

Bernhard, Thomas. *Gathering Evidence: A Memoir.* New York, 1986.

Bettauer, Hugo. *The City Without Jews.* Philadelphia, 1926.

Bihl, Wolfdieter. "Die Juden in der Habsburgermonarchie 1848-1918." *Studia Judaica Austriaca* 8 (1980).

Bilroth, Theodor. *Medical Sciences in German Universities.* New York, 1924.

Bloch, Josef S. *My Reminiscences.* Vienna and Berlin, 1923.

Botz, Gerhard. *Gewalt in der Politik.* Vienna, 1983.

Boyer, John. *Political Radicalism in Late Imperial Vienna: Origins of the Christian Social Movement, 1848-1897.* Chicago and London, 1981.

Bracher, Karl Dietrich. *The German Dictatorship.* New York, 1970.

Brandstaller, Trautl. "Juden Heute in Wien." *ORF Nachlese.* December 1986.

Braunthal, J. *The Tragedy of Austria.* London, 1948.

Bunzl, John and Beund Marin. *Antisemitismus in Österreich.* Innsbruck, 1983.

Canetti, Elias. *The Play of the Eyes.* New York, 1986.

_____. *The Torch in My Ear.* New York, 1982.

Clark, Ronald W. *Freud: The Man and the Cause.* New York, 1980.

Cohen, Israel. *Theodor Herzl.* New York and London, 1959.

Cowles, Virginia. *The Kaiser.* New York, 1963.

Dedijer, Vladimir. *The Road to Sarajevo*. New York, 1966.

Delloff, Linda-Marie. "Seeking the Truth in Austria." *The Christian Century*, August 27-September 3, 1986.

Der Spiegel. Cover story on Austrian fascism. April 14, 1986.

Dobrosycki, Luczon (editor). *Chronicle of the Lodz Ghetto*. New Haven, 1984.

Drucker, Peter F. *Adventures of a Bystander*. New York, 1978.

Eckstein, Benjamin. "Jews in the Mauthausen Concentration Camp." Yad Vashem: *Fourth International Congress Proceedings*, 1980.

Engelman, Bernt. *In Hitler's Germany*. New York, 1986.

Feis, Herbert. *Europe: The World's Banker 1870-1914*. New York, 1965.

Fest, Joachim C. *Hitler*. New York, 1975.

Fischer, Brigitte B. *My European Heritage*. Brookline, Massachusetts, 1986.

Fischer, Ernst. *An Opposing Man*. New York, 1974.

Fraenkel, Josef (editor). *The Jews of Austria*. London, 1967.

_____ (editor). *Robert Stricker*. London, 1950. (This book was privately printed by a group of Stricker's friends and admirers.)

Freud, Martin. *Sigmund Freud: Man and Father*. New York, 1958.

Fuchs, Albert. *Geistige Stromungen in Österreich 1867-1918*. Vienna, 1949.

Funder, Friedrich. *Von Gestern ins Heute*. Vienna, 1952.

Gedye, Richard. *Adam Muller Gutterbrunn and the Aryan Theater of Vienna, 1898-1903*. Göttingen, 1973.

Gilbert, Martin. *The Holocaust*. New York, 1985.

Goebbels, Josef. *The Goebbels Diaries*. London, 1948.

Goerlitz, Walter. *History of the German General Staff, 1657-1945*. New York, 1963.

Gold, Hugo. *Geschichte der Juden in Wien*. Tel Aviv, 1966.

Goldhammer, Leo. *Die Juden Wiens: Eine statistische Studie*. Vienna and Leipzig, 1927.

Grunberger, Richard. *The 12-Year Reich: A Social History of Nazi Germany, 1933- 1945*. New York, 1971.

Grunwald, Max. *Vienna*. Philadelphia, 1936.

Gstein, Heinz. *Judisches Wien*. Vienna and Munich, 1984.

Gunther, John. "Chancellor Dollfuss: Flyweight Champion of Europe." *Vanity Fair*, December 1933.

_____. *The Lost City*. New York, 1964.

Haffner, Sebastian. *The Meaning of Hitler*. Cambridge, 1983.

Hall, Murray G. *Der Fall Bettauer*. Vienna, 1978.

Hausler, Wolfgang. *Das Österreichische Judentum*. Vienna, 1974.

Hawlik, Johannes. *Der Bürgerkaiser*. Vienna and Munich, 1985.

Herzl, Theodor. *Diaries*. (Edited and translated by Marvin Lowenthal). New York, 1956.

Hilberg, Raul. *The Destruction of the European Jews* (revised ed.). New York, 1985.

Hilsenrad, Helen. *Brown Was the Danube*. South Brunswick, New Jersey, 1966.

Hitler, Adolf. *Mein Kampf*. Los Angeles, 1981.

Holland, Bernard. "Through Vienna's Glass, Darkly." *The New York Times*, September 18, 1986.

Hollensteiner, Johannes. *Gutachten über die staatliche Annerkennung orthodoxer-israelitischer Religionsgemeinden*. Vienna, June 3, 1935.

Holzbauer, A. J. "1945 — Davor/Danach Im Kino." In *Arbeitsmaterialien* (Program Book) issued by the Museum of the 20th Century, Vienna, in conjunction with the presentation of a series of Nazi films in 1986.

Jacob, Heinrich Eduard. "Fledermaus und Borsenkrach." *Program Book for Die Fledermaus.* Published by the Vienna State Opera, 1985.

Janik, Alan and Stephen Toulmin. *Wittgenstein's Vienna.* 1973.

Jenks, William A. *Vienna and the Young Hitler.* New York, 1960.

Johnston, William M. *The Austrian Mind: An Intellectual and Social History, 1848-1938.* Berkley, 1972.

Karner, Stefan. "Zür Sozialen Lage der österreichischen Arbeiterschaft unter dem Nationalsozialismus." *Aufrisse, 3* (1981).

Kollek, Teddy. *For Jerusalem.* New York, 1978.

Koppensteiner, Jurgen. *Österreich.* Munich, 1983.

Kramer, Jane. "Letter from Europe." *The New Yorker,* June 30, 1986.

Krausnick, Helmut. *Anatomy of the SS State.* New York, 1965.

Kreisky, Bruno. "Wie es Kam . . ." *Der Sozialistische Kampfer,* January/February 1986.

Lauterstein, Ingeborg. *Vienna Girl.* New York, 1986.

_____. *The Water Castle.* Boston, 1980.

Lendvai, Paul. "The New Austria and the Old Nazis." *Commentary,* September 1967.

Levin, Nora. *The Holocaust: The Destruction of European Jewry, 1933-1943.* New York, 1968.

Lewy, Guenter. *The Catholic Church and Nazi Germany.* London, 1964.

Lohrmann, Klaus (editor). *1000 Jahre Österreichisches Judentum.* Vienna, 1982. (Exhibition catalogue issued by the Institute of Jewish Studies of the University of Vienna. Contains several articles by respected scholars.)

Luza, Radomis. *Austro-German Relations in the Anschluss Era.* Princeton, 1975.

Lyons, Reverend James R. "Vienna: One Man's View." *Newsletter of the National Christian Leadership Conference for Israel.* Fall 1986.

Maas, Walter B. *Country Without a Name.* New York, 1979.

Maderegger, Sylvia. *Die Juden im Österreicheschen Standestaat, 1934-1938.* Vienna-Salzburg-Geyer, 1973.

Mahler, Raphael. *A History of Modern Jewry.* New York and London, 1971.

Marek, George R. *The Eagles Die.* New York, 1974.

Meisel, Gerhard. "Von Januskopf zür Wasserkopf." In the Catalogue of the 1985 Exhibition, *Traum und Wirklichkeit: Wien, 1870-1930.*

Meissl, Sebastian, et al. (editors). *Verdrängte Schuld, Verfehlte Sühne: Entnaziführung im Österreich, 1945-1955.* Vienna, 1986.

Mendes-Flohr, Paul R. et al. *The Jew in the Modern World.* New York, 1980.

Meyer, Ernie. "The Making of a Righteous Gentile." *The Jerusalem Post,* January 16, 1987.

Meysels, Lucian O. *In Meinem Salon ist Österreich.* Vienna and Munich, 1985.

Mikoletzky, Hanns Leo. *Österreichische Zeitgeschichte.* Vienna, 1969.

Miller, Judith. "Erasing the Past." *The New York Times Sunday Magazine,* November 16, 1986.

Mitchell, B. R. *European Historical Statistics, 1750-1970.* New York, 1975.

Monson, Karen. *Alma Mahler: Muse to Genius.* London, 1983.

Morton, Frederic. *A Nervous Splendor: Vienna 1888/1889.* London, 1979.

Moser, Jonny. "Antisemitismus und Zionismus in Wien des Fin de Siécle." *Traum und Wirklichkeit.* Exhibition Catalogue, 1985.

_____. "Die Katastrophe der Juden in Österreich 1938-1945 — Ihre Voraussitzunger und ihre Überwindung." *Studia Judaica Austriaca V,* 1977.

Neimark, Anne E. *One Man's Valor: Leo Baeck and the Holocaust.* New York, 1986.

Österreichischen Liga für Menscherechte. Der Fall Halsman. Vienna, 1931.

Papen, Franz von. *Memoirs.* New York, 1953.

Pauley, Bruce F. *Hitler and the Forgotten Nazis.* Chapel Hill, 1981.

Pawel, Ernst. *The Nightmare of Reason: A Life of Franz Kafka.* New York, 1984.

Penkower, Monty Noam. *The Jews Were Expendable.* Urbana and Chicago, 1983.

Perl, William R. *The Four-Front War.* New York, 1978.

Peters, Uwe Herrik. *Anna Freud: A Life Dedicated to Children.* New York, 1985.

Peyser, Joan. *Bernstein.* New York, 1987.

Pick, Robert. *The Last Days of Imperial Vienna.* New York, 1976.

Pollak, Walter (editor). *Tausand Jahre Österreich* . Vienna, 1974.

Prittie, Terrence. *Germans Against Hitler.* Boston, 1964.

Rabitsch, Gisela. "Das KL Mauthausen." *Studien zür Geschichte der Konzentrationslager.* Institut für Zeitgeschichte, University of Stuttgart, 1970.

Richter, Charles. "The Vienna Kehileth." *Adas Yereim 25 Years Anniversary Journal,* 1967.

Rosenkranz, Herbert. "Austrian Jewry: Between Forced Emigration and Deportation." *Proceedings of the Third International Conference of Yad Vashem, 1977.*

_____. *Verfolgung und Selbstbehauptung: Die Juden in Österreich 1938-1945.* Vienna and Munich, 1938.

Ross, Martin H. (Hans Ruzicka). *Marrano.* Boston, 1976.

Rozenblit, Marsha L. *The Jews of Vienna, 1864-1914.* Albany, 1983.

Rubin, E. *140 Jewish Marshals, Generals, Admirals.* London, 1952.

Ruzicka, Hans. See listing under Martin H. Ross.

Sachar, Howard M. *Diaspora.* New York, 1985.

Sandgruber, Roman. "Der Grosse Krach." In the catalogue of the 1985 exhibition, *Traum und Wirklichkeit: Wien, 1870-1930.*

Schacht, Hjalmar. *Confessions of a Financial Wizard.* Boston, 1956.

Schechter, Edmund. *Viennese Vignettes.* New York, 1983.

Schnitzler, Arthur. *My Youth in Vienna.* New York, 1970.

Schorske, Carl E. *Fin-de-Siecle Vienna.* New York, 1980.

Schubert, Kurt. "Der Weg zur Katastrophe." *Studia Judaica* (1977).

Schuschnigg, Kurt von (Requiem). *New York, 1946.*

_____. *The Brutal Takeover.* London, 1971.

Shimron, Ben. *Das Chajes Realgymnasium in Wien: 1919-1938.* Unpublished manuscript, Tel Aviv.

Shirer, William L. *The Nightmare Years, 1930-1940.*

Simon, Walter B. "The Jewish Vote in Austria." *Leo Baeck Yearbook, 1971.*

Spiel, Hilde. *Vienna's Golden Autumn, 1866-1938.* London, 1987.

Spira, Leopold. *Feinbild "Jud."* Vienna, 1981.

Stadler, Karl R. *Austria.* New York, 1971.

Steed, Henry Wickham. *Through Thirty Years, 1892-1922: A Personal Narrative.* Garden City, New York, 1924.

Stewart, Desmond. *Theodor Herzl: Artist and Politician.* Garden City, New York, 1974.

Stiefel, Dieter. *Entnazifizierung in Österreich.* Vienna, 1981.

Stourzh, Gerald. "Galten die Juden als Nationalität Altösterreichs?" *Studia Judaica Austriaca X* (1984).

Sully, Melamie. *Political Parties and Elections in Austria.* London, 1981.

Tietze, Hans. *Die Juden Wiens.* Vienna, 1933.

Toland, John. *Adolf Hitler.* Garden City, New York, 1976.

Traum und Wirklichkeit: Wien 1870-1930. Catalog of the Exhibition, Vienna, 1985.

Varon, Benno Weiser. "How, Though Jewish, I Did Not Become a Doctor." *Midstream,* November 1978.

_____. "Nazis Sitting in the Peanut Gallery." *The Jewish Week and the American Examiner,* March 30, 1984.

_____. "Unsentimental Journey To Vienna." *Commentary*, July 1955.

_____. "Vienna Remembers Its Famous Jews (Thank God, They're Dead)." *Zionist Voice*, October 1985.

_____. "Vienna Revisited." *Midstream*, May 1966.

Vaughan, Roger. *Herbert von Karajan*. New York, 1986.

Vogel, Martin. "Jugend-Alijah Noar Wien." *Die Gemeinde* (Vienna), September 20, 1978.

Walter, Bruno. *Theme and Variations*. New York, 1952.

Wasserman, Jakob. *My Life as German and Jew*. New York, 1933.

Wechsberg, Joseph. *The Vienna I Knew*. Garden City, New York, 1979.

Weinzierl, Erika. *Zu Wenig Gerechte: Österreicher und Judenverfolgung, 1938-1945*. Revised edition. Graz and Vienna, 1985.

Weizmann, Chaim. *Trial and Error*. New York, 1949.

Wiesenthal, Simon. *Schuld und Sühne der NS-Täter aus Österreich*. Dokumentationszentrum des Judischer Verfolgter des Naziregimes. Vienna, October 12, 1966.

Wistrich, Robert S. *Socialism and the Jews*. East Brunswick, New Jersey, 1982.

Zarek, Otto. *Splendor and Shame*. New York, 1941.

Zohn, Harry. ". . . ich bin ein Sohn der deutschen Sprache nur . . ." Vienna and Munich, 1986.

_____. "Reaction of Vienna's Jews to Herzl's Zionist Quest." Paper delivered at the Herzl Symposium in Vienna, May 1985.

Zuckerman, Carl. *A Part of Myself*. New York, 1966.

Zweig, Stefan. *The World of Yesterday*. New York, 1943.

PERSONAL COMMUNICATIONS

In preparing this book, the author has interviewed and/or corresponded with the following persons:

Max Alter
Helly Frost Barzilay
Harry N. Chameides
Grete Cohen
Max M. Diamant
Edith Ehrlich
Leonard Ehrlich
Eliahu Fried
Raphael Gat
Richard Geehr
William Geisler
Lisa Gidron
Mahum Gross
Eva Guez
Marta Halpert
Fritz Hodek
Alfred Hoelzel
Rhoda Kalman
G.H. Kirsch
Sidoni Korelek
Kurt Lieber
Ditta Jedlinsky Lowy
Louis Lowy
Hilde Wang Massler

Joseph Meisels
Esther Menczer
Menachem Menczer
Mordecai Menzcer
Jacob Metzer
Lucian Meysels
Jonny Moser
Ehud Nahir
Charles Richter
Zeev Wilhelm Ritter
Viktor Rosenfeld
Herbert Rosenkranz
Bertram R. Schader
Kurt Schubert
Benyamin Shimron
Ernst Simon
Franz Singer
William Stricker
Ellen Sommer Taxer
Benno Weiser Varon
Simon Wiesenthal
Leon Zelman
Fritzi Zohn
Harry Zohn

Index

Adler, Alfred, 54

Adler, Friedrich, 137

Adler, Viktor, 6, l6, 37, 54, 89, 90-91, 94, 124, 125, 137, 142

Aguadas Israel (Zionist organization), 129, 161, 164, 235

Aktion Reinhard, 317

Albia (fraternal society), 73

Aleichem, Sholem, 164

Allies: misinterpretation of *Anschluss*, 332-334

Alvado, N.D., 129

American Board of Mission to the Jews, 328f

Andersen, Benjamin M., 371f-372f

Anschluss, 198-199, 202, 259-275, 332-334

Anti-Judaism, 65-66, 90-9l: *See also* Anti-Semitism; Judaism.

Anti-Semitism: in Austria, 168, 214, 306-322, 352, 366-375; campaigns used by Social Democrats, 160-161, 167; capitalism as factor of, 64-65; of Catholic Church, 98, 214, 369; causes, 63-67, 70-76; of Christian Social party, 157, 158, 168, 175, 177-178; in cultural circles, 108; demonstrations of by Nazis, 173; during World War I, 137-140; economy and, 71, 149-153; following World War I, 168; following World War II, 346-364; in France, 67; in Galicia, 35; German, 214, 366-367; and German Peoples' Day, 154; in Great Britain, 67; *Heimwehr* and, 182; Hitler's conversion to, 110-111, 245; of Jews, 55-58, 82-83, 90-91; Linz Program, 94; of Lueger, 106-107; Nazis and, 200; newspapers and, 107, 171, 221; organizations against, 82-83, 89-92, 93-99, 121-123, 155; organizations promoting, 86, 88-91, 93-99, 228-230; racial, 63-67, 71-72, 87-89, 94, 98-99, 115-118, 123, 159, 204, 214, 224; religious, 63, 65-66, 77-80, 87, 214-215; of Seipel, 145-146, 148; socialism and, 124; at University of Vienna, 72-74, 107, 204-205, 230; Zionism and, 116-118 *See also* Anti-Judaism

Arafat, Yassir, 354

Arendt, Hannah, 61, 67, 106

Arnstein family, 54

Arstein, Fanny von, 32, 37

Arnsteiner, Adam Isaac, 30

Arnstein-Eskeles bank, 32

Aryan race, 108: *Ahnenpass*, 243

Asch, Sholem, 127

Ashtor, Eliahu, 176

Assimilanten, See Jews, Integrationist

Auerbach, Moshe, 278

Auschwitz (concentration camp), 291, 294, 298, 299

Austria: and anti-Nazi movement, 223; anti-Semitism in, 168, 214, 306-322, 352, 366-375; and Bukovina Settlement, 128; bureaucracy of, 16-17; characteristics of citizens, 10, 16-17, 20, 22-24, 321, 370-374; civil war of 1932, 216-218; constitution of 1867, 37; corruption in, 357-359; demographics of, 12-13; denazification problems in, 348; Depression of 1873, 11-71; and development of gas chambers, 317; economy during World War II, 330-331; economy following World War I, 146-150; economy in 1870s, 11-12; economy in 1937, 241; economy in late 1800s, 36; economy in late 1920s, 197-198; effects of Versailles Treaty on, 142-143; elections of 1927, 177-179; at end of World War II, 334-336; fascism in, 182, 218-219, 224; Gentile intellectual/cultural community response to *Anschluss*, 304-305; Germanism in, 49, 241; government legislation against Jews, 166-167; Grand Coalition, 142-145; Hungarian Settlement, 49; and Industrial Revolution, 11, 69-70; Jewish emigration from, 213-214; Kelsen constitution for, 144; lack of reference to World War II in literature and history of, 346; and National Socialist Workers Party (Nazis), 172, 174-175, 199-208, 210, 212-220, 222, 242, 248, 249, 253-254, 301-322, 344-346; nationalism in, 49; neo-Nazis in, 363; Parliament, 14, 33, 85-86, 94, 97, 127; and compensation to Israel for treatment of Jews, 351-352; and Peace Treaty of 1955, 349; and People's Party, 349,351;

Hohensteiner Report on separate *Gemeinde* for Orthodox Jews, 235

Holland, 269, 271, 280

Holland, Bernard, 352

Holocaust *See* Jews, mass extermination of

Holubek agitation, 77

Holy Roman Empire, 9

Home Defense Force *See Heimwehr*

"How Jews Lived Before 1938" (film), 293

Hungarian Settlement, 13, 49

Hungary, 51-52, 70: and communism in, 153; concern with growing Nazism, 247; response to Jews' expulsion from Austria, 261

Husserl, Edmund, 5, 18, 39, 40, 54

Illustrierte Neue Welt, 328f, 364

Illustrierte Wiener Volkszeitung, 86

Industrial Revolution, 69-70

Innitzer, Theodor Cardinal, 223, 228, 229, 323, 324, 325, 326, 331, 332

Integrationist Jews, 46-47, 50-51, 80-81, 121-125, 126, 165-167, 191-192, 219, 233, 234, 235, 244, 245, 250

Intermarriage, 54f, 313, 321, 324, 325, 326, 364

Israel: asks compensation for German Jews, 351   *See also* Palestine

Israelites and Other Anti-Semites (Beda), 130

Israelitische Kultusgemeinde, See Gemeinde

Italy: after World War I, 143; forms alliance with Germany, 239-240, 241; *See also* Mussolini, Benito

Iverson, Johannes, 328

Jabotinsky, Vladimir, 236-238, 243, 247

Janik, Alan, 20

Jehovah's Witnesses, 332

Jellinek, Rabbi Adolf, 42-43, 50, 78

Jenks, William A., 66

"Jew Süss" (film), 283

Jewish Agency, 354

Jewish Bureau *see Judenamt*

Jewish Chronicle of London, 116, 267

Jewish Community Council *See Gemeinde, Israelitische Kultusgemeinde*

Jewish Cultural Center, 249

Jewish Cultural League (Berlin), 312

Jewish Election Association, 167

Jewish Home for the Aged, 313

Jewish National Council, 165-167

Jewish Nationalist Party, 127, 128, 178

The Jewish Question as a Racial, Moral, and Cultural Question (Dühring), 64

The Jewish Question (Marx), 65

The Jewish State, 115, 117

The Jewish Swindle (Social Democrat book), 160

Jewish Telegraphic Agency, 178, 250

Jewish War Archives, 140

Jewish Welcome Service, 363

Jews: in academia, 39; anti-Judaism of, 90-91; anti-Semitism of, 55-58, 82-83, 90-91; assimilation of, 30-31, 55, 66, 190; in British army, 335; capitalism and, 64-65, 70-71, 72, 75, 83, 160; Catholic Church's negative beliefs concerning religious practices of, 78-80, 87, 91-92, 109; Christian, 324, 325; conflicts with Catholic Church, 50-51; conversion and reasons for conversion of, 53-55, 66, 72, 189, 190, 229, 321, 324-328; cultural contributions of, 39-41, 169, 224- 225; in Czechoslovakia, 51-52; denial of religious background, 53-55, 66; deportation of, 290-294; destruction of in 1421, 29; destruction of in 1670, 30; early reactions to Nazi demonstrations, 175; education of, 30, 38, 43, 52, 226, 230, 235, 285, 295; effects of Austrian civil war of 1932 on, 217-220; effects of economic depression on, 232; emancipation in 1867, 34-35; emigration from Austria, 213- 214, 268, 280-282, 364; as entrepreneurs during Industrial Revolution, 70-71; exclusion of in Austrian society, 226- 232, 243; forced labor of by Nazis, 285; Germanism and, 50-52, 81; Holocaust survivors, 341-344; in Hungary, 51-52; immigration procedures, 270, 273; immigration to Austria, 85, 86, 248; immigration to Belgium, 269;

Schlamme, Martha, 341f

Schmidt, Anton, 319-320

Schmidt, Guido, 303

Schmied, P. Wilhelm, 153

Schmitz, Richard, 214, 233

Schneider, Ernst, 75-76, 82, 85, 88

Schnitzler, Arthur, 57: on anti-Semitism, 58, 361, 375; on characteristics of the Viennese, 321, 370; as playwright, 4, 15, 39, 163, 358, 362; *The Road to the Open*, 24, 27, 56, 375; as student at University of Vienna

Schober, Johannes, 185, 198, 199

Scholz, Father Karl Roman, 333

Schönberg, Arnold, 3, 18, 39, 54, 55, 361

Schönerer, Georg Ritter von, 93-95, 96, 110

Schorske, Carl, 114

Schubert, Franz, 3, 42

Schubert, Kurt, 352

Schulz, Karl, 172

Schuschnigg, Kurt von, 220: allies with Social Democrats, 251- 252; anti-Semitic policies of, 226-232; decline in power of, 241-242, 249-253; holds plebiscite, 252-254, 303; and Jewish immigration to Palestine, 243; Jewish reaction to, 223-224; refusal to leave Austria, 253f; signs agreement with Hitler, 240, 249-250; signs pact with Italy, 239, 240-241

Schutzbund (Protective League), 144, 179, 200-201, 203; clashes with Dollfuss, 210, 216

Schwartz, Delmore, 365

Schwarz, Dr. Kaspar, 87-88

Schwarz, Rosa Rachel, 265

Das Schwarze Korps, 306

Schwarzwald, Eugenie, 136-137

Schwarzwald, Hermann, 57, 136

Schweitzer, Edmund, 129

Second Socialist International (1891), 90, 125

Seewald, Father Alexander, 326-327

Seipel, Ignaz, 142, 145-146, 148: and attitude toward Jews, 176, 177-179; and coalition government, 199; and support of German Nazis, 201, 204; and handling of Nazis, 178; and League of Nations loan, 148, 198, 202; refuses to allow Hitler into Austria, 178; and student riots, 159

Seitz, Karl, 152, 160, 179]

Selbst-Emancipazion (Pinsker), 113"

Self-Help Organization of Jewish Cripples", 280

Semmelweiss, Ignaz, 17

Seventh Day Adventists, 332

Seyss-Inquart, Dr. Arthur, 240, 249, 252, 253, 318, 346f, 347

Shimron, Ben, 165, 366, 368f

Shirer, William, 264, 302, 306

Shoemakers' Guild, 34, 74

Sicherheitsdienst (Gestapo branch), 316

Singer, Franz, 49f

Skorzeny, Otto, 316f

Sobibor (concentration camp), 317

Sobol, Joshua, 362

Soccer See Hakoah (soccer team)

Social Democrat Party, 6, 37, 124-125: after World War I, 142; and civil war of 1932, 216-218; and clashes with Nazis, 202, 206; and clashes with Dollfuss, 210; conflicts with Greater Germans and Christian Socials, 181-182; extra-legal armies of, 144, 156; gain majority in 1911 elections, 128; ideology of, 176, 177; Jews in, 56, 125-126, 189; rally to support Jews, 156; refusal to form coalition government, 199; Schuschnigg allies with, 251-252; and *Schutzbund*, 144; support of *Anschluss*, 304; under Austrian fascism, 231- 232; use of anti-Semitic campaigns, 160-161, 167; and *Volkswehr*, 156

Socialism: anti-Semitism and, 124; the Catholic Church and, 65; Hitler's views on, 110; Jews and, 64-65, 89-91, 124-125; Second Socialist International (1891), 90, 125; Zionism and, 124-125

Wise, Stephen, 289f

Wistrich, Robert, 70

Wittgenstein, Ludwig, 5, 18, 36, 39, 40, 297

Wollendorf (detention camp), 221

Wolter, Charlotte, 22

Women: in 1890s, 20-21; in education, 38

World Jewish Congress, 208, 236, 361

World War I: anti-Semitism and economics, 146-153; anti- Semitism following, 168; Austria in, 135-141; Austrian economy following, 146-150, 168; Austrian government following, 176-179; Christian Socials Party and, 142; effects of peace treaty on Austria, 142-143; Jewish population following, 150, 189; Jews in, 135-139; Social Democrat party in, 142; Vienna during, 135-141; Zionism and, 137, 164-165

World War II: *Anschluss,* 198-199, 202, 259-275, 332-334; anti-Semitism following, 346-364; Austria following, 330-331, 334-336, 345-355, 356-360; lack of reference to in Austrian literature or history, 346; Austria's treatment of Jews following, 335, 342, 344, 351, 360-364; and Austria's treatment of war criminals, 316, 347-350, 354; Catholic Church during, 221-222, 323-328, 331-332; and concentration camps, 221, 262, 263, 264, 278, 279, 289, 291, 294, 295, 296, 297-299, 317-318, 335-336, 342, 343, 346-347; and deportation of Jews, 290-294; Vienna during, 261-277; Vienna following, 334-336, 358-360; Zionism and, 237-240, 266-267   See also Hitler, Adolf; National Socialist Workers Party

World Zionist Organization, 129, 174-175, 187-188, 236

Yad Vashem (Jerusalem), 320, 321, 362, 366

Yarnell, Robert 328

"Yellow Star" edict, 286-287, 325-326

Youth Aliyah School, 295

Yugoslavia, 143, 269, 316

Zelman, Leon, 363

Zimmerman, Fred, 169

Zins, Sigmund, 82

Zion: Union of Austrian Societies for the Colonization of Palestine and Syria, 114

Zionism (Zionists), 46, 53, 139-140: division of in 1930s, 235- 238; domestic nationalism and, 126; emigration from Austria under Nazis, 266-267, 272, 273, 282, 289, 306, 312; and the *Gemeinde,* 122-123, 129, 207-208, 213; growth of in 1920s, 187-192; Herzl on, 115-118; integrationists and, 122-123, 233, 234, 235-238, 250; and Jewish Nationalist Party, 127, 128; Kreisky and, 354-355; New Zionist Organization, 237; newspapers, 117, 118, 191; organizations, 129, 174-175, 187- 188, 191, 236, 237, 238, 249, 271-273, 281; and Palestine Agency, 266, 268; post-World War I support for, 164-165; and racial anti Semitism, 116-118; reactions to World War I, 137; revisionist, 244, 269, 271-272; socialism and, 124-125; Stricker and, 139-140, 187, 188, 236, 238, 244; 20th anniversary of, 248-249; at University of Vienna, 119-121; and Viennese Jewish nationalism, 113, 127, 128; World Zionist Organization, 129, 174-175, 187-188, 236; *Zionistische Rundschau* (publication), 267
See also Palestine

Zionist Association for Secondary School Students, 191

Zionist Labor Group, 125

Zohn, Fritzi, 274

Zohn, Harry, 74f, 115, 116f

Zohn, Leon, 274

Zu Wenig Gerechte (Weinzierl), 321

Zuckerkandl, Berta, 185, 186, 214

Zuckerkandl, Emil, 81f, 129

Zuckerman, Hugo, 136

Zuckmayer, Carl, 220, 301, 309

Zweig, Stefan, 363: on Austrian independence, 143, 163, 224; on characteristics of the Viennese, 19, 22; on culture of Vienna, 4, 15, 40, 41, 367; opinion of Lueger, 106; on post-World War I Austria, 146; suicide of, 265; urges othes to flee Austria, 220, 243, 246